Legends and Tales

of

Ireland

LEGENDS AND TALES
OF
IRELAND

BY

SAMUEL LOVER, R.H.A.

AUTHOR OF

"Handy Andy," "Rory O'More," etc.

AND

THOMAS CROFTON CROKER

AUTHOR OF

"Popular Songs of Ireland," "Historical Songs of Ireland," etc.

THREE VOLUMES IN ONE—ILLUSTRATED

CRESCENT BOOKS
NEW YORK

Previously published by Simpkin, Marshall, Hamilton, Kent & Co

This edition published 1987 by Crescent Books
Distributed by Crown Publishers, Inc.
225 Park Avenue, South
New York, New York 10003

ISBN 0-517-62915-1

Printed and bound in Great Britain
h g f e d c b a

CONTENTS

SAMUEL LOVER'S
LEGENDS AND TALES OF IRELAND

CONTENTS

THOMAS CROFTON CROKER'S
FAIRY LEGENDS OF THE SOUTH OF IRELAND

LEGENDS OF THE SHEFRO—

CONTENTS

CONTENTS

SAMUEL LOVER'S

LEGENDS AND TALES

OF

IRELAND

PREFACE

THOUGH the sources whence these Stories are derived are open to every one, yet chance or choice may prevent thousands from making such sources available; and though the village crone and mountain guide have many hearers, still their circle is so circumscribed, that most of what I have ventured to lay before my reader is for the first time made tangible to the greater portion of those who do me the favour to become such.

Many of them were originally intended merely for the diversion of a few friends round my own fireside;—there, recited in the manner of those from whom I heard them, they first made their *début*, and the flattering reception they met on so minor a stage, led to their appearance before larger audiences;—subsequently, I was induced to publish two of them in the *Dublin Literary Gazette*, and the favourable notice from contemporary prints, which they received, has led to the publication of the present volume.

I should not have troubled the reader with this account of the "birth, parentage, and education" of my literary bantlings, but to have it understood that some of them are essentially *oral* in their character, and, I fear, suffer materially when reduced to writing. This I mention *en passant* to the critics; and if I meet but half as good-natured *readers* as I have hitherto found *auditors*, I shall have cause to be thankful. But, previously to the perusal of the following pages, there are a few observations that I feel are necessary, and which I shall make as concise as possible.

Most of the stories are given in the manner of the peasantry; and this has led to some peculiarities that might be objected to, were not the cause explained—namely, frequent digressions in the course of the narrative, occasional adjurations, and certain words unusually spelt. As regards the first, I beg to answer, that the stories would be deficient in national character without it; the Irish are so imaginative that they never tell a story straightforward, but constantly indulge in episode; for the second, it is only fair to say, that in most cases the Irish peasant's adjurations are not meant to be in the remotest degree irreverent, but arise merely from the impassioned manner of speaking which an excitable people are prone to; and I trust that such oaths as "thunder-and-turf," or maledictions, as "bad cess to you," will not be considered very offensive.

15

Nay, I will go further, and say, that their frequent exclamations of "Lord be praised,"—"God betune us and harm," etc., have their origin in a deeply reverential feeling, and a reliance on the protection of Providence. As for the orthographical dilemmas into which an attempt to spell their peculiar pronunciation has led me, I have ample and most successful precedent in Mr. Banim's works. Some general observations, however, it may not be irrelevant to introduce here, on the pronunciation of certain sounds in the English language by the Irish peasantry. And here I wish to be distinctly understood, that I speak only of the midland and western districts of Ireland—and chiefly of the latter.

They are rather prone to curtailing their words; *of*, for instance, is very generally abbreviated into *o'* or *i'*, except when a succeeding vowel demands a consonant; and even in that case they would substitute *v*. The letters *d* and *t*, as finals, they scarcely ever sound; for example, pond, hand, slept, kept, are pronounced *pon, han, slep, kep.* These letters, when followed by a vowel, are sounded as if the aspirate *h* intervened, as tender, letter—*tindher, letther.* Some sounds they sharpen, and *vice versâ.* The letter *e*, for instance, is mostly pronounced like *i* in the word litter, as *lind* for lend, *mind* for mend, etc.; but there are exceptions to this rule—Saint Kevin, for example, which they pronounce K*a*vin. The letter *o* they sound like *a* in some words, as off, *aff* or *av*—thus softening *f* into *v;* beyond, *beyant*—thus sharpening the final *d* to *t*, and making an exception to the custom of not sounding *d* as a final; in others they alter it to *ow*—as old, *owld.* Sometimes *o* is even converted into *i*—as spoil, *spile.* In a strange spirit of contrariety, while they alter the sound of *e* to that of *i*, they substitute the latter for the former sometimes—as hinder, *hendher*—cinder, *cendher; s* they soften into *z*—as us, *uz.* There are other peculiarities which this is not an appropriate place to dilate upon. I have noticed the most obvious. Nevertheless, even these are liable to exceptions, as the peasantry are quite governed by ear—as in the word *of*, which is variously sounded *o', i', ov, av,* or *iv,* as best suits their pleasure.

It is unnecessary to remark how utterly unsystematic I have been in throwing these few remarks together. Indeed, to classify (if it were necessary) that which has its birth in ignorance would be a very perplexing undertaking. But I wished to notice these striking peculiarities of the peasant pronunciation, which the reader will have frequent occasion to observe in the following pages; and, as a further assistance, I have added a short glossary.

GLOSSARY

ALPEEN—A cudgel.

BAD SCRAN—Bad food.

BAD WIN'
BAD CESS } Malediction. Cess is an abbreviation of success.

BAITHERSHIN—It may be so.

BALLYRAG—To scold.

CAUBEEN—An old hat. Strictly, a *little* old hat. *Een*, in Irish, is diminutive.

COLLEEN DHAS—Pretty girl.

COMETHER — Corruption of "Come hither." "Putting his comether" means forcing his acquaintance.

GOMMOCH—A simpleton.

HARD WORD—Hint.

HUNKERS—Haunches.

KIMMEENS—Sly tricks.

MACHREE—My dear.

MAVOURNEEN—My darling.

MUSHA!—An exclamation, as "Oh, my!" "Oh, la!"

NOGGIN—A small wooden drinking vessel.

PHILLELEW—An outcry.

SPALPEEN—A contemptible person.

STRAVAIG—To ramble.

ULICAN—The funeral cry.

WAKE — Watching the body of the departed previously to interment.

WEIRASTHRU!—Mary, have pity!

LEGENDS AND TALES

OF

IRELAND

---◄•►---

KING O'TOOLE AND ST. KEVIN

A LEGEND OF GLENDALOUGH

WHO has not read of St. Kevin, celebrated as he has been by
Moore in the melodies of his native land, with whose wild and
impassioned music he has so intimately entwined his name?
Through him, in the beautiful ballad whence the epigraph of
this story is quoted, the world already knows that the skylark,
through the intervention of the saint, never startles the morning
with its joyous note in the lonely valley of Glendalough.   In the
same ballad, the unhappy passion which the saint inspired, and
the "unholy blue" eyes of Kathleen, and the melancholy fate of
the heroine by the saint's being "unused to the melting mood,"
are also celebrated; as well as the superstitious *finale* of the
legend, in the spectral appearance of the love-lorn maiden :

> "And her ghost was seen to glide
> Gently o'er the fatal tide."

Thus has Moore given, within the limits of a ballad, the spirit
of two legends of Glendalough, which otherwise the reader might
have been put to the trouble of reaching after a more roundabout
fashion.   But luckily for those coming after him, one legend he
has left to be

> "—— touched by a hand more unworthy—"

and instead of a lyrical essence, the raw material in prose is
offered, nearly *verbatim*, as it was furnished to me by that
celebrated guide and *bore*, Joe Irwin, who traces his descent
in a direct line from the old Irish kings, and warns the public
in general that "there's a power of them spalpeens sthravaigin'

19

about, sthrivin' to put their *comether* upon the quol'ty (quality), and callin' themselves Irwin (knowin', the thieves o' the world, how his name had gone far and near, as the rale guide), for to deceave dacent people; but never for to b'lieve the likes—for it was only mulvatherin people they wor." For my part, I promised never to put faith in any but himself; and the old rogue's self-love being satisfied, we set out to explore the wonders of Glendalough. On arriving at a small ruin, situated on the south-eastern side of the lake, my guide assumed an air of importance, and led me into the ivy-covered remains, through a small square doorway, whose simple structure gave evidence of its early date: a lintel of stone lay across two upright supporters, after the fashion of such remains in Ireland.

"This, sir," said my guide, putting himself in an attitude, "is the chapel of King O'Toole—av coorse y'iv often heerd o' King O'Toole, your honour?"

"Never," said I.

"Musha, thin, do you tell me so?" said he. "By gor, I thought all the world, far and near, heerd o' King O'Toole! Well, well!—but the darkness of mankind is ontellible. Well, sir, you must know, as you didn't hear it afore, that there was wanst a king, called King O'Toole, who was a fine ould king in the ould ancient times, long ago; and it was him that ownded the Churches in the airly days."

"Surely," said I, "the Churches were not in King O'Toole's time?"

"Oh, by no manes, your honour—throth, it's yourself that's right enough there; but you know the place is called 'The Churches,' bekase they wor built *affher* by St. Kavin, and wint by the name o' the Churches iver more; and therefore, av coorse, the place bein' so called, I say that the king ownded the Churches—and why not, sir, seein' 'twas his birthright, time out o' mind, beyant the flood? Well, the king, you see, was the right sort—he was the *rale* boy, and loved sport as he loved his life, and huntin' in partic'lar; and from the risin' o' the sun, up he got, and away he wint over the mountains beyant affher the deer. And the fine times them wor; for the deer was as plinty thin—aye, throth, far plintyer than the sheep is now; and that's the way it was with the king, from the crow o' the cock to the song o' the redbreast.

"In this counthry, sir," added he, speaking parenthetically in an undertone, "we think it onlooky to kill the redbreast, for the robin is God's own bird."

Then, elevating his voice to its former pitch, he proceeded:

"Well, it was all mighty good, as long as the king had his health; but, you see, in coorse o' time, the king grewn ould, by raison he was stiff in his limbs, and when he got sthriken in years, his heart failed him, and he was lost intirely for want o' divarshin, bekase he couldn't go a-huntin' no longer; and, by dad, the poor king was obleeged at last for to get a goose to divart him."

Here an involuntary smile was produced by this regal mode of recreation, " the royal game of goose."

" Oh, you may laugh if you like," said he, half-affronted, "but it's thruth I'm tellin' you; and the way the goose divarted him was this-a-way : you see, the goose used for to swim acrass the lake, and go down divin' for throut (and not finer throut in all Ireland, than the same throut), and cotch fish on a Friday for the king, and flew every other day round about the lake divartin' the poor king, that you'd think he'd break his sides laughin' at the frolicksome tricks av his goose; so in coorse o' time the goose was the greatest pet in the counthry, and the biggest rogue, and divarted the king to no end, and the poor king was as happy as the day was long. So that's the way it was ; and all went on mighty well, antil, by dad, the goose got sthricken in years, as well as the king, and grewn stiff in the limbs, like her masther, and couldn't divart him no longer ; and then it was that the poor king was lost complate, and didn't know what in the wide world to do, seein' he was done out of all divarshin, by raison that the goose was no more in the flower of her blame.

" Well, the king was nigh-hand broken-hearted, and melancholy intirely, and was walkin' one mornin' by the edge of the lake, lamentin' his cruel fate, an' thinkin' o' drownin' himself that could get no divarshin in life, when all of a suddint, turnin' round the corner beyant, who should he meet but a mighty dacent young man comin' up to him.

" ' God save you,' says the king (for the king was a civil-spoken gintleman, by all accounts), 'God save you,' says he to the young man.

" ' God save you kindly,' says the young man to him back again ; 'God save you,' says he, ' King O'Toole.'

" ' Thrue for you,' says the king, 'I am King O'Toole,' says he, ' prince and plennypennytinchery o' these parts,' says he ; 'but how kem ye to know that ? ' says he.

" ' Oh, never mind,' says Saint Kavin.

"For you see," said Old Joe, in his undertone again, and looking very knowingly, "it *was* Saint Kavin, sure enough—the saint himself in disguise, and nobody else. ' Oh, never mind,' says he, ' I know more than that,' says he, ' nor twice that.'

" ' And who are you ? ' said the king, ' that makes so bowld— who are you, at all at all ? '

" ' Oh, never you mind,' says Saint Kavin, ' who I am ; you'll know more o' me before we part, King O'Toole,' says he.

" ' I'll be proud o' the knowledge o' your acquaintance, sir,' says the king, mighty p'lite.

" ' Troth, you may say that,' says Saint Kavin. ' And now, may I make bowld to ax, how is your goose, King O'Toole ? ' says he.

" ' Blur-an-agers, how kem you to know about my goose ? ' says the king.

" ' Oh, no matther ; I was given to undherstand it,' says Saint Kavin.

" ' Oh, that's a folly to talk,' says the king ; ' bekase myself and my goose is private frinds,' says he, ' and no one could tell you,' says he, ' barrin' the fairies.'

" ' Oh, thin, it wasn't the fairies,' says Saint Kavin ; ' for I'd have you to know,' says he, ' that I don't keep the likes o' sitch company.'

" ' You might do worse then, my gay fellow,' says the king ; ' for it's *they* could show you a crock o' money as aisy as kiss hand ; and that's not to be sneezed at,' says the king, ' by a poor man,' says he.

" ' Maybe I've a betther way of making money myself,' says the saint.

" ' By gor,' says the king, ' barrin' you're a coiner,' says he, ' that's impossible ! '

" ' I'd scorn to be the like, my lord ! ' says Saint Kavin, mighty high, ' I'd scorn to be the like,' says he.

" ' Then, what are you,' says the king, ' that makes money so aisy, by your own account ? '

" ' I'm an honest man,' says Saint Kavin.

" ' Well, honest man,' says the king, ' and how is it you make your money so aisy ? '

" ' By makin' ould things as good as new,' says Saint Kavin.

" ' Blur-an-ouns, is it a tinker you are ? ' says the king.

" ' No,' says the saint ; ' I'm no tinker by thrade, King O'Toole ; I've a betther thrade than a tinker,' says he—' what would you say,' says he, ' if I made your old goose as good as new ? '

" My dear, at the word o' makin' his goose as good as new, you'd think the poor ould king's eyes was ready to jump out iv his head, ' and,' says he—' troth, thin, I'd give you more money nor you could count,' says he, ' if you did the like ; and I'd be beboulden to you into the bargain.'

" ' I scorn your dirty money,' says Saint Kavin.

" ' Faith then, I'm thinkin' a thrifle o' change would do you no harm,' says the king, lookin' up sly at the old *caubeen* that Saint Kavin had on him.

" ' I have a vow agin' it,' says the saint ; ' and I am book sworn,' says he, ' never to have goold, silver, or brass in my company.'

" 'Barrin' the thrifle you can't help,' says the king, mighty cute, and looking him straight in the face.

" 'You just hot it,' says Saint Kavin; 'but though I can't take money,' says he, 'I could take a few acres o' land, if you'd give them to me.'

" 'With all the veins o' my heart,' says the king, 'if you can do what you say.'

" 'Thry me!' says Saint Kavin. 'Call down your goose here,' says he, 'and I'll see what I can do for her.'

" 'With that the king whistled, and down kem the poor goose, all as one as a hound, waddlin' up to the poor ould cripple, her masther, and as like him as two *pays*. The minute the saint clapt his eyes an the goose, 'I'll do the job for you,' says he, 'King O'Toole!'

" 'By *Jaminee*,' says King O'Toole, 'if you do, bud I'll say you're the cleverest fellow in the sivin parishes.'

" 'Oh, by dad,' says Saint Kavin, 'you must say more nor that —my horn's not so soft all out,' says he, 'as to repair your ould goose for nothin'; what'll you gi' me, if I do the job for you?— that's the chat,' says Saint Kavin.

" 'I'll give you whatever you ax,' says the king; 'isn't that fair?'

" 'Divil a fairer,' says the saint; 'that's the way to do business. Now,' says he, 'this is the bargain I'll make with you, King O'Toole: will you gi' me all the ground the goose flies over the first offer afther I make her as good as new?'

" 'I will,' says the king.

" 'You won't go back o' your word?' says Saint Kavin.

" 'Honour bright!' says King O'Toole, howldin' out his fist."

Here old Joe, after applying his hand to his mouth, and making a sharp, blowing sound (something like "*thp*"), extended it to illustrate the action.

" 'Honour bright,' says Saint Kavin back agin, 'it's a bargain,' says he. 'Come here!' says he to the poor ould goose—'come here, you unfort'nate ould cripple,' says he, 'and it's *I* that'll make you the sportin' bird.'

"With that, my dear, he tuk up the goose by the two wings— 'Criss o' my crass and you,' says he, markin' her to grace with the blessed sign at the same minute—and throwin' her up in the air, 'whew!' says he, jist givin' her a blast to help her; and with that, my jewel, she tuk to her heels, flyin' like one o' the aigles themselves, and cuttin' as many capers as a swallow before a shower of rain. Away she wint down there, right fornist you, along the side o' the clift, and flew over Saint Kavin's bed (that is where Saint Kavin's bed is *now*, but was not *thin*, by raison it wasn't made, but was conthrived afther by Saint Kavin himself,

that the women might lave him alone), and on with her undher
Lugduff, and round the ind av the lake there, far beyant where
you see the watherfall (though indeed it's no watherfall at all now,
but only a poor dhribble iv a thing; but if you seen it in the
winther, it id do your heart good, and it roarin' like mad, and as
white as the dhriven snow, and rowlin' down the big rocks before
it, all as one as childher playin' marbles)—and on with her thin
right over the lead mines o' Luganure (that is where the lead
mines is *now*, but was not *thin*, by raison they worn't discovered,
but was all goold in Saint Kavin's time).

"Well, over the ind o' Luganure she flew, stout and sturdy,
and round the other ind av the *little* lake, by the Churches (that is,
av coorse, where the Churches is *now*, but was not *thin*, by raison
they wor not built, but afth;erwards by Saint Kavin), and over
the big hill here over your head, where you see the big clift—
(and that clift in the mountain was made by *Fan Ma Cool*, where
he cut it acrass with a big swoord that he got made a purpose
by a blacksmith out o' Ruthdrum, a cousin av his own, for to
fight a joyant [giant] that darr'd him an the Curragh o' Kildare;
and he thried the swoord first an the mountain, and cut it down
into a gap, as is plain to this day; and faith, sure enough, it's
the same sauce he sarv'd the joyant, soon and suddent, and
chopped him in two like a pratie, for the glory of his sowl and
owld Ireland)—well, down she flew over the clift, and fluttherin'
over the wood there at Poulanass (where I showed you the purty
watherfall—and by the same token, last Thursday was a twelvemonth sence, a young lady, Miss Rafferty by name, fell into the same
watherfall, and was nigh-hand drownded—and indeed would be
to this day, but for a young man that jumped in afther her;
indeed, a smart slip iv a young man he was—he was out o'
Francis Street, I hear, and coorted her sence, and they wor
married, I'm given to undherstand—and indeed a purty couple
they wor).   Well, as I said, afther fluttherin' over the wood a
little bit, to *plaze* herself, the goose flew down, and lit at the fut
o' the king, as fresh as a daisy, afther flyin' roun' his dominions,
just as if she hadn't flew three perch.

"Well, my dear, it was a beautiful sight to see the king
standin' with his mouth open, lookin' at his poor ould goose
flyin' as light as a lark, and betther nor ever she was; and
when she lit at his fut, he patted her an the head, and '*Mavourneen*,' says he, 'but you are the *darlint* o' the world.'

"'And what do you say to me,' says Saint Kavin, 'for makin'
her the like?'

"'By gor,' says the king, 'I say nothin' bates the art o' man,
barrin' the bees.'

"'And do you say no more nor that?' says Saint Kavin.

" ' And that I'm beholden to you,' says the king.

" ' But will you gi'e me all the ground the goose flewn over?' says Saint Kavin.

" ' I will,' says King O'Toole. ' And you're welkim to it,' says he, ' though it's the last acre I have to give.'

" ' But you'll keep your word thrue?' says the saint.

" ' As thrue as the sun,' says the king.

" ' It's well for you,' says Saint Kavin, mighty sharp—' it's well for you, King O'Toole, that you said that word,' says he; ' for if you didn't say that word, *the divil receave the bit o' your goose id ever fly agin,*' says Saint Kavin.

"Oh! you needn't laugh," said old Joe, half offended at detecting the trace of a suppressed smile; "you needn't laugh, *for it's thruth I'm tellin' you.*

"Well, whin the king was as good as his word, Saint Kavin was *plazed* with him, and thin it was that he made himself known to the king. 'And,' says he, ' King O'Toole, you're a dacent man,' says he, ' for I only kem here to *thry you.* You don't know me,' says he, ' bekase I'm disguised.'[1]

" ' Troth, then, you're right enough,' says the king. ' I didn't perceave it,' says he; ' for, indeed, I never seen the sign o' sper'ts an you.'

" ' Oh! that's not what I mane,' says Saint Kavin. ' I mane I'm deceavin' you all out, and that I'm not myself at all.'

" ' Blur-an-agers! thin,' says the king, ' if you're not yourself, who are you?'

" ' I'm Saint Kavin,' said the saint, blessin' himself.

" ' Oh, queen iv heaven!" says the king, makin' the sign o' the crass betune his eyes, and fallin' down on his knees before the saint. ' Is it the great Saint Kavin,' says he, ' that I've been discoorsin' all this time without knowin' it,' says he, ' all as one as if he was a lump iv a *gossoon?* And so you're a saint?' says the king.

" ' I am,' says Saint Kavin.

" ' By gor, I thought I was only talking to a dacent boy,' says the king.

" ' Well, you know the differ now,' says the saint. ' I'm Saint Kavin,' says he, ' the greatest of all the saints.'

"For Saint Kavin, you must know, sir," added Joe, treating me to another parenthesis, "Saint Kavin is counted the greatest of all the saints, bekase he went to school with the prophet Jeremiah.

"Well, my dear, that's the way that the place kem, all at wanst, into the hands of Saint Kavin; for the goose flewn round

---

[1] A person in a state of drunkenness is said to be *disguised.*

every individyial acre o' King O'Toole's property, you see, *bein'*
let into the saycret by Saint Kavin, who was mighty *cute ;* and
so, when he *done* the ould king out iv his property for the glory
of God, he was *plazed* with him, and he and the king was the best
o' frinds ivermore afther (for the poor ould king was *doatin'*, you
see), and the king had his goose as good as new to divart him as
long as he lived ; and the saint supported him afther he kem into
his property, as I tould you, antil the day iv his death—and that
was soon afther ; for the poor goose thought he was ketchin' a
throut one Friday, but, my jewel, it was a mistake he made, and
instead of a throut, it was a thievin' horse-eel, and, by gor !
instead iv the goose killin' a throut for the king's supper, by
dad ! the eel killed the king's goose, and small blame to him ;
but he didn't ate her, bekase he darn't ate what Saint Kavin
laid his blessed hands on.

" Howsumdever, the king never recovered the loss iv his goose,
though he had her stuffed (I don't mane stuffed with pratees and
inyans, but as a curosity) and presarved in a glass case for his
own divarshin ; and the poor king died on the next Michaelmas
Day, which was remarkable. *Throth, it's thruth I'm tellin' you ;*
and when he was gone, Saint Kavin gev him an illigant wake and
a beautiful berrin'; and more betoken, he *said mass for his sowl,*
and tuk care av his goose."

LOUGH CORRIB

It chanced, amongst some of the pleasantest adventures of a
tour through the West of Ireland, in 1825, that the house of Mr.
—— of —— received me as a guest.   The owner of the mansion
upheld the proverbial reputation of his country's hospitality, and
his lady was of singularly winning manners, and possessed of much
intelligence — an intelligence arising not merely from the
cultivation resulting from careful education, but originating also
from the attention which persons of good sense bestow upon the
circumstances which come within the range of their observation.

Thus, Mrs. ——, an accomplished Englishwoman, instead of
sneering at the deficiencies which a poorer country than her own
laboured under, was willing to be amused by observing the
difference which exists in the national character of the two
people, in noticing the prevalence of certain customs, superstitions,
etc. etc. ; while the popular tales of the neighbourhood had for
her a charm which enlivened a sojourn in a remote district that
must otherwise have proved lonely.

To this pleasure was added that of admiration of the natural
beauties with which she was surrounded ; the noble chain of the
Mayo mountains, linking with the majestic range of those of

Joyce's country, formed no inconsiderable source of picturesque beauty and savage grandeur; and when careering over the waters of Lough Corrib that foamed at their feet, she never sighed for the grassy slopes of Hyde Park, nor that unruffled pond, the Serpentine river.

In the same boat which often bore so fair a charge have I explored the noble Lough Corrib to its remotest extremity, sailing over the depths of its dark waters, amidst solitudes whose echoes are seldom awakened but by the scream of the eagle.

From this lady I heard some characteristic stories and prevalent superstitions of the country. Many of these she had obtained from an old boatman, one of the crew that manned Mr. ——'s boat; and often, as he sat at the helm, he delivered his "round, unvarnished tale"; and, by the way, in no very measured terms either, whenever his subject happened to touch upon the wrongs his country had sustained in her early wars against England, although his liege-lady was a native of the hostile land. Nevertheless, the old Corribean (the name somehow has a charmingly savage sound about it) was nothing loath to have his fling at "the invaders"—a term of reproach he always cast upon the English.

Thus skilled in legendary lore, Mrs. —— proved an admirable guide to the "lions" of the neighbourhood; and it was previously to a projected visit to the Cave of Cong that she entered upon some anecdotes relating to the romantic spot, which led her to tell me that one legend had so particularly excited the fancy of a young lady, a friend of hers, that she wrought it into the form of a little tale, which, she added, had not been considered ill done. "But," said she, "'tis true we were all friends who passed judgment, and only drawing-room critics: You shall therefore judge for yourself, and hearing it before you see the cave, will at least rather increase your interest in the visit." And forthwith drawing from a little cabinet a manuscript, she read to me the following tale—much increased in its effect by the sweet voice in which it was delivered.

A LEGEND OF LOUGH MASK

THE evening was closing fast as the young Cormac O'Flaherty had reached the highest acclivity of one of the rugged passes of the steep mountains of Joyce's country. He made a brief pause —not to take breath, fair reader—Cormac needed no breathing time, and would have considered it little short of an insult to have had such a motive attributed to the momentary stand he made, and none that knew the action of the human figure would have thought it; for the firm footing which one beautifully-formed leg held with youthful firmness on the mountain path,

while the other, slightly thrown behind, rested on the half-bent
foot, did not imply repose, but rather suspended action. In
sooth, youth Cormac, to the eye of the painter, might have
seemed a living *Antinous*—all the grace of that beautiful
antique, all the youth, all the expression of suspended motion
were there, with more of vigour and impatience. He paused—
not to take breath, Sir Walter Scott; for, like your own Malcolm
Græme,

> "Right up Ben Lomond could he press,
> And not a sob his toil confess;"

and our young O'Flaherty was not to be outdone in breasting up
a mountain side by the boldest Græme of them all.

But he lingered for a moment to look back upon a scene at
once sublime and gorgeous; and cold must the mortal have
been who could have beheld and had not paused.

On one side the Atlantic lay beneath him, brightly reflecting
the glories of an autumnal setting sun, and expanding into a
horizon of dazzling light; on the other lay the untrodden wilds
before him, stretching amidst the depths of mountain valleys,
whence the sunbeam had long since departed, and mists were
already wreathing round the overhanging heights, and veiling
the distance in vapoury indistinctness—as though you looked
into some wizard's glass, and saw the uncertain conjuration of
his wand. On the one side all was glory, light, and life—on the
other all was awful, still, and almost dark. It was one of
Nature's sublimest moments, such as are seldom witnessed, and
never forgotten.

Ere he descended the opposite declivity, Cormac once more
bent back his gaze; and now it was not one exclusively of
admiration. There was a mixture of scrutiny in his look, and
turning to Diarmid, a faithful adherent of his family, and only
present companion, he said: "That sunset forebodes a coming
storm; does it not, Diarmid?"

"Ay, truly does it," responded the attendant; "and there's
no truth in the clouds if we haven't it soon upon us."

"Then let us speed," said Cormac; "for the high hill and the
narrow path must be traversed ere our journey be accomplished."
And he sprang down the steep and shingly pass before him,
followed by the faithful Diarmid.

> "'Tis sweet to know there is an eye to mark
> Our coming—and grow brighter when we come."

And there *was* a bright eye watching for Cormac, and many a
love-taught look did Eva cast over the waters of Lough Mask,
impatient for the arrival of the O'Flaherty. "Surely he will be
here this evening," thought Eva; "yet the sun is already low,
and no distant oars disturb the lovely quiet of the lake. But

may he not have tarried beyond the mountains—he has friends there?" recollected Eva. But soon the maiden's jealous fancy whispered: "He has friends *here* too." And she reproached him for his delay; but it was only for a moment.

"The accusing spirit blushed," as Eva continued her train of conjecture. "'Tis hard to part from pressing friends," thought she, "and Cormac is ever welcome in the hall, and heavily closes the portal after his departing footsteps."

Another glance across the lake. 'Tis yet unrippled by an oar. The faint outline of the dark grey mountains, whose large masses lie unbroken by the detail which daylight discovers; the hazy distance of the lake, whose extremity is undistinguishable from the overhanging cliffs which embrace it; the fading of the western sky; the last lonely rook winging his weary way to the adjacent wood; the flickering flight of the bat across her windows—all—all told Eva that the night was fast approaching; yet Cormac was not come. She turned from the casement with a sigh. Oh! only those who love can tell how anxious are the moments we pass in watching the approach of the beloved one.

She took her harp. Every heroine, to be sure, has a harp; but this was not the pedal harp, that instrument *par excellence* of heroines, but the simple harp of her country, whose single row of brazen wires had often rung to many a sprightly planxty, long, long before the double action of Erard had vibrated to some fantasia from Rossini or Meyerbeer, under the brilliant finger of a Bochsa or a Labarre.

But now the harp of Eva did not ring forth the spirit-stirring planxty, but yielded to her gentlest touch one of the most soothing and plaintive of her native melodies; and to her woman sensibility, which long expectation had excited, it seemed to breathe an unusual flow of tenderness and pathos, which her heated imagination conjured almost into prophetic wailing. Eva paused—she was alone; the night had closed—her chamber was dark and silent. She burst into tears, and when her spirits became somewhat calmed by this gush of feeling, she arose, and dashing the lingering tear-drops from the long lashes of the most beautiful blue eyes in the world, she hastened to the hall, and sought in the society of others to dissipate those feelings by which she had been overcome.

The night closed over the path of Cormac, and the storm he anticipated had swept across the waves of the Atlantic, and now burst in all its fury over the mountains of Joyce's country. The wind rushed along in wild gusts, bearing in its sweeping eddy heavy dashes of rain, which soon increased to a continuous deluge of enormous drops, rendering the mountain gullies the channel of temporary rivers, and the path that wound along the verge of each precipice so slippery as to render its passage death to the timid or unwary, and dangerous even to the firmest or most practised foot. But our hero and his attendant strode on ; the torrent was resolutely passed, its wild roar audible above the loud thunder - peals that rolled through the startled echoes of the mountains ; the dizzy path was firmly trod, its dangers rendered more perceptible by the blue lightnings, half revealing the depths of the abyss beneath, and Cormac and Diarmid still pressed on towards the shores of Lough Mask, unconscious of the interruption that yet awaited them, fiercer than the torrent, and more deadly than the lightning.

As they passed round the base of a projecting crag, that flung its angular masses athwart the ravine through which they wound, a voice of brutal coarseness suddenly arrested their progress with the fiercely uttered word of " Stand ! "

Cormac instantly stopped—as instantly his weapon was in his hand ; and with searching eye he sought to discover through the gloom what bold intruder dared cross the path of the O'Flaherty. His tongue now demanded what his eye failed him to make known, and the same rude voice that first addressed him answered : " Thy mortal foe ! Thou seek'st thy bride, fond boy, but never shalt thou behold her—never shalt thou share the bed of Eva."

" Thou liest, foul traitor ! " cried Cormac fiercely. " Avoid my path ; avoid it, I say, for death is in it ! "

" Thou say'st truly," answered the unknown, with a laugh of horrid meaning. " Còme on, and thy words shall be made good ! "

At this moment a flash of lightning illumined the whole glen with momentary splendour, and discovered to Cormac, a few paces before him, two armed men of gigantic stature, in one of whom he recognised Emman O'Flaherty, one of the many branches of that ancient and extensive family, equally distinguished for his personal prowess and savage temper.

" Ha ! " exclaimed Cormac, " is it Emman Dubh ? " for the black hair of Emman had obtained for him this denomination of *Black Edward*, a name fearfully suitable to him who bore it.

" Yes," answered he tauntingly, " it is Emman Dubh who waits the coming of his *fair* cousin. You have said death is in your path. Come on and meet it."

Nothing daunted, however shocked at discovering the midnight waylayer of his path in his own relative, Cormac answered : " Emman Dubh, I have never wronged you ; but since you thirst for my blood, and cross my path, on your own head be the penalty. Stand by me, Diarmid," said the brave youth, and rushing on his Herculean enemy, they closed in mortal combat.

Had the numbers been equal, the colossal strength of Emman

might have found its overmatch in the activity of Cormac, and his skill in the use of his weapon. But oh, the foul, the treacherous Emman! He dared his high - spirited rival to advance but to entrap him into an ambuscade; for as he rushed upon his foe, past the beetling rock that hung over his path, a third assassin, unseen by the gallant Cormac, lay in wait, and when the noble youth was engaged in the fierce encounter, a blow, dealt him in the back, laid the betrothed of Eva lifeless at the feet of the savage and exulting Emman.

Restlessly had Eva passed that turbulent night—each gust of the tempest, each flash of living flame and burst of thunder awakened her terrors, lest Cormac, the beloved of her soul, were exposed to its fury; but in the lapses of the storm hope ventured to whisper he yet lingered in the castle of some friend beyond the mountains. The morning dawned, and silently bore witness to the commotion of the elements of the past night: The riven branch of the naked tree, that in one night had been shorn of its leafy beauty; the earth strewn with foliage half green, half yellow, ere yet the autumnal alchemy had converted its summer verdure quite to gold, gave evidence that an unusually early storm had been a forerunner of the equinox. The general aspect of Nature, too, though calm, was cold; the mountains wore a dress of sombre grey, and the small, scattered clouds were straggling over the face of heaven, as though they had been rudely riven asunder, and the short and quick lash of the waters upon the shore of Lough Mask might have told to an accustomed eye that a longer wave and a whiter foam had broken on its strand a few hours before.

But what is that upthrown upon the beach? And who are those who surround it in such consternation? It is the little skiff that was moored at the opposite side of the lake on the preceding eve, and was to have borne Cormac to his betrothed bride. And they who identify the shattered boat are those to whom Eva's happiness is dear; for it is her father and his attendants, who are drawing ill omens from the tiny wreck. But they conceal the fact, and the expecting girl is not told of the evil-boding discovery. But days have come and gone, and Cormac yet tarries. At length 'tis past a doubt; and the father of Eva knows his child is widowed ere her bridal—widowed in heart, at least. And who shall tell the fatal tale to Eva? Who shall cast the shadow o'er her soul, and make the future darkness? Alas! ye feeling souls that ask it, that pause ere you can speak the word that blights for ever, pause no longer, for Eva knows it. Yes; from tongue to tongue—by word on word from many a quivering lip, and meanings darkly given, the dreadful certainty at last arrived to the bewildered Eva.

It was nature's last effort at comprehension; her mind was filled with the one fatal knowledge—Cormac was gone for ever; and that was the only mental consciousness that ever after employed the lovely Eva.

The remainder of the melancholy tale is briefly told. Though quite bereft of reason, she was harmless as a child, and was allowed to wander round the borders of Lough Mask, and its immediate neighbourhood. A favourite haunt of the still beautiful maniac was the Cave of Cong, where a subterranean river rushes from beneath a low natural arch in the rock, and passing for some yards over a strand of pebbles, in pellucid swiftness, loses itself in the dark recesses of the cavern with the sound of a rapid and turbulent fall. This river is formed by the waters of Lough Mask becoming engulfed at one of its extremities, and hurrying through a subterranean channel until they rise again in the neighbourhood of Cong, and become tributary to Lough Corrib Here the poor girl would sit for hours; and believing that her beloved Cormac had been drowned in Lough Mask, she hoped, in one of those half-intelligent dreams which haunt a distempered brain, to arrest his body, as she fancied it must pass through the Cave of Cong, borne on the subterranean river.

Month after month passed by; but the nipping winter and the gentle spring found the lovely Eva still watching by the stream, like some tutelary water-nymph beside her sacred fountain. At length she disappeared—and though the strictest search was made, the broken-hearted Eva was never heard of more; and the tradition of the country is, that the fairies took pity on a love so devoted, and carried away the faithful girl to join her betrothed in fairyland!

Mrs. —— closed the manuscript, and replaced it in the little cabinet.

"Most likely," said I, "poor Eva, if ever such a person existed—"

"If!" said the fair reader. "Can you be so ungrateful as to question the truth of my legend, after all the trouble I have had in reading it to you? Get away! A sceptic like you is only fit to hear the commonplaces of the daily press."

"I cry your pardon, fair lady," said I. "I am most orthodox in legendary belief, and question not the existence of your Eva. I was only about to say that perchance she might have been drowned in and carried away by the river she watched so closely."

"Hush, hush!" said the fair chronicler. "As you hope for favour or information in our fair counties of Galway or Mayo, never *dare* to question the truth of a legend—never venture a '*perhaps*' for the purpose of making a tale more reasonable, nor endeavour to substitute the reign of common sense in hopes of superseding the empire of the fairies. Go to-morrow to the Cave of Cong, and if you return still an unbeliever, I give you up as an irreclaimable infidel."

THE WHITE TROUT

A LEGEND OF CONG

THE next morning I proceeded alone to the cave, to witness the natural curiosity of its subterranean river, my interest in the visit being somewhat increased by the foregoing tale. Leaving my horse at the little village of Cong, I bent my way on foot through the fields, if you may venture to give that name to the surface of this immediate district of the county Mayo, which, presenting large flat masses of limestone, intersected by patches of verdure, gives one the idea much more of a burial-ground covered with monumental slabs than a formation of Nature. Yet (I must make this remark *en passant*) such is the richness of the pasture in these little verdant interstices, that cattle are fattened upon it in a much shorter time than on a meadow of the most cultured aspect; and though to the native of Leinster this *land* (if we may be pardoned a premeditated *bull*) would appear all *stones*, the Mayo farmer knows it from experience to be a profit-able tenure. Sometimes deep clefts occur between these laminæ of limestone rock, which, closely overgrown with verdure, have not infrequently occasioned serious accidents to man and beast; and one of these chasms, of larger dimensions than usual, forms the entrance to the celebrated cave in question.

Very rude steps of unequal height, partly natural and partly artificial, lead the explorer of its quiet beauty, by an abrupt descent, to the bottom of the cave, which contains an enlightened area of some thirty or forty feet, whence a naturally vaulted passage opens, of the deepest gloom. The depth of the cave may be about equal to its width at the bottom; the mouth is not more than twelve or fifteen feet across; and pendent from its margin clusters of ivy and other parasite plants hang and cling in all the fantastic variety of natural festooning and tracery. It is a truly beautiful and poetical little spot, and particularly interesting to the stranger from being unlike anything else one has ever seen, and having none of the noisy and vulgar pretence of regular *show-places*, which calls upon you every moment to exclaim " Prodigious ! "

An elderly and decent-looking woman had just filled her pitcher with the deliciously cold and clear water of the subterranean river that flowed along its bed of small, smooth, and many-coloured pebbles, as I arrived at the bottom ; and perceiving at once that I was a stranger, she paused, partly perhaps with the pardonable pride of displaying her local knowledge, but more from the native peasant politeness of her country, to become the temporary *Cicerone* of the cave. She spoke some words of Irish, and hurried forth on her errand a very handsome and active boy, of whom she informed me she was the great-grandmother.

"Great-grandmother !" I repeated, in unfeigned astonishment.

"Yes, your honour," she answered, with evident pleasure sparkling in her eyes, which time had not yet deprived of their brightness, or the soul-subduing influence of this selfish world bereft of their kind-hearted expression.

"You are the youngest woman I have ever seen," said I, "to be a great-grandmother."

"Troth, I don't doubt you, sir," she answered.

"And you seem still in good health, and likely to live many a year yet," said I.

"With the help of God, sir," said she reverently.

"But," I added, "I perceive a great number of persons about here of extreme age. Now, how long generally do the people in this country live ?"

"Troth, sir," said she, with the figurative drollery of her country, "we live here as long as we like."

"Well, that is no inconsiderable privilege," said I ; "but you, nevertheless, must have married very young ?"

"I was not much over sixteen, your honour, when I had my first child at my breast."

"That was beginning early," said I.

"Thrue for you, sir ; and faith, Noreen (that's my daughter, sir)—Noreen herself lost no time either ; I suppose she thought she had as good a right as the mother before her—she was married at seventeen, and a likely couple herself and her husband was. So you see, sir, it was not long before I was a granny. Well, to make the saying good, 'As the ould cock crows, the young bird cherrups,' and faiks, the whole breed, seed, and generation tuk after the owld woman (that's myself, sir) ; and so, in coorse of time, I was not only a granny, but a *grate* granny ; and, by the same token, here comes my darling Paudeen Bawn, with what I sent him for."

Here the fine little fellow I have spoken of, with his long fair hair curling about his shoulders, descended into the cave, bearing some faggots of bogwood, a wisp of straw, and a lighted sod of turf.

"Now, your honour, it's what you'll see the pigeon-hole to advantage."

"What pigeon-hole !" said I.

"Here where we are," she replied.

"Why is it so called ?" I inquired.

"Because, sir, the wild pigeons often build in the bushes and the ivy that's round the mouth of the cave, and in here too," said she, pointing into the gloomy depth of the interior.

"Blow that turf, Paudeen ;" and Paudeen, with distended cheeks and compressed lips, forthwith poured a few vigorous blasts on the sod of turf, which soon flickered and blazed, while the kind old woman lighted her faggots of bogwood at the flame.

"Now, sir, follow me," said my conductress.

"I am sorry you have had so much trouble on my account," said I.

"Oh, no throuble in life, your honour, but the greatest of pleasure;" and so saying, she proceeded into the cave, and I followed, carefully choosing my steps by the help of her torch-light along the slippery path of rock that overhung the river. When she had reached a point of some little elevation, she held up her lighted pine branches, and waving them to and fro, asked me could I see the top of the cave.

The effect of her figure was very fine, illumined as it was in the midst of utter darkness by the red glare of the blazing faggots ; and as she wound them round her head, and shook their flickering sparks about, it required no extraordinary stretch of imagination to suppose her, with her ample cloak of dark drapery, and a few straggling tresses of grey hair escaping from the folds of a rather Eastern head-dress, some sibyl about to commence an awful rite, and evoke her ministering spirits from the dark void, or call some water-demon from the river, which rushed unseen along, telling of its wild course by the turbulent dash of its waters, which the reverberation of the cave rendered still more hollow.

She shouted aloud, and the cavern-echoes answered to her summons. "Look !" said she—and she lighted the wisp of straw, and flung it on the stream. It floated rapidly away, blazing in wild undulations over the perturbed surface of the river, and at length suddenly disappeared altogether. The effect was most picturesque and startling ; it was even awful. I might almost say sublime !

Her light being nearly expired, we retraced our steps, and emerging from the gloom, stood beside the river, in the enlightened area I have described.

"Now, sir," said my old woman, "we must thry and see the white throut ; and you never seen a throut o' that colour yet, I warrant."

I assented to the truth of this.

"They say it's a fairy throut, yer honour, and tells mighty quare stories about it."

" What are they ? " I inquired.

" Troth, it's myself doesn't know the half o' them—only partly ;
but sthrive and see it before you go, sir, for there's them that
says it isn't lucky to come to the cave and lave it without seein'
the white throut. And if you're a bachelor, sir, and didn't get a
peep at it, throth, you'd never be married, and sure that 'id be a
murther."

" Oh," said I, " I hope the fairies would not be so spiteful—"

" Whisht, whisht ! " said she, looking fearfully around ; then,
knitting her brows, she gave me an admonitory look, and put her
finger on her lip, in token of silence, and then coming sufficiently
near me to make herself audible in a whisper, she said, " Never
speak ill, your honour, of the good people—beyant all, in sitch a
place as this—for it's in the likes they always keep; and one doesn't
know who may be listenin'. God keep uz ! But look, sir, look ! "
and she pointed to the stream—" there she is."

" Who—what ? " said I.

" The throut, sir."

I immediately perceived the fish in question, perfectly a trout
in shape, but in colour a creamy white, heading up the stream, and
seeming to keep constantly within the region of the enlightened
part of it.

" There it is, in that very spot evermore," continued my guide,
" and never anywhere else."

" The poor fish, I suppose, likes to swim in the light," said I.

" Oh, no, sir," said she, shaking her head significantly, " the
people here has a mighty owld story about that throut."

" Let me hear it, and you will oblige me."

" Och ! it's only laughin' at me you'd be, and call me an ould
fool, as the misthiss beyant in the big house often did afore,
when she first kem among us—but she knows the differ now."

" Indeed I shall not laugh at your story," said I, " but on the
contrary, shall thank you very much for your tale."

" Then sit down a minnit, sir," said she, throwing her apron
upon the rock, and pointing to the seat, " and I'll tell you to the
best of my knowledge." And seating herself on an adjacent patch
of verdure, she began her legend.

" There was wanst upon a time, long ago, a beautiful young
lady that lived in a castle up by the lake beyant, and they say
she was promised to a king's son, and they wor to be married ;
when, all of a suddent, he was murthered, the crathur (Lord help
us), and threwn into the lake abow, and so, of coorse, he couldn't
keep his promise to the fair lady—and more's the pity.

" Well, the story goes that she went out iv her mind bekase
av losin' the king's son ; for she was tindher-hearted, God help
her ! like the rest iv us, and pined away after him, until, at last,

no one about seen her, good or bad, and the story wint that the fairies took her away.

"Well, sir, in coorse o' time the white throut, God bless it! was seen in the sthrame beyant, and sure the people didn't know what to think av the crathur, seein' as how a *white* throut was never heerd av afore nor sence; and years upon years the throut was there, just where you seen it this blessed minnit, longer nor I can tell—aye, troth, and beyant the memory o' th' ouldest in the village.

"At last the people began to think it must be a fairy—for what else could it be?—and no hurt nor harm was iver put an the white throut, antil some wicked sinners of sojers kem to these parts, and laughed at all the people, and gibed and jeered them for thinkin' o' the likes; and one o' them in partic'lar (bad luck to him; God forgi' me for sayin' it!) swore he'd catch the throut and ate it for his dinner—the blackguard!

"Well, what would you think o' the villiany of the sojer?— Sure enough he cotch the throut; and away wid him home, and puts an the fryin'-pan, and into it he pitches the purty little thing. The throut squeeled all as one as a Christian crathur, and, my dear, you'd think the sojer id split his sides laughin'— for he was a harden'd villian; and when he thought one side was done, he turns it over to fry the other; and what would you think, but the divil a taste of a burn was an it at all at all; and sure the sojer thought it was a *quare* throut that couldn't be briled. 'But,' says he, 'I'll give it another turn by-and-by'— little thinkin' what was in store for him—the haythen!

"Well, when he thought that side was done, he turns it again —and lo and behould you, the divil a taste more done that side was nor the other. 'Bad luck to me,' says the sojer, 'but that bates the world!' says he; 'but I'll thry you agin, my darlint,' says he, 'as cunnin' as you think yourself,'—and so, with that, he turns it over and over; but the divil a sign av the fire was an the purty throut. 'Well,' says the desperate villian (for sure, sir, only he was a desperate villian *entirely*, he might know he was doin' a wrong thing, seein' that all his endayvours was no good)—'well,' says he, 'my jolly little throut, maybe you're fried enough, though you don't seem over-well dress'd; but you may be better than you look, like a singed cat, and a tit-bit, afther all,' says he; and with that he ups with his knife and fork to taste a piece o' the throut—but, my jew'l, the minnit he puts his knife into the fish, there was a murtherin' screech, that you'd think the life id lave you if you heerd it, and away jumps the throut out av the fryin'-pan into the middle o' the flure; and an the spot where it fell, up riz a lovely lady—the beautifullest young crathur that eyes ever seen, dressed in white, with a band o' goold in her hair, and a sthrame o' blood runnin' down her arm.

" ' Look where you cut me, you villian,' says she, and she held out her arm to him—and, my dear, he thought the sight id lave his eyes.

" ' Couldn't you lave me cool and comfortable in the river where you snared me, and not disturb me in my duty ? ' says she.

" Well, he thrimbled like a dog in a wet sack, and at last he stammered out somethin', and begged for his life, and ax'd her ladyship's pardin, and said he didn't know she was an duty, or he was too good a sojer not to know betther nor to meddle wid her.

" ' I *was* on duty, then,' says the lady ; ' I was watchin' for my thrue love, that is comin' by wather to me,' says she ; ' an' if he comes while I am away, an' that I miss iv him, I'll turn you into a pinkeen, and I'll hunt you up and down for evermore, while grass grows or wather runs.'

" Well, the sojer thought the life id lave him at the thoughts iv his bein' turned into a pinkeen, and begged for marcy ; and with that, says the lady :

" ' Renounce your evil coorses,' says she, ' you villian, or you'll repint it too late ; be a good man for the futhur, and go to your duty reg'lar. And now,' says she, ' take me back, and put me into the river agin, where you found me.'

" ' Oh, my lady,' says the sojer, ' how could I have the heart to drownd a beautiful lady like you ? '

" But before he could say another word, the lady was vanished, and there he saw the little throut an the ground. Well, he put it an a clane plate, and away he run for the bare life, for fear her lover would come while she was away ; and he run, and he run, ever till he came to the cave agin, and threw the throut into the river. The minnit he did, the wather was as red as blood for a little while, by raison av the cut, I suppose, until the sthrame washed the stain away ; and to this day there's a little red mark an the throut's side where it was cut.

" Well, sir, from that day out the sojer was an althered man, and reformed his ways, and wint to his duty reg'lar, and fasted three times a week—though it was never fish he tuk an fastin' days ; for afther the fright he got, fish id never rest an his stomach, God bless us !—savin' your presence. But anyhow, he was an althered man, as I said before ; and in coorse o' time he left the army, and turned hermit at last ; and they say he *used to pray evermore for the sowl of the White Throut.*"

———

THE BATTLE OF THE BERRINS;

OR,

THE DOUBLE FUNERAL

I WAS sitting alone in the desolate churchyard of ——, intent upon my "silent art," lifting up my eyes from my portfolio only to direct them to the interesting ruin I was sketching, when the deathlike stillness that prevailed was broken by a faint and wild sound, unlike anything I had ever heard in my life. I confess I was startled. I paused in my occupation, and listened in breathless expectation. Again this seemingly unearthly sound vibrated through the still air of evening, more audibly than at first, and partaking of the vibratory quality of tone I have noticed in so great a degree as to resemble the remote sound of the ringing of many glasses crowded together.

I arose and looked around. No being was near me, and again this heart-chilling sound struck upon my ear, its wild and wailing intonation reminding me of the Æolian harp. Another burst was wafted up the hill; and then it became discernible that the sound proceeded from many voices raised in lamentation.

It was the *ulican*. I had hitherto known it only by report. For the first time now its wild and appalling cadence had ever been heard, and it will not be wondered at by those acquainted with it that I was startled on hearing it under such circumstances.

I could now perceive a crowd of peasants of both sexes winding along a hollow way that led to the churchyard where I was standing, bearing amongst them the coffin of the departed; and ever and anon a wild burst of the *ulican* would arise from the throng, and ring in wild and startling *unison* up the hill, until, by a gradual and plaintive descent through an *octave*, it dropped into a subdued wail; and they bore the body onward the while, not in the measured and solemn step that custom (at least our custom) deems decent, but in a rapid and irregular manner, as if the violence of their grief hurried them on and disdained all form.

The effect was certainly more impressive than that of any other funeral I had ever witnessed, however much the "pride, pomp, and circumstance" of such arrays had been called upon to produce a studied solemnity; for no hearse with sable plumes, nor chief mourners, nor pall-bearers, ever equalled in *poetry* or *picturesque* these poor people, bearing along on their shoulders in the stillness of evening the body of their departed friend to its "long home"—the women raising their arms above their heads in the untaught action of grief, their dark and ample

THE BATTLE OF THE BERRINS

cloaks waving wildly about, agitated by the varied motions of their wearers, and their wild cry raised in lament

"Most musical, most melancholy."

At length they reached the cemetery, and the coffin was borne into the interior of the ruin, where the women still continued to wail for the dead, while half-a-dozen athletic young men immediately proceeded to prepare a grave. And seldom have I seen finer fellows, or men more full of activity; their action, indeed, bespoke so much life and vigour as to induce an involuntary and melancholy contrast with the object on which that action was bestowed.

Scarcely had the spade upturned the green sod of the burial-ground, when the wild peal of the *ulican* again was heard at a distance. The young men paused in their work, and turned their heads, as did all the bystanders, towards the point whence the sound proceeded.

We soon perceived another funeral procession wind round the foot of the hill, and immediately the grave-makers renewed their work with redoubled activity, while exclamations of anxiety on their part for the completion of their work, and of encouragement from the lookers-on, resounded on all sides; and such ejaculations as "Hurry, boys, hurry!"—"Stir yourself, Paddy!" —"That's your sort, Mike!"—"Rouse your sowl!" etc., etc., resounded on all sides. At the same time, the second funeral party that was advancing no sooner perceived the churchyard already occupied, than they directly quickened their pace, as the wail rose more loudly and wildly from the train; and a detachment bearing pick and spade forthwith sallied from the main body, and dashed with headlong speed up the hill. In the meantime, an old woman, with streaming eyes and dishevelled hair, rushed wildly from the ruin where the first party had borne their coffin, towards the young athletes I have already described as working with "might and main," and addressing them with all the passionate intensity of her country, she exclaimed : " Sure you wouldn't let them have the advantage of us, that-a-way, and lave my darlin' boy wanderhin' about, dark an' 'lone in the long nights. Work, boys! work! for the bare life, and the mother's blessin' be an you, and let my poor Paudeen have rest."

I thought the poor woman was crazed, as indeed her appearance and vehemence of manner, as well as the (to me) unintelligible address she had uttered, might well induce me to believe, and I questioned one of the bystanders accordingly.

" An' is it why she's goin' wild about it, you're axin'? " said the person I addressed, in evident wonder at my question. "Sure then I thought all the world knew that, let alone a gintleman like you, that ought to be knowledgable. And sure she doesn't want the poor boy to be walkin', as of coorse he must, barrin' they're smart."

"What do you mean?" said I. "I don't understand you."

"Whisht! whisht!" said he; "here they come, by the powers, and the Gallaghers at the head of them," as he looked towards the new-comers' advanced-guard, who had now gained the summit of the hill, and, leaping over the boundary-ditch of the cemetery, advanced towards the group that surrounded the grave, with rapid strides and a resolute air.

"Give over there, I bid you," said a tall and ably-built man of the party to those employed in opening the ground, who still plied their implements with energy.

"Give over, or it'll be worse for you. Didn't you hear me, Rooney?" said he, as he laid his muscular hand on the arm of one of the party he addressed, and arrested him in his occupation.

"I did hear you," said Rooney; "but I didn't heed you."

"I'd have you keep a civil tongue in your head," said the former.

"You're mighty ready to give advice that you want yourself," rejoined the latter, as he again plunged the spade into the earth.

"Lave off, I tell you!" said our Hercules, in a higher tone; "or, by this and that, I'll make you sorry!"

"Arrah! what brings you here at all," said another of the grave-makers, "breedin' a disturbance?"

"What brings him here but mischief?" said a grey-haired man, who undertook, with national peculiarity, to answer one interrogatory by making another. "There's always a quarrel whenever there's a Gallagher." For it was indeed one of "the Gallaghers" that the peasant I spoke to noticed as being "at the head o' them," who was assuming so bold a tone.

"You may thank your grey hairs that I don't make you repent o' your words," said Gallagher, and his brow darkened as he spoke.

"Time was," said the old man, "when I had something surer than grey hairs to make such as you respect me;" and he drew himself up with an air of patriarchal dignity, and displayed in his still expansive chest and commanding height the remains of a noble figure, that bore testimony to the truth of what he had just uttered. The old man's eye kindled as he spoke—but 'twas only for a moment; and the expression of pride and defiance was succeeded by that of coldness and contempt.

"I'd have beat you blind the best day ever you seen," said Gallagher, with an impudent swagger.

"Troth you wouldn't, Gallagher!" said a contemporary of the old man; "but your consait bates the world!"

"That's thrue," said Rooney. "He's a great man intirely, in

his own opinion. I'd make a power of money if I could *buy* Gallagher at *my* price and *sell* him at his *own*."

A low and jeering laugh followed this hit of my friend Rooney; and Gallagher assumed an aspect so lowering that a peasant, standing near me, turned to his companion and said significantly: "By gor, Ned, there'll be wigs an the green afore long!"

And he was quite right.

The far-off speck on the horizon, whence the prophetic eye of a sailor can foretell the coming storm, is not more nicely discriminated by the mariner than the symptoms of an approaching fray by an Irishman; and scarcely had the foregoing words been uttered, than I saw the men tucking up their long frieze coats in a sort of jacket fashion—thus getting rid of their *tails*, like game-cocks before a battle. A more menacing grip was taken by the bearer of each stick (a usual appendage of Hibernians); and a general closing-in of the bystanders round the nucleus of dissatisfaction made it perfectly apparent that hostilities must soon commence.

I was not long left in suspense about such a catastrophe, for a general outbreaking soon took place, commencing in the centre with the principals already noticed, and radiating throughout the whole circle, until a general action ensued, and the belligerents were dispersed in various hostile groups over the churchyard.

I was a spectator from the topmost step of a stile leading into the burial-ground, deeming it imprudent to linger within the precincts of the scene of action, when my attention was attracted by the appearance of a horseman, who galloped up the little stony road, and was no sooner at my side than he dismounted, exclaiming at the top of his voice: "Oh, you reprobates! *lave* off, I tell you, you heathens! Are you Christians at all?"

I must here pause a moment to describe the person of the horseman in question. He was a tall, thin, pale man, having a hat which, from exposure to bad weather, had its broad, slouching brim crimped into many fantastic involutions, its crown somewhat depressed in the middle, and the edges of the same exhibiting a napless paleness, very far removed from its original black; no shirt-collar sheltered his angular jaw-bones— a narrow white cravat was drawn tightly round his spare neck; a single-breasted coat of rusty black, with standing collar, was tightly buttoned nearly up to his chin, and a nether garment of the same, with large silver knee-buckles, meeting a square-cut and buckram-like pair of black leather boots, with heavy, plated spurs, that had seen the best of their days, completed the picture. His horse was a small, well-built hack, whose long, rough coat would have been white, but that soiled litter had stained it to a dirty yellow; and taking advantage of the liberty which the abandoned rein afforded, he very quietly turned him to the little fringe of grass which bordered each side of the path, to make as much profit of his time as he might, before his rider should resume his seat in the old high-pommelled saddle which he had vacated in uttering the ejaculations I have recorded.

This person, then, hastily mounting the stile on which I stood, with rustic politeness said : "By your leave, sir," as he pushed by me in haste, and jumping from the top of the wall, proceeded with long and rapid strides towards the combatants, and brandishing a heavy thong whip which he carried, he began to lay about him with equal vigour and impartiality on each and every of the peace - breakers, both parties sharing in the castigation thus bestowed, with the most even, and, I might add, *heavy*-handed justice.

My surprise was great on finding that all the blows inflicted by this new belligerent, instead of being resented by the assaulted parties, seemed taken as if resistance against this potent chastiser were vain, and in a short time they all fled before him, like so many frightened school-boys before an incensed pedagogue, and huddled themselves together in a crowd, which at once became pacified at his presence.

Seeing this result, I descended from my perch and ran towards the scene that excited my surprise in no ordinary degree. I found this new-comer delivering to the multitude he had quelled a severe reproof of their "unchristian doings," as he termed them and it became evident that he was the pastor of the flock, and it must be acknowledged a very turbulent flock he seemed to have of it.

This admonition was soon ended. It was certainly impressive, and well calculated for the audience to whom it was delivered, as well from the simplicity of its language as the solemnity of its manner, which was much enhanced by the deep and somewhat sepulchral voice of the speaker. "And now," added the pastor, "let me ask you for what you were fighting like so many wild Indians ? for surely your conduct is liker to savage creatures than men that have been bred up in the hearing of God's word."

A pause of a few seconds followed this question ; and at length someone ventured to answer from amongst the crowd that it was "in regard of the berrin."

"And is not so solemn a sight," asked the priest, "as the burial of the departed enough to keep down the evil passions of your hearts ? "

"Troth then, and plaze your Riverince, it was nothin' ill-nathured in life, but only a good-nathured turn we wor doin for poor Paudeen Mooney that's departed ; and sure it's to your Riverince we'll be goin' immadiantly for the masses for the poor boy's sowl." Thus making interest in the offended quarter with an address for which the Irish peasant is pre-eminently distinguished.

"Tut! tut!" rapidly answered the priest, anxious, perhaps, to silence this very palpable appeal to his own interest. "Don't talk to me about doing a good-natured turn. Not," added he, in a subdued undertone, "but that prayers for the souls of the departed faithful are enjoined by the Church; but what has that to do with your scandalous and lawless doings that I witnessed this minute, and you yourself," said he, addressing the last speaker, "one of the busiest with your alpeen? I'm afraid you're rather fractious, Rooney. Take care that I don't speak to you from the altar."

"Oh, God forbid that your Riverince id have to do the like!" said the mother of the deceased, already noticed, in an imploring tone, and with the big tear-drops chasing each other down her cheeks; "and sure it was only they wanted to put my poor boy in the ground *first*, and no wondher sure, as your Riverince *knows*, and not to have my poor Paudeen—"

"Tut, tut! woman!" interrupted the priest, waving his hand rather impatiently, "don't let me hear any folly."

"I ax your Riverince's pardon, and sure it's myself that id be sorry to offind my clargy—God's blessin' be an them night and day! But I was only goin' to put in a word for Mikee Rooney, and sure it wasn't him at all, nor wouldn't be any of us, only for Shan Gallagher, that wouldn't lave us in peace."

"Gallagher!" said the priest, in a deeply reproachful tone. "Where is he?"

Gallagher came not forward, but the crowd drew back, and left him revealed to the priest. His aspect was that of sullen indifference, and he seemed to be the only person present totally uninfluenced by the presence of his pastor, who now advanced towards him, and extending his attenuated hand in the attitude of denunciation towards the offender, said very solemnly:

"I have already spoken to you in the house of worship, and now, once more, I warn you to beware. Riot and battle are found wherever you go, and if you do not speedily reform your course of life, I shall expel you from the pale of the Church, and pronounce sentence of excommunication upon you from the altar."

Everyone appeared awed by the solemnity and severity of this address from the onset, but when the word "excommunication" was uttered, a thrill of horror seemed to run through the assembled multitude; and even Gallagher himself, I thought, betrayed some emotion on hearing the terrible word. Yet he evinced it but for a moment, and turning on his heel, he retired from the ground with something of the swagger with which he entered it. The crowd opened to let him pass, and opened widely, as if they sought to avoid contact with one so fearfully denounced.

"You have two coffins here," said the clergyman; "proceed, therefore, immediately to make two graves, and let the bodies be interred at the same time, and I will read the service for the dead."

No very great time was consumed in making the necessary preparation. The "narrow beds" were made, and as their tenants were consigned to their last long sleep, the solemn voice of the priest was raised in the "De Profundis"; and when he had concluded the short and beautiful psalm, the friends of the deceased closed the graves, and covered them neatly with fresh-cut sods, which is what *Paddy* very metaphorically calls

"Putting the daisy quilt over him."

The clergyman retired from the churchyard, and I followed his footsteps for the purpose of introducing myself to "his reverence," and seeking from him an explanation of what was still a most unfathomable mystery to me, namely, the cause of the quarrel, which, from certain passages in his address to the people, I saw he understood, though so slightly glanced at. Accordingly, I overtook the priest, and as the old Irish song has it,

"To him I obnoxiously made my approaches."

He received me with courtesy, which, though not savouring much of intercourse with polished circles, seemed to spring whence all true politeness emanates—from a good heart.

I begged to assure him it was not an impertinent curiosity which made me desirous of becoming acquainted with the cause of the fray which I had witnessed, and he had put a stop to in so summary a manner, and hoped he would not consider it an intrusion if I applied to him for that purpose.

"No intrusion in life, sir," answered the priest very frankly, and with a rich *brogue*, whose intonation was singularly expressive of good nature. It was the specimen of brogue I have never met but in one class, the Irish gentleman of the last century—an accent which, though it possessed all the characteristic traits of "the brogue," was at the same time divested of the slightest trace of vulgarity. This is not to be met with now, or at least very rarely. An attempt has been made by those who fancy it genteel to graft the English accent upon the Broguish stem— and a very bad fruit it has produced. The truth is, the accents of the two countries could never be happily blended; and far from making a pleasing amalgamation, it conveys the idea that the speaker is endeavouring to *escape* from his own accent for

what he considers a superior one; and it is this attempt to be
fine which so particularly allies the idea of vulgarity with the
tone of brogue so often heard in the present day.

Such, I have said, was *not* the brogue of the Rev. Phelim
Roach, or Father Roach, as the peasants called him; and his
voice, which I have earlier noticed as almost sepulchral, I found
derived that character from the feeling of the speaker when
engaged in an admonitory address; for when employed on
colloquial occasions, it was no more than what might be called a
rich and deep manly voice. So much for Father Roach, who
forthwith proceeded to enlighten me on the subject of the funeral,
and the quarrel arising therefrom.

"The truth is, sir, these poor people are possessed of many
foolish superstitions; and however we may, as *men*, pardon them,
looking upon them as fictions originating in a warm imagination,
and finding a ready admission into the minds of an unlettered
and susceptible peasantry, we cannot, as pastors of the flock,
admit their belief to the poor people committed to our care."

This was quite new to me—to find a clergyman of the religion
I had hitherto heard of as being *par excellence* abounding in
superstition denouncing the very article in question. But let
me not interrupt Father Roach.

"The superstition I speak of," continued he, "is one of the
many these warm-hearted people indulge in, and is certainly very
poetical in its texture."

"But, sir," interrupted my newly-made acquaintance, pulling
forth a richly chased gold watch of antique workmanship, that at
once suggested ideas of the " *bon vieux temps,*" "I must ask your
pardon—I have an engagement to keep at the little hut I call
my home, which obliges me to proceed there forthwith. If you
have so much time to spare as will enable you to walk with me
to the end of this little road, it will suffice to make you acquainted
with the nature of the superstition in question."

I gladly assented; and the priest, disturbing the nibbling
occupation of his hack, threw the rein over his arm, and the
docile little beast, following him on one side as quietly as I did
on the other, he gave me the following account of the cause of
all the previous riot, as we wound down the little stony path
that led to the main road.

"There is a belief among the peasantry in this particular
district that the ghost of the last person interred in the churchyard is obliged to traverse, unceasingly, the road between this
earth and purgatory, carrying water to slake the burning thirst
of those confined in that 'limbo large'; and that the ghost is
thus obliged to walk

'Through the dead waste and middle of the night,'

until some fresh arrival of a tenant to the 'narrow house' supplies a fresh ghost to 'relieve guard,' if I may be allowed so military an expression ; and thus the supply of water to the sufferers in purgatory is kept up unceasingly."

Hence it was that the fray had arisen, and the poor mother's invocation, "that her darling boy should not be left to wander about the churchyard dark and lone in the long nights," became at once intelligible. Father Roach gave me some curious illustrations of the different ways in which this superstition influenced his " poor people," as he constantly called them. But I suppose my readers have had quite enough of the subject, and I shall therefore say no more of other " cases in point," contented with having given them one example, and recording the existence of a superstition which, however wild, undoubtedly owes its existence to an affectionate heart and a poetic imagination.

FATHER ROACH

I FOUND the company of Father Roach so pleasant that I accepted an invitation which he gave me when we arrived at the termination of our walk to breakfast the next morning at the little hut, as he called the unpretending but neat cottage he inhabited, a short mile distant from the churchyard where we first met. I repaired, accordingly, the next morning at an early hour to my appointment, and found the worthy, pastor ready to receive me. He met me at the little avenue (not that I mean to imply an idea of grandeur by the term) which led from the main road to his dwelling. It was a short, narrow road, bordered on each side by alder bushes, and an abrupt, awkward turn placed you in front of the humble dwelling of which he was master ; the area before it, however, was clean, and the offensive dunghill, the intrusive pig, and barking cur-dog were not the distinguishing features of this, as unfortunately they too often are of other Irish cottagers.

On entering the house, an elderly and comfortably clad woman curtsied as we crossed the threshold, and I was led across an apartment, whose

" Neatly sanded floor—"

(an earthen one, by the way)—we traversed diagonally to an opposite corner, where an open door admitted us into a small but comfortable *boarded* apartment, where breakfast was laid, unostentatiously but neatly, and inviting to the appetite, as far as that could be stimulated by a white cloth, most promising fresh butter, a plate of evidently fresh eggs, and the best of cream, whose rich white was most advantageously set off by the plain blue ware of which the ewer was composed ; add to this an ample cake of fresh griddle bread, and

"Though last, not least,"

the savoury smell that arose from a rasher of bacon, which announced itself through the medium of more senses than one ; for its fretting and fuming in the pan, playing many an ingenious variation upon "fiz and whiz ! "

"Gave dreadful note of preparation."

But I must not forget to notice the painted tin tea canister of mine host, which was emblazoned with the talismanic motto of

"O'Connell and Liberty ; "

and underneath the semi-circular motto aforesaid appeared the rubicund visage of a lusty gentleman in a green coat, holding in his hand a scroll inscribed with the dreadful words, "Catholic rent,"

"Unpleasing most to Brunswick ears,"

which was meant to represent no less a personage than the "Great Liberator" himself.

While breakfast was going forward, the priest and myself had made no inconsiderable advances towards intimacy. Those who have mingled much in the world have often, no doubt, experienced, like myself, how much easier it is to enter at once, almost, into friendship with some, before the preliminaries of common acquaintance can be established with others.

Father Roach was one of the former species. We soon sympathised with each other ; and becoming, as it were, at once possessed of the keys of each other's freemasonry, we mutually unlocked our confidence. This led to many an interesting conversation with the good father while I remained in his neighbourhood. He gave me a sketch of his life in a few words. It was simply this : He was a descendant of a family that had once been wealthy and of large possessions in the very county where, as he said himself, he was "a pauper."

"For what else can I call myself," said the humble priest, "when I depend on the gratuitous contributions of those who are little better than paupers themselves for my support ? But God's will be done."

His forefathers had lost their patrimony by repeated forfeitures, under every change of power that had distracted the unfortunate island of which he was a native ; and for him and his brothers nothing was left but personal exertion.

"The elder boys would not remain here," said he, "where their religion was a barrier to their promotion. They went abroad, and offered their swords to the service of a foreign power. They fought and fell under the banners of Austria, who disdained not the accession of all such strong arms and bold hearts that left their native soil to be better appreciated in a stranger land.

"I, and a younger brother, who lost his father ere he could feel the loss, remained in poor Ireland. I was a sickly boy, and was constantly near my beloved mother—God rest her soul!— who early instilled into my infant mind deeply reverential notions of religion, which at length imbued my mind so strongly with their influence that I determined to devote my life to the priesthood. I was sent to St. Omer to study, and on my return was appointed to the ministry, which I have ever since exercised to the best of the ability that God has vouchsafed to his servant."

Such was the outline of Father Roach's personal and family history.

In some of the conversations which our intimacy originated, I often sought for information touching the peculiar doctrines of his Church, and the discipline which its followers are enjoined to adopt.

I shall not attempt to weary the reader with an account of our arguments—for the good Father Roach was so meek as to condescend to an argument with one unlearned as myself, and a heretic to boot—nor to detail some anecdotes that to me were interesting on various points in question. I shall reserve but *one fact*—and a most singular one it is—to present to my readers on the subject of confession.

Speaking upon this point, I remarked to Father Roach, that of all the practices of the Roman Catholic Church, that of confession I considered the most beneficial within the range of its discipline.

He concurred with me in admitting it as highly advantageous to the sinner. I ventured to add that I considered it very beneficial also to the person sinned against.

"Very true," said Father Roach; "restitution is often made through its agency."

"But in higher cases than those you allude to," said I; "for instance, the detection of conspiracies, unlawful meetings, etc. etc."

"Confession," said he, somewhat hesitatingly, "does not immediately come into action in the way you allude to."

I ventured to hint, rather cautiously, that in this kingdom, where the Roman Catholic religion was not the one established by law, there might be some reserve between penitent and confessor on a subject where the existing government might be looked upon something in the light of a step-mother.

A slight flush passed over the priest's pallid face. "No, no," said he; "do not suspect us of any foul play to the power under which we live. No! But recollect, the doctrine of our Church is this—that whatsoever penance may be enjoined on the offending penitent by his confession, his crime, however black, must in all cases he held sacred, when its acknowledgment is made under the seal of confession."

"In all cases?" said I.

"Without an exception," answered he.

"Then, would you not feel it your duty to give a murderer up to justice?"

The countenance of Father Roach assumed an instantaneous change, as if a sudden pang shot through him—his lip became suddenly ashy pale, he hid his face in his hands, and seemed struggling with some deep emotion. I feared I had offended, and feeling quite confused, began to stammer out some nonsense, when he interrupted me.

"Do not be uneasy," said he. "You have said nothing to be ashamed of, but your words touched a chord"—and his voice trembled as he spoke—"that cannot vibrate without intense pain;" and wiping away a tear that glistened in each humid eye, "I shall tell you a story," said he, "that will be the strongest illustration of such a case as you have supposed." And he proceeded to give me the following narrative:

THE PRIEST'S STORY

I HAVE already made known unto you that a younger brother and myself were left to the care of my mother—best and dearest of mothers! said the holy man, sighing deeply, and clasping his hands fervently, while his eyes were lifted to heaven, as if love made him conscious that the spirit of her he lamented had found its eternal rest there—thy gentle and affectionate nature sunk under the bitter trial that an all-wise Providence was pleased to visit thee with! Well, sir, Frank was my mother's darling; not that you are to understand, by so saying, that she was of that weak and capricious tone of mind which lavished its care upon one at the expense of others—far from it; never was a deep store of maternal love more equally shared than among the four brothers; but when the two seniors went away, and I was some time after sent for my studies to St. Omer, Frank became the object upon which all the tenderness of her affectionate heart might exercise the little maternal cares that hitherto had been divided amongst many. Indeed, my dear Frank deserved it all; his was the gentlest of natures, combined with a mind of singular strength and brilliant imagination. In short, as the phrase has it, he was "the flower of the flock," and great things were expected from him. It was some time after my return from St. Omer, while preparations were making for advancing Frank in the pursuit which had been selected as the business of his life, that every hour which drew nearer to the moment of his departure made him dearer, not only to us, but to all who knew him, and each friend claimed a day that Frank should spend with him, which always passed in recalling the happy hours they had already spent together, in assurances given and received of kindly remembrances that still should be cherished, and in mutual wishes for success, with many a hearty prophecy from my poor Frank's friends, "that he would one day be a great man."

One night, as my mother and myself were sitting at home beside the fire, expecting Frank's return from one of these parties, my mother said, in an unusually anxious tone: "I wish Frank was come home."

"What makes you think of his return so soon?" said I.

"I don't know," said she; "but somehow, I'm uneasy about him."

"Oh, make yourself quiet," said I, "on that subject; we cannot possibly expect Frank for an hour to come yet."

Still, my mother could not become calm, and she fidgeted about the room, became busy in doing nothing, and now and then would go to the door of the house to listen for the distant tramp of Frank's horse; but Frank came not.

More than the hour I had named as the probable time of his return had elapsed, and my mother's anxiety had amounted to a painful pitch; and I began myself to blame my brother for so long and late an absence. Still, I endeavoured to calm her, and had prevailed on her to seat herself again at the fire, and commenced reading a page or two of an amusing book, when suddenly she stopped me, and turned her head to the window in the attitude of listening.

"It is! it is!" said she; "I hear him coming."

And now the sound of a horse's feet in a rapid pace became audible. She rose from her chair, and with a deeply aspirated "Thank God!" went to open the door for him herself. I heard the horse now pass by the window; in a second or two more the door was opened, and instantly a fearful scream from my mother brought me hastily to her assistance. I found her lying in the hall in a deep swoon. The servants of the house hastily crowded to the spot, and gave her immediate aid. I ran to the door to ascertain the cause of my mother's alarm, and there I saw Frank's horse panting and foaming, and the saddle empty. That my brother had been thrown and badly hurt was the first thought that suggested itself; and a car and horse were immediately ordered to drive in the direction he had been returning; but in a few minutes our fears were excited to the last degree by discovering there was blood on the saddle.

We all experienced inconceivable terror at the discovery, but not to weary you with details, suffice it to say that we commenced a diligent search, and at length arrived at a small by-way that turned from the main road, and led through a bog, which was the nearest course for my brother to have taken homewards, and we accordingly began to explore it. I was mounted on the horse my brother had ridden, and the animal snorted violently, and exhibited evident symptoms of dislike to retrace this by-way, which, I doubted not, he had already travelled that night; and this very fact made me still more apprehensive that some terrible occurrence must have taken place to occasion such excessive repugnance on the part of the animal. However, I urged him onward, and telling those who accompanied me to follow with what speed they might, I dashed forward, followed by a faithful dog of poor Frank's. At the termination of about half a mile, the horse became still more impatient of restraint, and started at every ten paces; and the dog began to traverse the little road, giving an occasional yelp, sniffing the air strongly, and lashing his sides with his tail, as if on some scent. At length he came to a stand, and beat about within a very circumscribed space—yelping occasionally, as if to draw my attention.

I dismounted immediately, but the horse was so extremely restless that the difficulty I had in holding him prevented me from observing the road by the light of the lantern which I carried. I perceived, however, it was very much trampled hereabouts, and bore evidence of having been the scene of a struggle. I shouted to the party in the rear, who soon came up and lighted some faggots of bogwood which they brought with them to assist in our search, and we now more clearly distinguished the marks I have alluded to. The dog still howled, and indicated a particular spot to us; and on one side of the path, upon the stunted grass, we discovered a quantity of fresh blood, and I picked up a pencil-case that I knew had belonged to my murdered brother—for I now was compelled to consider him as such; and an attempt to describe the agonised feelings which at that moment I experienced would be in vain. We continued our search for the discovery of his body for many hours without success, and the morning was far advanced before we returned home. How changed a home from the preceding day! My beloved mother could scarcely be roused for a moment from a sort of stupor that seized upon her when the paroxysm of frenzy was over which the awful catastrophe of the fatal night had produced. If ever heart was broken, hers was. She lingered but a few weeks after the son she adored, and seldom spoke during the period, except to call upon his name.

But I will not dwell on this painful theme. Suffice it to say she died ; and her death, under such circumstances, increased the sensation which my brother's mysterious murder had excited. Yet, with all the horror which was universally entertained for the crime, and the execrations poured upon its atrocious per- petrator, still the doer of the deed remained undiscovered, and even I, who of course was the most active in seeking to develop the mystery, not only could catch no clue to lead to the discovery of the murderer, but failed even to ascertain where the mangled remains of my lost brother had been deposited.

It was nearly a year after the fatal event that a penitent knelt to me, and confided to the ear of his confessor the misdeeds of an ill-spent life ; I say of his whole life—for he had never before knelt at the confessional.

Fearful was the catalogue of crime that was revealed to me— unbounded selfishness, oppression, revenge, and lawless passion had held unbridled influence over the unfortunate sinner, and sensuality in all its shapes, even to the polluted home and betrayed maiden, had plunged him deeply into sin.

I was shocked—I may even say I was disgusted, and the culprit himself seemed to shrink from the recapitulation of his crimes, which he found more extensive and appalling than he had dreamed of, until the recital of them called them all up in fearful array before him. I was about to commence an admonition, when he interrupted me—he had more to communicate. I desired him to proceed. He writhed before me. I enjoined him in the name of the God he had offended, and who knoweth the inmost heart, to make an unreserved disclosure of his crimes before he dared to seek a reconciliation with his Maker. At length, after many a pause and convulsive sob, he told me, in a voice almost suffocated by terror, that he had been guilty of bloodshed. I shuddered, but in a short time I recovered myself, and asked how and where he had deprived a fellow-creature of life ? Never, to the latest hour of my life, shall I forget the look which the miserable sinner gave me at that moment. His eyes were glazed, and seemed starting from their sockets with terror ; his face assumed a deadly paleness—he raised his clasped hands up to me in the most imploring action, as if supplicating mercy, and with livid and quivering lips he gasped out—"'Twas I who killed your brother !"

Oh, God ! how I felt at that instant ! Even now, after the lapse of years, I recollect the sensation : it was as if the blood were flowing back upon my heart, until I felt as if it would burst; and then, a few convulsive breathings, and back rushed the blood again through my tingling veins. I thought I was dying; but suddenly I uttered an hysteric laugh, and fell back senseless in my seat.

When I recovered, a cold sweat was pouring down my forehead, and I was weeping copiously. Never before did I feel my manhood annihilated under the influence of an hysterical affection. It was dreadful.

I found the blood-stained sinner supporting me, roused from his own prostration by a sense of terror at my emotion; for when I could hear anything, his entreaties that I would not discover upon him were poured forth in the most abject strain of supplication. "Fear not for your miserable life," said I; "the seal of confession is upon what you have revealed to me, and so far you are safe; but leave me for the present, and come not to me again until I send for you." He departed.

I knelt and prayed for strength to Him who alone could give it, to fortify me in this dreadful trial. Here was the author of a brother's murder, and a mother's consequent death, discovered to me in the person of my penitent. It was a fearful position for a frail mortal to be placed in; but as a consequence of the holy calling I professed, I hoped, through the blessing of Him whom I served, to acquire fortitude for the trial into which the ministry of His gospel had led me.

The fortitude I needed came through prayer, and when I thought myself equal to the task, I sent for the murderer of my brother. I officiated for him as our Church has ordained—I appointed penances to him, and in short, dealt with him merely as any other confessor might have done.

Years thus passed away, and during that time he constantly attended his duty; and it was remarked through the country that he had become a quieter person since Father Roach had become his confessor. But still he was not liked—and indeed, I fear he was far from a reformed man, though he did not allow his transgressions to be so glaring as they were wont to be; and I began to think that terror and cunning had been his motives in suggesting to him the course he had adopted, as the opportunities which it gave him of being often with me as his confessor were likely to lull every suspicion of his guilt in the eyes of the world; and in making me the depositary of his fearful secret, he thus placed himself beyond the power of my pursuit, and interposed the strongest barrier to my becoming the avenger of his bloody deed.

Hitherto I have not made you acquainted with the cause of that foul act. It was jealousy. He found himself rivalled by my brother in the good graces of a beautiful girl of moderate circumstances, whom he would have wished to obtain as his wife, but to whom Frank had become an object of greater interest; and I doubt not, had my poor brother been spared, that marriage would ultimately have drawn closer the ties that were so savagely severed. But the ambuscade and the knife had done their deadly work; for the cowardly villain had lain in wait for him on the lonely bog-road he guessed he would travel on that fatal night, and springing from his lurking-place, he stabbed my noble Frank in the back.

Well, sir, I fear I am tiring you with a story which, you cannot wonder, is interesting to me; but I shall hasten to a conclusion.

One gloomy evening in March I was riding along the very road where my brother had met his fate, in company with his murderer. I know not what brought us together in such a place, except the hand of Providence, that sooner or later brings the murderer to justice; for I was not wont to pass the road, and loathed the company of the man who happened to overtake me upon it. I know not whether it was some secret visitation of conscience that influenced him at the time, or that he thought the lapse of years had wrought upon me so far as to obliterate the grief for my brother's death, which had never been, till that moment, alluded to, however remotely, since he confessed his crime. Judge then my surprise when, directing my attention to a particular point in the bog, he said:

"'Tis close by that place that your brother is buried."

I could not, I think, have been more astonished had my brother appeared before me.

"What brother?" said I.

"Your brother Frank," said he; "'twas there I buried him, poor fellow, after I killed him."

"Merciful God!" I exclaimed, "thy will be done," and seizing the rein of the culprit's horse, I said: "Wretch that you are! you have owned to the shedding of the innocent blood that has been crying to Heaven for vengeance these ten years, and I arrest you here as my prisoner."

He turned ashy pale as he faltered out a few words to say I had promised not to betray him.

"'Twas under the seal of confession," said I, "that you disclosed the deadly secret, and under that seal my lips must have been for ever closed; but now, even in the very place where your crime was committed, it has pleased God that you should arraign yourself in the face of the world, and the brother of your victim is appointed to be the avenger of his innocent blood."

He was overwhelmed by the awfulness of this truth, and

unresistingly he rode beside me to the adjacent town of ——,
where he was committed for trial.

The report of this singular and providential discovery of a
murder excited a great deal of interest in the country; and as
I was known to be the culprit's confessor, the bishop of the
diocese forwarded a statement to a higher quarter, which
procured for me a dispensation as regarded the confessions of
the criminal, and I was handed this instrument, absolving me
from further secrecy, a few days before the trial. I was the
principal evidence against the prisoner. The body of my
brother had, in the interim, been found in the spot his murderer
had indicated, and the bog preserved it so far from decay as to
render recognition a task of no difficulty. The proof was so
satisfactorily adduced to the jury that the murderer was found
guilty and executed, ten years after he had committed the
crime.

The judge pronounced a very feeling comment on the nature
of the situation in which I had been placed for so many years,
and passed a very flattering eulogium upon what he was pleased
to call "my heroic observance of the obligation of secrecy by
which I had been bound."

Thus, sir, you see how sacred a trust that of a fact revealed
under confession is held by our Church, when even the avenging
a brother's murder was not sufficient warranty for its being
broken.

THE KING AND THE BISHOP

A LEGEND OF CLONMACNOISE

THERE are few things more pleasant to those who are doomed to
pass the greater part of their lives in the dust and din and smoke
of a city than to get on the top of a stage-coach early some fine
summer morning, and whirl along through the yet unpeopled
streets, echoing from their emptiness to the rattle of the welcome
wheels that are bearing you away from your metropolitan prison,
to the

"Free blue streams and the laughing sky"

of the sweet country. How gladly you pass the last bridge over one
of the canals! and then, deeming yourself fairly out of town, you
look back once only on its receding "groves of chimneys," and
settling yourself comfortably in your seat, you cast away care,
and look forward in gleeful anticipation of your three or four
weeks in the tranquillity and freedom of a country ramble.

Such have my sensations often been—not a little increased, by-
the-by, as I hugged closer to my side my portfolio, well stored

with paper, and heard the rattle of my pencils and colours in the tin sketching box in my pocket. Such were they when last I started one fresh and lovely summer's morning, on the Ballinasloe coach, and promised myself a rich treat in a visit to Clonmacnoise, or "the Churches," as the place is familiarly called by the peasantry. Gladly I descended from my lofty station on our dusty conveyance, when it arrived at Shannonbridge, and engaging a boat, embarked on the noble river whence the village takes its name, and proceeded up the wide and winding stream to the still sacred and once celebrated Clonmacnoise, the second monastic foundation established in Ireland, once tenanted by the learned and the powerful, now scarcely known but to the mendicant pilgrim, the learned antiquary, or the vagrant lover of the picturesque.

Here, for days together, have I lingered, watching its noble, "ivy-mantled" tower, reposing in shadow, or sparkling in sunshine, as it spired upward in bold relief against the sky; or admiring the graceful involutions of the ample Shannon that wound beneath the gentle acclivity on which I stood, through the plashy meadows and the wide waste of bog, whose rich brown tones of colour faded into blue on the horizon; or in noting the red-tanned sail of some passing turf-boat, as it broke the monotony of the quiet river, or in recording with my pencil the noble stone cross, or the tracery of some mouldering ruin,

> " Where ivied arch, or pillar lone,
> Plead haughtily for glories gone,"

though I should not say "haughtily," for poor old Clonmacnoise pleads with as much humility as the religion which reared her now does; and which, like her, interesting in the attitude of decay, teaches and appeals to our sympathies and our imagination, instead of taking the strongholds of our reason by storm, and forcing our assent by overwhelming batteries of irrefragable proof, before it seeks to win our will by tender and impassioned appeals to the heart. But I wander from Clonmacnoise. It is a truly solemn and lonely spot; I love it almost to a folly, and have wandered day after day through its quiet cemetery, till I have almost made acquaintance with its ancient grave-stones.

One day I was accosted by a peasant who had watched for a long time, in silent wonder, the draft of the stone cross, as it grew into being beneath my pencil; and finding the man "apt," as the ghost says to Hamlet, I entered into conversation with him. To some remark of mine touching the antiquity of the place, he assured me "it was a fine *ould* place, in the *ould* ancient times." In noticing the difference between the two round towers—for there are *two* very fine ones at Clonmacnoise, one on the top of the hill, and one close beside the plashy bank of the river—he accounted for the difference by a piece of legendary information with which he favoured me, and which may, perhaps, prove of sufficient importance to interest the reader.

"You see, sir," said he, "the one down there beyant, at the river side, was built the first, and finished complate entirely, for the roof is an it, you see; but when that was built, the bishop thought that another id look very purty on the hill beyant, and so he bid the masons set to work, and build up another tower there.

"Well, away they went to work, as busy as nailers; troth it was jist like a bee-hive, every man with his hammer in his hand, and sure the tower was completed in due time. Well, when the last stone was laid on the roof, the bishop axes the masons how much he was to pay them, and they ups and towld him their price; but the bishop, they say, was a neygar [niggard]— God forgi' me for saying the word of so holy a man!—and he said they axed too much, and he wouldn't pay them. With that, my jew'l, the masons said they would take no less; and what would you think, but the bishop had the cunnin' to take away the ladthers that was reared up agin the tower.

"'And now,' says he, 'my gay fellows,' says he, 'the divil a down out o' that you'll come antil you larn manners, and take what's offered to yees,' says he; 'and when yees come down in your price you may come down yourselves into the bargain.'

"Well, sure enough, he kep his word, and wouldn't let man nor mortyel go nigh them to help them; and faiks the masons didn't like the notion of losing their honest airnins, and small blame to them; but sure they wor starvin' all the time, and didn't know what in the wide world to do, when there was a fool chanc'd to pass by, and seen them.

"'Musha! but you look well there,' says the innocent, 'an' how are you?' says he.

"'Not much the better av your axin,' says they.

"'Maybe you're out there,' says he. So he questioned them, and they tould him how it was with them, and how the bishop tuk away the ladthers, and they couldn't come down.

"'Tut, you fools!' says he; 'sure isn't it aisier to take down two stones nor to put up one?'

"Wasn't that mighty cute o' the fool, sir? And wid that, my dear sowl, no sooner said than done. Faiks, the masons began to pull down their work, and whin they went an for some time, the bishop bid them stop, and he'd let them down; but faiks, before he gev in to them they had taken the roof clane off; and that's the raison that one tower has a roof, sir, and the other has none."

But before I had seen Clonmacnoise and its towers, I was intimate with the most striking of its legends by favour of the sinewy boatman who rowed me to it. We had not long left

Shannonbridge, when, doubling an angle of the shore, and stretching up a reach of the river where it widens, the principal round tower of Clonmacnoise became visible.

"What tower is that?" said I to my Charon.

"That's the big tower of Clonmacnoise, sir," he answered; "an' if your honour looks sharp, a little to the right of it, lower down, you'll see the ruins of the ould palace."

On a somewhat closer inspection, I did perceive the remains he spoke of, dimly discernible in the distance; and it was not without his indication of their relative situation to the tower that I could have distinguished them from the sober grey of the horizon behind them, for the evening was closing fast, and we were moving eastward.

"Does your honour see it yit?" said my boatman.

"I do," said I.

"God spare you your eye-sight," responded he, "for troth it's few gintlemen could see the ould palace this far off, and the sun so low, barrin' they were used to *sportin'*, and had a sharp eye for the birds over a bog, or the like o' that. Oh, then, it's Clonmacnoise, your honour, that's the holy place," continued he, "mighty holy in the ould ancient times, and mighty great too, wid the sivin churches, let alone the two towers, and the bishop, and plinty o' priests, and all to that."

"Two towers?" said I; "then I suppose one has fallen?"

"Not at all, sir," said he; "but the other one that you can't see is beyant in the hollow by the river-side."

"And it was a great place, you say, in the *ould ancient times?*"

"Troth it was, sir, and is still, for to this day it *bates* the world in regard o' pilgrims."

"Pilgrims!" I ejaculated.

"Yes, sir," said the boatman, with his own quiet manner, although it was evident to a quick observer that my surprise at the mention of pilgrims had not escaped him.

I mused a moment. Pilgrims, thought I, in the *British* dominions, in the nineteenth century—strange enough!

"And so," continued I aloud, "you have pilgrims at Clonmacnoise?"

"Troth we have, your honour, from the top of the north and the farthest corner of Kerry; and you may see them any day in the week, let alone the pathern [patron] day, when all the world, you'd think, was there."

"And the palace," said I, "I suppose belonged to the bishop of Clonmacnoise?"

"Some says 'twas the bishop, your honour, and indeed it is them that has larnin' says so; but more says 'twas a king had it long ago, afore the Churches was there at all, at all; and sure enough it looks far oulder nor the Churches, though them is ould enough, God knows. All the knowledgable people I ever heerd talk of it says that; and now, sir," said he, in an expostulatory tone, " wouldn't it be far more nath'ral that the bishop id live in the Churches? And sure," continued he, evidently leaning to the popular belief, "id stands to *raison* that a king id live in a palace, and why *shud* it be called a palace if a king didn't live there ?"

Satisfying himself with this most logical conclusion, he pulled his oar with evident self-complacency; and as I have always found, I derived more legendary information by yielding some-what to the prejudice of the narrator, and by abstaining from inflicting any wound on his pride (so Irish a failing) by laughing at or endeavouring to combat his credulity, I seemed to favour his conclusions, and admitted that a king must have been the *ci-devant* occupant of the palace. So much being settled, he proceeded to tell me that "there was a mighty *quare* story" about the last king that ruled Clonmacnoise; and having expressed an eager desire to hear the *quare story*, he seemed quite happy at being called on to fulfil the office of chronicler; and pulling his oar with an easier sweep, lest he might disturb the quiet hearing of his legend by the rude splash of the water, he prepared to tell his tale, and I to devour up his discourse.

" Well, sir, they say there was a king wanst lived in the palace beyant, and a sportin' fellow he was, and *Cead mile failte* was the word in the palace; no one kem but was welkim, and I go bail the sorra one left it without the *deoch an' doris*. Well, to be sure, the king, av coorse, had the best of eatin' and drinkin', and there was bed and boord for the stranger, let alone the welkim for the neighbours—and a good neighbour he was by all accounts, until, as bad luck would have it, a crass ould bishop (the saints forgi' me for saying the word !) kem to rule over the Churches. Now, you must know, the king was a likely man, and as I said already, he was a sportin' fellow, and by coorse a great favourite with the women; he had a smile and a wink for the crathers at every hand's turn, and the soft word, and the— The short and the long of it is, he was the *divil* among the girls.

" Well, sir, it was all mighty well, antil the ould bishop I mintioned arrived at the Churches; but whin he kem, he tuk great scandal at the goings-an of the king, and he determined to cut him short in his coorses all at wanst; so with that whin the king wint to his duty, the bishop ups and he tells him that he must mend his manners, and all to that; and when the king said that the likes o' that was never tould him afore by the best priest o' them all, ' More shame for them that *wor* before me,' says the bishop.

" But to make a long story short, the king looked mighty black at the bishop, and the bishop looked twice blacker at him again, and so on, from bad to worse, till they parted the bittherest of inimies : and the king, that was the best o' friends to the Churches afore, swore be this and be that he'd vex them for it, and that he'd be even with the bishop afore long.

"Now, sir, the bishop might jist as well have kept never mindin' the king's little *kimmeens* with the girls, for the story goes that he had a little failin' of his own in regard of a dhrop, and that he knew the differ betune wine and wather, for, poor ignorant crathurs, it's little they knew about whisky in them days. Well, the king used often to send *lashins* o' wine to the Churches, by the way, as he said, that they should have plinty of it for celebrating the mass—although he knew well that it was a little of it went far that-a-way, and that their Riverinces was fond of a hearty glass as well as himself—and why not, sir, if they'd let him alone—for, says the king, as many a one said afore, and will again, I'll make a child's bargain with you, says he : do you let me alone, and I'll let you alone ; *manin'* by that, sir, that if they'd say nothin' about the girls, he would give them plinty of wine.

"And so it fell out a little before he had the *scrimmage* with the bishop, the king promised them a fine store of wine that was comin' up the Shannon in boats, sir, and big boats they wor, I'll go bail—not all as one as the little *drolleen* [wren] of a thing we're in now, but nigh-hand as big as a ship ; and there was three of these fine boats-full comin'—two for himself, and one for the Churches ; and so says the king to himself, ' The divil receave the dhrop of that wine they shall get,' says he, ' the dirty beggarly neygars ; bad cess to the dhrop,' says he, ' my big-bellied bishop, to nourish your jolly red nose. I said I'd be even with you,' says he, ' and so I will ; and if you spoil my divarshin, I'll spoil yours, and turn about is fair play, as the divil said to the smoke-jack.' So with that, sir, the king goes and he gives ordhers to his sarvants how it wid be when the boats kem up the river with the wine—and more especial to one in partic'lar they called Corny, his own man, by raison he was mighty stout, and didn't love priests much more nor himself.

" Now, Corny, sir, let alone bein' stout, was mighty dark, and if he wanst said the word, you might as well sthrive to move the rock of Dunamaise as Corny, though without a big word at all, at all, but as *quite* [quiet] as a child. Well, in good time, up kem the boats, and down runs the monks, all as one as a flock o' crows over a cornfield, to pick up whatever they could for themselves ; but troth the king was afore them, for all his men was there, and Corny at their head.

"'*Dominus vobiscum!*' (which manes, God save you, sir!) says one of the monks to Corny, 'we kem down to save you the throuble of unloading the wine which the king, God bless him! gives to the Church.'

"'Oh, no throuble in life, plaze your Riverince,' says Corny, 'we'll unload it ourselves, your Riverince,' says he.

"So with that they began unloading, first one boat, and then another; but sure enough, every individual cashk of it went up to the palace, and not a one to the Churches; so whin they seen the second boat a'most empty, quare thoughts began to come into their heads; for before this offer the first boat-load was always sent to the bishop, after a dhrop was taken to the king, which, you know, was good manners, sir; and the king, by all accounts, was a gentleman, every inch of him. So, with that, says one of the monks:

"'My blessin' an you, Corny, my son,' says he, 'sure it's not forgettin' the bishop you'd be, nor the Churches,' says he, 'that stands betune you and the divil.'

"Well, sir, at the word divil, 'twas as good as a play to see the look Corny gave out o' the corner of his eye at the monk.

"'Forget yez,' says Corny, 'throth it's long afore me or my *masther*,' says he (nodding his head a bit at the word), 'will forget the bishop of Clonmacnoise. Go an with your work, boys,' says he to the men about him; and away they wint, and soon finished unloadin' the second boat; and with that they began at the third.

"'God bless your work, boys,' says the bishop; for, sure enough, 'twas the bishop himself kem down to the river side, having got the *hard word* of what was goin' an. 'God bless your work,' says he, as they heaved the first barrel of wine out of the boat. 'Go, help them, my sons,' says he, turning round to half-a-dozen strappin' young priests as was standing by.

"'No occasion in life, plaze your Riverince,' says Corny; 'I'm intirely obleeged to your lordship, but we're able for the work ourselves,' says he. And without sayin' another word, away went the barrel out of the boat, and up on their shoulders, or whatever way they wor takin' it, and up the hill to the palace.

"'Hillo!' says the bishop, 'where are yiz goin' with that wine?' says he.

"'Where I tould them,' says Corny.

"'Is it to the palace?' says his Riverince.

"'Faith, you jist hit it,' says Corny.

"'And what's that for?' says the bishop.

"'For fun,' says Corny, no ways *frikened* at all by the dark look the bishop gave him. And sure it's a wondher the fear of the Church didn't keep him in dread—but Corny was the divil intirely.

"'Is that the answer you give your clargy, you reprobate?' says the bishop. 'I'll tell you what it is, Corny,' says he, 'as sure as you're standin' there I'll excommunicate you, my fine fellow, if you don't keep a civil tongue in your head.'

"'Sure it wouldn't be worth your Riverince's while,' says Corny, 'to excommunicate the likes o' me,' says he, 'while there's the king my masther to the fore, for your holiness to play bell, book, and candle-light with.'

"'Do you mane to say, you scruff of the earth,' says the bishop, 'that your masther, the king, put you up to what you're doing?'

"'Divil a thing else I mane,' says Corny.

"'You *villian!*' says the bishop, 'the king never did the like.'

"'Yes, but I did, though,' says the king, puttin' in his word fair an aisy; for he was lookin' out o' his dhrawing-room windy, and run down the hill to the river when he seen the bishop goin', as he thought, to put his *comether* upon Corny.

"'So,' says the bishop, turnin' round quite short to the king—'so, my lord,' says he, 'am I to understand this villian has your commands for his purty behavor?'

"'He has my commands for what he done,' says the king, quite stout; 'and more be token, I'd have you to know he's no villian at all,' says he, 'but a thrusty sarvant, that does his masther's biddin'.'

"'And don't you intind sendin' any of this wine over to my Churches beyant?' says the bishop.

"'The divil receave the dhrop,' says the king.

"'And what for?' says the bishop.

"'Bekase I've changed my mind,' says the king.

"'And won't you give the Church wine for the holy mass?' says the bishop.

"'The mass!' says the king, eyin' him mighty sly.

"'Yes, sir—the mass,' says his Riverince, colouring up to the eyes—'the mass.'

"'Oh, *baithershin!*' says the king.

"'What do you mane?' says the bishop—and his nose got blue with fair rage.

"'Oh, nothin',' says the king, with a toss of his head.

"'Are you a gintleman?' says the bishop.

"'Every inch o' me,' says the king.

"'Then sure no gintleman goes back of his word,' says the other.

"'I won't go back o' my word, either,' says the king. 'I promised to give wine for the mass,' says he, 'and so I will.

Send to my palace every Sunday mornin', and you shall have a bottle of wine, and that's plinty; for I'm thinkin',' says the king, 'that so much wine lyin' beyant there is neither good for your bodies nor your sowls.'

"'What do you mane?' says the bishop, in a great passion, for all the world like a turkey-cock.

"'I mane, that when your wine-cellar is so full,' says the king, 'it only brings the fairies about you, and makes away with the wine too fast,' says he, laughin'; 'and the fairies to be about the Churches isn't good, your Riverince,' says the king; 'for I'm thinkin',' says he, 'that some of the spiteful little divils has given your Riverince a blast, and burnt the ind of your nose.'

"With that, my dear, you couldn't hould the bishop with the rage he was in; and says he, 'You think to dhrink all that wine —but you're mistaken,' says he. 'Fill your cellars as much as you like,' says the bishop, '*but you'll die in drooth yit;*' and with that he went down on his knees and cursed the king (God betune us and harm!) and shakin' his fist at him, he gother [gathered] all his monks about him, and away they wint home to the Churches.

"Well, sir, sure enough, the king fell sick of a suddent, and all the docthors in the country round was sent for; but they could do him no good at all, at all—and day by day he was wastin' and wastin', and pinin' and pinin', till the flesh was worn off his bones, and he was as bare and as yellow as a kite's claw; and then, what would you think, but the drooth came an him sure enough, and he was callin' for dhrink every *minit,* till you'd think he'd dhrink the *sae* dhry.

"Well, when the clock struck twelve that night, the drooth was an him worse nor ever, though he dhrunk as much that day —ay, troth, as much as would turn a mill; and he called to his servants for a dhrink of *grule* [gruel].

"'The grule's all out,' says they.

"'Well, then, give me some *whay*,' says he.

"'There's none left, my lord,' says they.

"'Then give me a dhrink of wine,' says he.

"'There's none in the room, dear,' says the nurse-tindher.

"'Then go down to the wine-cellar,' says he, 'and get some.'

"With that, they wint to the wine-cellar—but, jew'l machree, they soon run back into his room, with their faces as white as a sheet, and tould him there was not one dhrop of wine in all the cashks in the cellar.

"'Oh, murther! murther!' says the king, '*I'm dyin' of drooth,*' says he.

"And then, God help iz! they bethought themselves of what the bishop said, and the curse he laid an the king.

"'You've no grule?' says the king.

"'No,' says they.

"'Nor *whay?*'

"'No,' says the sarvants.

"'Nor wine?' says the king.

"'Nor wine either, my lord,' says they.

"'Have you no *tay?*' says he.

"'Not a dhrop,' says the nurse-tindher.

"'Then,' says the king, 'for the tindher marcy of God, gi' me a dhrink of wather.'

"And what would you think, sir, but there wasn't a dhrop of wather in the place.

"'Oh, murther! murther!' says the king, 'isn't it a poor case that a king can't get a dhrink of wather in his own house? Go then,' says he, 'and get me a jug of wather out of the ditch.'

"For there was a big ditch, sir, all round the palace. And away they run for wather out of the ditch, while the king was roarin' like mad for the drooth, and his mouth like a coal of fire. And sure, sir, the story goes, they couldn't find any wather in the ditch!

"'Millia murther! millia murther!' cries the king, 'will no one take pity an a king that's *dyin' for the bare drooth?*'

"And they all thrimbled again, with the fair fright, when they heerd this, and thought of the ould bishop's prophecy.

"'Well,' says the poor king, 'run down to the Shannon,' says he, 'and sure, at all events, you'll get wather there,' says he.

"Well, sir, away thcy run with pails and noggins down to the Shannon, and (God betune us and harm!) what do you think, sir, but the river Shannon was dhry! So, av coorse, when the king heer the Shannon was gone dhry, it wint to his heart; and he thought o' the bishop's curse an him—and givin' one murtherin' big *screech* that split the walls of the palace, as may be seen to this day, he died, sir—makin' the bishop's words good, that '*he would die of drooth yit!*'

"And now, sir," says my historian, with a look of lurking humour in his dark grey eye, "isn't that mighty wondherful— *iv it's true?*"

JIMMY THE FOOL

As some allusion has been made in the early part of the foregoing story to a fool, this, perhaps, is the fittest place to say something of fools in general. Be it understood, I only mean fools by profession; for, were amateur fools included, an essay on fools in general would be no trifling undertaking. And further, I mean to limit myself within still more circumscribed bounds by treating of the subject only as it regards that immediate part of his Majesty's dominions called Ireland.

In Ireland the fool, or natural, or innocent (for by all those names he goes), as represented in the stories of the Irish peasantry, is very much the fool that Shakespeare occasionally embodies ; and even in the present day many a witticism and sarcasm given birth to by these mendicant Touchstones would be treasured in the memory of our *beau monde*, under the different heads of brilliant or biting, had they been uttered by a Bushe or a Plunket. I recollect a striking piece of imagery employed by one of the tribe on his perceiving the approach of a certain steward, who, as a severe task-master, had made himself disliked amongst the peasantry employed on his master's estate. This man had acquired a nickname (Irishmen, by the way, are celebrated for the application of *sobriquets*), which nick-name was "Danger"; and the fool, stand-ing one day amidst a parcel of workmen, who were cutting turf, perceived this said steward crossing the bog towards them.

"Ah, ah! by dad, you must work now, boys," said he, "here comes Danger. Bad luck to you, Daddy Danger, you dirty blood-sucker! sure the earth's heavy with you." But suddenly stopping in his career of commonplace abuse, he looked with an air of contemplative dislike towards the man, and deliberately said : "There you are, Danger! and may I never break bread, *if all the turf in the bog 'id warm me to you.*"

Such are the occasional bursts of figurative language uttered by our fools, who are generally mendicants; or perhaps it would be fitter to call them dependents, either on some particular family, or on the wealthy farmers of the district. But they have a great objection that such should be supposed to be the case, and are particularly jealous of their independence. An example of this was given me by a friend who patronised one that was rather a favourite of the gentlemen in the neighbourhood, and a constant attendant at every fair within ten or fifteen miles, where he was sure to pick up a good deal of money from his gentlemen friends. Aware of this fact, Mr. ——, meeting Jimmy one morning on the road, and knowing what errand he was bound on, asked him where he was going.

"I'm goin' to the fair, your honour."

"Why, what can bring *you* there?"

"Oh, I've business there."

"What business—?"

"I'll tell you to-morrow."

"Ah! Jimmy," said the gentleman, "I see how it is—you're going to the fair to ask all the gentlemen for money."

"Indeed I'm not : I'm no beggar — Jimmy wouldn't be a beggar. Do you think I've nothin' else to do but beg?"

JIMMY THE FOOL

"Well, what else brings you to the fair?"

"Sure, I'm goin' to sell a cow there," said Jimmy, quite delighted at fancying he had successfully baffled the troublesome inquiries of the Squire; and not willing to risk another question or answer, he uttered his deafening laugh, and pursued his road to the fair.

From the same source I heard that they are admirable couriers, which my friend very fairly accounted for by attributing it to the small capability of comprehension in the constitution of their minds, which, rendering them unable to embrace more than one idea at a time, produces a singleness of purpose that renders them valuable messengers. As an instance of this, he told me that a gentleman in his neighbourhood once sent a certain fool to the town of ——, with a packet of great consequence and value, to his banker, with a direction to the bearer not to hand it to any person but Mr. —— himself, and not to return without seeing him.

It so happened Mr. —— had gone to Dublin that morning; and no assurances nor persuasion, on the part of that gentleman's confidential clerk, could induce the fool to hand him the parcel—thus observing strict obedience to the commands of his master. But he adhered still more literally to his commission; for when he was told Mr. —— had gone to Dublin, and that, therefore, he could not give him the packet, he said: "Oh, very well, Jimmy 'ill go back again;" but when he left the office, he took the road to Dublin, instead of homewards, having been bidden *not to return without delivering it,* and ran the distance to the capital (about one hundred and forty miles), in so short a time, that he arrived there but a few hours after the gentleman he followed, and never rested until he discovered where he was lodged, and delivered to him the parcel, in strict accordance with his instructions.

They are affectionate also. I have heard of a fool who, when some favourite member of a family he was attached to died, went to the churchyard, and sat on the grave, and there wept bitterly, and watched night and day; nor could he be forced from the place, nor could the calls of hunger and thirst induce him to quit the spot for many days; and such was the intensity of grief on the part of the affectionate creature, that he died in three months afterwards.

But they can be revengeful too, and entertain a grudge with great tenacity. The following is a ridiculous instance of this: A fool, who had been severely bitten by a gander, that was unusually courageous, watched an opportunity when his enemy was absent, and getting amongst the rising family of the gander, he began to trample upon the goslings, and was caught in the fact of murdering them wholesale, by the enraged woman who had reared them.

"Ha, Jimmy, you villian! is it murtherin' my lovely goslin's you are, you thief of the world? Bad scram to you, you thick-headed vagabone."

"Divil mend them, granny," shouted Jimmy, with a laugh of idiotic delight, as he leaped over a ditch, out of the reach of the henwife, who rushed upon him with a broomstick, full of dire intent upon Jimmy's skull.

"Oh, you moroadin' thief!" cried the exasperated woman shaking her uplifted broomstick at Jimmy in impotent rage "wait till Maurice ketches you—that's all."

"Divil mend them, granny," shouted Jimmy—"ha! ha!—why did their daddy bite me?"

The peasantry believe a fool to be insensible to fear from any ghostly visitation; and I heard of an instance where the experiment was made on one of these unhappy creatures, by dressing a strapping fellow in a sheet, and placing him in a situation to intercept "poor Jimmy" on his midnight path, and try the truth of this generally-received opinion, by endeavouring to intimidate him. When he had reached the appointed spot, a particularly lonely and narrow path, and so hemmed in by high banks on each side as to render escape difficult, Mr. Ghost suddenly reared his sheeted person as Jimmy had half ascended a broken stile, and with all the usual terrific formulæ of "Boo," "Fee-fa-fum,' etc., etc., demanded who dared to cross that path? The answer:

"I'm poor Jimmy," was given in his usual tone.

"I'm Raw-head and Bloody-bones," roared the ghost.

"Ho! ho! I often heerd o' you," said Jimmy.

"Baw," cried the ghost, advancing—"I'll kill you—I'll kill you—I'll kill you."

"The divil a betther opinion I had iv you," said Jimmy.

"Boo!" says Raw-head, "I'll eat you—I'll eat you."

"The divil do you good with me," says Jimmy. And so the ghost was at a nonplus, and Jimmy won the field.

I once heard of a joint-stock company having been established between a fool and a blind beggar-man, and for whom the fool acted in the capacity of guide. They had share and share alike in the begging concern, and got on tolerably well together, until one day the blind man had cause to suspect Jimmy's honour. It happened that a mail-coach passing by, the blind man put forth all his begging graces to induce the "quality" to "extind their charity," and succeeded so well, that not only some copper, but a piece of silver was thrown by the wayside. Jimmy, I'm sorry to say, allowed "the filthy lucre of gain" so far to predominate, that in picking up these gratuities, he appropriated the silver coin to his own particular pouch, and brought the halfpence only for division to his blind friend; but the sense of hearing was so nice in the latter, that he detected the sound of the falling silver, and asked Jimmy to produce it. Jimmy denied the fact stoutly. "Oh, I heerd it fall," said the blind man. "Then you were betther off than poor Jimmy," said our hero; "for you *heerd* it, but poor Jimmy didn't *see* it." "Well, look for it," says the blind man. "Well, well, but you're cute, daddy," cried Jimmy; "you're right enough, I see it now;" and Jimmy affected to pick up the sixpence, and handed it to his companion.

"Now we'll go an to the Squire's," said the blind man, "and they'll give us somethin' to eat;" and he and his idiot companion were soon seated outside the kitchen-door of the Squire's house, waiting for their expected dish of broken meat and potatoes.

Presently Jimmy was summoned, and he stepped forward to receive the plate that was handed him; but in its transit from the kitchen-door to the spot where the blind man was seated, Jimmy played foul again, by laying violent hands on the meat, and leaving potatoes only in the dish. Again the acute sense of the blind man detected the fraud; he sniffed the scent of the purloined provision; and after poking with hurried fingers amongst the potatoes, he exclaimed: "Ha! Jimmy, Jimmy, I smelt meat." "Deed and deed, no," said Jimmy, who had, in the meantime, with the voracity of brutal hunger, devoured his stolen prey. "That's a lie, Jimmy," said the blind man—"that's like the sixpence. Ha! you thievin' rogue, to cheat a poor blind man, you villian;" and forthwith he aimed a blow of his stick at Jimmy with such good success, as to make the fool bellow lustily. Matters, however, were accommodated; and both parties considered that the beef and the blow pretty well balanced one another, and so accounts were squared.

After their meal at the Squire's, they proceeded to an adjoining village; but in the course of their way thither, it was necessary to pass a rapid, and sometimes swollen, mountain-stream, and the only means of transit was by large blocks of granite placed at such intervals in the stream as to enable a passenger to step from one to the other, and hence called "stepping-stones." Here, then, it was necessary, on the blind man's part, to employ great caution, and he gave himself up to the guidance of Jimmy, to effect his purpose. "You'll tell me where I'm to step," said he, as he cautiously approached the brink. "Oh, I will, daddy," said Jimmy; "give me your hand."

But Jimmy thought a good opportunity had arrived for disposing of one whom he found to be an over-intelligent companion, and leading him to a part of the bank where no friendly stepping-stone was placed, he cried: "Step out now, daddy." The poor blind man obeyed the command, and tumbled plump into the water. The fool screamed with delight, and clapped his hands. The poor deluded blind man floundered for some time in the stream, which, fortunately, was not sufficiently deep to be dangerous; and when he scrambled to the shore, he laid about him with his stick and tongue, in dealing blows and anathemas, all intended for Jimmy. The former Jimmy carefully avoided by running out of the enraged man's reach.

"Oh, my curse light an you, you black-hearted thraitor," said the dripping old beggar, "that has just wit enough to be wicked, and to play such a hard-hearted turn to a poor blind man."

"Ha! ha! daddy," cried Jimmy, "*you could smell the mate—why didn't you smell the wather?*"

THE CATASTROPHE

JOHN DAW, of the county ——, gent., who, from his propensity to look down his neighbours' chimneys, was familiary called Mr. Jackdaw, was a man who (to adopt a figure of speech which he often used himself), could see as far into a millstone as most people. He could play at politics, as boys play at marbles; and Mr. Daw could be down upon any king's taw as best suited his pleasure, and prove he was quite right to boot, provided you would only listen to his arguments, and not answer them. Though, to say the truth, Mr. Daw seldom meddled with so august a personage as a king—he was rather of Shakespeare's opinion that

"There's a divinity doth hedge a king;"

and after the fall of Napoleon, whom he could abuse to his heart's content, with all the hackneyed epithets of tyrant, monster, etc., without any offence to *legitimacy*, his rage against royalty was somewhat curtailed of its "fair proportions." But still, politics always afforded him a very pretty allowance of hot water to dabble in. Of course, he who could settle the affairs of nations with so much satisfaction to himself, could also superintend those of his neighbours; and the whole county, if it knew but all, had weighty obligations to Mr. Daw for the consideration he bestowed on the concerns of every man in it rather than his own. But the whole world is very ill-natured, and the county —— in particular; for while Mr. Daw thus exhibited so much interest in the affairs of his acquaintances, they only called him "bore, busybody, meddler," and other such-like amiable appellations.

No stolen "march of intellect" had ever been allowed to surprise the orthodox outposts of Mr. Daw's understanding. He was for the good old times—none of your heathenish innovations for him! The word liberality was an abomination in his ears, and strongly reminded him of "Popery, slavery, arbitary power, brass money, and wooden shoes."

Two things he hated in particular—cold water and papists; he thought them both bad for "the constitution." Now, the former of the aforesaid Mr. Daw took special good care should never make any innovation on his, and the bitterest regret of his life was that he had it not equally in his power to prevent the latter from making inroads upon that of the nation.

A severe trial of Mr. Daw's temper existed in the situation which a certain Roman Catholic chapel held on the road which led from his house to the parochial Protestant church. This chapel was a singularly humble little building, whose decayed roof of straw gave evidence of the poverty and inability of the flock who crowded within it every Sunday to maintain a more seemly edifice for the worship of God. It was situated immediately on the roadside, and so inadequate was it in size to contain the congregation which flocked to it for admittance, that hundreds of poor people might be seen every Sabbath kneeling outside the door, and stretching in a crowd so dense across the road as to occasion considerable obstruction to a passenger thereon. This was always a source of serious annoyance to the worthy Mr. Daw; and one Sunday in particular, so great was the concourse of people, that he was absolutely obliged to stop his jaunting-car, and was delayed the enormous space of a full minute and a half before the offending worshippers could get out of the way. This was the climax of annoyance—it was insufferable. That he should have, every Sunday as he went to church, his Christian serenity disturbed by passing so heathenish a temple as a mass-house, and witness the adoration of "damnable idolaters," was bad enough; but that he, one of the staunchest Protestants in the county, one of the most unflinching of the sons of ascendancy, should be delayed on his way to church by a pack of "rascally rebelly papists," as he charitably called them, was beyond endurance, and he deeply swore he would never go to church by that road again to be obnoxious to so great an indignity. And he kept his word. He preferred going a round of five miles to the ample and empty church of ——, than again pass the confined and crowded little chapel.

This was rather inconvenient sometimes, to be sure, when autumn rains and winter snows were falling; but no matter. The scene of his degradation was not to be passed for any consideration, and many a thorough drenching and frost-bitten penalty were endured in the cause of ascendancy; but what then? He had the reward in his own breast, and he bore all with the fortitude of a martyr, consoling himself in the notion of his being a "suffering loyalist."

If he went out of his way to avoid one popish nuisance, he was "*put* out of his way" by another, namely, by having his residence

THE CATASTROPHE

in the vicinity of a convent; yea, within earshot of their vesper music lay his pleasure-ground, and a stone wall (a very strong and high one, to be sure), was all that interposed itself between his Protestant park and the convent garden.

Both of these lay upon the shore of the expansive Shannon; and "many a time and oft," when our hero was indulging in an evening stroll on the bank of the river, did he wish the poor nuns fairly at the bottom of it, as their neighbouring voices, raised perchance in some hymn to the Virgin, smote the tympanum of his offended ear.

He considered at length that this proximity to a convent, which at first he deemed such an hardship, might be turned to account in a way, of all others, congenial to his disposition, by affording him an opportunity of watching the movements of its inmates. Of the nefarious proceedings of such a body, of their numberless intrigues, etc., etc., he himself had no doubt, and he forthwith commenced a system of *espionnage*, that he might be enabled to produce proof for the conviction of others. During the day, there was a provoking propriety preserved about the place that excited Mr. Daw's wrath. "Ay, ay," would he mutter to himself, "they were always deep as well as dangerous— they're too cunning to commit themselves by anything that might be easily discovered; but wait, wait until the moonlight nights are past, and I'll warrant my watching shan't go for nothing."

Under the dewy damps of night, many an hour did Mr. Daw hold his *surveillance* around the convent bounds, but still Fortune favoured him not in this enterprise, and not one of the delinquencies which he had no doubt were going forward had he the good fortune to discover. No scarf was waved from the proscribed casements, no ladder of ropes was to be found attached to the forbidden wall, no boat, with muffled oar, stealthily skimming along the waters, could be detected in the act of depositing "a gallant gay Lothario" in the Hesperian garden, where, he doubted not, many an adventurous Jason plucked forbidden fruit.

Chance, however, threw in his way a discovery, which all his premeditated endeavours had formerly failed to accomplish, for one evening, just as the last glimmer of departing day was streaking the west, Mr. Daw, in company with a friend (a congenial soul), when returning after a long day's shooting, in gleeful anticipation of a good dinner, heard a sudden splash in the water, apparently proceeding from the extremity of the convent wall, to which point they both directly hurried. What the noise originated in we shall soon see, but a moment's pause must be first given to say a word or two of Mr. Daw's friend.

He was a little bustling man, always fussing about something or other, eternally making frivolous excuses for paying visits at unseasonable hours, for the purpose of taking people by surprise, and seeing what they were about, and everlastingly giving people advice ; and after any unpleasant accident, loss of property, or other casualty, he was always ready with an assurance that " if that had been his case he would have done so and so," and gave ample grounds for you to understand that you were very little more or less than a fool, and he the wisest of men since the days of Solomon.

But curiosity was his prevailing foible. When he entered a room, his little twinkling eyes went peering round the chamber to ascertain if anything worth notice was within eyeshot, and when failure ensued, in that case he himself went on a voyage of discovery into every corner, and with excuses so plausible, that he flattered himself nobody saw what he did. For example, he might commence thus : " Ha, Miss Emily, you've got a string broken in your harp, I see," and forthwith he posted over to the instrument ; and while he was clawing the strings, and declaring it was "a monstrous sweet harp," he was reconnoitring the quarter where it stood with the eye of a lynx. Unsuccessful there, he would proceed, mayhap, to the table, where some recently received letters were lying, and stooping down over one with its seal upwards, exclaim : " Dear me ! what a charming device ! Let me see—what is it ?—a padlock, and the motto ' Honour keeps the key.' Ah ! very pretty, indeed—excellent." And then he would carelessly turn over the letter to see the postmark and superscription, to try if he could glean any little *hint* from them. " So, so ! a foreign postmark. I see—ha ! I daresay, now, this is from your cousin—his regiment's abroad, I believe ? Eh ! Miss Emily ?" (rather knowingly). Miss Emily might reply slyly : " I thought you admired the *motto* on the seal ?" "Oh, yes—a—very true, indeed—a very pretty motto," and so on.

This little gentleman was, moreover, very particular in his dress. The newest fashions were sure to be exhibited on his diminutive person, and from the combined quality of *petit maître* and eavesdropper, he enjoyed a *sobriquet* as honourable as Mr. Daw, and was called *Little Beau Peep*.

Upon one occasion, however, while minding his neighbours' affairs with an exemplary vigilance, some sheep-stealers made free with a few of his flock, and though so pre-eminently prompt in the suggestion of preventions or remedies in similar cases when his friends were in trouble, he could not make the slightest successful movement towards the recovery of his own property. All his *dear friends* were, of course, delighted ; and so far did they carry their exultation in his mishap, that someone, a night or two after his disaster, pasted on his hall-door the following quotation from a celebrated nursery ballad :

" Little Beau Peep
Has lost his sheep,
And does not know where to find them."

He had a little dog, too, that was as great a nuisance as himself, and emulated his master in his prying propensities; he was very significantly called " Ferret," and not unfrequently had he been instrumental in making mischievous discoveries. One in particular I cannot resist noticing :

Mrs. Fitz-Altamont was a lady of high descent—in short, the descent had been such a long one, that the noble family of Fitz-Altamont had descended very low indeed ; but Mrs. Fitz-Altamont would never let " the aspiring blood of Lancaster sink in the ground "; and accordingly, was always reminding her acquaintance how very noble a stock she came from, at the very moment, perhaps, she was making some miserable show of gentility. In fact, Mrs. Fitz-Altamont's mode of living reminded one very much of worn-out plated ware, in which the copper makes a very considerable appearance ; or, as Goldsmith says of the French, she

" Trimm'd her robe of frieze with copper lace."

Her children had been reared from their earliest infancy with lofty notions ; they started, even from the baptismal font, under the shadow of high-sounding names ; there were Alfred, Adolphus, and Harold, her magnanimous boys, and Angelina and Iphigenia, her romantic girls.

Judge, then, of the mortification of Mrs. Fitz-Altamont, when one day, seated at rather a homely early dinner, Little Beau Peep popped in upon them. How he contrived such a surprise is not stated—whether by a surreptitious entry through a back window, or, fairy-like, through a key-hole, has never been clearly ascertained—but certain it is, he detected the noble family of Fitz-Altamont in the fact of having been dining upon—EGGS !—yes, sympathetic reader—EGGS ! The *denouement* took place thus : Seated before this unseemly fare, the noise of Beau Peep was heard in the hall by the affrighted Fitz-Altamonts. No herd of startled deer was ever half so terrified by the deep bay of the ferocious staghound as " the present company " at the shrill pipe of the cur, Beau Peep ; and by a simultaneous movement of thought and action they at once huddled everything upon the table, topsy-turvy, into the table-cloth, and crammed it with precipitous speed under the sofa ; and scattering the chairs from their formal and indicative position round the table, they met their "*dear friend*" Beau Peep with smiles, as he gently opened the door in his own insinuating manner, to say that, "just as he was in the neighbourhood, he would not pass by his esteemed friend, Mrs. Fitz-Altamont, without calling to pay his respects."

Both parties were "*delighted*" to see each other, and Mr. Beau Peep seated himself on the sofa, and his little dog "Ferret" lay down between his feet; and whether it was from a spice of his master's talent for discovery, or a keen nose that Nature gave him, we know not; but after sniffing once or twice, he made a sudden dart beneath the sofa, and in an instant, emerged from under its deep and dirty flounce, dragging after him the table-cloth, which, unfolding in its course along the well-darned carpet, disclosed "a beggarly account of empty" egg-shells.

We shall not attempt to describe the *finale* of such a scene; but Mrs. Fitz-Altamont, in speaking to a friend on the subject, when the affair had "got wind," and demanded an explanation, declared she never was so "horrified" in her life. It was just owing to her own foolish good-nature; she had allowed *all* her servants (she had *one*) to go to the fair in the neighbourhood, and had ordered John to be at home at a certain hour from the town, with marketing. But John did not return; and it happened so unfortunately—such a thing never happened before in her house—there was not an atom in the larder but eggs, and they just were making a little *lunch*, when that provoking creature, Mr. Terrier, broke in on them.

"My dear madam, if you had only seen it: Alfred *had* eaten his egg—Adolphus *was* eating his egg—Harold was in the act of *cracking* his egg—and I was just putting some salt in my egg (indeed, I spilt the salt a moment before, and was certain something unlucky was going to happen)—and the dear, romantic girls, Angelina and Iphigenia, were at the moment boiling their eggs, when that dreadful little man got into the house. It's very laughable, to be sure—he! he! he!—when one knows all about it; but *really*, I was never so provoked in my life."

We ask pardon for so long a digression; but an anxiety to show what sort of person Little Beau Peep was has betrayed us into it; and we shall now hurry to the development of our story.

We left Beau Peep and Jack Daw hurrying off towards the convent wall, where it was washed by the river, to ascertain what caused the loud splash in the water which they heard, and has already been noticed. On arriving at the extremity of Mr. Daw's grounds, they perceived the stream yet agitated, apparently from the sudden immersion of something into it; and on looking more sharply through the dusk, they saw, floating rapidly down the current, a basket, at some distance, but not so far away as to prevent their hearing a faint cry, evidently proceeding from it;

and the next moment they heard a female voice say, in the adjoining garden of the convent: "There, let it go; the nasty creature, to do such a horrid thing—"

"Did you hear that?" said Mr. Daw.

"I did," said Beau Peep.

"There's proof positive," said Daw. "The villainous papist jades, one of them has had a child, and some of her dear sisters are drowning it for her, to conceal her infamy."

"No doubt of it," said Beau Peep.

"I knew it all along," said Jack Daw. "Come, my dear friend," added he, "let us hasten back to O'Brien's cottage, and he'll row us down the river in his boat, and we may yet be enabled to reach the basket in time to possess ourselves of the proof of all this popish profligacy."

And off they ran to O'Brien's cottage; and hurrying O'Brien and his son to unmoor their boat, in which the gentlemen had passed a considerable part of the day in sporting, they jumped into the skiff, and urged the two men to pull away as fast as they could after the prize they hoped to obtain. Thus, though excessively hungry, and anxious for the dinner that was awaiting them all the time, their appetite for scandal was so much more intense, that they relinquished the former in pursuit of the latter.

"An' where is it your honour's goin'?" demanded O'Brien.

"Oh, a little bit down the river here," answered Mr. Daw; for he did not wish to let it be known what he was in quest of, or his suspicions touching it, lest the peasants might baffle his endeavours at discovery, as he was sure they would strive to do in such a case, for the honour of the creed to which they belonged.

"Throth, then, it's late your honour's a-goin' an' the wather this time o' day, and the night comin' an."

"Well, never mind that you, but pull away."

"By my sowl, I'll pull like a young cowlt, if that be all, and Jim too, sir (that's your sort, Jamie); but at this gate o' goin', the sorra far off the rapids will be, long, and sure if we go down them now, the dickens a back we'll get to-night."

"Oh, never mind that," said Daw; "we can return by the fields."

As O'Brien calculated, they soon reached the rapids, and he called out to Jim to "studdy the boat there;" and with skilful management the turbulent descent was passed in safety, and they glided onwards again, under the influence of their oars, over the level waters.

"Do you see it yet?" asked one of the friends to the other, who replied in the negative.

"Maybe it's the deep hole your honour id be lookin' for?"

queried O'Brien, in that peculiar vein of inquisitiveness which the Irish peasant indulges in, and through which he hopes, by presupposing a motive of action, to discover in reality the object aimed at.

" No," answered Daw, rather abruptly.

" Oh, it's only bekase it's a choice place of settin' night-lines," said O'Brien ; "and I was thinkin' maybe it's for that your honour id be."

" Oh ! " said Beau Peep, " 'tis nothing more than is caught by night-lines we're seeking—eh, Daw ? "

" Aye, aye ; and, by Jove, I think I see it a little way before us —pull, O'Brien, pull ! " and the boat trembled under the vigorous strokes of O'Brien and his son, and in a few minutes they were within an oar's length of the basket, which by this time was nearly sinking, and a moment or two later had deprived Jack Daw and Beau Peep of the honour of the discovery, which they were now on the eve of completing.

" Lay hold of it," said Mr. Daw ; and Beau Peep, in " making a long arm " to secure the prize, so far overbalanced himself that he went plump, head foremost, into the river ; and had it not been for the activity and strength of the elder O'Brien, this our pleasant history must have turned out a tragedy of the darkest dye, and many a subsequent discovery of the indefatigable Beau Peep remained in the unexplored depths of uncertainty. But, fortunately for the lovers of family secrets, the inestimable Beau Peep was drawn, dripping, from the river, by O'Brien, at the same time that Jack Daw, with the boat-hook, secured the basket.

" I've got it ! " exclaimed Daw, in triumph.

" Aye, and *I've got it*, too," chattered forth poor Beau Peep.

" What's the matter with you, my dear friend ? " said Daw, who, in his anxiety to obtain the basket, never perceived the fatality that had befallen his friend.

" I've been nearly drowned, that's all," whined forth the unhappy little animal, as he was shaking the water out of his ears.

" Throth, it was looky I had my hand so ready," said O'Brien, " or faith, maybe it's more nor a basket we'd have to be lookin' for."

" My dear fellow," said Daw, " let us go ashore immediately, and, by the exercise of walking, you may counteract the bad effects that this accident may otherwise produce. Get the boat ashore, O'Brien, as fast as possible. But we have got the basket, however, and that's some consolation for you."

" Yes," said the shivering little scandal-hunter ; " I don't mind the drenching, since we have secured that."

" Why, thin," said O'Brien, as he pulled towards the shore,

'may I make so bould as to ax your honour what curiosity there is in an ould basket, to make yiz take so much throuble, and nigh-hand drowndin' yourselves afore you cotcht it?"

"Oh, never you mind," said Mr. Daw; "you shall soon know all about it. By-the-by, my dear friend," turning to Terrier, "I think we had better proceed, as soon as we get ashore, to our neighbour Sturdy's—his is the nearest house we know of. There you may be enabled to change your wet clothes; and he being a magistrate, we can swear our informations against the delinquents in this case."

"Very true," said the unfortunate Beau Peep, as he stepped ashore, assisted by O'Brien, who, when the gentlemen proceeded some paces in advance, said to his son, who bore the dearly-won basket, that "the poor little whelp (meaning Beau Peep) looked for all the world like a dog in a wet sack."

On they pushed at a smart pace, until the twinkling of lights through some neighbouring trees announced to them the vicinity of Squire Sturdy's mansion. The worthy Squire had just taken his first glass of wine after the cloth had been drawn, when the servant announced the arrival of Mr. Daw and his half-drowned friend, who were at once ushered into the dining-room.

"Good heavens!" exclaimed the excellent lady of the mansion (for the ladies had not yet withdrawn), on perceiving the miserable plight of Beau Peep, "what has happened?"

"Indeed, madam," answered our little hero, "an unfortunate accident on the water—"

"Oh, ho!" said the Squire; "I should think that quite in your line—just exploring the secrets of the river? Why, my dear sir, if you go on at this rate, making discoveries by water as well as by land, you'll rival Columbus himself before long." And Miss Emily, of whom we have already spoken, whispered her mamma that she had often heard of a diving-bell (*belle*), but never before of a diving *beau*.

"Had you not better change your clothes?" said Mrs. Sturdy to the shivering Terrier.

"Thank you, madam," said he, somewhat loftily, being piqued at the manner of his reception by the Squire; "I shall wait till an investigation has taken place in my presence of a circumstance which I have contributed to bring to light; and my discoveries by water may be found to be not undeserving of notice."

"I assure you, Mr. Sturdy," added Mr. Daw, in his most impressive manner, "we have an information to swear to before you of the most vital importance, and betraying the profligacy of *certain people* in so flagrant a degree that I hope it may at length open the eyes of those that are wilfully blind to the interests of their king and their country."

This fine speech was meant as a hit at Squire Sturdy, who was a blunt, honest man—who acted in most cases, to the best of his ability, on the admirable Christian maxim of loving his neighbour as himself.

"Well, Mr. Daw," said the Squire, "I am all attention to hear your information—"

"May I trouble you," said Daw, "to retire to your study, as the matter is rather of an indelicate nature, and not fit for ladies' ears?"

"No, no. We'll stay here, and Mrs. S. and my daughters will retire to the drawing-room. Go, girls, and get the tea ready;" and the room was soon cleared of the ladies, and the two O'Briens were summoned to wait upon the Squire in the dining-room, with the important basket.

When they entered, Mr. Daw, with a face of additional length and solemnity, unfolded to Squire Sturdy how the attention of his friend and himself had been attracted by a basket flung from the convent garden; how they ran to the spot; how they heard a faint cry; "and then, sir," said he, "we were at once awake to the revolting certainty that the nuns had thus intended to destroy one of their own illegitimate offspring."

"Cross o' Christ about us!" involuntarily muttered forth the two O'Briens, making the sign of the cross at the same time on their foreheads.

"But have you any proof of this?" asked the magistrate.

"Yes, sir," said Beau Peep triumphantly; "we have proof—proof positive! Bring forward that basket," said he to the boatman. "There, sir, is the very basket containing the evidence of their double guilt—first, the guilt of unchastity, and next, the guilt of infanticide; and it was in laying hold of the basket that I met the accident, Mr. Sturdy, that has occasioned you so much mirth. However, I believe you will acknowledge now, Mr. Sturdy, that my discoveries by water have been rather important—"

Here Mr. Daw broke in by saying that the two boatmen were witnesses to the fact of finding the basket.

"Oh! by this and that," roared out O'Brien, "the devil resave the bit of a child I seen, I'll be upon my oath! And I wouldn't say that in a lie—"

"Be silent, O'Brien," said the magistrate. "Answer me, Mr. Daw, if you please, one or two questions:

"Did one or both of you see the basket thrown from the convent garden?"

"Both of us."

"And you heard a faint cry from it?"

"Yes; we heard the cry of an infant."

"You then rowed after the basket, in O'Brien's boat?"

"Yes."

"Is this the basket you saw the gentleman pick up, O'Brien?"

"By my sowl, I can't exactly say, your honour, for I was picking up Mr. Terrier."

"It was you, then, that saved Mr. Terrier from drowning?"

"Yes, sir, undher God—"

"Fortunate that O'Brien was so active, Mr. Terrier. Well, O'Brien, but that is the same basket you have carried here from the river?"

"Throth, I don't know where I could change it an the road, sir—"

"Well, let us open the basket and see what it contains"—and O'Brien commenced unlacing the cords that bound up the wicker-tomb of the murdered child; but so anxious was Mr. Daw for prompt production of his evidence, that he took out his pen-knife and cut the fastenings.

"Now, take it out," said Mr. Daw; and every eye was riveted on the basket as O'Brien, lifting the cover and putting in his hand, said:

"Oh, then, but it's a beautiful baby!" and he turned up a look of the tenderest pity at the three gentlemen.

"Pull it out here!" said Mr. Daw imperatively; and O'Brien, with the utmost gentleness, lifting the lifeless body from the basket, produced—A DROWNED CAT!

"Oh, then, isn't it a darlint?" said O'Brien, with the most provoking affectation of pathos in his voice, while sarcasm was playing on his lip, and humour gleaming from his eye, as he witnessed with enjoyment the vacant stare of the discomfited Daw and Beau Peep, and exchanged looks with the worthy Squire, who had set up a horse-laugh the instant the poor pussy had made her appearance; and the moment he could recover his breath, exclaimed: "Why, by the L—d, it's a dead cat!" and hereupon the sound of smothered laughter reached them from outside the half-closed door, where the ladies, dear creatures! had stolen to listen, having been told that something not proper to hear was going forward.

The two grand inquisitors were so utterly confounded that neither had a word to say, and as soon as the Squire had recovered from his immoderate fit of laughing, he said: "Well, gentlemen, this is a most important discovery you have achieved! I think I must despatch an express to Government on the strength of it."

"Oh, wait a bit, your honour," said O'Brien, "there's more o' them yit;" and he took from out of the basket a handful of dead kittens.

Now, it happened that the cat had kittened in the convent

that day, and as it not unfrequently happens, the ferocious animal had destroyed some of her offspring, which so disgusted the nuns that they bundled cat and kittens into an old basket, and threw them all into the river, and thus the "faint cry," and the words of the sisters, "The nasty creature, to do such a horrid thing," are at once explained.

"Why, this is worse than you anticipated, gentlemen," said the Squire, laughing, "for here not only one, but several lives have been sacrificed."

"Mr. Sturdy," said Mr. Daw, very solemnly, "let me tell you that if—"

"Tut! tut! my dear sir," said the good-humoured Squire, interrupting him, "the wisest in the world may be deceived now and then; and no wonder your sympathies should have been awakened by the piercing cries of the helpless little sufferers."

"Throth, the sign's an it," said O'Brien. "It's aisy to see that the gintlemen has no childher of their own, for if they had, by my sowl, it's long before they'd mistake the cry of a dirty cat for a Christian child."

This was a bitter hit of O'Brien's, for neither Mrs. Daw nor Mrs. Terrier had ever been "as ladies wish to be who love their lords."

"I think," said the Squire, "we may now dismiss this affair; and after you have changed your clothes, Mr. Terrier, a good glass of wine will do you no harm, for I see no use of letting the decanters lie idle any longer, since this *mysterious* affair has been elucidated."

"Throth, then, myself was thinkin' it a quare thing all along, for though sometimes a girl comes before your worship to sware a child agin a man, by the powers, I never heerd av a gintleman comin' to swear a child agin a woman yit—"

"Come, gentlemen," said the Squire, "the wine waits for us, and O'Brien and his son shall each have a glass of whisky to drink repose to the souls of the cats."

"Good luck to your honour," said O'Brien, "and the misthress too—ah, by dad, it's *she* that knows the differ betune a cat and a child; and more power to your honour's elbow—"

But no entreaties on the part of Squire Sturdy could induce the discomfited Daw and Terrier to accept the Squire's proffered hospitality. The truth was, they were both utterly crestfallen, and as the ladies had overheard the whole affair, they were both anxious to get out of the house at fast as they could; so the Squire bowed them out of the hall-door—they wishing him a very civil good-night, and apologising for the trouble they had given him.

"Oh, don't mention it," said the laughing Squire; "really, I have been very much amused; for of all the strange cases that have ever come within my knowledge, I have never met with so very curious a *cat*—astrophe!"

THE DEVIL'S MILL

BESIDE the River Liffey stands the picturesque ruins of a mill, overshadowed by some noble trees, that grow in great luxuriance at the water's edge. Here, one day, I was accosted by a silver-haired old man that for some time had been observing me, and who, when I was about to leave the spot, approached me and said: "I suppose it's after takin' off the ould mill you'd be, sir?"

I answered in the affirmative.

"Maybe your honour id let me get a sight iv it," said he.

"With pleasure," said I, as I untied the strings of my portfolio, and drawing the sketch from amongst its companions, presented it to him. He considered it attentively for some time, and at length exclaimed:

"Throth, there it is, to the life—the broken roof and the wather-coorse; ay, even to the very spot where the gudgeon of the wheel was wanst, let alone the big stone at the corner, that was laid the first by *himself;*" and he gave the last word with mysterious emphasis, and handed the drawing back to me with a "thankee, sir!" of most respectful acknowledgment.

"And who was 'himself,'" said I, "that laid that stone?" feigning ignorance, and desiring to "draw him out," as the phrase is.

"Oh, then, maybe it's what you'd be a stranger here?" said he

"Almost," said I.

"And you never hear tell of L——'s mill," said he, "and how it was built?"

"Never," was my answer.

"Throth, then, I thought young and ould, rich and poor, knew that—far and near."

"I don't, for one," said I; "but perhaps," I added, bringing forth some little preparation for a lunch that I had about me, and producing a small flask of whisky—"perhaps you will be so good as to tell me, and take a slice of ham, and drink my health," offering him a dram from my flask, and seating myself on the sod beside the river.

"Thank you kindly, sir," says he; and so, after "warming his heart," as he said himself, he proceeded to give an account of the mill in question.

"You see, sir, there was a man wanst, in times back, that

owned a power of land about here—but God keep uz, they said he didn't come by it honestly, but did a crooked turn whenever 'twas to sarve himself—and sure he *sould the pass*, and what luck or grace could he have afther that?"

"How do you mean he sold the pass?" said I.

"Oh, sure your honour must have heerd how the pass was sould, and he bethrayed his king and counthry."

"No, indeed," said I.

"Och, well," answered my old informant, with a shake of the head, which he meant, like Lord Burleigh in the *Critic*, to be very significant, "it's no matther now, and I don't care talkin' about it; and laist said is soonest mended—howsomever, he got a power of money for that same, and lands and what not; but the more he got, the more he craved, and there was no ind to his sthrivin' for goold evermore, and thirstin' for the lucre of gain.

"Well, at last, the story goes, the divil (God bless us!) kem to him, and promised him hapes o' money, and all his heart could desire, and more too, if he'd sell his soul in exchange."

"Surely he did not consent to such a dreadful bargain as that?" said I.

"Oh, no, sir," said the old man, with a slight play of muscle about the corners of his mouth, which, but that the awfulness of the subject suppressed it, would have amounted to a bitter smile—"oh, no, he was too cunnin' for that, bad as he was—and he was bad enough, God knows—he had some regard for his poor sinful sowl, and he would not give himself up to the divil, all out; but the villian, he thought he might make a bargain with the *ould chap*, and get all he wanted, and keep himself out of harm's way still; for he was mighty cute—and throth, he was able for Ould Nick any day.

"Well, the bargain was struck, and it was this-a-way: The divil was to give him all the goold ever he'd ask for, and was to let him alone as long as he could; and the timpter promised him a long day, and said 'twould be a great while before he'd want him, at all, at all; and whin that time kem, he was to keep his hands aff him, as long as the other could give him some work he couldn't do.

"So when the bargain was made, 'Now,' says the Colonel to the divil, 'give me all the money I want.'

"'As much as you like,' says Ould Nick. 'How much will you have?'

"'You must fill me that room,' says he, pointin' into a murtherin' big room, that he emptied out on purpose—'you must fill me that room,' says he, 'up to the very ceilin' with goolden guineas.'

" ' And welkim,' says the divil.

" With that, sir, he began to shovel in the guineas into the room like mad ; and the Colonel towld him, that as soon as he was done, to come to him in his own parlour below, and that he would then go up and see if the divil was as good as his word, and had filled the room with the goolden guineas. So the Colonel went downstairs, and the ould fellow worked away as busy as a nailer, shovellin' in the guineas by hundherds and thousands.

" Well, he worked away for an hour and more, and at last he began to get tired ; and he thought it *mighty odd* that the room wasn't fillin' fasther. Well, afther restin' for a while, he began agin, and he put his shouldher to the work in airnest ; but still the room was no fuller, at all, at all.

" ' Och ! bad luck to me,' says the divil ; ' but the likes of this I never seen,' says he, ' far and near, up and down—the dickens a room I ever kem across afore,' says he, ' I couldn't cram while a cook would be crammin' a turkey, till now ; and here I am,' says he, ' losin' my whole day, and I with such a power o' work an my hands yit, and this room no fuller than if I began five minutes ago.'

" By gor, while he was spakin', he seen the hape o' guineas in the middle of the flure growing *littler and littler* every minit ; and at last they wor disappearing, for all the world, like corn in the hopper of a mill.

" ' Ho ! ho !' says Ould Nick, ' is that the way wid you,' says he ; and with that he run over to the hape of goold—and what would you think, but it was runnin' down through a great big hole in the flure that the Colonel made through the ceilin' in the room below ; and that was the work he was at afther he left the divil, though he purtended he was only waitin' for him in his parlour ; and there the divil, when he looked down through the hole in the flure, seen the Colonel, not content with the *two* rooms full of guineas, but with a big shovel throwin' them into a closet a one side of him as fast as they fell down. So putting his head through the hole, he called down to the Colonel :

" ' Hillo ! neighbour,' says he.

" The Colonel look up, and grew as white as a sheet when he seen he was found out, and the red eyes starin' down at him through the hole.

" ' Musha, bad luck to your impudence !' says Ould Nick ; ' is it sthrivin' to chate *me* you are,' says he, ' you villian ? '

" ' Oh ! forgive me this wanst,' says the Colonel, ' and upon the honour of a gintleman,' says he, ' I'll never—'

" ' Whisht ! whisht ! you thievin' rogue,' says the divil, ' I'm not angry with you, at all, at all ; but only like you the betther, bekase you're so cute. Lave off slaving yourself there,' says he, 'you have got goold enough for this time; and whenever you want more, you have only to say the word, and it shall be yours at command.'

"So, with that the divil and he parted for that time; and myself doesn't know whether they used to meet often afther or not; but the Colonel never wanted money, anyhow, but went on prosperous in the world—and as the saying is, if he took the dirt out o' the road, it id turn to money wid him; and so, in coorse of time, he bought great estates, and was a great man entirely—not a greater in Ireland, throth."

Fearing here a digression on landed interest, I interrupted him to ask how he and the fiend settled their accounts at last?

"Oh, sir, you'll hear that all in good time. Sure enough it's terrible, and wondherful it is at the ind, and mighty improvin'— glory be to God!"

"Is that what you say," said I, in surprise, "because a wicked and deluded man lost his soul to the tempter?"

"Oh, the Lord forbid, your honour! but don't be impatient, and you'll hear all. They say, at last, after many years of prosperity, that the old Colonel got stricken in years, and he began to have misgivin's in his conscience for his wicked doin's, and his heart was heavy as the fear of death came upon him; and sure enough, while he had such murnful thoughts, the divil kem to him, and tould him *he should go wid him.*

"Well, to be sure the ould man was frekened, but he plucked up his courage and his cuteness, and towld the divil, in a bantherin' way, jokin' like, that he had partic'lar business thin, that he was goin' to a party, and hoped an *ould friend* wouldn't inconvaynience him, that a-way—"

"Well," said I, laughing at the "put off" of *going to a party,* "the devil, of course would take no excuse, and carried him off in a flash of fire?"

"Oh, no, sir," answered the old man, in something of a reproving, or, at least, offended tone—"that's the finish, I know very well, of many a story such as we're talkin' of, but that's not the way of this, *which is thruth every word,* what I tell you."

"I beg your pardon for the interruption," said I.

"No offince in life, sir," said the venerable chronicler, who was now deep in his story, and would not be stopped.

"Well, sir," continued he, "the divil said he'd call the next day, and that he must be ready; and sure enough, in the evenin' he kem to him; and when the Colonel seen him, he reminded him of his bargain that as long as he could give him some work he couldn't do, he wasn't obleeged to go.

" ' That's thrue,' says the divil.

" ' I'm glad you're as good as your word, anyhow,' says the Colonel.

" ' I never bruk my word yit,' says the ould chap, cocking up his horns consaitedly—' honour bright,' says he.

" ' Well, then,' says the Colonel, ' build me a mill, down there by the river,' says he, ' and let me have it finished by to-morrow mornin'.'

" ' Your will is my pleasure,' says the ould chap, and away he wint; and the Colonel thought he had nick'd Ould Nick at last, and wint to bed quite aisy in his mind.

" But, *jewel machree,* sure the first thing he heerd the next mornin' was, that the whole counthry round was runnin' to see a fine bran-new mill, that was an the riverside, where, the evenin' before, not a thing at all, at all but rushes was standin', and all, of coorse, wondherin' what brought it there; and some sayin' 'twas not lucky, and many more throubled in their mind, but one and all agreein' it was no *good;* and that's the very mill forninst you, that you were takin' aff, and the stone that I noticed is a remarkable one—a big coign-stone—that they say the divil himself laid first, and has the mark of four fingers and a thumb an it, to this day.

" But when the Colonel heerd it, he was more throubled than any, of coorse, and 'began to conthrive what else he could think iv, to keep himself out iv the claws of the *ould one.* Well, he often heerd tell that there was one thing the divil never could do, and I dar say you heerd it too, sir—that is, that he couldn't make a rope out of the sands of the sae; and so when the *ould one* kem to him the next day and said his job was done, and that now the mill was built, he must either tell him somethin' else he wanted done, or come away wid him.

" So the Colonel said he saw it was all over wid him; ' but,' says he, ' I wouldn't like to go wid you alive, and sure, it's all the same to you, alive or dead ?'

" ' Oh, that won't do,' says his frind; ' I can't wait no more,' says he.

" ' I don't want you to wait, my dear frind,' says the Colonel; " all I want is, that you'll be plazed to kill me before you take me away.'

" ' With pleasure," says Ould Nick.

" ' But will you promise me my choice of dyin' one partic'lar way ?' says the Colonel.

" ' Half a dozen ways, if it plazes you,' says he.

" ' You're mighty obleegin', says the Colonel ; ' and so,' says he, ' I'd rather die by bein' hanged with a rope *made out of the sands of the sae,*' says he, lookin' mighty knowin' at the *ould fellow.*

" ' I've always one about me,' says the divil, ' to obleege my frinds,' says he ; and with that he pulls out a rope made of sand, sure enough.

" ' Oh, it's game you're makin',' says the Colonel, growin' as white as a sheet.

" ' The *game is mine*, sure enough,' says the ould fellow, grinnn', with a terrible laugh.

" ' That's not a sand-rope at all,' says the Colonel.

" ' Isn't it?' says the divil, hittin' him acrass the face with the ind iv the rope, and the sand (for it *was* made of sand, sure enough) went into one of his eyes, and made the tears come with the pain.

" ' That bates all I ever seen or heerd,' says the Colonel, sthrivin' to rally, and make another offer—' is there anything you *can't* do?'

" ' Nothin' you can tell me,' says the divil,' 'so you may as well lave off your palaverin', and come along at wanst.'

" ' Will you give me one more offer ? ' says the Colonel.

" ' You don't desarve it,' says the divil, ' but I don't care if I do ; ' for you see, sir, he was only playin' wid him, and tantalising the ould sinner.

" ' All fair,' says the Colonel, and with that he ax'd him could he stop a woman's tongue.

" ' Thry me,' says Ould Nick.

" ' Well, then,' says the Colonel, ' make my lady's tongue be quiet for the next month, and I'll thank you.'

" ' She'll never throuble you agin,' says Ould Nick ; and with that the Colonel heerd roarin' and cryin', and the door of his room was throwin' open, and in ran his daughter, and fell down at his feet, telling him her mother had just dhropped dead.

" The minit the door opened, the divil runs and hides himself behind a big elbow-chair ; and the Colonel was frekened almost out of his siven sinses, by raison of the sudden death of his poor lady, let alone the jeopardy he was in himself, seein' how the divil had *forestall'd* him every way ; and after ringin' his bell, and callin' to his servants, and recoverin' his daughter out of her faint, he was goin' away wid her out o' the room, whin the divil caught hould of him by the skirt of the coat, and the Colonel was obleeged to let his daughter be carried out by the sarvants, and shut the door afther them.

" ' Well,' says the divil, and he grinn'd and wagg'd his tail, and all as one as a dog when he's plaz'd—' what do you say now ? ' says he.

" ' Oh,' says the Colonel, ' only lave me alone antil I bury my poor wife,' says he, ' and I'll go with you then, you villian,' says he.

" ' Don't call names,' says the divil ; ' you had better keep a civil tongue in your head,' says he ; ' and it doesn't become a gintleman to forget good manners.'

"Well, sir, to make a long story short, the divil purtended to let him off, out of kindness, for three days, antil his wife was buried ; but the raison of it was this, that when the lady, his daughter, fainted, he loosened the clothes about her throat, and in pulling some of her dhress away, he tuk off a goold chain that was an her neck, and put it in his pocket, and the chain had a diamond crass on it, the Lord be praised ! and the divil darn't touch him while he had the *sign of the crass* about him.

"Well, the poor Colonel, God forgive him ! was grieved for the loss of his lady, and she had an *iligant berrin*, and they say that when the prayers was readin' over the dead, the ould Colonel took it to heart like anything, and the word o' God kem home to his poor sinful sowl at last.

"Well, sir, to make a long story short, the ind if it was that for the three days o' grace that was given to him the poor deluded ould sinner did nothin' at all but read the Bible from mornin' till night, and bit or sup didn't pass his lips all the time, he was so intint upon the holy Book, but sat up in an ould room in the far ind of the house, and bid no one disturb him an no account, and struv to make his heart bould with the words iv life ; and sure it was somethin' strinthened him at last, though as the time drew nigh that the *inimy* was to come, he didn't feel aisy. And no wondher ! And, by dad ! the three days was past and gone in no time, and the story goes that at the dead hour o' the night, when the poor sinner was readin' away as fast as he could, my jew'l ! his heart jumped up to his mouth at gettin' a tap on the shoulder.

"' Oh, murther ! ' says he. ' Who's there ? ' for he was afeard to look up.

"' It's me,' says the *ould one*, and he stood right forninst him, and his eyes like coals o' fire lookin' him through, and he said, with a voice that a'most split his ould heart : ' Come ! ' says he.

"' Another day ! ' cried out the poor Colonel.

"' Not another hour,' says Sat'n.

"' Half an hour ? '

"' Not a quarther,' says the divil, grinnin', with a bitther laugh. ' Give over your readin', I bid you,' says he, ' and come away wid me.'

"' Only gi' me a few minits,' says he:

"' Lave aff your palavering, you snakin' ould sinner,' says Sat'n. ' You know you're bought and sould to me, and a purty bargain I have o' you, you ould baste,' says he, ' so come along at wanst,' and he put out his claw to ketch him ; but the Colonel tuk a fast hould o' the Bible, and begg'd hard that he'd let him alone, and wouldn't harm him antil the bit o' candle that was just blinkin' in the socket before him was burned out.

" ' Well, have it so, you dirty coward !' says Ould Nick, and with that he spit an him.

"But the poor ould Colonel didn't lose a minit—for he was cunnin' to the ind—but snatched the little taste o' candle that was forninst him out o' the candlestick, and puttin' it an the holy Book before him, he shut down the cover of it and quinched the light. With that the divil gave a roar like a bull, and vanished in a flash o' fire, and the poor Colonel fainted away in his chair ; but the sarvants heerd the noise—for the divil tore aff the roof o' the house when he left it—and run into the room, and brought their master to himself agin. And from that day out he was an althered man, and used to have the Bible read to him every day, for he couldn't read himself any more, by raison of losin' his eyesight when the divil hit him with the rope of sand in the face, and afther spit an him—for the sand wint into one eye, and he lost the other that-a-way, savin' your presence.

"So you see, sir, afther all, the Colonel, undher heaven, was too able for the divil, and by readin' the good Book his sowl was saved, and, glory be to God ! *isn't that mighty improvin' ?*"

THE GRIDIRON ;

OR,

PADDY MULLOWNEY'S TRAVELS IN FRANCE

MATHEWS, in his " Trip to America," gives a ludicrous representation of an Irishman who has left his own country on the old-fashioned speculation of "seeking his fortune," and who, after various previous failures in the pursuit, at length goes into the back settlements, with the intention of becoming interpreter-general between the Yankees and the Indian tribes; but the Indians reject his proffered service, "*the poor ignorant craytures,*" as he himself says, "*just because* he did not understand the language." We are told, moreover, that Goldsmith visited the land of dykes and dams, for the purpose of teaching the Hollanders *English,* quite overlooking (until his arrival in the country made it obvious), that he did not know a word of *Dutch* himself. I have prefaced the following story thus, in the hope that the "*precedent,*" which covers so many absurdities in *law,* may be considered available by the *author,* as well as the *suitor,* and may serve a turn in the court of criticism, as well as in the common pleas.

A certain old gentleman in the west of Ireland, whose love of the ridiculous quite equalled his taste for claret and fox-hunting, was wont, upon certain festive occasions, when opportunity offered, to amuse his friends by *drawing out* one of his servants, who was exceeding fond of what he termed his *"thravels,"* and in whom a good deal of whim, some queer stories, and perhaps, more than all, long and faithful services, had established a right of loquacity. He was one of those few trusty and privileged domestics who, if his master unheedingly uttered a rash thing in a fit of passion, would venture to set him right. If the Squire said: "I'll turn that rascal off," my friend Pat would say: "Throth, you won't, sir;" and Pat was always right, for if any altercation arose upon the "subject matter in hand," he was sure to throw in some good season, either from former services, general good conduct, or the delinquent's "wife and childher," that always turned the scale.

But I am digressing. On such merry meetings as I have alluded to, the master, after making certain "approaches," as a military man would say, as the preparatory steps in laying siege to some *extravaganza* of his servant, might, perchance, assail Pat thus: "By-the-by, Sir John" (addressing a distinguished guest), "Pat has a very curious story which something you told me to-day reminds me of. You remember, Pat" (turning to the man, evidently pleased at the notice thus paid to himself)—" you remember that queer adventure you had in France?"

"Throth, I do, sir," grins forth Pat.

"What!" exclaims Sir John, in feigned surprise, "was Pat ever in France?"

"Indeed he was," cries mine host; and Pat adds: "Ay, and farther, plaze your honour."

"I assure you, Sir John," continues my host, "Pat told me a story once that surprised me very much, respecting the ignorance of the French."

"Indeed!" rejoins the baronet. "Really, I always supposed the French to be a most accomplished people."

"Throth, then, they're not, sir," interrupts Pat.

"Oh, by no means," adds mine host, shaking his head emphatically.

"I believe, Pat, 'twas when you were crossing the Atlantic?" says the master, turning to Pat with a seductive air, and leading into the "full and true account" (for Pat had thought fit to visit *North Amerikay*, for "a raison he had," in the autumn of the year 'ninety-eight).

"Yes, sir," says Pat, "the broad Atlantic," a favourite phrase of his, which he gave with a brogue as broad almost as the Atlantic itself.

"It was the time I was lost in crassin' the broad Atlantic, a-comin' home," began Pat, decoyed into the recital; "whin the

winds began to blow, and the sae to rowl, that you'd think the
Colleen dhas (that was her name) would not have a mast left but
what would rowl out of her.

"Well, sure enough, the masts went by the boord at last, and
the pumps were choak'd (divil choak them for that same), and av
coorse the wather gained an us; and throth, to be filled with
wather is neither good for man or baste; and she was sinkin' fast,
settlin' down, as the sailors call it; and faith I never was good at
settlin' down in my life, and I liked it then less nor ever;
accordingly, we prepared for the worst, and put out the boat, and
got a sack o' bishkets, and a cashk o' pork, and a kag o' wather,
and a thrifle o' rum aboord, and any other little matthers we
could think iv in the mortial hurry we wor in—and faith, there
was no time to be lost, for, my darlint, the *Colleen dhas* went down
like a lump o' lead, afore we wor many strokes o' the oar away
from her.

"Well, we dhrifted away all that night, and next mornin' we
put up a blanket an the ind av a pole as well as we could, and
then we sailed iligant; for we darn't show a stitch o' canvass the
night before, bekase it was blowin' like bloody murther, savin'
your presence, and sure, it's the wondher of the world we worn't
swally'd alive by the ragin' sae.

"Well, away we wint, for more nor a week, and nothin' before
our two good-lookin' eyes but the canophy iv heaven, and the
wide ocean—the broad Atlantic—not a thing was to be seen but
the sae and the sky; and though the sae and the sky is mighty
purty things in themselves, throth, they're no great things when
you've nothin' else to look at for a week together—and the barest
rock in the world, so it was land, would be more welkim.   And
then, soon enough, throth, our provisions began to run low—the
bishkits, and the wather, and the rum—throth, *that* was gone first
of all, God help uz!—and oh, it was thin that starvation began
to stare us in the face.   'Oh, murther, murther, captain darlint,'
says I; 'I wish we could see land anywhere,' says I.

"'More power to your elbow, Paddy, my boy,' says he, 'for
sitch a good wish, and throth, it's myself wishes the same.'

"'Oh,' says I, 'that it may plaze you, sweet queen iv heaven,
supposing it was only a *dissolute* island,' says I, 'inhabited wid
Turks, sure they wouldn't be such bad Christhans as to refuse us
a bit and a sup.'

"'Whisht, whisht, Paddy!' says the captain, 'don't be talkin'
bad of anyone,' says he; 'you don't know how soon you may
want a good word put in for yourself, if you should be called to
quarthers in th' other world all of a suddint,' says he.

"'Thrue for you, captain darlint,' says I—I called him darlint,
and make free wid him, you see, bekase disthress makes uz all

equal—'thrue for you, captain jewel—God betune uz and harm,
I owe no man any spite—and throth, that was only thruth.
Well, the last bishkit was sarved out, and by gor, the *wather itself*
was all gone at last, and we passed the night mighty cowld—well,
at the brake o' day, the sun riz most beautiful out o' the waves,
that was as bright as silver and as clear as crysthal. But it was
only the more cruel upon us, for we wor beginnin' to feel *terrible*
hungry ; when all at wanst I thought I spied the land—by gor, I
thought I felt my heart up in my throat in a minit, and 'Thunder
and turf, captain,' says I, 'look to leeward,' says I.

" ' What for ?' says he.

" ' I think I see the land,' says I.   So he ups with his bring-'m-
near (that's what the sailors call a spy-glass, sir), and looks out,
and sure enough, it was.

" ' Hurra !' says he, ' we're all right now.   Pull away, my boys,'
says he.

" ' Take care you're not mistaken,' says I ; 'maybe it's only a
fog-bank, captain darlint,' says I.

" ' Oh, no,' says he, ' it's the land in airnest.'

" ' Oh, then, whereabouts in the wide world are we, captain ?'
says I ; 'maybe it id be in *Roosia*, or *Proosia*, or the Garman
Oceant,' says I.

" ' Tut, you fool !' says he—for he had that consaited way wid
him, thinkin' himself cleverer than anyone else — ' tut, you
fool,' says he, ' that's *France*,' says he.

" ' Tare an ouns !' says I, ' do you tell me so ?   And how do you
know it's France it is, captain dear ?' says I.

" ' Bekase this is the Bay o' Bishky we're in now,' says he.

" ' Throth, I was thinkin' so myself,' says I, ' by the rowl it
has ; for I often heerd av it in regard of that same ;' and throth,
the likes av it I never seen before nor since, and with the help o'
God, never will.

" Well, with that my heart began to grow light ; and when I
seen my life was safe, I began to grow twice hungrier nor ever.
' So,' says I, ' captain jewel, wish we had a gridiron.'

" ' Why, then,' says he, ' thunder an' turf,' says he, ' what puts
a gridiron into your head ?'

" ' Bekase I'm starvin' with the hunger,' says I.

" ' And sure, bad luck to you,' says he, ' you couldn't ate a
gridiron,' says he, ' barrin' you wor a *pelican o' the wildherness*,'
says he.

" ' Ate a gridiron !' says I.   ' Och, in throth, I'm not sitch a
gommoch all out as that, anyhow.   But sure, if we had a gridiron,
we could dress a beef-stake,' says I.

" ' Arrah ! but where's the beef-stake ?' says he.

" ' Sure, couldn't we cut a slice aff the pork ?' says I.

" ' By gor, I never thought o' that,' says the captain.   ' You're a clever fellow, Paddy,' says he, laughin'.

" ' Oh, there's many a thrue word said in joke,' says I.

" ' Thrue for you, Paddy,' says he.

" ' Well, then,' says I, ' if you put me ashore there beyant ' (for we were nearin' the land all the time), ' and sure, I can ax thim for to lind me the loan of a gridiron,' says I.

" ' Oh, by gor, the butther's comin' out o' the stirabout in airnest now,' says he.   ' You gommoch,' says he, ' sure I towld you before that's France—and sure they're all furriners there,' says the captain.

" ' Well,' says I, ' and how do you know but I'm as good a furriner myself as any o' thim.'

" ' What do you mane ? ' says he.

" ' I mane,' says I, ' what I towld you, that I'm as good a furriner myself as any o' thim ? '

" ' Make me sinsible,' says he.

" ' By dad, maybe that's more nor me, or greater nor me, could do,' says I—and we all began to laugh at him, for I thought I'd pay him off for his bit o' consait about the Garman Oceant.

" ' Lave aff your humbuggin',' says he, ' I bid you, and tell me what it is you mane, at all, at all.'

" ' *Parly voo frongsay*,' says I.

" ' Oh, your humble sarvant,' says he.   ' Why, by gor, you're a scholar, Paddy.'

" ' Throth, you may say that,' says I.

" ' Why, you're à clever fellow, Paddy,' says the captain, jeerin' like.

" ' You're not the first that said that,' says I, ' whether you joke or no.'

" ' Oh, but I'm in airnest,' says the captain.   ' And do you tell me, Paddy,' says he, ' that you spake Frinch ? '

" ' *Parly voo frongsay*,' says I.

" ' By gor, that bangs Banagher, and all the world knows Banagher bangs the divil—I never met the likes o' you, Paddy,' says he.   ' Pull away, boys, and put Paddy ashore, and maybe we won't get a good bellyful before long.'

" So with that it was no sooner said than done.   They pulled away, and got close into shore in less than no time, and run the boat up in a little creek—and a beautiful creek it was, with a lovely white sthrand—an iligant place for ladies to bathe in the summer ; and out I got—and it's stiff enough in my limbs I was, afther bein' cramp'd up in the boat, and perished with the cowld and hunger ; but I conthrived to scramble on, one way or t'other, tow'rds a little bit iv wood that was close to the shore, and the smoke curlin' out of it, quite timptin' like.

" ' By the powdhers o' war, I'm all right,' says I, ' there's a house there;' and sure enough there was, and a parcel of men, women, and childher, eating their dinner round a table, quite convaynient. And so I wint up to the door, and I thought I'd be very civil to thim, as I heerd the Frinch was always mighty p'lite intirely, and I thought I'd show them I knew what good manners was.

"So I took aff my hat, and making a low bow, says I: 'God save all here,' says I.

"Well, to be sure, they all stopt ating at wanst, and begun to stare at me, and faith, they almost look'd me out o' countenance; and I thought to myself it was not good manners at all, more betoken from furriners, which they call so mighty p'lite; but I never minded that in regard o' wantin' the gridiron; and so says I: 'I beg your pardon,' says I, 'for the liberty I take, but it's only bein' in disthress in regard of ating,' says I, 'that I make bowld to throuble yez, and if you could lind me the loan of a gridiron,' says I, 'I'd be entirely obleeged to ye.'

"By gor, they all stared at me twice worse nor before; and with that, says I, knowin' what was in their minds: 'Indeed, it's thrue for you,' says I, 'I'm tatthered to pieces, and God knows I look quare enough; but it's by raison of the storm,' says I, 'which dhruv us ashore here below, and we're all starvin',' says I.

"So then they began to look at each other agin; and myself, seeing at wanst dirty thoughts was in their heads, and that they tuk me for a poor beggar, comin' to crave charity, with that, says I: 'Oh, not at all,' says I, 'by no manes; we have plenty o' mate ourselves, there below; and we'll dhress it,' says I, 'if you would be plazed to lind us the loan of a gridiron,' says I, makin' a low bow.

"Well, sir, with that, throth, they stared at me twice worse nor ever, and faith, I began to think that maybe the captain was wrong, and that it was not France, at all, at all; and so says I: 'I beg pardon, sir,' says I, to a fine ould man, with a head of hair as white as silver, 'maybe I'm undher a mistake,' says I; 'but I thought I was in France, sir. Aren't you furriners?' says I—'*Parly voo frongsay?*'"

"'We munseer,' says he.

"'Then, would you lind me the loan of a gridiron,' says I, 'if you plaze?'

"Oh, it was thin that they stared at me as if I had siven heads; and faith, myself began to feel flusthered like and onaisy, and so says I, makin' a bow and scrape agin: 'I know it's a liberty I take, sir,' says I, 'but it's only in the regard of bein' cast away; and if you plaze, sir,' says I, '*parly voo frongsay?*'

"'We munseer,' says he, mighty sharp.

" 'Then, would you lind me the loan of a gridiron?' says I, 'and you'll obleege me.'

"Well, sir, the ould chap began to munseer me, but the divil a bit of a gridiron he'd gi' me; and so I began to think they wor all neygars, for all their fine manners; and throth, my blood begun to rise, and says I: 'By my sowl, if it was you was in disthress,' says I, 'and if it was to ould Ireland you kem, it's not only the gridiron they'd give you, if you ax'd it, but something to put an it too, and the dhrop o' dhrink into the bargain, and *cead mile failte.*'

"Well, the word *cead mile failte* seemed to sthreck his heart, and the ould chap cocked his ear, and so I thought I'd give him another offer, and make him sinsible at last; and so says I, wanst more, quite slow, that he might undherstand : '*Parly—voo—frongsay*, munseer?'

" 'We munseer,' says he.

" 'Then lind me the loan of a gridiron,' says I, 'and bad scram to you.'

"Well, bad win to the bit of it he'd gi' me, and the ould chap begins bowin' and scrapin', and said something or other about a long tongs.

" 'Phoo! the divil sweep yourself and your tongs,' says I. 'I don't want a tongs, at all, at all; but can't you listen to raison,' says I, '*Parly voo frongsay ?*'

" 'We munseer.'

" 'Then lind me the loan of a gridiron,' says I, 'and howld your prate.'

"Well, what would you think but he shook his ould noddle, as much as to say he wouldn't, and so says I : 'Bad cess to the likes o' that I ever seen! Throth, if you wor in my counthry it's not that-a-way they'd use you. The curse o' the crows an you, you ould sinner,' says I; 'the divil a longer I'll darken your door.'

"So he seen I was vex'd, and I thought, as I was turnin' away, I seen him begin to relint, and that his conscience throubled him, and says I, turnin' back : 'Well, I'll give you one chance more, you ould thief! Are you a Chrishthan, at all, at all? Are you a furriner?' says I, 'that all the world calls so p'lite. Bad luck to you! Do you undherstand your own language? *Parly voo frongsay ?*' says I.

" 'We munseer,' says he.

" 'Then, thunder an' turf,' says I, 'will you lind me the loan of a gridiron?'

"Well, sir, the divil resave the bit of it he'd gi' me, and so with that the 'curse o' the hungry an you, you ould neygarly villian,' says I. 'The back o' my hand and the sowl o' my fut to you, that you may want a gridiron yourself yit,' says I; 'and wherever I go, high and low, rich and poor, shall hear o' you,' says I. And with that I left them there, sir, and kem away; and in throth, it's often sense that *I thought that it was remarkable.*"

PADDY THE PIPER

THE only introduction I shall attempt to the following "*extrava-ganza*" is to request the reader to suppose it to be delivered by a frolicking Irish peasant in the richest brogue and most dramatic manner.

"I'll tell you, sir, a mighty quare story, and it's as thrue as I'm standin' here, and that's no lie.

"It was in the time of the *'ruction*, whin the long summer days, like many a fine fellow's precious life, was cut short by raison of the martial law, that wouldn't let a dacent boy be out in the evenin', good or bad; for whin the day's work was over, divil a one of uz dar go to meet a frind over a glass, or a girl at the dance, but must go home and shut ourselves up, and never budge, nor rise latch, nor dhraw boult, antil the morning kem agin.

"Well, to come to my story. 'Twas afther night-fall, and we wor sittin' round the fire, and the praties wor boilin', and the noggins of butthermilk was standin' ready for our suppers, whin a knock kem to the door.

"'Whisht!' says my father. 'Here's the sojers come upon uz now,' says he. 'Bad luck to thim, the villians! I'm afeared they seen a glimmer of the fire through the crack in the door,' says he.

"'No,' says my mother, 'for I'm afther hangin' an ould sack and my new petticoat agin it a while ago.'

"'Well, whisht, anyhow,' says my father, 'for there's a knock agin,' and we all held our tongues till another thump kem to the door.

"'Oh, it's a folly to purtind any more,' says my father; 'they're too cute to be put off that-a-way,' says he. 'Go, Shamus,' says he to me, 'and see who's in it.'

"'How can I see who's in it in the dark?' says I.

"'Well,' says he, 'light the candle, thin, and see who's in it, but don't open the door, for your life, barrin' they brake it in,' says he, 'exceptin' to the sojers, and spake thim fair, if it's thim.'

"So with that I wint to the door, and there was another knock.

"'Who's there?' says I.

"'It's me,' says he.

"'Who are you?' says I.

PADDY THE PIPER

" ' A frind,' says he.

" ' *Baithershin !* ' says I—' who are you, at all ? '

" ' Arrah ! don't you know me ? ' says he.

" ' Divil a taste,' says I.

" ' Sure I'm Paddy the Piper,' says he.

" ' Oh, thunder an' turf,' says I, ' is it you, Paddy, that's in it ? '

" ' Sorra one else,' says he.

" ' And what brought you at this hour ? ' says I.

" ' By gar,' says he, ' I didn't like goin' the roun' by the road,' says he, ' and so I kem the short cut, and that's what delayed me,' says he.

" ' Oh, bloody wars ! ' says I. ' Paddy, I wouldn't be in your shoes for the king's ransom,' says I ; ' for you know yourself it's a hangin' matther to be cotched out these times,' says I.

" ' Sure, I know that,' says he, ' God help me ; and that's what I kem to you for,' says he ; ' and let me in for ould acquaintance sake,' says poor Paddy.

" ' Oh, by this and that,' says I, ' I darn't open the door for the wide world ; and sure you know it ; and throth, if the Husshians or the Yeos ketches you,' says I, ' they'll murther you, as sure as your name's Paddy.'

" ' Many thanks to you,' says he, ' for your good intintions ; but, plaze the pigs, I hope it's not the likes o' that is in store for me, anyhow.'

" ' Faix, then,' says I, ' you had betther lose no time in hidin' yourself,' says I ; ' for throth, I tell you, it's a short thrial and a long rope the Husshians would be afther givin' you—for they've no justice, and less marcy, the villians ! '

" ' Faith, thin, more's the raison you should let me in, Shamus,' says poor Paddy.

" ' It's a folly to talk,' says I. ' I darn't open the door.'

" ' Oh, then, millia murther ? ' says Paddy, ' what'll become of me, at all, at all ? ' says he.

" ' Go aff into the shed,' says I, ' behin' the house, where the cow is, and there there's an iligant lock o' straw that you may go sleep in,' says I, ' and a fine bed it id be for a lord, let alone a piper.'

" So off Paddy set to hide in the shed, and throth, it wint to our hearts to refuse him, and turn him away from the door, more by token when the praties was ready—for sure, the bit and the sup is always welkim to the poor thraveller. Well, we all wint to bed, and Paddy hid himself in the cow-house ; and now I must tell you how it was with Paddy :

" You see, afther sleeping for some time, Paddy wakened up thinkin' it was mornin', but it wasn't mornin' at all, but only the

light o' the moon that deceaved him ; but at all evints, he wanted
to be stirrin' airly, bekase he was goin' off to the town hard by,
it bein' fair day, to pick up a few ha'pence with his pipes—for
the divil a betther piper was in all the counthry round nor Paddy ;
and everyone gave it up to Paddy that he was iligant an the
pipes, and played ' Jinny bang'd the Weaver ' beyant tellin', and
the ' Hare in the Corn,' that you'd think the very dogs was in it
and the horsemen ridin' like mad.

"Well, as I was sayin', he set off to go to the fair, and he wint
meandherin' along through the fields, but he didn't go far, antil
climbin' up through a hedge, when he was comin' out at t'other
side, his head kem plump agin somethin' that made the fire
flash out iv his eyes. So with that he looks up—and what do
you think it was, Lord be marciful to uz! but a corpse hangin'
out of a branch of a three.

"'Oh, the top o' the mornin' to you, sir,' says Paddy, 'and is
that the way with you, my poor fellow ? Throth, you tuk a start
out o' me,' says poor Paddy ; and 'twas thrue for him, for it
would make the heart of a stouter man nor Paddy jump to see
the like, and to think of a Chrishthan crathur being hanged up,
all as one as a dog.

"Now, 'twas the rebels that hanged this chap—bekase, you
see, the corpse had got clothes an him, and that's the raison that
one might know it was the rebels—by raison that the Husshians
and the Orangemen never hanged anybody wid good clothes an
him, but only the poor and definceless crathurs like uz ; so, as I
said before, Paddy knew well it was the *boys* that done it ; ' and,'
says Paddy, eyin' the corpse, 'by my sowl, thin, but you have
a beautiful pair o' boots an you,' says he, ' and it's what I'm
thinkin' you won't have any great use for thim no more ; and
sure, it's a shame to the likes o' me,' says he, 'the best piper in
the sivin counties, to be trampin' wid a pair of ould brogues not
worth three *traneeens*, and a corpse with such an iligant pair o'
boots, that wants someone to wear thim. So, with that, Paddy
lays hould of him by the boots, and began a-pullin' at thim, but
they wor mighty stiff ; and whether it was by raison of their
bein' so tight, or the branch of the three a-jiggin' up an' down,
all as one as a weighdee buckettee, an' not lettin' Paddy cotch
any right hoult o' thim—he could get no *advantage* o' thim at all
—and at last he gev it up, and was goin' away, whin lookin'
behind him agin, the sight of the iligant fine boots was too much
for him, and he turned back, determined to have the boots, anyhow, by fair means or foul ; and I'm loath to tell you now how
he got thim—for indeed it was a dirty turn, and throth, it was
the only dirty turn I ever knew Paddy to be guilty av ; and you
see it was this a-way ; 'pon my sowl, he pulled out a big knife,

and by the same token, it was a knife with a fine buck-handle and a murtherin' big blade, that an uncle o' mine, that was a gardener at the lord's, made Paddy a prisint av; and more by token, it was not the first mischief that knife done, for it cut love between thim, that was the best of frinds before; and sure, 'twas the wondher of everyone, that two knowledgable men, that ought to know betther, would do the likes, and give and take sharp steel in frindship; but I'm forgettin'—well, he outs with his knife, and what does he do, but he cuts off the legs of the corpse; 'and,' says he, 'I can take off the boots at my convaynience;' and throth, it was, as I said before, a dirty turn.

"Well, sir, he tuck'd the legs undher his arms, and at that minit the moon peeped out from behind a cloud—'Oh! is it there you are?' says he to the moon, for he was an impidint chap—and thin, seein' that he made a mistake, and that the moonlight deceaved him, and that it wasn't the airly dawn, as he conceaved; and bein' friken'd for fear himself might be cotched and trated like the poor corpse he was afther a malthreating, if *he* was found walking the counthry at that time—by gar, he turned about, and walked back agin to the cow-house, and hidin' the corpse's legs in the sthraw, Paddy wint to sleep agin. But what do you think? the divil a long Paddy was there, antil the sojers came in airnest, and by the powers, they carried off Paddy—and faith, it was only sarvin' him right for what he done to the poor corpse.

"Well, whin the mornin' kem, my father says to me: 'Go, Shamus,' says he, 'to the shed, and bid poor Paddy come in, and take share o' the praties, for I go bail, he's ready for his breakquest by this, anyhow!'

"Well, out I wint to the cow-house, and called out 'Paddy!' and afther callin' three or four times, and gettin' no answer, I wint in, and called agin, and divil an answer I got still. 'Blood-an-agers!' says I. 'Paddy, where are you, at all, at all?' and so, castin' my eyes about the shed, I seen two feet stickin' out from undher the hape o' straw—'Musha! thin,' says I, 'bad luck to you, Paddy, but you're fond of a warm corner, and maybe you haven't made yourself as snug as a flay in a blanket? but I'll disturb your dhrames, I'm thinkin',' says I, and with that I laid hould of his heels (as I thought, God help me!), and givin' a good pull to waken him, as I intinded, away I wint, head over heels, and my brains was a'most knocked out agin' the wall.

"Well, whin I recovered myself, there I was, an the broad o' my back, and two things stickin' out o' my hands like a pair o' Husshian's horse-pist'ls—and I thought the sight 'id lave my eyes when I seen they wor two mortial legs.

"My jew'l, I threw them down like a hot pratie, and jumpin' up, I roared out millia murther. 'Oh, you murtherin' villian,' says I, shakin' my fist at the cow; 'oh, you unnath'ral *baste*,' says I, 'you've ate poor Paddy, you thievin' cannible; you're worse than a neygar,' says I; 'and bad luck to you, how dainty you are, that nothin' 'id sarve you for your supper but the best piper in Ireland. *Weirasthru! weirasthru!* what'll the whole counthry say to such an unnath'ral murther? And you lookin' as innocent there as a lamb, and atin' your hay as quite as if nothin' happened.' With that I run out—for throth, I didn't like to be near her—and goin' into the house, I tould them all about it.

"'Arrah! be aisy,' says my father.

"'Bad luck to the lie I tell you,' says I.

"'Is it ate, Paddy?' says they.

"'Divil a doubt of it,' says I.

"'Are you sure, Shamus?' says my mother.

"'I wish I was as sure of a new pair o' brogues,' says I. 'Bad luck to the bit she has left iv him but his two legs.'

"'And do you tell me she ate the pipes too?' says my father.

"'By gor, I b'lieve so,' says I.

"'Oh, the divil fly away wid her,' says he. 'What a cruel taste she has for music!'

"'Arrah!' says my mother, 'don't be cursin' the cow that gives the milk to the childher.'

"'Yis, I will,' says my father. 'Why shouldn't I curse sich an nnnath'ral baste?'

"'You oughtn't to curse any livin' thing that's undher your roof,' says my mother.

"'By my sowl, thin,' says my father, 'she shan't be undher my roof any more; for I'll sind her to the fair this minit,' says he, 'and sell her for whatever she'll bring. Go aff,' says he, 'Shamus, the minit you've ate your breakquest, and dhrive her to the fair.'

"'Throth, I don't like to dhrive her,' says I.

"'Arrah, don't be makin' a gommagh of yourself,' says he.

"'Faith, I don't,' says I.

"'Well, like or no like,' says he, 'you must dhrive her.'

"'Sure, father,' says I, 'you could take more care iv her yourself.'

"'That's mighty good,' says he, 'to keep a dog and bark myself;' and faith, I rec'llected the sayin' from that hour. 'Let me have no more words about it,' says he, 'but be aff wid you.'

"So aff I wint—and it's no lie I'm tellin' whin I say it was sore agin my will I had anything to do with sich a villian of a baste. But howsomever, I cut a brave long wattle, that I might dhrive the manather iv a thief, as she was, without bein' near her, at all, at all.

"Well, away we wint along the road, and mighty throng it

wuz wid the boys and the girls—and in short, all sorts, rich and poor, high and low, crowdin' to the fair.

"'God save you,' says one to me.

"'God save you, kindly,' says I.

"'That's a fine baste you're dhrivin',' says he.

"'Throth, she is,' says I; though God knows it wint agin my heart to say a good word for the likes of her.

"'It's to the fair you're goin', I suppose,' says he, 'with the baste?' (He was a snug-lookin' farmer, ridin' a purty little grey hack.)

"'Faith, thin, you're right enough,' says I. 'It is to the fair I'm goin'.'

"'What do you expec' for her?' says he.

"'Faith, thin, myself doesn't know,' says I—and that was thrue enough, you see, bekase I was bewildhered like about the baste entirely.

"'That's a quare way to be goin' to market,' says he; 'and not to know what you expec' for your baste.'

"'Och,' says I—not likin' to let him suspict there was anything wrong wid her—'och,' says I, in a careless sort of a way, 'sure, no one can tell what a baste 'ill bring, antil they come to the fair,' says I, 'and see what price is goin'.'

"'Indeed, that's nath'ral enough,' says he. 'But if you wor bid a fair price before you come to the fair, sure you might as well take it,' says he.

"'Oh, I've no objection in life,' says I.

"'Well, thin, what 'ill you ax for her?' says he.

"'Why, thin, I wouldn't like to be onraisonable,' says I—(for the thruth was, you know, I wanted to get rid iv her)—'and so I'll take four pounds for her,' says I, 'and *no less*.'

"'No less!' says he.

"'Why, sure, that's chape enough,' says I.

"'Throth, it is,' says he; 'and I'm thinkin' it's *too* chape it is,' says he; 'for if there wasn't somethin' the matter, it's not for that you'd be sellin' the fine milch cow, as she is to all appearance.'

"'Indeed, thin,' says I, 'upon my conscience, she *is* a fine milch cow.'

"'Maybe,' says he, 'she's gone off her milk, in regard that she doesn't feed well?'

"'Och, by this and that,' says I, 'in regard of feedin' there's not the likes of her in Ireland. So make your mind aisy; and if you like her for the money, you may have her.'

"'Why, indeed, I'm not in a hurry,' says he, 'and I'll wait to see how they go in the fair.'

"'With all my heart,' says I, purtendin' to be no ways consarned—but in throth, I began to be afeard that the people was

seein' somethin' unnath'ral about her, and that we'd never get
rid of her, at all, at all.   At last we kem to the fair, and a great
sight o' people was in it—throth, you'd think the whole world was
there, let alone the standin's o' gingerbread and iligant ribbins,
and makin's o' beautiful gownds, and pitch-and-toss, and merry
go-rouns, and tints with the best av dhrink in thim, and the
fiddles playin' up t' incourage the boys and girls; but I never
minded thim at all, but detarmint to sell the thievin' rogue av a
cow afore I'd mind any divarshin in life; so an I dhriv her into
the thick av the fair, whin all of a suddint, as I kem to the
door av a tint, up sthruck the pipes to the tune av 'Tattherin' Jack
Welsh,' and, my jew'l, in a minit the cow cock'd her ears, and was
makin' a dart at the tint.

"'Oh, murther!' says I, to the boys standin' by, 'hould her,
says I, 'hould her—she ate one piper already, the vagabone, and
bad luck to her, she wants another.'

"'Is it a cow for to ate a piper?' says one o' thim.

"'Divil a bit o' lie in it, for I seen his corpse myself, and
nothin' left but the two legs,' says I; 'and it's a folly to be
sthrivin' to hide it, for I *see* she'll never lave it aff—as poor Paddy
Grogan knows to his cost, Lord be marciful to him!'

"'Who's that takin' my name in vain?' says a voice in the
crowd; and with that, shovin' the throng a one side, who the divil
should I see but Paddy Grogan, to all appearance.

"'Oh, hould him too,' says I.   'Keep him av me, for it's
not himself at all, but his ghost,' says I; 'for he was kilt last
night to my sartin knowledge, every inch av him, all to his legs.'

"Well, sir, with that, Paddy—for it *was* Paddy himself, as it
kem out afther—fell a laughin', that you'd think his sides 'ud
split; and whin he kem to himself, he ups and he tould uz how it
was, as I tould you already; and the likes av the fun they made
av me was beyant tellin' for wrongfully misdoubtin' the poor cow,
and layin' the blame iv atin' a piper an her.   So we all wint into
a tint to have it explained, and by gor, it tuk a full gallon o'
sper'ts t' explain it; and we dhrank health and long life to Paddy
and the cow, and Paddy played that day beyant all tellin',
and many a one said the likes was never heerd before or sence,
even from Paddy himself—and av coorse, the poor slandhered cow
was dhruv home agin, and many a quite day she had wid
us afther that; and whin she died, throth, my father had sitch a
regard for the poor thing, that he had her skinned, and an iligant
pair of breeches made out iv her hide, and it's in the fam'ly
to this day; and isn't it mighty remarkable it is, what I'm goin'
to tell you now, but it's as thrue as I'm here, and from that out,
anyone that has them breeches an, the minit a pair o' pipes sthrikes
up, they çan't rest, but goes jiggin' and jiggin' in their sate, and

never stops as long as the pipes is playin'—and there," said he, slapping the garment in question that covered his sinewy limb, with a spank of his brawny hand that might have startled nerves more tender than mine—"there, there is the very breeches that's an me now, and a fine pair they are this minit."

THE PRIEST'S GHOST

" A SAD tale's best for winter," saith the epigraph ; and it was by the winter's hearth that I heard the following *ghost-story*, rendered interesting from the air of reverential belief with which it was delivered from the withered lips of an old woman.

Masses for the souls of the dead are among the most cherished items of the Roman Catholic peasant's belief ; and it was to prove how sacred a duty the mass for the " soul of the faithful departed " is considered before the eternal judgment-seat, that the tale was told, which I shall endeavour to repeat as nearly as my memory will serve, in the words of the original narrator. It was a certain eve of St. John, as well as I can remember, that the old dame gave as the date of the supernatural occurrence.

"Whin Mary O'Malley, a friend of my mother's (God rest her sowl!) and it was herself tould me the story : Mary O'Malley was in the chapel hearin' vespers an the eve o' Saint John, whin, you see, whether it was that she was dhrowsy or tired afther the day's work—for she was all 'day teddin' the new-cut grass, for 'twas haymakin' sayson—or whether it was *ordhered*, and that it was all for the glory of God, and the repose of a throubled sowl, or how it was, it doesn't become me to say, but howsomever, Mary fell asleep in the chapel, and sound enough she slep', for never a wink she wakened antil every individhial craythur was gone, and the chapel doors was locked. Well, you may be sure, it's poor Mary O'Malley was freken'd, and thrimbl'd till she thought she'd ha' died on the spot, and sure, no wondher, considerin' she was locked up in a chapel all alone, and in the dark, and no one near her.

Well, afther a time she recovered herself a little, and she thought there was no use in life in settin' up a phillelew, sthrivin' to make herself heerd, for she knew well no livin' sowl was within call ; and so, on a little considheration, whin she got over the first fright at being left alone that-a-way, good thoughts kem into her head to comfort her ; and sure she knew she was in God's own house, and that no bad sper't daar come there. So, with that she knelt down agin, and repeated her crados and pather-and-aves, over and over, antil she felt quite sure in the purtection of hiv'n, and then, wrappin' herself up in her cloak, she thought she might lie down and sthrive to sleep till mornin', whin, 'may the Lord keep us!' piously ejaculated the old woman, crossing herself most devoutly, 'all of a suddint a light shined into the chapel as bright as the light of day, and with that poor Mary, lookin' up, seen it shinin' out of the door of the vesthry, and immediately out walked out of the vesthry a priest dhressed in black vestments, and goin' slowly up to the althar, he said : 'Is there anyone here to answer this mass?'

Well, my poor dear Mary thought the life 'id lave her, for she dhreaded the priest was not of this world, and she couldn't say a word ; and whin the priest ax'd three times was there no one there to answer the mass, and got no answer, he walked back agin into the vesthry, and in a minit all was dark agin ; but before he wint, Mary thought he looked towards her, and she said she'd never forget the melancholy light of his eyes, and the look he gave her quite pitiful like, and she said she never heerd before nor since such a wondherful deep voice.

Well, sir, the poor craythur, the minit the sper't was gone—for it was a sper't, God be good to us !—that minit the craythur fainted dead away; and so I suppose it was with her from one faint into another, for she knew nothin' more about anything antil she recovered and kem to herself in her mother's cabin, afther being brought home from the chapel next mornin' whin it was opened for mass, and she was found there.

I hear, thin, it was as good as a week before she could lave her bed, she was so overcome by the mortial terror she was in that blessed night, blessed as it was, bein' the eve of a holy saint, and more by token, the manes of givin' repose to a throubled sper't ; for you see, whin Mary tould what she had seen and heerd to her clargy, his Riverence, undher God, was enlightened to see the maynin' of it all ; and the maynin' was this, that he undherstood from hearin' of the priest appearin' in black vestments, that it was for to say mass for the dead that he kem there ; and so he supposed that the priest durin' his lifetime had forgot to say a mass for the dead that he was bound to say, and that his poor sowl couldn't have rest antil that mass was said, and that he must walk antil the duty was done.

So Mary's clargy said to her, that as the knowledge of this was made through her, and as his Riverence said she was chosen, he ax'd her would she go and keep another vigil in the chapel, as his Riverence said—and thrue for him—for the repose of a sowl. So Mary, bein' a stout girl, and always good, and relyin' on doin' what she thought was her duty in the eyes of God, said she'd watch another night, but hoped she wouldn't be ax'd to stay long in the chapel alone. So the priest tould her 'twould do if she was there a little afore twelve o'clock at night ; for you know, sir, that people never appears antil afther twelve, and from that till cock-crow. And so accordingly Mary wint on the night of the vigil, and before twelve down she knelt in the chapel, and began a-countin' of her beads, and the craythur, she thought every minit was an hour antil she'd be relaysed.

Well, she wasn't kep' long; for soon the dazzlin' light burst from out of the vesthry door, and the same priest kem out that appeared afore, and in the same melancholy voice he ax'd, when he mounted the althar: 'Is there anyone here to answer this mass?'

Well, poor Mary sthruv to spake, but the craythur thought her heart was up in her mouth, and not a word could she say, and agin the word was ax'd from the althar, and still she couldn't say a word; but the sweat ran down her forehead as thick as the winther's rain, and immediately she felt relieved, and the impression was taken aff her heart like, and so, whin for the third and last time the appearance said: 'Is there *no* one here to answer this mass?' poor Mary mutthered out 'Yis' as well as she could.

Oh, often I heerd her say the beautiful sight it was to see the lovely smile upon the face of the sper't as he turned round and looked kindly upon her, saying these remarkable words: 'It's twenty years,' says he, 'I have been askin' that question, and no one answered till this blessed night, and a blessin' be on her that answered, and now my business on earth is finished,' and with that he vanished before you could shut your eyes.

So never say, sir, it's no good praying for the dead; for you see that even the sowl of a priest couldn't have pace for forgettin' so holy a thing as a mass for the sowl of the faithful departed."

NEW POTATOES

IN the merry month of June, or thereabouts, the aforesaid melody may be heard, in all the wailing intonation of its *minor third*, through every street of Dublin.

We Irish are conversational, the lower orders particularly so, and the hawkers who frequent the streets often fill the lapses that occur between their cries by a current conversation with some passing friend, occasionally broken by the deponent "labouring in her calling" and yelling out: "Brave lemons" or "Green *pays*," in some awkward interval, frequently productive of very ludicrous effects.

Such was the case, as I happened to overhear a conversation between Katty, a *black-eyed* dealer in "New pittayatees!" and her friend Sally, who had "Fine fresh Dublin Bay herrings!" to dispose of. Sally, to do her justice, was a very patient hearer, and did not interrupt her friend with her own cry in the least;

whether it was from being interested in her friend's little mis-fortunes, or that Katty was one of those "out-and-outers" in story-telling, who, when once they begin, will never leave off, nor even allow another to edge in a word as "thin as a sixpence," I will not pretend to say; but certain it is, Katty, in the course of her history, had it all her own way, like "a bull in a chaynee-shop," as she would have said herself.

Such is the manner in which the following sketch from Nature came into my possession. That it is altogether slang, I premise; and give all fastidious persons fair warning, that if a picture from low life be not according to their taste, they can leave it unread, rather than blame me for too much fidelity in my outline. So here goes at a *scena*, as the Italians say.

"MY NEW PITTAYATEES!"

Enter Katty, with a grey cloak, a dirty cap, and a black eye; a sieve of potatoes *on* her head, and a "trifle o' sper'ts" *in* it. Katty meanders down Patrick Street.

KATTY—"*My new Pittayatees!—My-a-new Pittayatees!—My new*—"—(*Meeting a friend.*)—Sally darlin', is that you?

SALLY—Throth, it's myself; and what's the matther wid you, Katty?

KAT.—'Deed, my heart bruk cryin'—"*New pittayatees*"—cryin' afther that vagabone.

SAL.—Is it Mike?

KAT.—Throth, it's himself indeed.

SAL.—And what is it he done?

KAT.—Och! he ruined me with his—"*New pittayatees*"—with his goin's-an—the ould thing, my dear.

SAL.—Throwin' up his little finger, I suppose?

KAT.—Yis, my darlint; he kem home th' other night, blazin' blind dhrunk, cryin' out—"*New pit-tay-a-tees!*"—roarin' and bawlin', that you'd think he' rise the roof aff o' the house.

"Bad luck attend you; bad cess to you, you pot-walloppin' varmint," says he (maynin' me, i' you plaze)—"wait till I ketch you, you sthrap, and it's I'll give you your fill iv"—'*New pittayatees!*'—"your fill iv a licking, if ever you got it," says he.

So, with that, I knew the villian was *mulvathered;* let alone the heavy fut o' the miscrayint an the stairs, that a child might know he was done for—"*My new pitttayaees!*"—Throth, he was done to a turn, like a mutton-kidney.

SAL.—Musha! God help you, Katty.

KAT.—Oh, wait till you hear the ind o' my—"*New pittayatees!*" —o' my throubles, and it's then you'll open your eyes—"*My new pittayatees!*"

SAL.—Oh, bud I pity you.

KAT.—Oh, wait—wait, my jewel—wait till you hear what became o'—"*My new pittayatees!*"—wait till I tell you the ind of it. Where did I lave aff? Oh, ay, at the stairs.

Well, as he was comin' upstairs (knowin' how it 'd be), I thought it best to take care o' my—"*New pittayatees!*"—to take care o' myself; so with that I put the bowlt an the door, betune me and danger, and kep' listenin' at the key-hole; and sure enough, what should I hear but—"*New pittayatees!*"—but the vagabone gropin' his way round the cruked turn in the stair, and tumblin' afther into the hole in the flure an the landin', and whin he come to himself, he gev a thunderin' thump at the door. "Who's there?" says I. Says he—"*New pittayatees!*"—"Let me in," says he, "you vagabone (swarin' by what I wouldn't mintion), or by this and that, I'll *massacray* you," says he, "within an inch o'—'*New pittayatees!*'—within an inch o' your life," says he. "Mikee darlint," says I, sootherin' him.

SAL.—Why would you call sitch a 'tarnal vagabone darlint?

KAT.—My jew'l, didn't I tell you I thought it best to soother him with—"*New pittayatees!*"—with a tindher word; so, says I, "Mikee, you villian, you're disguised," says I; "you're disguised, dear."

"You lie," says he, "you impident sthrap, I'm not disguised; but, if I'm disguised itself," says he, "I'll make you know the differ," says he.

Oh! I thought the life id lave me, when I heerd him say the word; and with that I put my hand an—"*My new pittayatees!*" —an the latch o' the door, to purvint it from slippin'; and he ups and he gives a wicked kick at the door, and says he: "If you don't let me in this minit," says he, "I'll be the death o' your —'*New pittayatees!*'—o' yourself and your dirty breed," says he. Think o' that, Sally dear, to abuse my relations.

SAL.—Oh, the ruffin.

KAT.—Dirty breed, indeed! By my sowkins, they're as good as his any day in the year, and was never behoulden to—"*New pittayatees!*"—to go a-beggin' to the mendicity for their dirty— "*New pittayatees!*"—their dirty washin's o' pots, and sarvints' lavin's, and dogs' bones, all as one as that cruk'd disciple of his mother's cousin's sisther, the ould dhrunken asperseand, as she is.

SAL.—No, in throth, Katty dear.

KAT.—Well, where was I? Oh, ay, I left off at—"*New pittayatees!*"—I left off at my dirty breed. Well, at the word "dirty breed," I knew full well the bad dhrop was up in him— and faith, it's soon and suddint he made me sinsible av it, for the first word he said was—"*New pittayatees!*"—the first word he said was to put his shouldher to the door, and in he bursted the door, fallin' down in the middle o' the flure, cryin' out—"*New pittayatees !*"—cryin' out: "Bad luck attind you," says he. "How dar you refuse to lit me into my own house, you sthrap," says he, "agin the law o' the land," says he, scramblin' up on his pins agin, as well as he could; and as he was risin', says I—"*New pittayatees !*"—says I to him (screeching out loud, that the neighbours in the flure below might hear me), "Mikee, my darlint," says I.

"Keep the pace, you vagabone," says he; and with that he hits me a lick av a—"*New pittayatees !*"—a lick av a stick he had in his hand, and down I fell (and small blame to me), down I fell an the flure cryin'—"*New pittayatees !*"—cryin' out: "Murther! murther!"

SAL.—Oh, the hangin' bone villian!

KAT.—Oh, that's not all! As I was risin', my jew'l, he was goin' to sthrek me agin; and with that I cried out—"*New pittayatees !*"—I cried out: "Fair-play, Mikee," says I; "don't sthrek a man down;" but he wouldn't listen to raison, and was goin' to hit me agin, whin I put up the child that was in my arms betune me and harm. "Look at your babby, Mikee," says I. "How do I know that, you flag-hoppin' jade," says he. (Think o' that, Sally jew'l — misdoubtin' my vartue, and I an honest woman, as I am. God help me!!!)

SAL.—Oh! but you're to be pitied, Katty dear.

KAT.—Well, puttin' up the child betune me and harm, as he was risin' his hand—"Oh!" says I, "Mikee darlint, don't sthrek the babby;" but, my dear, before the word was out o' my mouth, he sthruk the babby. (I thought the life 'id lave me.) And iv coorse, the poor babby, that never spuk a word, began to cry— "*New pittayatees !*"—began to cry and roar and bawl, and no wondher.

SAL.—Oh, the haythen, to go sthrek the child.

KAT.—And, my jew'l, the neighbours in the flure below, hearin' the skrimmage, kem runnin' up the stairs, cryin' out—"*New pittayatees*"—cryin' out: "Watch, watch, Mikee M'Evoy," says they. "Would you murther your wife, you villian?" "What's that to you?" says he. "Isn't she my own?" says he, "and if I plaze to make her feel the weight o' my—'*New pittayatees*'—the weight o' my fist, what's that to you?" says he. "It's none o' your business, anyhow, so keep your tongue in your jaw, and your toe in your pump, and 'twill be betther for your—'*New pittayatees*'— 'twill be betther for your health, I'm thinkin'," says he; and with that he looked cruked at thim, and squared up to one o' thim—a poor definceless craythur—a tailor.

"Would you fight your match?" says the poor innocent man.

"Lave my sight," says Mikee, "or, by jingo, I'll put a stitch in your side, my jolly tailor," says he.

"Yiv put a stitch in your wig already," says the tailor, "and that'll do for the present writin'."

And with that, Mikee was goin' to hit him with a—"*New pittayatee*"—a lift-hander; but he was cotch howld iv before he could let go his blow; and who should stand up forninst him, but—"*My new pittayatees*"—but the tailor's wife (and by my sowl, it's she that's the sthrapper, and more's the pity she's thrown away upon one o' the sort); and says she : "Let *me* at him," says she, "it's I that's used to give a man a lickin' every day in the week; you're bowld an the head now, you vagabone," says she; "but if I had you alone," says she, "no matther if I wouldn't take the consait out o' your—'*New pittayatees*'—out o' your braggin' heart;" and that's the way she wint an ballyraggin' him; and by gor, they all tuk patthern afther her, and abused him, my dear, to that degree, that I vow to the Lord, the very dogs in the sthreet wouldn't lick his blood.

SAL.—Oh, my blissin' on thim.

KAT.—And with that, one and all, they begun to cry—"*New pittayatees !*"—they began to cry him down; and, at last, they all swore out: "Hell's bell attind your berrin," says they, "you vagabone," as they just tuk him up by the scruff o' the neck, and threw him down the stairs; every step he'd take, you'd think he'd brake his neck (Glory be to God !), and so I got rid o' the ruffin; and then they left me cryin'—"*New pittayatees !*"—cryin' afther the vagabone—though the angels knows well he wasn't desarvin' o' one precious dhrop that fell from my two good-lookin' eyes— and oh ! but the condition he left me in.

SAL.—Lord look down an you !

KAT.—And a purty sight it id be, if you could see how I was lyin' in the middle o' the flure, cryin'—*New pittayatees !*"—cryin' and roarin', and the poor child, with his eye knocked out, in the corner, cryin'—"*New pittayatees !*"—and indeed, everyone in the place was cryin'—"*New pittayatees !*"—was cryin' murther.

SAL.—And no wondher, Katty dear.

KAT.—Oh, bud that's not all. If you seen the condition the place was in afther it; it was turned upside down, like a beggar's breeches. Throth, I'd rather be at a bull-bait than at it—enough to make an honest woman cry—"*New pittayatees !*"—to see the daycent room rack'd and ruin'd, and my cap tore off my head into tatthers—throth, you might riddle bull-dogs through it; and bad luck to the hap'orth he left me, but a few—"*New pittayatees !*" —a few coppers; for the morodin' thief spint all his—"*New pittayatees !*"—all his wages o' the whole week in makin' a baste iv himself; and God knows but that comes aisy to him ! and divil

a thing had I to put inside my face, nor dhrop to dhrink, barrin'
a few—"*New pittayatees !*"—a few grains o' tay, and the ind iv a
quarther o' sugar, and my eyes as big as your fist, and as black as
the pot (savin' your presence), and a beautiful dish iv—"*New
pittayatees !*"—dish iv delf, that I bought only last week in
Temple Bar, bruk in three halves in the middle o' the ruction—
and the rint o' the room not ped—and I dipindin' only an—"*New
pittayatees*"—an cryin' a sieve-full o' praties, or schreechin' a lock
o' savoys, or the like.

But I'll not brake your heart any more, Sally dear. God's
good, and never opens one door but He shuts another, and that's
the way iv it; and strinthins the wake with—"*New pittayatees*"—
with His purtection—and may the widdy and the orphin's blessin'
be an His name, I pray!—and my thrust is in Divine Providence, that was always good to me—and sure, I don't despair; but
not a night that I kneel down to say my prayers, that I don't
pray for—"*New pittayatees*"—for all manner o' bad luck to attind
that vagabone, Mikee M'Evoy. My curse light an him this blessed
minit; and—

[*A voice at a distance calls " Potatoes."*]

KAT.—Who calls? (*Perceives her customer.*) Here, ma'am!
Good-bye, Sally darlint—good-bye! "*New pittay-a-tees.*"

[*Exit Katty by the Cross Poddle.*]

PADDY THE SPORT

DURING a sojourn of some days in the county of ——, visiting a
friend, who was anxious to afford as much amusement to his
guests as country sports could furnish, "the dog and gun" were,
of course, put into requisition; and the subject of this sketch was
a constant attendant on the shooting-party.

He was a tall, loose-made, middle-aged man, rather on the elder
side of middle-age, perhaps—fond of wearing an oil-skinned hat
and a red waistcoat—much given to lying and tobacco, and
an admirable hand at filling a game-bag or emptying a whisky-
flask; and if game was scarce in the stubbles, Paddy was sure to
create plenty of another sort for his master's party, by the marvellous stories he had ever at his command. Such was "Paddy
the Sport," as the country people invariably called him.

Paddy was fond of dealing in mystification, which he practised
often on the peasants, whom he looked upon as an inferior class of
beings to himself—considering that his office of sportsman con-
ferred a rank upon him that placed him considerably above them,
to say nothing of the respect that was due to one so adroit in the
use of the gun as himself; and by the way, it was quite a scene

to watch the air of self-complacency that Paddy, after letting fly both barrels into a covey, and dropping his brace of birds as dead as a stone, quietly let down the piece from his shoulder and commenced reloading, looking about him the while with an admirable carelessness, and when his piece was ready for action again, returning his ramrod with the air of a master, and then, throwing the gun into the hollow of his arm, walk forward to the spot where the birds were lying, and pick them up in the most business-like manner.

But to return to Paddy's love of mystification. One day I accompanied him, or perhaps it would be fitter to say he acted as guide, in leading me across a country to a particular point, where I wanted to make a sketch. His dogs and gun, of course, bore him company, though I was only armed with my portfolio ; and we beat across the fields, merrily enough, until the day became overcast, and a heavy squall of wind and rain forced us to seek shelter in the first cottage we arrived at. Here the good woman's apron was employed in dusting a three-legged stool to offer to "the gintleman," and "Paddy the Sport" was hailed with welcome by everyone in the house, with whom he entered into conversation in his usual strain of banter and mystification.

I listened for some time to the passing discourse ; but the bad weather still continuing, I began to amuse myself, until it should clear, in making an outline of a group of dogs that were stretched upon the floor of the cabin, in a small green-covered sketching-book that I generally carry about me for less important memoranda. This soon caused a profound silence around me ; the silence was succeeded by a broken whispering, and Mr. Paddy, at last approaching me with a timidity of manner I could not account for, said : "Sure, sir, it wouldn't be worth your while to mind puttin' down the pup?" pointing to one that had approached the group of dogs, and had commenced his awkward gambols with his seniors.

I told him I considered the pup as the most desirable thing to notice ; but scarcely were the words uttered, until the old woman cried out : "Terry, take that cur out o' that—I'm sure I don't know what brings all the dogs here ;" and Terry caught up the pup in his arms, and was running away with him, when I called after him to stop ; but 'twas in vain. He ran like a hare from me ; and the old lady, seizing a branch of a furze-bush from a heap of them that were stowed beside the chimney-corner for fuel, made an onset on the dogs, and drove them yelping from the house.

I was astonished at this, and perceived that the air of everyone in the cottage was altered towards me ; and, instead of the civility which had saluted my entrance, estranged looks, or direct ones of no friendly character, were too evident. I was about to inquire the cause, when Paddy the Sport, going to the door, and casting a weather-wise look abroad, said: "I think, sir, we may as well be goin'—and indeed, the day's clearin' up fine afther all, and 'ill be beautiful yit. Good-bye to you, Mrs. Flannerty"—and off went Paddy; and I followed immediately, having expressed my thanks to the aforesaid Mrs. Flannerty, making my most engaging adieu, which, however, was scarcely returned.

On coming up with my conductor, I questioned him touching what the cause might be of the strange alteration in the manner of the cottagers, but all his answers were unsatisfactory or evasive.

We pursued our course to the point of destination. The day cleared, as was prophesied—Paddy killed his game—I made my sketch—and we bent our course homeward as the evening was closing. After proceeding for a mile or two, I pointed to a tree in the distance, and asked Paddy what very large bird it could be that was sitting in it.

After looking sharply for some time, he said: "*It* a bird, is it? —throth, it's a bird that never flew yet."

"What is it, then?" said I.

"It's a dog that's hangin'," said he.

And he was right — for as we approached, it became more evident every moment. But my surprise was excited when, having scarcely passed the suspended dog, another tree rose up in my view, in advance, decorated by a pendent brace of the same breed.

"By the powers! there's two more o' thim," shouted Paddy. "Why, at this rate, they've had more sportin' nor myself," said he. And I could see an expression of mischievous delight playing over the features of Mr. Paddy as he uttered the sentence.

As we proceeded, we perceived almost every second bush had been converted into a gallows for the canine race; and I could not help remarking to my companion that we were certainly in a very hang-dog country.

"Throth, thin, you may thank yourself for it," said he, laughing outright; for up to this period his mirth, though increasing at every fresh execution perceived, had been smothered.

"Thank myself!" said I—"how?'

"By my sowl, you frekened the whole country this mornin'," said he, "with that little green book of yours—"

"Is it my sketch-book?" said I.

"By gor, all the people thought it was a *ketch*-book, sure enough, and that you wor goin' round the counthry to ketch all the dogs in it, and make thim pay—"

"What do you mean?" said I.

"Is it what I mane you want to know, sir?—throth, thin, I don't know how I can tell it to a gintleman, at all, at all."

"Oh, you may tell me."

"By gor, sir, I wouldn't like offindin' your honour; but you see (since you must know, sir), that whin *you tuk* that little green book out iv your pocket, *they tuk* you for—savin' your presence—by gor, I don't like tellin' you."

"Tut, nonsense, man," said I.

"Well, sir (since you *must* know), by dad, they tuk you—I beg your honour's pardon—but, by dad, they tuk you for a tax-gatherer."

"A tax-gatherer!"

"Divil a lie in it; and whin they seen you takin' off the dogs, they thought it was to count thim, for to make thim pay for thim; and so, by dad, they thought it best, I suppose, to hang them out o' the way."

"Ha! Paddy," said I, "I see this is a piece of your knavery, to bewilder the poor people."

"Is it me?" says Paddy, with a look of assumed innocence, that avowed, in the most provoking manner, the inward triumph of Paddy in his own hoax.

"'Twas too much, Paddy," said I, "to practise so far on innocent people."

"Innocent!" said Paddy. "They're just about as innocent as a coal o' fire in a bag o' flax."

"And the poor animals, too!" said I.

"Is it the blackguard curs?" said Paddy, in the most sportsmanlike wonder at my commiserating any but a spaniel or pointer. "Throth, thin, sir, to tell you thruth, I let thim go an in their mistake, and I seen all along how 'twould be, and, 'pon my conscience, but a happy riddance the counthry will have o' sich riff-raff varmint of cabin curs. Why, sir, the mangy mongrels goes about airly in the sayson, moroding through the corn, and murthers the young birds and does not let them come to their full time, to be killed in their nath'ral way, and ruinin' gintlemen's sport into the bargain, and sure, hangin' is all that's good for them."

So much for Paddy's mystifying powers. Of this *coup* he was not a little vain, and many a laugh he has made at my expense afterwards, by telling the story of the "painter gintleman that was mistuk for a tax-gatherer."

Paddy being a professed story-teller, and a notorious liar, it may be naturally inferred that he dealt largely in fairy-tales and ghost-stories. Talking of fairies one day, for the purpose of exciting him to say something of them, I inquired if there were many fairies in that part of the country ?

"Ah! no, sir!" said he, with the air of a sorrowing patriot—"not now. There was wanst a power of fairies used to keep about the place; but sence the *rale* quol'ty—the good ould families—has left it, and the upstarts has kem into it—the fairies has quitted it all out, and wouldn't stay here, but is gone farther back into Connaught, where the ould blood is."

"But I daresay you have seen them sometimes ?"

"No, indeed, sir. I never saw thim, barrin' wanst, and that was whin I was a boy; but I heerd them often."

"How did you know it was fairies you heard ?"

"Oh, what else could it be ? Sure, it was crossin' out over a road I was in the time o' the ruction, and heard full a thousand men marchin' down the road, and by dad, I lay down in the gripe o' the ditch, not wishin' to be seen, nor liken to be throublesome to thim; and I watched who they wor, and was peepin' out iv a turf o' rishes, when what should I see but nothin' at all, to all appearance, but the thrampin' o' min, and a clashin' and a jinglin', that you'd think the infanthry and yeomanthry and cavalthry was in it, and not a sight iv anything to be seen but the brightest o' moonlight that ever kem out o' the hivins."

"And that was all ?"

"Divil a more; and by dad, 'twas more nor I'd like to see or hear agin."

"But you never absolutely saw any fairies ?"

"Why, indeed, sir, to say that I seen thim, that is with my own eyes, wouldn't be thrue, barrin wanst, as I said before, and that's many a long day ago, whin I was a boy, and I and another chap was watchin' turf in a bog; and whin the night was fallin' and we were goin' home, 'What would you think,' says I, 'Charley, if we wor to go home by old Shaughnessey's field, and stale a shafe o' pays ?' So he agreed, and off we wint to stale the pays; but whin we got over the fince, and was creepin' along the furrows for fear of bein' seen, I heerd some one runnin' afther me, and I thought we wor cotch, myself and the boy, and I turned round, and with that I seen two girls dhressed in white—throth I never see sitch white in my born days—they wor as white as the blown snow, and runnin' like the wind, and I knew at wanst that they wor fairies, and I threw myself down an my face, and by dad, I was afeard to look up for nigh half an hour."

I inquired of him what kind of faces these fine girls had.

"Oh, the divil a stim o' their faytures I could see, for the minit I clapt my eyes an thim, knowin' they wor fairies, I fell down, and darn't look at them twicet."

"It was a pity you did not remark them," said I.

"And do you think it's a fool I am, to look twicet at a fairy, and maybe have my eyes whipt out iv my head, or turned into stones, or stone blind, which is all as one."

"Then you can scarcely say you saw them?" said I.

"Oh, by dad, I can say I seen thim, and sware it for that matther; at laste, there was somethin' I seen as white as the blown snow."

"Maybe they were ghosts, and not fairies," said I. "Ghosts, they say, are always seen in white."

"Oh, by all that's good, they warn't ghosts, and that I know full well, for I know the differ betune ghosts and fairies."

"You have had experience, then, in both, I suppose."

"Faix, you may say that. Oh, I had a wondherful great *appearance* wanst that kem to me, or at laste to the house where I was, for, to be sure, it wasn't to me it kem—why should it? But it was whin I was livin' at the lord's in the next county, before I kem to live with his honour here, that I saw the appearance."

"In what shape did it come?"

"Throth, thin, I can't well tell you what shape; for you see whin I heerd it comin' I put my head undher the clothes, and never looked up, nor opened my eyes until I heerd it was gone."

"But how do you know that it was a ghost?"

"Oh, sure, all the counthry knew the house was throubled, and indeed, that was the raison I had for lavin' it, for when my lord turned me off ho was expectin' that I'd ax to be tuk back agin, and faith, sorry he was, I go bail, that I didn't, but I wouldn't stay in the place and it hanted!"

"Then it *was* haunted!"

"To be sure it was; sure, I tell you, sir, the sper't kem to me."

"Well, Paddy that was only civil—returning a visit; for I know you are fond of going to the spirits occasionally."

"Musha, bud your honour is always jokin' me about the dhrop. Oh, bud faith, the sper't kem to me, and whin I hid my head undher the clothes, sure, didn't I feel the sper't sthrivin' to pull them aff o' me. But wait and I'll tell you how it was. You see, myself and another sarvant was sleepin' in one room, and by the same token, a thievin' rogue he was the same sarvant, and I heerd a step comin' down the stairs, and they wor stone stairs, and the latch was riz, but the door was locked, for I turned the key in it myself; and when the sper't seen the latch was fast, by dad, the key was turned in the door (though it was inside, av coorse), and the sper't walked in, and I heerd the appearance walkin' about the place, and it kem and shuk me; but as I tould you, I shut my eyes, and rowled my head up in the clothes; well, with that it went and raked the fire, (for I suppose it was cowld), but the fire was a'most gone out, and with that it went to the turf-bucket to see if there was any sods there to throw an the fire; but not a sod there was left, for we wor sittin' up late indeed (it being the young lord's birthday, and we wor drinkin' his health), and when it couldn't find any turf in the bucket, bad cess to me, but it began to kick the buckets up and down the room for spite, and divil sich a clatter I ever heerd as the sper't made, kickin' the turf-bucket like a futball round the place; and whin it was tired plazin' itself that-a-way, the appearance came and shuk me agin, and I roared and bawled at last, and thin away it wint, and slammed the door afther it, that you'd think it id pull the house down."

"I'm afraid, Paddy," said I, "that this was nothing more than a troublesome dream."

"Is it a dhrame, your honour! That a dhrame! By my sowl, that id be a quare dhrame! Oh, in throth, it was no dhrame it was, but an appearance; but indeed, afther, I often thought it was an appearance for death, for the young lord never lived to see another birthday. Oh, you may look at me, sir, but it's th'uth. Aye, and I'll tell you what's more, the young lord, the last time I seen him out, was one day he was huntin', and he came in from the stables, through the back-yard, and passed through that very room to go up by the back-stairs, and as he wint in through that very door that the appearance slammed afther it—what would you think, but he slammed the door afther him the very same way; and indeed, I thrimbled when I thought iv it. He was in a hurry, to be sure; but I think there was some maynin' in it "—and Paddy looked mysterious.

After the foregoing satisfactory manner in which Paddy showed so clearly that he understood the difference between a ghost and a fairy, he proceeded to enlighten me with the further distinction of a spirit, from either of them. This was so very abstruse, that I shall not attempt to take the elucidation of the point out of Paddy's own hands; and should you, gentle reader, ever have the good fortune to make his acquaintance, Paddy, I have no doubt, will clear up the matter as fully and clearly to your satisfaction as he did to mine. But I must allow Paddy to proceed in his own way.

"Well, sir, before I go an to show you the differ betune the fairies and sper'ts, I must tell you about a mighty quare thrick the fairies was goin' to play at the lord's house, where the appearance kem to me, only that the nurse (and she was an aunt o' my own) had the good-luck to baulk thim. You see, the way it was, was this: The child was a man-child, and it was the first boy was in the family for many a long day; for they say there was a prophecy standin' agin the family that there should be no son to

inherit; but at last there was a boy, and a lovely fine babby it
was, as you'd see in a summer's day; and so, one evenin', that
the fam'ly, my lord and my lady, and all o' thim, was gone out,
and gev the nurse all sorts o' charges about takin' care o' the
child, she was not long alone, whin the housekeeper kem to her
and ax'd her to come downstairs, where she had a party; and
they expected to be mighty pleasant, and was to have great
goin's an; and so the nurse said she didn't like lavin' the child,
and all to that; but howsomever, she was beguiled into the
thing; and she said at last that as soon as she left the child out
iv her lap, where she was hushin' it to sleep, foreninst the fire,
that she'd go down to the rest o' the sarvants and take share o'
what was goin'.

"Well, at last the child was fast asleep, and the nurse laid it
an the bed, as careful as if it was goolden diamonds, and tucked
the curtains roun' about the bed, and made it as safe as Newgate,
and thin she wint down, and joined the divarshin—and merry
enough they wor, at playin' iv cards, and dhrinkin' punch, and
dancin', and the like o' that.

"But I must tell you, that before she wint down at all, she left
one o' the housemaids to stay in the room, and charged her, on
her apparel, not to lave the place until she kem back; but for
all that, her fears wouldn't let her be aisy; and indeed, it was
powerful lucky that she had an inklin' o' what was goin' an.
For what id you think, but the blackguard iv a housemaid, as
soon as she gets the nurse's back turned, she ups and she goes to
another party was in the sarvants' hall, wid the undher-sarvants;
for whin the lord's back was turned, you see, the house was all as
one as a play-house, fairly turned upside down.

"Well, as I said, the nurse (undher God) had an inklin' o'
what was to be; for though there was all sorts o' divarshin goin'
an in the housekeeper's room, she could not keep the child out iv
her head, and she thought she heerd the screeches av it ringin' in
her ear every minit, although she knew full well she was far
beyant where the cry o' the child could be heerd—but still the
cry was as plain in her ear as the earring she had in it; and so
at last she grewn so onaisy about the child, that she was goin' upstairs agin—but she was stopped by one, and another coaxed her,
and another laughed at her, till at last she grew ashamed of doin'
what was right (and God knows, but many a one iv uz is laughed
out o' doin' a right thing), and so she sat down agin—but the cry
in her ears wouldn't let her be aisy; and at last she tuk up her
candle, and away she wint upstairs.

"Well, afther passin' the two first flights, sure enough she
heerd the child a-screechin', that id go to your heart; and with
that she hurried up so fast that the candle a'most wint out with

the draught; and she run into the room and wint up to the bed, callin' out, *My lanna ban'n*, and all to that, to soother the child; and pullin' open the bed-curtain to take the darlin' up—but what would you think, not a sign o' the child was in the bed, good, bad, or indifferent; and she thought the life id lave her; for thin she was afeard the child dhropped out o' the bed—though she thought the curtains was tucked so fast and so close that no accident could happen; and so she run round to the other side to take up the child (though, indeed, she was afeard she'd see it with its brains dashed out), and lo and behould you, divil a taste av it was there, though she heerd it screechin' as if it was murtherin'; and so thin she didn't know what in the wide world to do; and she run rootin' into every corner o' the room lookin' for it; but bad cess to the child she could find—whin, all iv a suddint, turnin' her eyes to the bed agin, what did she perceave but the fut-carpet that wint round the bed, goin' by little and little undher it, as if someone was pullin' it; and so she made a dart at the carpet, and cotch hould o' the ind iv it—and with that, what should she see but the babby lyin' in the middle o' the fut-carpet, as if it was dhrawin' down into the flure undher the bed. One half o' the babby was out o' sight already, undher the boords, whin the nurse seen it, and it screechin' like a sae-gull, and she laid houl' iv it; and faith, she often towl' myself that she was obleeged to give a good sthrong pull before she could get the child from the fairies."

"Then it was the fairies were taking the child away?" said I.

"Who else would it be?" said Paddy. "Sure, the carpet wouldn't be runnin' undher the bed itself, if it wasn't pulled by the fairies; besides, I towl' you there was a prophecy stannin' agin the male boys of the lord's fam'ly."

"I hope, however, *that* boy lived?"

"Oh yes, sir, the charm was bruk that night, for the other childher used to be tuk away always by the fairies, and that night the child 'id have been tuk only for the nurse that was givin' (undher God) to undherstan' the screechin' in her ears, and arrived betimes to ketch howlt o' the carpet and baulk the fairies, for all knowledgable people I ever heerd says that if you baulk the fairies *wanst*, they'll lave you alone evermore."

"Pray, did she *see* any of the fairies that were stealing the child?"

"No, sir; the fairies doesn't love to be seen, and seldom at all you get a sight iv them; and that's the differ I was speakin' iv to you betune fairies and sper'ts. Now, the sper'ts is always seen in some shape or other; and maybe it id be a bird, or a shafe o' corn, or a big stone, or a hape o' dung, or the like o' that, and never know 'twas a sper't at all, antil you wor made sinsible av it somehow or other. Maybe it id be that you wor comin' home from a friend's house late at night, and you might fall down and couldn't keep a leg undher you, and not know why, barrin' it was a sper't misled you, and maybe it's in a ditch you'd find yourself asleep in the mornin' when you woke."

"I daresay, Paddy, that same has happened to yourself before now ? "

"Throth, and you may say that, sir; but the commonest thing in life is for a sper't for to take the shape iv a dog—which is a favourite shape with sper'ts—and indeed, Tim Mooney, the miller in the next town, was a'most frekened out iv his life by a sper't that-a-way; and he'd ha' been murthered, only he had the good-loock to have a *rale* dog wid him—and a rale dog is the finest thing in the world against sper'ts."

"How do you account for that, Paddy ? '

"Bekase, sir, the dog's the most sinsible, and the bowldest baste, barrin' the cock, which is bowldher for his size than any o' God's craythurs, and so, whin the cock crows, all evil sper'ts vanishes; and the dog bein', as I said, bowld and sinsible also, is mighty good; besides, you couldn't make a cock your companion—it wouldn't be nath'ral to raison, you know—and therefore, a dog is the finest thing in the world for a man to have with him in throublesome places; but I must tell you, that though sper'ts dhreads a dog, a fairy doesn't mind him, for I have heerd o' fairies ridin' a dog, all as one as a monkey; and a lanthern also is good, for the sper't o' darkness dhreads the light. But this is not tellin' you about Mooney, the miller: He was comin' home, you see, from a neighbour's, and had to pass by a rath, and when he was just kem to the rath, his dog that was wid him (and a brave dog he was, by the same token) began to growl and gev a low bark, and with that, the miller seen a great big baste of a black dog comin' up to thim, and walks a one side av him all as one, as if he was his masther; with that Mooney's own dog growled agin, and runs betune his masther's legs, and there he staid walkin' on wid him, for to purtect him; and the miller was frekened a'most out iv his life, and his hair stood up sthraight an his head, that he was obleeged to put his hand up to his hat and shove it down an his head, and three times it was that way, that his hair was risin' the hat aff his head with the fright, and he was obleeged to howld it down, and his dog growlin' all the time, and the black thief iv a dog keepin' dodgin' him along, and his eyes like coals o' fire, and the terriblest smell of sulphur, I hear, that could be, all the time, till at last they came to a little sthrame that divided the road, and there, my dear, the sper't disappeared, not bein' able to pass runnin' wather; for sper'ts, sir, is always waken'd with wather."

"That I believe," said I; "but I think, Paddy, you seldom put spirits to so severe a trial."

"Ah, thin, but your honour will you never give over jeerin' me about the dhrop. But in throth, what I'm tellin' you is thrue about it—runnin' wather desthroys sper'ts."

"Indeed, Paddy, I know that is your opinion."

"Oh, murther, murther! there I made a slip agin, and never seen it till your honour had the advantage o' me. Well, no matther, it's good, anyway; but indeed, I think it has so good a good name iv its own that it's a pity to spile it, baptizin' it any more."

Such were the marvellous yarns that Paddy was constantly spinning. Indeed, he had a pride, I rather think, in being considered equally expert at "the long bow" as at the rifle; and if he had not a bouncer to astonish his hearers with, he endeavoured that his ordinary strain of conversation, or his answer to the commonest question, should be of a nature to surprise them. Such was his reply one morning to his master, when he asked Paddy what was the cause of his being so hoarse.

"Indeed, sir," answered Paddy, "it's a cowld I got, and indeed, myself doesn't know how I cotch cowld, barrin' that I slep' in a field last night and forgot to shut the gate afther me."

"Ah, Paddy," said the Squire, "the old story—you were drunk as usual, and couldn't find your way home. You are a shocking fellow, and you'll never get on as long as you give yourself up to whisky."

"Why, thin, your honour, sure that's the raison I ought to get an the fasther, for isn't a 'spur in the head worth two in the heel,' as the ould sayin' is?"

Here a laugh from the Squire's guests turned the scale in Paddy's favour.

"I give you up, Paddy," said the master; "you're a sad dog, worse than Larry Lanigan."

"Oh, murther! Is it Lanigan you'd be afther comparin' me to?" said Paddy. "Why, Lanigan is the complatest dhrinker in Ireland; by my sowkins, more whisky goes through Lanigan than any other *worm* in the county. Is it Lanigan? Faiks, that's the lad could take the consait out iv a gallon o' sper'ts without quittin' it. Throth, Lanigan is just the very chap that id go to first mass every mornin' in the year if holy wather was whisky."

This last reply left Paddy in possession of the field, and no further attack was made upon him on the score of his love of "the dhrop!" and this triumph on his part excited him to exert himself in creating mirth for the gentlemen who formed the shooting party. One of the company retailed that well-known joke made by Lord Norbury, viz., when a certain gentleman declared that he had shot twenty hares before breakfast, his lordship replied that he *must have fired at a wig.*

Here Paddy declared that he thought "it was no great shootin'" to kill twenty hares, for that he had shot seventy-five brace of rabbits in one day.

"Seventy-five brace!" was laughed forth from everyone present.

"Bad loock to the lie in it," said Paddy.

"Oh, be easy, Paddy," said his master.

"There it is now, and you won't b'live me? Why, thin, in throth, it's not that I'm proud iv it, I tell you, for I don't think it was any great things iv shootin', at all, at all."

Here a louder burst of merriment than the former hailed Paddy's declaration.

"Well, now," said Paddy, "if yez be quiet and listen to me, I'll explain it to your satisfaction. You see, it was in one iv the islans aff the shore there"—and he pointed seawards—"it was in one o' the far islans out there, where rabbits are so plinty, and runnin' so thick that you can scarcely see the grass."

"Because the island is all sand," said his master.

"No, indeed, now, though you thought you had me there," said Paddy, very quietly. "It's not the sandy islan at all, bud one farther out."

"Which of them?"

"Do you know the little one with the black rock?"

"Yes."

"Well, it's not that. But you know—"

"Arrah! can't you tell his honour," said a peasant who was an attendant on the party, to carry the game—"can't you tell his honour at wanst, and not be delayin'."

Paddy turned on this plebeian intruder with the coolest contempt and said: "Hurry no man's cattle; get a jackass for yourself," and then resumed: "Well, sir, but you know the islan with the sharp headlan'—"

"Yes."

"Well, it's not that either; but if you—"

"At that rate, Paddy," said the Squire, "we shall never hear which island this wonderful rabbit burrow is in. How would you steer for it after passing Innismoyle?"

"Why, thin, you should steer about nor'-west, and when you cleared the black rocks you'd have the sandy islan bearin' over your larboard bow, and thin you'd see the islan I spake av, when you run about as far as—"

"Pooh! pooh!" said the Squire, "you're dreaming, Paddy; there's no such island at all."

"By my sowl, there is, beggin' your honour's pardon."

" It's very odd I never saw it."

" Indeed it's a wondher, sure enough."

" Oh, it can't be," said the Squire.   " How big is it ? "

" Oh, by dad, it's as big as ever it'll be," said Paddy, chuckling.

This answer turned the laugh against the Squire again, who gave up further cross-questioning of Paddy, whose readiness of converting his answers into jokes generally frustrated any querist who was hardy enough to engage with Paddy in the hope of puzzling him.

" Paddy," said the Squire, "after that wonderful rabbit adventure, perhaps you would favour the gentlemen with that story you told me once about a fox ? "

" Indeed and I will, plaze your honour," said Paddy ; " though I know full well the divil a one word iv it you b'live, nor the gintlemen won't either, though you're axin' me for it, but only want to laugh at me, and call me a big liar whin my back's turned."

" Maybe we wouldn't wait for your back being turned, Paddy, to honour you with that title."

" Oh, indeed, I'm not sayin' you wouldn't do it as soon fore-ninst my face, your honour, as you often did before, and will agin, plaze God, and welkim—"

" Well, Paddy, say no more about that, but let's have the story."

" Sure, I'm losin' no time, only tellin' the gintlemen beforehand that it's what they'll be callin' it, a lie—and indeed, it's ancommon, sure enough ; but you see, gintlemen, you must remimber that the fox is the cunnin'est baste in the world, barrin' the wran—"

Here Paddy was questioned why he considered the wren as cunning a *baste* as the fox.

" Why, sir, bekase all birds build their nest wid one hole to it only, excep'n the wran ; but the wran builds two holes to the nest, and so that if any inimy comes to disturb it upon one door, it can go out an the other.   But the fox is cute to that degree, that there's many mortial a fool to him—and by dad, the fox could buy and sell many a Christian, as you'll soon see by-and-by, when I tell you what happened to a wood-ranger that I knew wanst, and a dacent man he was, and wouldn't say the thing in a lie.

" Well, you see, he kem home one night mighty tired—for he was out wid a party in the domain, cock-shootin' that day ; and whin he got back to his lodge, he threw a few logs o' wood an the fire to make himself comfortable, an he tuk whatever little matther he had for his supper ; and afther that he felt himself so tired that he wint to bed.   But you're to undherstan' that though he wint to bed, it was more for to rest himself like than

to sleep, for it was airly ; and so he jist went into bed, and there
he divarted himself lookin' at the fire, that was blazin' as merry
as a bonfire on the hearth.

"Well, as he was lyin' that-a-way, jist thinkin' o' nothin' at
all, what should come into the place but a fox. But I must tell
you, what I forgot to tell you before, that the ranger's house was
on the bordhers o' the wood, and he had no one to live wid him
but himself, barrin' the dogs that he had the care iv, that was his
only companions, and he had a hole cut an the door, with a
swingin' boord to it, that the dogs might go in or out accordin'
as it plazed thim ; and by dad, the fox came in, as I tould you,
through the hole in the door, as bowld as a ram, and walked over
to the fire, and sat down foreninst it.

"Now, it was mighty provokin' that all the dogs was out—
they wor rovin' about the wood, you see, lookin' for to catch
rabbits to ate, or some other mischief, and so it happened that
there wasn't as much as one individual dog in the place ; and
by gor, I'll go bail, the fox knew that right well before he put his
nose inside the ranger's lodge.

"Well, the ranger was in hopes some o' the dogs id come home
and ketch the chap, and he was loath to stir hand or fut himself,
afeard o' freghtenin' away the fox ; but, by gor, he could hardly
keep his timper, at all, at all, when he seen the fox take his pipe
aff o' the hob, where he left it afore he wint to bed, and puttin'
the bowl o' the pipe into the fire to kindle it (it's as thrue as I'm
here) he began to smoke foreninst the fire, as nath'ral as any
other man you ever seen.

"'Musha, bad luck to your impidence, you long-tailed blaguard,
says the ranger, ' and is it smokin' my pipe you are ? Oh, thin,
by this and by that, if I had my gun convaynient to me, it's fire
and smoke of another sort, and what you wouldn't bargain for,
I'd give you,' says he. But still he was loath to stir, hopin' the
dogs id come home ; and ' By gor, my fine fellow,' says he to the
fox, ' if one o' the dogs comes home, salpethre wouldn't save you,
and that's a sthrong pickle.'

"So with that he watched antil the fox wasn't mindin' him,
but was busy shakin' the cindhers out o' the pipe whin he was
done wid it, and so the ranger thought he was goin' to go immediately afther gitten' an air o' the fire and a shough o' the pipe ;
and so says he : ' Faiks, my lad, I won't let you go so aisy as all
that, as cunnin' as you think yourself;' and with that he made
a dart out o' bed and run over to the door, and got betune it
and the fox ; and ' Now,' says he, ' your bread's baked, my buck,
and maybe my lord won't. have a fine run out o' you, and the
dogs at your brish every yard, you morodin' thief, and the divil
mind you,' says he, ' for your impidence—for sure, if you hadn't

the impidence of a highwayman's horse, it's not into my very
house, undher my nose, yu'd daar for to come ;' and with that
he began to whistle for the dogs ; and the fox, that stood eyin'
him all the time while he was spakin', began to think it was time
to be joggin' whin he heard the whistle, and says the fox to
himself : 'Throth, indeed, you think yourself a mighty great
ranger now,' says he, 'and you think you're very cute, but upon
my tail, and that's a big oath, I'd be long sorry to let sich a
mallet-headed bog-throtter as yourself take a dirty advantage o'
me, and I'll engage,' says the fox, 'I'll make you lave the door
soon and suddint ;' and with that he turned to where the
ranger's brogues was lyin' hard beside the fire, and what would
you think, but the fox tuk up one o' the brogues, and wint over
to the fire and threw it into it.

"'I think that'll make you start,' says the fox.

"'Divil resave the start,' says the ranger—'that won't do, my
buck,' says he ; 'the brogue may burn to cindhers,' says he, 'but
out o' this I won't stir ;' and thin, puttin' his fingers into his
mouth, he gev a blast iv a whistle you'd hear a mile off, and
shouted for the dogs.

"'So that won't do,' says the fox. 'Well, I must thry another
offer,' says he ; and with that he tuk up the other brogue, and
threw *it* into the fire too.

"'There, now,' says he, 'you may keep the other company,'
says he ; 'and there's a pair o' ye now, as the divil said to his
knee-buckles.'

"'Oh, you thievin' varmint,' says the ranger, 'you won't lave
me a tack to my feet ; but no matther,' says he, 'your head's
worth more nor a pair o' brogues to me, any day ; and by the
Piper o' Blessin'town, you're money in my pocket this minit,' says
he ; and with that the fingers was in his mouth agin, and he was
goin' to whistle, whin, what would you think, but up sits the fox
an his hunkers, and puts his two forepaws into his mouth, makin'
game o' the ranger—(bad luck to the lie I tell you).

"Well, the ranger, and no wondher, although in a rage he was,
couldn't help laughin' at the thought o' the fox mockin' him, and
by dad, he tuk sitch a fit o' laughin', that he couldn't whistle, and
that was the cuteness o' the fox to gain time ; but whin his first
laugh was over, the ranger recovered himself, and gev another
whistle ; and so says the fox : 'By my sowl,' says he, 'I think it
wouldn't be good for my health to stay here much longer, and I
mustn't be thriflin' with that blackguard ranger any more,' says
he, 'and I must make him sinsible that it is time to let me go ;
and though he hasn't undherstan'in' to be sorry for his brogues, I'll
go bail I'll make him lave that,' says he, 'before he'd say *sparables*'
—and with that, what do you think the fox done ? By all that's

good—and the ranger himself tould me out iv his own mouth, and said he would never have b'lived it, only he seen it—the fox tuk a lighted piece iv a log out o' the blazin' fire, and run over wid it to the ranger's bed, and was goin' to throw it into the sthraw, and burn him out of house and home; so when the ranger seen that, he gev a shout out iv him:

"'Hilloo! hilloo! you murdherin' villian,' says he, 'you're worse nor Captain Rock; is it goin' to burn me out you are, you red rogue iv a Ribbonman?' and he made a dart betune him and the bed, to save the house from bein' burned; but, my jew'l, that was all the fox wanted—and as soon as the ranger quitted the hole in the door that he was standin' foreninst, the fox let go the blazin' faggit, and made one jump through the door and escaped.

"But before he wint, the ranger gev me his oath, that the fox turned round and gev him the most contemptible look he ever got in his life, and showed every tooth in his head with laughin'; and at last he put out his tongue at him, as much as to say: "You've missed me, like your mammy's blessin','' and off wid him! —like a flesh o' lightnin'.'"

BARNY O'REIRDON, THE NAVIGATOR
CHAPTER I
OUTWARD-BOUND

A VERY striking characteristic of an Irishman is his unwillingness to be outdone. Some have asserted that this arises from vanity, but I have ever been unwilling to attribute an unamiable motive to my countrymen where a better may be found, and one equally tending to produce a similar result, and I consider a deep-seated spirit of emulation to originate this peculiarity. Phrenologists might resolve it by supposing the organ of the love of approbation to predominate in our Irish craniums, and it may be so; but as I am not in the least a metaphysician, and very little of a phrenologist, I leave those who choose to settle the point in question, quite content with the knowledge of the fact with which I started, viz., the unwillingness of an Irishman to be outdone. This spirit, it is likely, may sometimes lead men into ridiculous positions; but it is equally probable, that the desire of surpassing one another has given birth to many of the noblest actions, and some of the most valuable inventions; let us, therefore, not fall out with it.

Now, having vindicated the *motive* of my countrymen, I will prove the total absence of national prejudice in so doing, by giving an illustration of the ridiculous consequences attendant upon this Hibernian peculiarity.

Barny O'Reirdon was a fisherman of Kinsale, and a heartier fellow never hauled a net or cast a line into deep water; indeed

Barny, independently of being a merry boy among his companions, a lover of good fun and good whisky, was looked up to, rather, by his brother fishermen, as an intelligent fellow, and few boats brought more fish to market than Barny O'Reirdon's ; his opinion on certain points in the craft was considered law, and in short, in his own little community, Barny was what is commonly called a leading man. Now, your leading man is always jealous in an inverse ratio to the sphere of his influence, and the leader of a nation is less incensed at a rival's triumph than the great man of a village. If we pursue this descending scale, what a desperately jealous person the oracle of oyster-dredgers and cockle-women must be ! Such was Barny O'Reirdon.

Seated one night at a public-house, the common resort of Barny and other marine curiosities, our hero got entangled in debate with what he called a strange sail—that is to say, a man he had never met before, and whom he was inclined to treat rather magisterially upon nautical subjects ; at the same time, that the stranger was equally inclined to assume the high hand over him, till at last the new-comer made a regular outbreak by exclaiming :

"Ah, tare-an-ouns, lave off your balderdash, Mr. O'Reirdon. By the powdhers o' war it's enough, so it is, to make a dog bate his father, to hear you goin' an as if you war Curlumberus or Sir Crustyphiz Wran, when ivery one knows the divil a farther you iver wor nor ketchin' crabs or drudgin' oysters."

"Who tould you that, my Watherford Wondher ? " rejoined Barny. "What the dickins do you know about saefarin' farther nor fishin' for sprats in a bowl wid your grandmother ? "

"Oh, baithershin," says the stranger.

"And who made you so bowld with my name ? " demanded O'Reirdon.

"No matther for that," said the stranger ; "but if you'd like for to know, sure, it's your cousin Molly Mullins knows me well, and maybe I don't know you and yours as well as the mother that bore you—aye, in throth ; and sure, I know the very thoughts o' you as well as if I was inside o' you, Barny O'Reirdon."

"By my sowl, thin, you know betther thoughts than your own, Mr. Whippersnapper, if that's the name you go by."

"No, it's not the name I go by. I've as good a name as your own, Mr. O'Reirdon, for want of a betther, and that's O'Sullivan."

"Throth, there's more than there's good o' them," said Barny.

"Good or bad, I'm a cousin o' your own twice removed by the mother's side."

"And is it the Widda O'Sullivan's boy you'd be that left this come Candlemas four years ? "

"The same."

"Throth, thin, you might know betther manners to your eldhers, though I'm glad to see you, anyhow, agin ; but a little thravellin' puts us beyant ourselves sometimes," said Barny, rather contemptuously.

"Throth, I niver bragged out o' myself yit, and it's what I say, that a man that's only a-fishin' aff the land all his life has no business to compare in the regard o' thracthericks wid a man that has sailed to Fingal."

This silenced any further argument on Barny's part.   Where Fingal lay was all Greek to him ; but unwilling to admit his ignorance, he covered his retreat with the usual address of his countrymen, and turned the bitterness of debate into the cordial flow of congratulation at seeing his cousin again.

The liquor was freely circulated, and the conversation began to take a different turn, in order to lead from that which had nearly ended in a quarrel between O'Reirdon and his relation.

The state of the crops, county cess, road jobs, etc., became topics, and various strictures as to the utility of the latter were indulged in, while the merits of the neighbouring farmers were canvassed.

"Why, thin," said one, "that field o' whate o' Michael Coghlan is the finest field o' whate mortial eyes was ever set upon—divil the likes iv it myself ever seen far or near."

"Throth, thin, sure enough," said another, "it promises to be a fine crap, anyhow ; and myself can't help thinkin' it quare that Mickee Coghlan, that's a plain-spoken, quite [quiet] man, and simple like, should have finer craps than Pether Kelly o' the big farm beyant, that knows all about the great saycrets o' the airth, and is knowledgable to a degree, and has all the hard words that iver was coined at his fingers'-ends."

"Faith, he has a power o' *blasthogue* about him, sure enough," said the former speaker, "if that could do him any good, but he isn't fit to hould a candle to Michael Coghlan in the regard o' farmin'."

"Why, blur-an-angers," rejoined the upholder of science, "sure, he met the Scotch steward that the lord beyant has, one day, that I hear is a wondherful edicated man, and was brought over here to show us all a patthern—well, Pether Kelly met him one day, and by gor, he discoorsed him to that degree that the Scotch chap hadn't a word left in his jaw."

"Well, and what was he the betther o' having more prate than a Scotchman ? " asked the other.

"Why," answered Kelly's friend, "I think it stands to raison that the man that done out the Scotch steward ought to know somethin' more about farmin' than Mickee Coghlan."

"Augh ! don't talk to me about knowing," said the other,

rather contemptuously. " Sure, I gev in to you that he has a power o' prate, and the gift o' the gab, and all to that. I own to you that he has *the-o-ry* and the *che-mis-thery*, but he hasn't the *craps*. Now, the man that has the craps is the man for my money."

" You're right, my boy," said O'Reirdon, with an approving thump of his brawny fist on the table. " It's a little talk goes far —*doin'* is the thing."

" Ah, yiz may run down larnin' if yiz like," said the undismayed stickler for theory versus practice, " but larnin' is a fine thing, and sure, where would the world be at all only for it ; sure, where would the staymers [steamboats] be, only for larnin' ? "

" Well," said O'Reirdon, " and the divil may care if we never seen them ; I'd rather dipind an wind and canvas any day than the likes o' them. What are they good for, but to turn good sailors into kitchen-maids, all as one, bilin' a big pot o' wather and oilin' their fire-irons, and throwin' coals an the fire ? Augh ! thim staymers is a disgrace to the sae ; they're for all the world like ould fogies, smokin' from mornin' till night, and doin' no good."

" Do you call it doin' no good to go fasther nor ships iver wint before ? "

" Pooh ! sure, Solomon, queen o' Sheba, said there was time enough for all things."

" Thrue for you," said O'Sullivan. " *Fair and aisy goes far in a day*, is a good ould sayin'."

" Well, maybe you'll own to the improvemint they're makin' in the harbour o' Howth, beyant in Dublin, is some good."

" We'll see whether it'll be an improvemint first," said the obdurate O'Reirdon.

" Why, man alive, sure you'll own it's the greatest o' good it is, takin' up the big rocks out o' the bottom o' the harbour."

" Well, and where's the wondher of that ? Sure, we done the same here."

" Oh, yis ; but it was whin the tide was out and the rocks was bare ; but up in Howth, they cut away the big rocks from undher the sae intirely."

" Oh, be aisy ; why, how could they do that ? "

" Aye, there's the matther, that's what larnin' can do ; and wondherful it is intirely ! and the way it is, is this, as I hear it, for I never seen it, but hard it described by the lord to some gintlemen and ladies one day in his garden where I was helpin' the gardener to land some salary (celery). You see the ingineer goes down undher the wather intirely, and can stay there as long as he plazes."

" Whoo ! and what o' that ? Sure, I heerd the long sailor say that come from the Aysthern Injees, that the ingineers there can a'most live undher wather; and goes down lookin' for dimonds, and has a sledge-hammer in their hand, brakin' the dimonds when they're too big to take them up whole, all as one as men brakin' stones an the road."

"Well, I don't want to go beyant that; but the way the lord's ingineer goes down is, he has a little bell wid him, and while he has that little bell to ring, hurt nor harm can't come to him."

"Arrah, be aisy."

"Divil a lie in it."

"Maybe it's a blessed bell," said O'Reirdon, crossing himself.

"No, it is not a blessed bell."

"Why, thin, now do you think me sitch a born nath'ral as to give in to that; as if the ringin' iv a bell, barrin' it was a blessed bell, could do the like. I tell you it's unpossible."

"Ah, nothin's unpossible to God."

"Sure, I wasn't denyin' that; but I say the bell is unpossible."

"Why," said O'Sullivan, "you see he's not altogether complate in the demonstheration o' the mashine; it is not by the ringin' o' the bell it is done, but—"

"But what?" broke in O'Reirdon impatiently. "Do you mane for to say there is a bell in it, at all, at all?"

"Yes, I do," said O'Sullivan.

"I tould you so," said the promulgator of the story.

"Aye," said O'Sullivan; "but it is not by the ringin' iv the bell it is done."

"Well, how is it done, thin?" said the other, with a half offended, half supercilious air.

"It is done," said O'Sullivan, as he returned the look with interest, "it is done intirely be jommethry."

"Oh! I undherstan' it now," said O'Reirdon, with an inimitable affectation of comprehension in the "Oh!"—"but to talk of the ringin' iv a bell doin' the like is beyant the beyants intirely, barrin', as I said before, it was a blessed bell, glory be to God!"

"And so you tell me, sir, it is jommethry," said the twice discomfited man of science.

"Yes, sir," said O'Sullivan, with an air of triumph, which rose in proportion as he saw he carried the listeners along with him—"jommethry."

"Well, have it your own way. There's them that won't hear raison sometimes, nor have belief in larnin'; and you may say it's jommethry if you plaze; but I heerd them that knows betther than iver you knew say—"

"Whisht, whisht! and bad cess to you both," said O'Reirdon, "what the dickens are yiz goin' to fight about now, and sitch good liquor before yiz? Hillo! there, Mrs. Quigley, bring uz another quart, i' you plaze; aye, that's the chat, another quart. Augh! yiz may talk till you're black in the face about your invintions, and your staymers, and bell-ringin', and gash, and railroads; but here's long life and success to the man that invinted the impairil [imperial] quart; that was the rale beautiful invintion"—and he took a long pull at the replenished vessel, which strongly indicated that the increase of its dimensions was a very agreeable *measure* to such as Barny.

After the introduction of this and *other* quarts, it would not be an easy matter to pursue the conversation that followed. Let us, therefore, transfer our story to the succeeding morning, when Barny O'Reirdon strolled forth from his cottage, rather later than usual, with his eyes bearing *eye*-witness to the carouse of the preceding night. He had not a headache, however. Whether it was that Barny was too experienced a campaigner under the banners of Bacchus, or that Mrs. Quigley's boast was a just one, namely: "That of all the drink in her house, there wasn't a headache in a hogshead of it," is hard to determine, but I rather incline to the strength of Barny's head.

The above-quoted declaration of Mrs. Quigley is the favourite inducement held out by every boon companion in Ireland at the head of his own table. "Don't be afraid of it, my boys! It's the right sort. There's not a headache in a hogshead of it."

This sentiment has been very seductively rendered by Moore, with the most perfect unconsciousness on his part of the likeness he was instituting. Who does not remember:

> "Friend of my soul, this goblet sip,
>   'Twill chase the pensive tear;
> 'Tis not so sweet as woman's lip,
>   But oh, 'tis more sincere:
> Like her delusive beam,
>   'Twill steal away the mind;
> But like affection's dream,
>   It leaves no sting behind."

Is not this very elegantly saying: "There's not a headache in a hogshead of it?" But I am forgetting my story all this time.

Barny sauntered about in the sun, at which he often looked up, under the shelter of compressed bushy brows and long-lashed eyelids, and a shadowing hand across his forehead, to see "what time o' day" it was; and from the frequency of this action, it was evident the day was hanging heavily with Barny. He retired at last to a sunny nook in a neighbouring field, and stretching himself at full length, basked in the sun, and began "to chew the cud of sweet and bitter thought." He first reflected on his own undoubted weight in his little community, but still he could not get over the annoyance of the preceding night, arising from his being silenced by O'Sullivan—"a chap," as he said himself, "that lift the place four years agon a brat iv a boy, and to think iv his comin' back and outdoin' his elders, that saw him runnin' about the place, a gassoon, that one could tache a few months before;" 'twas too bad.   Barny saw his reputation was in a ticklish position, and began to consider how his disgrace could be retrieved.   The very name of Fingal was hateful to him; it was a plague spot on his peace that festered there incurably. He first thought of leaving Kinsale altogether; but flight implied so much of defeat that he did not long indulge in that notion. No; he *would* stay, "in spite of all the O'Sullivans, kith and kin, breed, seed, and generation."   But at the same time, he knew he should never hear the end of that hateful place, Fingal; and if Barny had had the power, he would have enacted a penal statute, making it death to name the accursed spot, wherever it was; but not being gifted with such legislative authority, he felt Kinsale was no place for him, if he would not submit to be flouted every hour out of the four-and-twenty by man, woman, and child that wished to annoy him.   What was to be done? He was in the perplexing situation, to use his own words, "of the cat in the thripe-shop," he didn't know which way to choose. At last, after turning himself over in the sun several times, a new idea struck him.   Couldn't he go to Fingal himself, and then he'd be equal to that upstart, O'Sullivan?   No sooner was the thought engendered, than Barny sprang to his feet a new man; his eye brightened, his step became once more elastic, he walked erect, and felt himself to be all over Barny O'Reirdon once more. "Richard was himself again."

But where was Fingal?—there was the rub.   That was a profound mystery to Barny, which, until discovered, must hold him in the vile bondage of inferiority.   The plain-dealing reader will say: "Couldn't he ask?"   No, no; that would never do for Barny—that would be an open admission of ignorance his soul was above; and consequently, Barny set his brains to work to devise measures of coming at the hidden knowledge by some circuitous route that would not betray the end he was working for.   To this purpose, fifty stratagems were raised and demolished in half as many minutes in the fertile brain of Barny, as he strided along the shore; and as he was working hard at the fifty-first, it was knocked all to pieces by his jostling against someone whom he never perceived he was approaching, so immersed was he in his speculations, and on looking up, who should it prove to be but his friend, "the long sailor from the Aysthern Injees." This was quite a godsend to Barny, and much beyond what he could have hoped for.   Of all the men under the sun, the long sailor was the man in a million for Barny's net at that minute, and accordingly, he made a haul of him, and thought it the greatest catch he ever made in his life.

Barny and the long sailor were in close companionship for the remainder of the day, which was closed, as the preceding one, in a carouse; but on this occasion, there was only a duet performance in honour of the jolly god, and the treat was at Barny's expense. What the nature of their conversation during the period was, I will not dilate on, but keep it as profound a secret as Barny himself did, and content myself with saying that Barny looked a much happier man the next day. Instead of wearing his hat slouched, and casting his eyes on the ground, he walked about with his usual unconcern, and gave his nod and passing word of "*civilitude*" to every friend he met. He rolled his quid of tobacco about in his jaw with an air of superior enjoyment, and if disturbed in his narcotic amusement by a question, he took his own good time to eject "the leperous distilment" before he answered the querist, with a happy composure, that bespoke a man quite at ease with himself. It was in this agreeable spirit that Barny bent his course to the house of Peter Kelly, the owner of the "big farm beyant," before alluded to, in order to put in practice a plan he had formed for the fulfilment of his determination of rivalling O'Sullivan.

He thought it probable that Peter Kelly, being one of the "snuggest" men in the neighbourhood, would be a likely person to join him in a "spec," as he called it (a favourite abbreviation of his for the word of speculation); and accordingly, when he reached the "big farm-house," he accosted its owner with the usual "God save you." "God save you kindly, Barny," returned Peter Kelly, "an' what is it brings you here, Barny," asked Peter, "this fine day, instead o' bein' out in the boat?" "Oh, I'll be in the boat soon enough, and it's far enough too I'll be out in her; an' indeed, it's partly that same is bringin' me here to yourself."

"Why, do you want me to go along wid you, Barny?"

"Throth an' I don't, Mr. Kelly. You're a knowledgable man an land, but I'm afeard it's a bad bargain you'd be at sae."

"And what wor you talking about me and your boat for?"

"Why, you see, sir, it was in the regard of a little bit o' business, an' if you'd come wid me and take a turn in the pratie-field, I'll be behouldin' to you, and maybe you'll hear somethin' that won't be displazin' to you."

"An' welkim, Barny," said Peter Kelly.

When Barny and Peter were in the "pratie-field," Barny opened the trenches (I don't mean the potato-trenches), but in military parlance, he opened the trenches and laid siege to Peter Kelly, setting forth the extensive profits that had been realised by various "specs" that had been made by his neighbours in exporting potatoes. "And sure," said Barny, "why shouldn't *you* do the same, and they here ready to your hand? as much as to say, *why don't you profit by me, Peter Kelly?* And the boat is below there in the harbour, and I'll say this much, the divil a betther boat is betune this and herself."

"Indeed, I b'live so, Barny," said Peter, "for considhering where we stand at this present, there's no boat at all, at all betune us," and Peter laughed with infinite pleasure at his own hit.

"Oh, well, you know what I mane, anyhow, an' as I said before, the boat is a darlint boat, and as for him that commands her—I b'live I need say nothin' about that," and Barny gave a toss of his head and a sweep of his open hand, more than doubling the laudatory nature of his comment on himself.

But as the Irish saying is, "to make a long story short," Barny prevailed on Peter Kelly to make an export; but in the nature of the venture they did not agree. Barny had proposed potatoes; Peter said there were enough of them already where he was going; and Barry rejoined that "praties were so good in themselves there never could be too much o' thim anywhere." But Peter being a knowledgable man, and up to all the "saycrets o' the airth, and understanding the the-o-ry and the che-mis-thery," overruled Barny's proposition, and determined upon a cargo of *scalpeens* (which name they give to pickled mackerel), as a preferable merchandise, quite forgetting that Dublin Bay herrings were a much better and as cheap a commodity, at the command of the Fingalians. But in many similar mistakes the ingenious Mr. Kelly has been paralleled by other speculators. But that is neither here nor there, and it was all one to Barny whether his boat was freighted with potatoes or *scalpeens*, so long as he had the honour and glory of becoming a navigator, and being as good as O'Sullivan.

Accordingly, the boat was laden and all got in readiness for putting to sea, and nothing was now wanting but Barny's orders to haul up the gaff and shake out the gib of his hooker.

But this order Barny refrained to give, and for the first time in his life exhibited a disinclination to leave the shore. One of his fellow-boatmen at last said to him: "Why, thin, Barny O'Reirdon, what the divil is come over you, at all, at all? What's the maynin' of your loitherin' about here, and the boat ready, and a lovely fine breeze aff o' the land."

"Oh, never you mind: I bli've I know my own business, anyhow; an' it's hard, so it is, if a man can't ordher his own boat to sail when he plazes."

"Oh, I was only thinkin' it quare—and a pity more betoken, as I said before, to lose the beautiful breeze, and—"

"Well, just keep your thoughts to yourself, i' you plaze, and stay in the boat as I bid you, and don't be out of her on your apperl, by no manner o' manes, for one minit, for you see, I don't know when it may be plazin' to me to go aboord an' set sail."

"Well, all I can say is, I never seen you afeard to go to sae before."

"Who says I'm afeard?" said O'Reirdon. "You'd betther not say that agin, or in throth, I'll give you a leatherin' that won't be for the good o' your health—throth, for three sthraws this minit I'd lave you that your own mother wouldn't know you with the lickin' I'd give you; but I scorn your dirty insinuation. No man ever seen Barny O'Reirdon afeard yet, anyhow. Hould your prate, I tell you, and look up to your betthers. What do you know iv navigation? Maybe you think it's as easy for to sail an a voyage as to go a start fishin'," and Barny turned on his heel and left the shore.

The next day passed without the hooker sailing, and Barny gave a most sufficient reason for the delay, by declaring that he had a warnin' given him in a dhrame (glory be to God!), and that it was given him to understand (under heaven) that it wouldn't be loocky that day.

Well, the next day was Friday, and Barny, of course, would not sail any more than any other sailor who could help it, on this unpropitious day. On Saturday, however, he came, running in a great hurry down to the shore, and jumping aboard, he gave orders to make all sail, and taking the helm of the hooker, he turned her head to the sea, and soon the boat was cleaving the blue waters with a velocity seldom witnessed in so small a craft, and scarcely conceivable to those who have not seen the speed of a Kinsale hooker.

"Why, thin, you tuk the notion mighty suddint, Barny," said the fisherman next in authority to O'Reirdon, as soon as the bustle of getting the boat under way had subsided.

"Well, I hope it's plazin' to you at last," said Barny. "Throth, one 'ud think you were never at sae before, you wor in such a hurry to be off; as new-fangled a'most as a child with a play-toy."

"Well," said the other of Barny's companions—for there were but two with him in the boat—"I was thinkin' myself, as well as Jimmy, that we lost two fine days for nothin', and we'd be there a'most, maybe now, if we sail'd three days agon."

"Don't b'live it," said Barny emphatically. "Now, don't you know yourself that there is some days that the fish won't come near the lines at all, and that we might as well be castin' our nets an the dhry land as in the sae, for all we'll catch if we start an an unloocky day; and sure, I tould you I was waitin'

only till I had it given to me to undherstan' that it was loocky
to sail, and I go bail, we'll be there sooner than if we started
three days agon, for if you don't start with good loock before you,
faix, maybe it's never at all to the end o' your thrip you'll come."

"Well, there's no use in talkin' about it now, anyhow; but
when do you expec' to be there?"

"Why, you see we must wait antil I can tell how the wind is
like to hould on, before I can make up my mind to that."

"But you're sure now, Barny, that you're up to the coorse you
have to run?"

"See now, lay me alone and don't be crass-questionin' me—
tare-an-ouns, do you think me sitch a bladdherang as for to go
to shuperinscribe a thing I wasn't aiquil to?"

"No; I was only goin' to ax you what coorse you wor goin'
to steer?"

"You'll find out soon enough when we get there—and so I
bid you agin lay me alone—just keep your toe in your pump.
Sure, I'm here at the helm, and a woight an my mind, and it's
fitther for you, Jim, to mind your own business and lay me to
mind mine. Away wid you there and be handy; haul taught that
foresheet there, we must run close an the wind. Be handy, boys;
make everything dhraw."

These orders were obeyed, and the hooker soon passed to
windward of a ship that left the harbour before her, but could
not hold on a wind with the same tenacity as the hooker, whose
qualities in this particular render it peculiarly suitable for the
purposes to which it is applied, namely, pilot and fishing-boats.

We have said a ship left the harbour before the hooker had
set sail, and it is now fitting to inform the reader that Barny
had contrived, in the course of his last meeting with the "long
sailor," to ascertain that this ship, then lying in the harbour,
was going to the very place Barny wanted to reach. Barny's
plan of action was decided upon in a moment; he had now
nothing to do but to watch the sailing of the ship and follow
in her course. Here was, at once, a new mode of navigation
discovered.

The stars, twinkling in mysterious brightness through the
silent gloom of night, were the first encouraging, because *visible*,
guides to the adventurous mariners of antiquity. Since then,
the sailor, encouraged by a bolder science, relies on the *unseen*
agency of Nature, depending on the fidelity of an atom of iron
to the mystic law that claims its homage in the North. This
is one refinement of science upon another. But the beautiful
simplicity of Barny O'Reirdon's philosophy cannot be too much
admired. To follow the ship that is going to the same place.
Is not this navigation made easy?

But Barny, like many a great man before him, seemed not to be aware of how much credit he was entitled to for his invention, for he did not divulge to his companions the originality of his proceeding; he wished them to believe he was only proceeding in the commonplace manner, and had no ambition to be distinguished as the happy projector of so simple a practice.

For this purpose he went to windward of the ship and then fell off again, allowing her to pass him, as he did not wish even those on board the ship to suppose he was following in their wake; for Barny, like all people that are quite full of one scheme, and fancy everybody is watching them, dreaded lest anyone should fathom his motives. All that day Barny held on the same course as his leader, keeping at a respectful distance, however, "for fear 'twould look like dodging her," as he said to himself; but as night closed in, so closed in Barny with the ship, and kept a sharp look-out that she should not give him the slip in the dark. The next morning dawned, and found the hooker and ship companions still; and thus matters proceeded for four days, during the entire of which time they had not seen land since their first losing sight of it, although the weather was clear.

"By my sowl," thought Barny, "the Channel must be mighty wide in these parts, and for the last day or so we've been goin' purty free with a flowin' sheet, and I wondher we aren't closin' in wid the shore by this time; or maybe it's farther off than I thought it was." His companions, too, began to question Barny on the subject, but to their queries he presented an impenetrable front of composure, and said: "It was always the best plan to keep a good bowld offin'." In two days more, however, the weather began to be sensibly warmer, and Barny and his companions remarked that it was "goin' to be the finest sayson—God bless it!—that ever kem out o' the skies for many a long year, and maybe it's the whate wouldn't be beautiful, and a great plenty of it." It was at the end of a week that the ship which Barny had hitherto kept ahead of him showed symptoms of bearing down upon him, as he thought, and sure enough, she did; and Barny began to conjecture what the deuce the ship could want with him, and commenced inventing answers to the questions he thought it possible might be put to him in case the ship spoke to him. He was soon put out of suspense by being hailed and ordered to run under her lee, and the captain, looking over the quarter, asked Barny where he was going.

"Faith, then, I'm goin' an my business," said Barny.

"But where?" said the captain.

"Why, sure, an it's no matther where a poor man like me id be goin'," said Barny.

"Only I'm curious to know what the deuce you've been following my ship for, for the last week?"

"Follyin' your ship! Why, thin, blur an agers, do you think it's follyin' yiz I am?"

"It's very like it," said the captain.

"Why, did two people niver thravel the same road before?"

"I don't say they didn't; but there's a great different between a ship of seven hundred tons and a hooker."

"Oh, as for that matther," said Barny, "the same high road sarves a coach and four and a low-back car; the thravellin' tinker an' a lord a' horseback."

"That's very true," said the captain; "but the cases are not the same, Paddy, and I can't conceive what the devil brings *you* here."

"And who ax'd you to consayve anything about it?" asked Barny, somewhat sturdily.

"D—n me, if I can imagine what you're about, my fine fellow," said the captain; "and my own notion is, that you don't know where the d—l you're going yourself."

"Oh, *baithershin!*" said Barny, with a laugh of derision.

"Why, then, do you object to tell?" said the captain.

"Arrah, sure, captain, an' don't you know that sometimes vessels is bound to sail undher *saycret ordhers?*" said Barny, endeavouring to foil the question by badinage.

There was a universal laugh from the deck of the ship at the idea of a fishing-boat sailing under secret orders; for by this time, the whole broadside of the vessel was crowded with grinning mouths and wondering eyes at Barny and his boat.

"Oh, it's a thrifle makes fools laugh," said Barny.

"Take care, my fine fellow, that you don't be laughing at the wrong side of your mouth before long, for I've a notion that you're cursedly in the wrong box, as cunning a fellow as you think yourself. D—n your stupid head, can't you tell what brings you here?"

"Why, thin, by gor, one id think the whole sae belonged to you, you're so mighty bowld in axin' questions an it. Why, tare-an-ouns, sure I've as much right to be here as you, though I haven't as big a ship nor so fine a coat—but maybe I can take as good sailin' out o' the one, and has as bowld a heart under th' other."

"Very well," said the captain. "I see there's no use in talking to you, so go to the d—l your own way." And away bore the ship, leaving Barny in indignation and his companions in wonder.

"An' why wouldn't you tell him?" said they to Barny.

"Why, don't you see," said Barny, whose object was now to blind them, "don't you see, how do I know but maybe he might be goin' to the same place himself, and maybe he has a cargo of *scalpeens* as well as uz, and wants to get before us there."

"Thrue for you, Barny," said they. "By dad, you're right." And their inquiries being satisfied, the day passed as former ones had done, in pursuing the course of the ship.

In four days more, however, the provisions in the hooker began to fail, and they were obliged to have recourse to the *scalpeens* for sustenance, and Barney then got seriously uneasy at the length of the voyage, and the likely greater length, for anything he could see to the contrary ; and urged at last by his own alarms and those of his companions, he was enabled, as the wind was light, to gain on the ship, and when he found himself alongside he demanded a parley with the captain.

The captain, on hearing that the " hardy hooker," as she got christened, was under his lee, came on deck, and as soon as he appeared Barny cried out :

"Why, thin, blur an agers, captain dear, do you expec' to be there soon ? "

"Where ? " said the captain.

"Oh, you know yourself," said Barny.

"It's well for me I do," said the captain.

"Thrue for you, indeed, your honour," said Barny, in his most insinuating tone ; "but whin will you be at the ind o' your voyage, captain jewel ? "

"I daresay in about three months," said the captain.

"Oh, Holy Mother ! " ejaculated Barny ; "three months ! Arrah, it's jokin' you are, captain dear, and only want to freken me."

"How should I frighten you ? " asked the captain.

"Why, thin, your honour, to tell God's thruth, I heerd you were goin' *there*, an' as I wanted to go there too, I thought I couldn't do better nor to folly a knowledgable gintleman like yourself, and save myself the throuble iv findin' it out."

"And where do you think I *am* going ? " said the captain.

"Why, thin," said Barny, "isn't it to Fingal ? "

"No," said the captain ; " 'tis to *Bengal*."

"Oh, Gog's blakey ! " said Barny, "what'll I do now, at all, at all ? "

CHAPTER II

HOMEWARD-BOUND

THE captain ordered Barny on deck, as he wished to have some conversation with him on what he, very naturally, considered a most extraordinary adventure. Heaven help the captain ! he knew little of Irishmen, or he would not have been so astonished.

Barny made his appearance. Puzzling question, and more puzzling answer, followed in quick succession between the commander and Barny, who, in the midst of his dilemma, stamped about, thumped his head, squeezed his caubeen into all manner of shapes, and vented his despair anathematically:

"Oh, my heavy hathred to you, you tarnal thief iv a long sailor, it's a purty scrape yiv led me into. By gor, I thought it was *Fin*gal he said, and now I hear it is *Bin*gal. Oh, the devil sweep you for navigation, why did I meddle or make wid you, at all, at all! And my curse light on you, Terry O'Sullivan, why did I iver come acrass you, you onloocky vagabone, to put sitch thoughts in my head? An' so it's *Bin*gal, and not *Fin*gal, you're goin' to, captain."

"Yes, indeed, Paddy."

"An' might I be so bowld to ax, captain, is Bingal much farther nor Fingal?"

"A trifle or so, Paddy."

"Och, thin, millia murther, weirasthru, how 'ill I iver get there, at all, at all?" roared out poor Barny.

"By turning about, and getting back the road you've come, as fast as you can."

"Is it back? Oh, Queen iv Heaven! an' how will I iver get back?" said the bewildered Barny.

"Then you don't know your course, it appears?"

"Oh, faix, I knew it iligant, as long as your honour was before me."

"But you don't know your course back?"

"Why, indeed, not to say rightly all out, your honour."

"Can't you steer?" said the captain.

"The divil a betther hand at the tiller in all Kinsale," said Barny, with his usual brag.

"Well, so far so good," said the captain. "And you know the points of the compass—you have a compass, I suppose?"

"A compass! by my sowl, an' it's not let alone a compass, but a *pair* a compasses I have, that my brother, the carpinthir, left me for a keepsake whin he wint abroad; but indeed, as for the points o' thim, I can't say much, for the childher spylt thim intirely rootin' holes in the flure."

"What the plague are you talking about?" asked the captain.

"Wasn't your honour discoorsin' me about the points o' the compasses?"

"Confound your thick head!" said the captain. "Why, what an ignoramus you must be, not to know what a compass is, and you at sea all your life? Do you even know the cardinal points?"

"The cardinals! faix, an' it's a great respect I have for them, your honour. Sure, arn't they belongin' to the Pope?"

"Confound you, you blockhead!" roared the captain, in a rage; "'twould take the patience of the Pope and the cardinals, and the cardinal virtues into the bargain, to keep one's temper with you. Do you know the four points of the wind?"

"By my sowl, I do, and more."

"Well, never mind more, but let us stick to four. You're sure you know the four points of the wind?"

"By dad, it would be a quare thing if a saefarin' man didn't know somethin' about the wind, anyhow. Why, captain dear, you must take me for a nath'ral intirely to suspect me o' the like o' not knowin' all about the wind. By gor, I know as much o' the wind a'most as a pig."

"Indeed, I believe so," laughed out the captain.

"Oh, you may laugh if you plaze, and I see by the same that you don't know about the pig, with all your edication, captain."

"Well, what about the pig?"

"Why, sir, did you never hear a pig can see the wind?"

"I can't say that I did."

"Oh, thin, he does; and for that raison who has a right to know more about it?"

"You don't for one, I daresay, Paddy; and maybe you have a pig aboard to give you information."

"Sorra taste, your honour, not so much as a rasher o' bacon; but it's maybe your honour never seen a pig tossin' up his snout, consaited like, and running like mad afore a storm."

"Well, what if I have?"

"Well, sir, that is when they see the wind a-comin'."

"Maybe so, Paddy, but all this knowledge in piggery won't find you your way home; and if you take my advice, you will give up all thoughts of endeavouring to find your way back, and come on board. You and your messmates, I daresay, will be useful hands, with some teaching; but at all events, I cannot leave you here on the open sea, with every chance of being lost."

"Why, thin, indeed, and I'm beholden to your honour; and it's the hoighth o' kindness, so it is, your offer; and it's nothin' else but a gintleman you are, every inch o' you; but I hope it's not so bad wid us yet, as to do the likes o' that."

"I think it's bad enough," said the captain, "when you are without a compass, and knowing nothing of your course, and nearly a hundred and eighty leagues from land."

"An' how many miles would that be, captain?"

"Three times as many."

"I never larned the rule o' three, captain, and maybe your honour id tell me yourself."

"That is rather more than five hundred miles."

"Five hundred miles!" shouted Barny. "Oh, the Lord look down on us! how 'ill we iver get back!"

"That's what I say," said the captain; "and therefore I recommend you come aboard with me."

"And where 'ud the hooker be all the time?" said Barny.

"Let her go adrift," was the answer.

"Is it the darlint boat? Oh, by dad, I'll never hear o' that at all."

"Well, then, stay in her and be lost. Decide upon the matter at once, either come on board or cast off;" and the captain was turning away as he spoke, when Barny called after him:

"Arrah, thin, your honour, don't go jist for one minit antil I ax you one word more. If I wint wid you, whin would I be home agin?"

"In about seven months."

"Oh, thin, that puts the wig an it at wanst. I darn't go at all."

"Why, seven months are not long in passing."

"Thrue for you, in throth," said Barny, with a shrug of his shoulders. "Faix, it's myself knows, to my sorrow, the half-year comes round mighty suddint, and the lord's agint comes for the thrifle o' rint; and faix, I know by Molly that nine months is not long in goin' over either," added Barny, with a grin.

"Then what's your objection as to the time?" asked the captain.

"Arrah, sure, sir, what would the woman that owns me do while I waz away? and maybe it's break her heart the craythur would, thinkin' I was lost intirely; and who'd be at home to take care o' the childher, and airn thim the bit and the sup, whin I'd be away? and who knows, but it's all dead they'd be afore I got back? Och hone! sure the heart id fairly break in my body if hurt or harm kem to thim through me. So say no more, captain dear, only give me a thrifle o' directions how I'm to make an offer at gettin' home, and it's myself that will pray for you night, noon, and mornin' for that same."

"Well, Paddy," said the captain, "as you are determined to go back, in spite of all I can say, you must attend to me well while I give you as simple instructions as I can. You say you know the four points of the wind—north, south, east, and west."

"Yis, sir."

"How do you know them? for I must see that you are not likely to make a mistake. How do you know the points?"

"Why, you see, sir, the sun, God bless it! rises in the aist, and sets in the west, which stands to raison; and when you stand bechuxt the aist and the west, the north is forninst you."

"And when the north is forninst you, as you say, is the east on your right or your left hand?"

"On the right hand, your honour."

"Well, I see you know that much, however. Now," said the captain, "the moment you leave the ship, you must steer a north-east course, and you will make some land near home in about a week, if the wind holds as it is now, and it is likely to do so; but, mind me, if you turn out of your course in the smallest degree, you are a lost man."

"Many thanks to your honour!"

"And how are you off for provisions?"

"Why, thin, indeed, in the regard o' that same we are in the hoighth o' distress, for exceptin' the scalpeens, sorra taste passed our lips for these four days."

"Oh, you poor devils!" said the commander, in a tone of sincere commiseration. "I'll order you some provisions on board before you start."

"Long life to your honour! and *I'd like to drink the health* of so noble a gintleman."

"I understand you, Paddy, you shall have grog too."

"Musha, the heavens shower blessin's an you, I pray the Virgin Mary and the twelve apostles—Matthew, Mark, Luke, and John —not forgettin' Saint Pathrick."

"Thank you, Paddy; but keep all your prayers for yourself, for you need them all to help you home again."

"Oh, never fear, whin the thing is to be done, I'll do it, by dad, with a heart and a half. And sure, your honour, God is good, an' will mind dissolute craythurs like uz, on the wild oceant as well as ashore."

While some of the ship's crew were putting the captain's benevolent intentions to Barny and his companions into practice, by transferring some provisions to the hooker, the commander entertained himself by further conversation with Barny, who was the greatest original he had ever met. In the course of their colloquy, Barny drove many hard queries at the captain, respecting the wonders of the nautical profession, and at last put the question to him plump.

"Oh, thin, captain dear, and how is it, at all, at all, that you make your way over the wide saes intirely to them furrin parts?"

"You would not understand, Paddy, if I attempted to explain to you."

"Sure enough, indeed, your honour, and I ask your pardon, only I was curious to know; and sure, no wonder."

"It requires various branches of knowledge to make a navigator."

"Branches," said Barny, "by gor, I think it id take *the whole three o' knowledge* to make it out. And that place you are going to, sir, that *Bin*gal (oh, bad luck to it for a *Bin*gal, it's the sore *Bin*gal to me!), is it so far off as you say?"

"Yes, Paddy; half round the world."

"Is it round in airnest, captain dear? Round about?"

"Aye, indeed."

"Oh, thin, arn't you afeard that whin you come to the top and that you're obleeged to go down, that you'd go sliddherin' away intirely, and never be able to stop, maybe. It's bad enough, so it is, goin' downhill by land, but it must be the dickens all out by wather."

"But there is no hill, Paddy. Don't you know that water is always level?"

"By dad, it's very *flat*, anyhow; and by the same token it's seldom I throuble it; but sure, your honour, if the wather is level, how do you make out that it is *round* you go?"

"That is part of the knowledge I was speaking to you about," said the captain.

"Musha, bad luck to you, knowledge, but you're a quare thing! and where is it Bingal, bad cess to it, would be, at all, at all?"

"In the East Indies."

"Oh, that is where they make the *tay*, isn't it, sir?"

"No; where the tea grows is farther still."

"Farther! why, that must be the ind of the world intirely. And they don't make it, then, sir, but it grows, you tell me."

"Yes, Paddy."

"Is it like hay, your honour?"

"Not exactly, Paddy; what puts hay in your head?"

"Oh, only bekase I hear them call it Bo*hay*."

"A most logical deduction, Paddy."

"And is it a great deal farther, your honour, the *tay* country is?"

"Yes, Paddy; China it is called."

"That's, I suppose, what we call Chaynee, sir?"

"Exactly, Paddy."

"By dad, I never could come at it rightly before, why it was nath'ral to dhrink tay out o' chaynee. I ax your honour's pardin for bein' throublesome, but I heerd tell from the long sailor iv a place they call Japan, in thim furrin parts; and *is* it there, your honour?"

"Quite true, Paddy."

"And I suppose it's there the blackin' comes from."

"No, Paddy; you're out there."

"Oh, well, I thought it stood to raison, as I heerd of japan blackin', sir, that it would be there it kem from, besides, as the blacks themselves—the naygurs I mane—is in thim parts."

"The negroes are in Africa, Paddy, much nearer to us."

"God betune uz and harm! I hope I would not be too near thim," said Barny.

"Why, what's your objection?"

"Arrah, sure, sir, they're hardly mortials at all, but has the mark o' the bastes an thim."

"How do you make out that, Paddy?"

"Why, sure, sir, and didn't Nathur make thim wid wool on their heads, plainly makin' it undherstood to Chrishthans that they wur little more nor cattle."

"I think your head is a-wool-gathering now, Paddy," said the captain, laughing.

"Faix, maybe so, indeed," answered Barny good-humouredly; "but it's seldom I ever went out to look for wool and kem home shorn, anyhow," said he, with a look of triumph.

"Well, you won't have that to say for the future, Paddy," said the captain, laughing again.

"My name's not Paddy, your honour," said Barny, returning the laugh, but seizing the opportunity to turn the joke aside, that was going against him—"my name isn't Paddy, sir, but Barny."

"Oh, if it was Solomon, you'll be bare enough when you go home this time; you have not gathered much this trip, Barny."

"Sure, I've been gathering knowledge, anyhow, your honour," said Barny, with a significant look at the captain, and a complimentary tip of his hand to his caubeen; "and God bless you for being so good to me."

"And what's your name besides Barny?" asked the captain.

"O'Reirdon, your honour—Barny O'Reirdon's my name."

"Well, Barny O'Reirdon, I won't forget your name nor yourself in a hurry, for you are certainly the most original navigator I ever had the honour of being acquainted with."

"Well," said Barny, with a triumphant toss of his head, "I have done out Terry O'Sullivan, at any rate; the divil a half so far he ever was, and that's a comfort. I have muzzled his clack for the rest iv his life, and he won't be comin' over us wid the pride iv his *Fing*al, while I'm to the fore, that was a'most at *Bing*al."

"Terry O'Sullivan—who is he, pray?" said the captain.

"Oh, he's a scut iv a chap that's not worth your axin' for—he's not worth your honour's notice—a braggin', poor craythur. Oh, wait till I get home, and the divil a more braggin' they'll hear out of his jaw."

"Indeed, then, Barny, the sooner you turn your face towards home the better," said the captain; "since you will go, there is no need in losing more time."

"Thrue for you, your honour—and sure, it's well for me had

the luck to meet with the likes o' your honour, that explained the ins and the outs iv it to me, and laid it all down as plain as prent."

"Are you sure you remember my directions?" said the captain.

"Throth, an I'll niver forget them to the day o' my death, and is bound to pray, more betoken, for you and yours."

"Don't mind praying for me till you get home, Barny; but answer me, how are you to steer when you shall leave me?"

"The nor'-aist coorse, your honour—that's the coorse agin the world."

"Remember that! never alter that course till you see land— let nothing make you turn out of a north-east course."

"Throth, an' that id be the dirty turn, seein' that it was yourself that ordered it. Oh, no; I'll depend my life an the *nor'-aist coorse*, and God help anyone that comes betune me and it—I'd run him down if he was my father."

"Well, good-bye, Barny."

"Good-bye, and God bless you, your honour, and send you safe!"

"That's a wish you want more for yourself, Barny—never fear for me, but mind yourself well."

"Oh, sure, I'm as good as at home wanst I know the way, barrin' the wind is conthrary; sure the nor-aist coorse 'ill do the business complate. Good-bye, your honour, and long life to you, and more power to your elbow, and a light heart and a heavy purse to you evermore, I pray the blessed Virgin and all the saints, amin!" and so saying, Barny descended the ship's side, and once more assumed the helm of the "hardy hooker."

The two vessels now separated on their opposite courses. What a contrast their relative situations afforded! Proudly the ship bore away under her lofty and spreading canvas, cleaving the billows before her, manned by an able crew, and under the guidance of experienced officers. The finger of science to point the course of her progress, the faithful chart to warn of the hidden rock and the shoal, the log line and the quadrant to measure her march and prove her position. The poor little hooker cleft not the billows, each wave lifted her on its crest like a seabird; but three inexperienced fishermen to manage her; no certain means to guide them over the vast ocean they had to traverse, and the holding of the "fickle wind" the only *chance* of their escape from perishing in the wilderness of waters. By the one, the feeling excited is supremely that of man's power; by the other, of his utter helplessness. To the one, the expanse of ocean could scarcely be considered "trackless"; to the other, it was a waste indeed.

Yet the cheer that burst from the ship, at parting, was answered as gaily from the hooker as though the odds had not been so fearfully against her, and no blither heart beat on board the ship than that of Barny O'Reirdon.

Happy light-heartedness of my poor countrymen! They have often need of all their buoyant spirits! How kindly they have been fortified by Nature against the assaults of adversity; and if they blindly rush into dangers, they cannot be denied the possession of gallant hearts to fight their way out of them.

But each hurrah became less audible; by degrees the cheers dwindled into faintness, and finally were lost in the eddies of the breeze.

The first feeling of loneliness that poor Barny experienced was when he could no longer hear the exhilarating sound. The plash of the surge, as it broke on the bows of his little boat, was uninterrupted by the kindred sound of human voice; and as it fell upon his ear, it smote upon his heart. But he rallied, waved his hat, and the silent signal was answered from the ship.

"Well, Barny," said Jimmy, "what was the captain sayin' to you all the time you wor wid him?"

"Lay me alone," said Barny. "I'll talk to you when I see her out o' sight, but not a word till thin. I'll look afther him, the rale gintleman that he is, while there's a topsail of his ship to be seen, and then I'll send my blessin' afther him, and pray for his good fortune wherever he goes, for he's the right sort, and nothin' else." And Barny kept his word, and when his straining eye could no longer trace a line of the ship, the captain certainly had the benefit of "a poor man's blessing."

The sense of utter loneliness and desolation had not come upon Barny until now; but he put his trust in the goodness of Providence, and in a fervent mental outpouring of prayer, resigned himself to the care of his Creator. With an admirable fortitude, too, he assumed a composure to his companions that was a stranger to his heart; and we all know how the burden of anxiety is increased when we have none with whom to sympathise. And this was not all. He had to affect ease and confidence, for Barny had not only no dependence on the firmness of his companions to go through the undertaking before them, but dreaded to betray to them how he had imposed on them in the affair. Barny was equal to all this. He had a stout heart, and was an admirable actor; yet for the first hour after the ship was out of sight he could not quite recover himself, and every now and then, unconsciously, he would look back with a wistful eye to the point where last he saw her. Poor Barny had lost his leader.

The night fell, and Barny stuck to the helm as long as Nature could sustain want of rest, and then left it in charge of one of his companions, with particular directions how to steer, and ordered, if any change in the wind occurred, that they should instantly wake him. He could not sleep long, however, the fever of anxiety was upon him, and the morning had not long dawned when he awoke. He had not well rubbed his eyes and looked about him, when he thought he saw a ship in the distance approaching them. As the haze cleared away, she showed distinctly bearing down towards the hooker. On board the ship, the hooker, in such a sea, caused surprise as before, and in about an hour she was so close as to hail, and order the hooker to run under her lee.

"The divil a taste," said Barny, "I'll not quit my *nor'-aist coorse* for the king of Ingland, nor Bonyparty into the bargain. Bad cess to you, do you think I've nothing to do but to plaze you?"

Again he was hailed.

"Oh, bad luck to the toe I'll go to you."

Another hail.

"Spake loudher you'd betther," said Barny jeeringly, still holding on his course.

A gun was fired ahead of him.

"By my sowl, you spoke loudher that time, sure enough," said Barny.

"Take care, Barny," cried Jimmy and Peter together. "Blur an agers, man, we'll be kilt if you don't go to them."

"Well, an we'll be lost if we turn out iv our *nor'-aist coorse*, and that's as broad as it's long. Let them hit iz if they like ; sure, it 'ud be a pleasanther death nor starvin' at sae. I tell you agin, I'll turn out o' my *nor'-aist coorse* for no man.'

A shotted gun was fired. The shot hopped on the water as it passed before the hooker.

"Phew ! you missed it, like your mammy's blessin'," said Barny.

"Oh, murther !" said Jimmy, "didn't you see the ball hop aff the wather forninst you. Oh, murther ! what 'ud we ha' done if we wor there, at all, at all ?"

"Why, we'd have taken the ball at the hop," said Barny, laughing, "accordin' to the ould sayin'."

Another shot was ineffectually fired.

"I'm thinking that's a Connaughtman that's shootin'," said Barny, with a sneer. The allusion was so relished by Jimmy and Peter that it excited a smile in the midst of their fears from the cannonade.

Again the report of the gun was followed by no damage.

"Augh ! never heed them !" said Barny contemptuously. "It's a barkin' dog that never bites, as the ould sayin' says," and the hooker was soon out of reach of further annoyance.

"Now, what a pity it was, to be sure," said Barny, "that I

wouldn't go aboord to plaze them.   Now, who's right?   Ah, lave
me alone always, Jimmy ; did you iver know me wrong yet ? "

" Oh, you may hillow now that you're out o' the wood," said
Jimmy ; " but accordin' to my idays, it was runnin' a grate rishk
to be conthrary wid them at all, and they shootin' balls afther us."

" Well, what matther ? " said Barny, " since they wor only
blind gunners, *an' I knew it ;* besides, as I said afore, I won't turn
out o' my *nor'-aist coorse* for no man."

" That's a new turn you tuk lately," said Peter.   " What's the
raison you're runnin' a nor'-aist coorse now, an' we never hear'd
iv it afore at all, till afther you quitted the big ship ? "

" Why, thin, are you sitch an ignoramus all out," said Barny,
" as not for to know that in navigation you must lie an a great
many different tacks before you can make the port you
steer for ? "

" Only I think," said Jimmy, " that it's back intirely we're
goin' now, and I can't make out the rights o' that at all."

" Why," said Barny, who saw the necessity of mystifying his
companions a little, " you see, the captain tould me that I kum
a round, an' rekimminded me to go th' other way."

" Faix, it's the first I ever heard o' goin' a round by sae,"
said Jimmy.

" Arrah, sure, that's part o' the saycrets o' navigation, and the
varrious branches o' knowledge that is requizit for a navigathor ;
an' that's what the captain—God bless him !—and myself was
discoorsin' an aboord ; and, like a rale gintleman as he is,
' Barny,' says he. ' Sir,' says I. ' You've come the round,' says
he. ' I know that,' says I, ' bekase I like to keep a good bowld
offin,' says I, ' in conthrary places.' ' Spoke like a good saeman,'
says he. ' That's my prenciples,' says I. ' They're the right
sort,' says he. ' But,' says he, ' (no offince), I think you wor
wrong,' says he, ' to pass the short turn in the ladieshoes,' says
he. ' I know,' says I, ' you mane beside the three-spike headlan'.'
' That's the spot,' says he ; ' I see you know it.' ' As well as I
know my father,' says I."

" Why, Barny," said Jimmy, interrupting him, " we see no
headlan' at all."

" Whist, whist ! " said Barny, " bad cess to you ; don't thwart
me.   We passed it in the night, and you couldn't see it.   Well,
as I was saying, ' I knew it as well as I know my father,' says I ;
' but I gev the preferrince to go the round,' says I. ' You're a
good saeman for that same,' says he, ' an' it would be right at
any other time than this present,' says he, ' but it's onpossible
now, tee-totally, on account o' the war,' says he. ' Tare alive,'
says I ; ' what war ? ' ' An' didn't you hear o' the war ? ' says he.
' Divil a word,' says I. ' Why,' says he, ' the naygurs has made

war on the king o' Chaynee,' says he, ' bekase he refused them any
more tay; an' with that, what did they do,' says he, ' but they put a
lumbaago on all the vessels that sails the round, an' that's the
raison,' says he, ' I carry guns, as you may see; and I'd rekimmind you,' says he, ' to go back, for you're not able for thim, an'
that's just the way iv it.' An' now, wasn't it loocky that I kem
acrass him at all, or maybe we might be cotch by the naygurs,
and ate up alive."

" Oh, thin, indeed, and that's thrue," said Jimmy and Peter;
" and when will we come to the short turn ?"

" Oh, never mind," said Barny, " you'll see it when you get
there; but wait till I tell you more about the captain and the
big ship. He said, you know, that he carried guns afeard o' the
naygurs, and in throth, it's the hoight o' care he takes o' them
same guns; and small blame to him, sure they might be the
salvation of him. 'Pon my conscience, they're taken betther care
of than any poor man's child. I hear'd him cautionin' the sailors
about them, and givin' them ordhers about their clothes."

" Their clothes !" said his two companions at once, in much
surprise; " is it clothes upon cannons ?"

" It's thruth I'm tellin' you," said Barny. " Bad luck to the
lie in it, he was talkin' about their aprons and their breeches."

" Oh, think o' that !" said Jimmy and Peter, in surprise.

" An' 'twas all iv a piece," said Barny, " that an' the rest o' the
ship all out. She was as nate as a new pin. Throth, I was a'most
ashamed to put my fut an the deck, it was so clane, and she
painted every colour in the rainbow; and all sorts o' curosities
about her; and instead iv a tiller to steer her, like this darlin
craythur iv ours, she goes wid a wheel, like a coach, all as one;
and there's the quarest thing you iver seen, to show the way, as
the captain gev me to undherstan', a little round, rowly-powly
thing in a bowl, that goes waddlin' about as if it didn't know
its own way, much more nor show anybody theirs. Throth,
myself thought that if that's the way they're obleeged to go, that
it's with a great deal of *fear and thrimblin'* they find it out."

Thus it was that Barny continued most marvellous accounts of
the ship and the captain to his companions, and by keeping their
attention so engaged, prevented their being too inquisitive as to
their own immediate concerns, and for two days more Barny and
the hooker held on their respective courses undeviatingly.

The third day, Barny's fears for the continuity of his *nor'-aist
coorse* were excited, as a large brig hove in sight, and the nearer she
approached, the more directly she came athwart Barny's course.

" May the divil sweep you," said Barny, " and will nothin' else
sarve you than comin' forninst me that-a-way? Brig-a-hoy there!"
shouted Barny, giving the tiller to one of his messmates, and

standing at the bow of his boat. "Brig-a-hoy there!—bad luck to you, go 'long out o' my *nor'-aist coorse*." The brig, instead of obeying his mandate, hove to, and lay right ahead of the hooker. "Oh, look at this!" shouted Barny, and he stamped on the deck with rage—"look at the blackguards where they're stayin', just a-purpose to ruin an unfort'nate man like me. My heavy hathred to you, *quit* this minit, or I'll run down an yes, and if we go to the bottom, we'll hant you for evermore—go 'long out o' that, I tell you. The curse o' Crummil an you, you stupid vagabones, that won't go out iv a man's nor'-aist coorse!"

From cursing Barny went to praying as he came closer. "For the tendher marcy o' heaven and lave my way. May the Lord reward you, and get out o' my nor'-aist coorse! May angels make your bed in heaven and don't ruinate me this-a-way." The brig was immovable, and Barny gave up in despair, having cursed and prayed himself hoarse, and finished with a duet volley of prayers and curses together, apostrophising the hard case of a man being "*done out of his nor'-aist coorse.*"

"A-hoy there!" shouted a voice from the brig; "put down your helm, or you'll be aboard of us. I say, let go your jib and foresheet—what are you about, you lubbers?"

'Twas true that the brig lay so fair in Barny's course that he would have been aboard, but that instantly the manœuvre above alluded to was put in practice on board the hooker, as she swept to destruction towards the heavy hull of the brig, and she luffed up into the wind alongside her. A very pale and somewhat emaciated face appeared at the side, and addressed Barny.

"What brings you here?" was the question.

"Throth, thin, and I think I might betther ax what brings *you* here, right in the way o' my *nor'-aist coorse*."

"Where do you come from?"

"From Kinsale; and you didn't come from a betther place, I go bail."

"Where are you bound to?"

"To Fingal."

"Fingal—where's Fingal?"

"Why, thin, ain't you ashamed o' yourself an not to know where Fingal is?"

"It is not in these seas."

"Oh, that's all you know about it," says Barny.

"You're a small craft to be so far at sea. I suppose you have provision on board?"

"To be sure we have; throth, if we hadn't, this id be a bad place to go a-beggin'."

"What have you eatable?"

"The finest o' scalpeens."

"What are scalpeens?"

"Why, you're mighty ignorant intirely," said Barny. "Why, scalpeens is pickled mackerel."

"Then you must give us some, for we have been out of everything eatable these three days; and even pickled fish is better than nothing."

It chanced that the brig was a West India trader, which unfavourable winds had delayed much beyond the expected period of time on her voyage, and though her water had not failed, everything eatable had been consumed, and the crew reduced almost to helplessness. In such a strait, the arrival of Barny O'Reirdon and his scalpeens was a most providential succour to them, and a lucky chance for Barny, for he got in exchange for his pickled fish a handsome return of rum and sugar, much more than equivalent to their value. Barny lamented much, however, that the brig was not bound for Ireland, that he might practise his own peculiar system of navigation; but as staying with the brig could do no good, he got himself put into his *nor'-aist coorse* once more, and ploughed away towards home.

The disposal of his cargo was a great godsend to Barny in more ways than one. In the first place, he found the most profitable market he could have had; and secondly, it enabled him to cover his retreat from the difficulty which still was before him of not getting to Fingal after all his dangers, and consequently being open to discovery and disgrace. All these beneficial results were not thrown away upon one of Barny's readiness to avail himself of every point in his favour; and accordingly, when they left the brig, Barny said to his companions: "Why, thin, boys, 'pon my conscience, but I'm as proud as a horse wid a wooden leg this minit, that we met thim poor unfort'nate craythers this blessed day, and was enabled to extind our charity to thim. Sure, an' it's lost they'd be only for our comin' across thim, and we, through the blessin' o' God, enabled to do an act of marcy—that is, feedin' the hungry; and sure, every good work we do here is before uz in heaven—and that's a comfort, anyhow. To be sure, now that the scalpeens is sould, there's no use in goin' to Fingal, and we may as well jist go home."

"Faix, I'm sorry myself," said Jimmy, "for Terry O'Sullivan said it was an iligant place intirely, an' I wanted to see it."

"To the divil wid Terry O'Sullivan," said Barny. "How does he know what's an iligant place? What knowledge has he of iligance? I'll go bail, he never was half as far a-navigatin' as we—he wint the short cut, I go bail, and never daar'd for to vinture the round, as I did."

"By dad, we wor a great dale longer, anyhow, than he tould me he was."

"To be sure we wor," said Barny, "he wint skulkin' by the short cut, I tell you, and was afeard to keep a bowld offin' like me. But come, boys, let uz take a dhrop o' that bottle o' sper'ts we got out o' the brig. By gor, it's well we got some bottles iv it; for I wouldn't much like to meddle wid that darlint little kag iv it antil we get home." The rum was put on its trial by Barny and his companions, and in their critical judgment was pronounced quite as good as the captain of the ship had bestowed upon them, but that neither of those specimens of spirit was to be compared to whisky. "By dad," says Barny, "they may rack their brains a long time before they'll make out a purtier invintion than *potteen*—that rum may do very well for thim that has the misforthin not to know betther; but the whisky is a more nath'ral sper't, accordin' to my idays." In this, as in most other of Barny's opinions, Peter and Jimmy coincided.

Nothing particular occurred for the two succeeding days, during which time Barny most religiously pursued his *nor'-aist coorse*, but the third day produced a new and important event. A sail was discovered on the horizon, and in the direction Barny was steering, and a couple of hours made him tolerably certain that the vessel in sight was an American, for though it is needless to say that he was not very conversant in such matters, yet from the frequency of his seeing Americans trading to Ireland, his eye had become sufficiently accustomed to their lofty and tapering spars, and peculiar smartness of rig, to satisfy him that the ship before him was of transatlantic build : nor was he wrong in his conjecture.

Barny now determined on a manœuvre, classing him amongst the first tacticians at securing a good retreat.

Moreau's highest fame rests upon his celebrated retrograde movement through the Black Forest.

Xenophon's greatest glory is derived from the deliverance of his ten thousand Greeks from impending ruin by his renowned retreat.

Let the ancient and the modern hero " repose under the shadow of their laurels," as the French have it, while Barny O'Reirdon's historian, with a pardonable jealousy for the honour of his country, cuts down a goodly bough of the classic tree, beneath which our Hibernian hero may enjoy his *otium cum dignitate*.

Barny calculated the American was bound for Ireland, and as she lay *almost* as directly in the way of his "nor'-aist coorse" as the West Indian brig, he bore up to and spoke to her.

He was answered by a shrewd Yankee captain.

"Faix, an' it's glad I am to see your honour agin," said Barny.

The Yankee had never been to Ireland, and told Barny so.

"Oh, throth, I couldn't forget a gintleman so aisy as that," said Barny.

"You're pretty considerably mistaken now, I guess," said the American.

"Divil a taste," said Barny, with inimitable composure and pertinacity.

"Well, if you know me so tarnation well, tell me what's my name." The Yankee flattered himself he had nailed Barny now.

"Your name, is it?" said Barny, gaining time by repeating the question. "Why, what a fool you are not to know your own name."

The oddity of the answer posed the American, and Barny took advantage of the diversion in his favour, and changed the conversation.

"By dad, I've been waitin' here these four or five days, expectin' some of you would be wantin' me."

"Some of us!—how do you mean?"

"Sure, an' arn't you from Amerikay?"

"Yes; and what then?"

"Well, I say I was waitin' for some ship or other from Amerikay, that 'ud be wantin' me. It's to Ireland you're goin', I dar'say."

"Yes."

"Well, I suppose you'll be wantin' a pilot," said Barny.

"Yes, when we get in shore; but not yet."

"Oh, I don't want to hurry you," said Barny.

"What port are you a pilot of?"

"Why, indeed, as for the matther o' that," said Barny, "they're all aiqual to me a'most."

"All?" said the American. "Why, I calculate you couldn't pilot a ship into all the ports of Ireland."

"Not all at wanst [once]," said Barny, with a laugh, in which the American could not help joining.

"Well, I say, what ports do you know best?"

"Why, thin, indeed," said Barny, "it would be hard for me to tell; but wherever you want to go, I'm the man that'll do the job for you complate. Where is your honour goin'?"

"I won't tell you that—but do you tell me what ports you know best?"

"Why, there's Watherford, and there's Youghall, an' Fingal."

"Fingal! Where's that?"

"So you don't know where Fingal is. Oh, I see you're a sthranger, sir—an' then there's Cork."

"You know Cove, then?"

"Is it the Cove o' Cork, why?"

" Yes."

" I was bred an' born there, and pilots as many ships into Cove as any other two min *out* of it."

Barny thus sheltered his falsehood under the idiom of his language.

" But what brought you so far out to sea ? " asked the captain.

" We wor lyin' out lookin' for ships that wanted pilots, and there kem an the terriblest gale o' wind off the land, an' blew us to sae out intirely, an' that's the way iv it, your honour."

" I calculate we got a share of the same gale ; 'twas from the nor'-east."

" Oh, directly ! " said Barny. " Faith, you're right enough, 'twas the *nor'-aist coorse* we wor an, sure enough ; but no matther now that we've met wid you—sure, we'll have a job home, anyhow."

" Well, get aboard, then," said the American.

" I will in a minit, your honour, whin I jist spake a word to my comrades here."

" Why, sure, it's not goin' to turn pilot you are ? " said Jimmy, in his simplicity of heart.

" Whist, you omadhaun ! " said Barny, " or I'll cut the tongue out o' you. Now, mind me, Pether. You don't undherstan' navigashin and the varrious branches o' knowledge, an' so all you have to do is to folly the ship whin I get into her, an' I'll show you the way home."

Barny then got aboard the American vessel, and begged of the captain, that as he had been out at sea so long, and had gone through a " power o' hardship intirely," that he would be permitted to go below and turn in to take a sleep, " for in throth, it's myself and sleep that is sthrangers for some time," said Barny ; " an' if your honour 'ill be plazed, I'll be thankful if you won't let them disturb me antil I'm wanted, for sure, till you see the land, there's no use for me in life, an' throth, I want a sleep sorely."

Barny's request was granted, and it will not be wondered at that, after so much fatigue of mind and body, he slept profoundly for four-and-twenty hours. He then was called, for land was in sight, and when he came on deck, the captain rallied him upon the potency of his somniferous qualities, and " calculated " he had never met anyone who could sleep " four-and-twenty hours on a stretch before."

" Oh, sir," said Barny, rubbing his eyes, which were still a little hazy, " whiniver *I* go to sleep *I pay attention to it.*"

The land was soon neared, and Barny put in charge of the ship, when he ascertained the first landmark he was acquainted with ; but as soon as the Head of Kinsale hove in sight, Barny gave a " whoo," and cut a caper that astonished the Yankees, and was quite inexplicable to them, though, I flatter myself, it is not to those who do Barny the favour of reading his adventures.

"Oh, there you are, my darlint ould head! an' where's the head like you? throth, it's little I thought I'd ever set eyes an your good-looking faytures agin. But God's good!"

In such half-muttered exclamations did Barny apostrophise each well-known point of his native shore, and when opposite the Harbour of Kinsale, he spoke the hooker, that was somewhat astern, and ordered Jimmy and Peter to put in there, and tell Molly immediately that he was come back, and would be with her as soon as he could, after piloting the ship into Cove. "But an your apperl, don't tell Pether Kelly o' the big farm, nor indeed, don't mintion to man nor mortial about the navigation we done antil I come home myself and make thim sensible of it, bekase, Jimmy and Pether, neither o' yiz is aiqual to it, and doesn't undherstan' the branches o' knowledge requizit for discoorsin' o' navigation."

The hooker put into Kinsale, and Barny sailed the ship into Cove. It was the first ship he ever had acted the pilot for, and his old luck attended him; no accident befel his charge, and what was still more extraordinary, he made the American believe he was absolutely the most skilful pilot on the station. So Barny pocketed his pilot's fee, swore the Yankee was a gentleman, for which the republican did not thank him, wished him good-bye, and then pushed his way home with what Barny swore was the easiest made money he ever had in his life. So Barny got himself paid for *piloting* the ship that *showed him the way home.*

All the fishermen in the world may throw their caps at his feat —none but an Irishman, I fearlessly assert, could have executed so splendid a *coup de finesse.*

And now, sweet readers (the ladies, I mean), did you ever think Barny would get home? I would give a hundred of pens to hear all the guesses that have been made as to the probable termination of Barny's adventure. They would furnish good material, I doubt not, for another voyage. But Barny did make other voyages, I can assure you; and perhaps he may appear in his character of navigator once more, if his daring exploits be not held valueless by an ungrateful world, as in the case of his great predecessor, Columbus.

As some *curious* persons (I *don't* mean the ladies) may wish to know what became of some of the characters who have figured in this tale, I beg to inform them that Molly continued a faithful wife and time-keeper, as already alluded to, for many years. That Peter Kelly was so pleased with his share in the profits arising from the trip, in the ample return of rum and sugar, that he freighted a large brig with scalpeens to the West Indies, and went supercargo himself.

All he got in return was the yellow fever.

Barny profited better by his share; he was enabled to open a public-house, which had more custom than any ten within miles of it.   Molly managed the bar very efficiently, and Barny "discoorsed" the customers most seductively; in short, Barny—at all times given to the *marvellous*—became a greater romancer than ever, and for years attracted even the gentlemen of the neighbourhood, who loved fun, to his house, for the sake of his magnanimous mendacity.

As for the hitherto triumphant Terry O'Sullivan, from the moment Barny's *Bingal* adventure became known, he was obliged to fly the country, and was never heard of more, while the hero of the hooker became a greater man than before, and never was addressed by any other title afterwards than that of THE COMMODORE.

THE BURIAL OF THE TITHE

IT was a fine morning in the autumn of 1832, and the sun had not yet robbed the grass of its dew, as a stout-built peasant was moving briskly along a small by-road in the county of Tipperary. The elasticity of his step bespoke the lightness of his heart, and the rapidity of his walk did not seem sufficient, even, for the exuberance of his glee, for every now and then the walk was exchanged for a sort of dancing shuffle, which terminated with a short, capering kick that threw up the dust about him, and all the while he whistled one of those whimsical jig-tunes with which Ireland abounds, and twirled his stick over his head in a triumphal flourish.   Then off he started again in his original pace, and hummed a rollicking song, and occasionally broke out into soliloquy :

"Why, thin, an' isn't it the grate day intirely for Ireland, that is in it this blessed day ?   Whoo! your sowl to glory, but we'll do the job complate "—and here he cut a caper.   "Divil a more they'll ever get, and it's only a pity they ever got any—but there's an ind o' thim now—they're cut down from this out "—and here he made an appropriate down-stroke of his shillelah through a bunch of thistles that skirted the road.   "Where will be their grand doin's now ?—eh ?—I'd like to know that.   Where'll be their lazy livery servants ?—ow ! ow !" and he sprang lightly over a stile.   "And what will they do for their coaches and four ?" Here a lark sprang up at his feet, and darted into the air with its thrilling rush of exquisite melody.   "Faith, you've given me my answer, sure enough, my purty lark; that's as much as to say they may go whistle for thim.   Oh, my poor fellows, how I pity yiz !" and here he broke into a "too ra la loo," and danced along the path ; then suddenly dropping into silence, he resumed

THE BURIAL OF THE TITHE

his walk, and applying his hand behind his head, cocked up his caubeen and began to rub behind his ear, according to the most approved peasant practice of assisting the powers of reflection. "Faix, and it's myself that's puzzled to know what'll the procthers and the process sarvers and 'praisers do at all. By gorra, they must go rob *an the road*, since they won't be let to rob any more *in the fields;* robbin' is all that is left for thim, for sure, they couldn't turn to any honest thrade afther the coorses they have been used to. Oh, what a power of miscrayants will be out of bread for the want of their ould thrade of false swearin'. Why, the vagabones will be lost, barrin' they're sent to *Bot*—and indeed, if a bridge could be built of false oaths, by my sowkins, they could sware thimselves there without wettin' their feet." Here he overtook another peasant, whom he accosted with the universal salutation of "God save you!" "God save you kindly," was returned for answer. "And is it yourself that's there, Mikee Noonan?" said the one first introduced to the reader.

"Indeed, it's myself and nobody else," said Noonan. "An' where is it you're goin' this fine mornin'?"

"An' is it yourself that's axin' that same, Mikee. Why, where is it I would be goin' but to the berrin'?"

"I thought so, in throth. It's yourself that is always ripe and ready for fun."

"And small blame to me."

"Why, thin, it was a mighty complate thing, whoever it was that thought of makin' a berrin' out of it."

"And don't you know?"

"Not to my knowledge."

"Why, thin, who 'ud you think now laid it all out?"

"Faix, I dunno—maybe 'twas Pether Conolly."

"No, it wasn't, though Pether's a cute chap. Guess again."

"Well, was it Phil Mulligan?"

"No, it wasn't, though you made a good offer at it, sure enough, for if it wasn't Phil, it was his sisther—"

"Tare alive, is it Biddy it was?"

"'Scure to the one else. Oh, she's the quarest craythur in life. There's not a thrick out that one's not up to, and more besides. By the powdhers o' war, she'd bate a field full o' lawyers at schkamin'—she's the divil's Biddy."

"Why, thin, but it was a grate iday intirely."

"You may say that, in throth—maybe it's we won't have the fun—but see who's before us there. Isn't it that ould Coogan?"

"Sure enough, by dad!"

"Why, thin, isn't he the rale fine ould cock to come so far to see the rights o' the thing."

"Faix, he was always the right sort. Sure, in Nointy-eight, as

I hear, he was malthrated a power, and his place rummaged, and himself a'most kilt, bekase he wouldn't inform an his neighbours."

"God's blessin' be an' him, an the likes av him, that wouldn't prove thraitor to a friend in disthress."

Here they came up with the old man to whom they alluded. He was the remains of a stately figure, and his white hair hung at some length round the back of his head and his temples, while a black and well-marked eyebrow overshadowed his keen grey eye; the contrast of the dark eyebrow to the white hair rendered the intelligent cast of his features more striking, and he was altogether a figure that one would not be likely to pass without notice. He was riding a small horse at an easy pace, and he answered the rather respectful salutation of the two foot-passengers with kindness and freedom. They addressed him as "*Mr.* Coogan," while to them he returned the familiar term "boys."

"And av coorse it's goin' to the berrin' you are, Mr. Coogan, and long life to you."

"Aye, boys. It's hard for an ould horse to leave off his thricks."

"Ould, is it? Faix, and it's yourself that has more heart in you this blessed mornin' than many a man that's not half your age."

"By dad, I'm not a cowlt, boys, though I kicked up my heels sometimes."

"Well, you'll never do it younger, sir; but sure, why wouldn't you be there when all the counthry is goin', I hear, and no wondher, sure. By the hole in my hat, it's enough, so it is, to make a sick man lave his bed to see the fun that'll be in it, and sure, it's right and proper, and shows the sperit that's in the counthry, when a man like yourself, Mr. Coogan, joins the poor people in doin' it."

"I like to stand up for the right," answered the old man.

"And always was a good warrant to do that same," said Larry, in his most laudatory tone.

"Will you tell us who's that fornint us an the road there?" asked the old man, as he pointed to a person that seemed to make his way with some difficulty, for he laboured under an infirmity of limb that caused a grotesque jerking action in his walk, if walk it might be called.

"Why, thin, don't you know him, Mr. Coogan? By dad, I thought there wasn't a parish in the county that didn't know poor Hoppy Houligan."

It has been often observed before, the love of *soubriquet* that the Irish possess; but let it not be supposed that their nicknames are given in a spirit of unkindness—far from it. A sense of the ridiculous is so closely interwoven in an Irishman's nature, that he will even jest upon his *own* misfortunes; and while he indulges in a joke (one of the few indulgences he can command), the person that excites it may as frequently be the object of his openheartedness as his mirth.

"And is that Hoppy Houligan?" said old Coogan. "I often heerd of him, to be sure, but I never seen him before."

"Oh, thin, you may see him before and behind now," said Larry; "and indeed, if he had a match for that odd skirt of his coat, he wouldn't be the worse iv it; and in throth, the cordheroys thimselves aren't a bit too good, and there's the laste taste in life of his—"

"Whisht," said the old man; "he is looking back, and maybe he hears you."

"Not he, in throth. Sure, he's partly bothered."

"How can he play the fiddle, thin, and he bothered?" said Coogan.

"Faix, and that's the very raison he *is* bothered; sure, he moidhers the ears off of him intirely with the noise of his own fiddle. Oh, he's a powerful fiddler."

"So I often heerd, indeed," said the old man.

"He bangs all the fiddlers in the counthry."

"And is in the greatest request," added Noonan.

"Yet he looks tatthered enough," said old Coogan.

"Sure, you never seen a well-dhrest fiddler yet," said Larry.

"Indeed, and now you remind me, I b'lieve not," said the old man. "I suppose they all get more kicks than ha'pence, as the saying is."

"Divil a many kicks Houligan gets; he's a great favourite intirely."

"Why is he in such disthress, thin?" asked Coogan.

"Faith, he's not in disthress at all; he's welkim everywhere he goes, and has the best of atin' and dhrinkin' the place affords, wherever he is, and picks up the coppers fast at the fairs, and is no way *necessitated* in life; though, indeed, it can't be denied as he limps along there, that he has a great many *ups* and *downs* in the world."

This person, of whom the preceding dialogue treats, was a celebrated fiddler in "these parts," and his familiar name of Hoppy Houligan was acquired, as the reader may already have perceived, from his limping gait. This limp was the consequence of a broken leg, which was one of the consequences of an affray, which is the certain consequence of a fair in Tipperary. Houligan was a highly characteristic specimen of an Irish fiddler. As Larry Lanigan said: "You never seen a well-dressed fiddler yet;" but Houligan was a particularly ill-fledged bird of the musical tribe. His corduroys have already been hinted at by Larry, as well as his coat, which had lost half the skirt, thereby partially revealing the aforesaid corduroys; or if one might be permitted to indulge in an image, the half-skirt that remained served to produce a partial eclipse of the disc of corduroy. This was what we painters call *picturesque.* By the way, the vulgar are always amazed that some tattered remains of anything is more prized by the painter than the freshest production in all its gloss of novelty. The fiddler's stockings, too, in the neglected falling of their folds round his leg, and the wisp of straw that fringed the opening of his gaping brogues, were valuable additions to the picture; and his hat— But stop—let me not presume; his hat it would be a vain attempt to describe. There are two things not to be described, which, to know what they are, you must see.

Those two things are Taglioni's dancing and an Irish fiddler's hat. The one is a wonder in *action;* the other, an enigma in *form.*

Houligan's fiddle was as great a curiosity as himself, and like its master, somewhat the worse for wear. It had been broken some scores of times, and yet, by dint of glue, was continued in what an antiquary would call "a fine state of preservation"; that is to say, there was rather more of glue than wood in the article. The stringing of the instrument was as great a piece of patchwork as itself, and exhibited great ingenuity on the part of its owner. Many was the knot above the finger-board and below the bridge—that is, when the fiddle was in its *best* order; for in case of fractures on the field of action—that is to say, at wake, patron, or fair, where the fiddler, unlike the girl he was playing for, had not two strings to his bow—in such case, I say, the old string should be knotted, wherever it might require to be, and I have heard it insinuated that the music was not a bit the worse of it. Indeed, the only economy that poor Houligan ever practised was in the strings of his fiddle, and those were an admirable exemplification of the proverb of "making both ends meet." Houligan's waistcoat, too, was a curiosity, or rather, a cabinet of curiosities; for he appropriated its pockets to various purposes—snuff, resin, tobacco, a clasp-knife with half a blade, a piece of flint, a *doodeen*, and some bits of twine and ends of fiddle-strings were all huddled together promiscuously. Houligan himself called his waistcoat Noah's ark; for as he said himself, there was a little of everything in it, barring money, and that would never stay in his company. His fiddle, partly enfolded in a scanty bit of old baize, was tucked under his left arm, and his right was employed in helping him to hobble along by means of a blackthorn stick, when he was overtaken by the three travellers already named, and saluted by all, with the addition of a query as to where he was going.

"An where would I be goin' but to the berrin'?" said Houligan.

"Throth, it's the same answer I expected," said Lanigan. "It would be nothin' at all without you."

"I've played at many a weddin'," said Houligan; "but I'm thinkin' there will be more fun at this berrin' than any ten weddin's."

"Indeed you may say that, Hoppy, aghra," said Noonan.

"Why, thin, Hoppy jewel," said Lanigan, "what did the skirt o' your coat do to you that you left it behind you, and wouldn't let it see the fun?"

"'Deed, thin, I'll tell you, Larry, my boy. I was goin' last night by the by-road that runs up at the back o' the ould house, nigh hand the Widdy Casey's, and I heerd that people was livin' in it since I thravelled the road last, and so I opened the ould iron gate that was as stiff in the hinge as a miser's fist, and the road ladin' up to the house lookin' as lonely as a churchyard, and the grass growin' out through it, and says I to myself: 'I'm thinkin' it's few darkens your doors,' says I. God be with the time the ould Squire was here, that staid at home and didn't go abroad out of his own counthry, lettin' the fine, stately ould place go to rack and ruin; and faix, I was turnin' back, and I wish I did, whin I seen a man comin' down the road, and so I waited till he kem near to me, and I axed if anyone was up at the house. 'Yis, says he; and with that I heerd terrible barkin' intirely, and a great big lump of a dog turned the corner of the house and stud growlin' at me. 'I'm afeard there's dogs in it,' says I to the man. 'Yis,' says he; 'but they're quite [quiet.]' So with that I wint my way, and he wint his way; but my jewel, the minit I got into the yard, nine great vagabones of dogs fell an me, and I thought they'd ate me alive; and so they would, I b'lieve, only I had a could bones o' mate and some praties that Mrs. Magrane—God bless her!—made me put in my pocket when I was goin' the road as I was lavin' her house that mornin' afther the christenin' that was in it, and sure enough, lashin's and lavin's was there. Oh, that's the woman has a heart as big as a king's, and her husband too, in throth; he's a dacent man, and keeps mighty fine dhrink in his house. Well, as I was sayin', the could mate and praties was in my pocket, and by gor, the thievin' morodin' villians o' dogs made a dart at the pocket and dragged it clane aff; and thin, my dear, with fightin' among thimselves, sthrivin' to come at the mate, the skirt o' my coat was in smidhereens in one minit—divil a lie in it—not a tatther in it was left together; and it's only a wondher I came off with my life."

"Faith, I think so," said Lanigan; "and wasn't it mighty providintial they didn't get at the fiddle. Sure, what would the counthry do thin?"

"Sure enough, you may say that," said Houligan; "and thin, my *bread* would be gone as well as my *mate*. But think o' the unnath'ral vagabone that tould me the dogs was quite; sure, he came back while I was there, and I ups and tould him what a shame it was to tell me the dogs was quite. 'So they are quite,' says he; 'sure, there's nine o' thim, and *only seven o' thim bites*.' 'Thank you,' says I."

There was something irresistibly comic in the quiet manner that Houligan said: "Thank you, says I;" and the account of his canine adventure altogether excited much mirth amongst his auditors. As they pursued their journey many a joke was passed and repartee returned, and the laugh rang loudly and often from the merry little group as they trudged along. In the course of the next mile's march their numbers were increased by some half-dozen, that, one by one, suddenly appeared by leaping over the hedge on the road, or crossing a stile from some neighbouring path. All these new-comers pursued the same route, and each gave the same answer when asked where he was going. It was universally this:

"Why, thin, where would I be goin' but to the berrin'?"

At a neighbouring confluence of roads straggling parties of from four to five were seen in advance, and approaching in the rear, and the highway soon began to wear the appearance it is wont to do on the occasion of a patron, a fair, or a market-day. Larry Lanigan was in evident enjoyment at this increase of numbers; and as the crowd thickened, his exultation increased, and he often repeated his ejaculation, already noticed in Larry's opening soliloquy: "Why, thin, an' isn't it a grate day intirely for Ireland!"

And now horsemen were more frequently appearing, and their numbers soon amounted to almost a cavalcade; and sometimes a car—that is to say, the car common to the country for agricultural purposes—might be seen, bearing a cargo of women; videlicet, "the good woman" herself, and her rosy-cheeked daughters, and maybe a cousin or two, with an *aid du camp* aunt to assist in looking after the young ladies. The roughness of the motion of this primitive vehicle was rendered as accommodating as possible to the gentler sex by a plentiful shake-down of clean straw on the car, over which a feather bed was laid, and the best quilt in the house over that, to make all smart, possibly a piece of hexagon patchwork of "the misthriss" herself, in which the tawdriest calico patterns served to display the taste of the rural sempstress, and stimulated the rising generation to feats of needlework. The car was always provided with a driver, who took such care upon himself "for a raison he had." He was almost universally what is called in Ireland "a clane boy"—that is to say, a well-made, good-looking young fellow, whose eyes were not put into his head for nothing; and these same eyes might be seen wandering backwards occasionally from his immediate charge, the dumb baste, to "take a squint" at some, or maybe *one*, of his passengers.

This explains the "raison he had" for becoming driver. Sometimes he sat on the crupper of the horse, resting his feet on the shafts of the car, and bending down his head to say something *tindher* to the *colleen* that sat next him, totally negligent of his duty as guide. Sometimes when the girl he wanted to be sweet on was seated at the back of the car, this relieved the horse from the additional burthen of his driver, and the clane boy would leave the horse's head and fall in the rear to *deludher* the craythur, depending on an occasional "hup" or "wo" for the guidance of the *baste*, when a too near proximity to the dyke by the roadside warned him of the necessity of his interference. Sometimes he was called to his duty by the open remonstrance of either the mother or aunt, or maybe a mischievous cousin, as thus:

"Why, thin, Dinny, what are you about, at all, at all? God betune me and harm, if you warn't within an inch o' puttin' uz all in the gripe o' the ditch. Arrah, lave off your gostherin' there, and mind the horse, will you; a purty thing it 'ud be if my bones was bruk. What are you doin' there at all, at the back o' the car, when it's at the baste's head you ought to be?"

"Arrah, sure, the baste knows the way herself."

"Faix, I b'lieve so, for it's little behoulden to you she is for showin' her. Augh!!—murther!!!—there we are in the gripe a'most."

"Lave off your screechin', can't you, and be quite. Sure the poor craythur only just wint over to get a mouthful o' the grass by the side o' the ditch."

"What business has she to be atin' now?"

"Bekase she's hungry, I suppose—and why isn't she fed betther?"

"Bekase rogues stales her oats, Dinny. I seen you in the stable by the same token yistherday."

"Sure enough, ma'am, for I wint there to look for my cowlt that was missin'."

"I thought it was *filly* you wor afther, Dinny," said a cousin, with a wink; and Dinny grinned, and his sweatheart blushed, while the rest of the girls tittered, the mother pretending not to hear the joke, and bidding Dinny go mind his business by attending to the horse.

But lest I should tire my reader by keeping him so long on the road, I will let him find the rest of his way as well as he can to a certain romantic little valley, where a comfortable farm-house was situated beside a small mountain stream that tumbled along noisily over its rocky bed, and in which some ducks, noisier than the stream, were enjoying their morning bath. The geese were indulging in dignified rest and silence upon the bank; a cock was crowing and strutting with his usual swagger amongst his hens; a pig was endeavouring to save his ears, not from this rural tumult, but from the teeth of a half-terrier dog, who was chasing him away from an iron pot full of potatoes which the pig had dared to attempt some impertinent liberties with; and a girl was bearing into the house a pail of milk which she had just taken from the cow that stood placidly looking on, an admirable contrast to the general bustle of the scene.

Everything about the cottage gave evidence of comfort on the part of its owner, and to judge from the numbers without and within the house, you would say he did not want for friends; for all, as they arrived at its door, greeted Phelim O'Hara kindly, and Phelim welcomed each new-comer with a heartiness that did honour to his grey hairs. Frequently passing to and fro, busily engaged in arranging an ample breakfast in the barn, appeared his daughter, a pretty, round-faced girl, with black hair and the long and silky-lashed dark-grey eyes of her country, where merriment loves to dwell, and a rosy mouth whose smiles served at once to display her good temper and her fine teeth; her colour gets fresher for a moment, and a look of affectionate recognition brightens her eye, as a lithe young fellow springs briskly over the stepping-stones that lead across the stream, and trips lightly up to the girl, who offers her hand in welcome. Who is the happy dog that is so well received by Honor O'Hara, the prettiest girl in that parish or the next, and the daughter of a "snug man" into the bargain? It is the reader's old acquaintance, Larry Lanigan; and maybe Larry did not give a squeeze extraordinary to the hand that was presented to him. The father received him well also; indeed, for that matter, the difficulty would have been to find a house in the whole district that Larry would *not* have been welcome in.

"So here you are at last, Larry," said old O'Hara. "I was wonderin' you were not here long ago."

"An' so I would, I thank you kindly," said Larry, "only I overtook ould Hoppy here, on the road, and sure, I thought I might as well take my time, and wait for poor Hoppy, and bring my welkim along with me;" and here he shoved the fiddler into the house before him.

"The girls will be glad to see the pair o' yiz," said the old man, following.

The interior of the house was crowded with guests, and the

usual laughing and courting so often described as common to such assemblages were going forward amongst the young people. At the farther end of the largest room in the cottage, a knot of the older men of the party were engaged in the discussion of some subject that seemed to carry deep interest along with it, and at the opposite extremity of the same room, a coffin of very rude construction lay on a small table; and around this coffin stood all the junior part of the company, male and female, and the wildness of their mirth, and the fertility of their jests, over this tenement of mortality and its contents, might have well startled a stranger for a moment, until he saw the nature of the deposit the coffin contained.

Enshrouded in a sheaf of wheat lay a pig, between whose open jaws a large potate was placed, and the coffin was otherwise grotesquely decorated.

The reader will wonder, no doubt, at such an exhibition, for certainly never was coffin so applied before; and it is therefore necessary to explain the meaning of all this, and I believe Ireland is the only country in the world where the facts I am about to relate could have occurred.

It may be remembered that some time previous to the date at which my story commences, His Majesty's ministers declared that there should be a "total extinction of tithes."

This declaration was received in Ireland by the great mass of the people with the utmost delight, as they fancied they should never have tithes to pay again. The peasantry in the neighbour-hood of Templemore formed the very original idea of BURYING THE TITHE. It is only amongst an imaginative people that such a notion could have originated; and indeed, there is something highly poetical in the conception. The tithe—that which the poor felt the keenest; that which they considered a tax on their industry; that which they looked upon as an hereditary oppression; that hateful thing, they were told, was to be extinct, and in joyous anticipation of the blessing, they determined to enact an emblematic interment of this terrible enemy. I think it is not too much to call this idea a fine one; and yet, in the execution of it, they invested it with the broadest marking of the grotesque. Such is the strange compound of an Irish peasant, whose anger is often vented in a jest, and whose mirth is sometimes terrible.

I must here pause for a moment, and request it to be distinctly understood that, in relating this story, in giving the facts connected with it, and in stating what the Irish peasants' feelings are respecting tithe, I have not the most distant notion of putting forward any opinions of my own on the subject. In the pursuit of my own quiet art, I am happily far removed from the fierce encounter of politics, and I do not wish to offend against the feelings or opinions of anyone in my little volume; and I trust therefore, that I may be permitted to give a sketch of a characteristic incident, as it came to my knowledge, without being mistaken for a partisan.

"I tell the tale as 'twas told to me."

I have said a group of seniors was collected at one end of the room, and as it is meet to give precedence to age, I will endeavour to give some idea of what was going forward amongst them.

There was one old man of the party whose furrowed forehead, compressed eyebrows, piqued nose, and mouth depressed at the corners, at once indicated to a physiognomist a querulous temper. He was one of your doubters upon all occasions, one of the unfailing elements of an argument; as he said himself, he was "dubersome" about everything; and he had hence earned the name of Daddy Dubersome amongst his neighbours. Well, Daddy began to doubt the probability that any such boon as the extinction of tithes was to take place, and said he was "sartin sure 'twas too good news to be thrue."

"Tare anounty," said another, who was the very antithesis of Daddy in his credulous nature; "sure, didn't I see it myself in *prent*."

"I was tould often that things was in prent," returned Daddy drily, "that comes out lies afther, to my own knowledge."

"But sure," added a third, "sure, didn't the Prime Ear himself lay it all out before the Parleymint?"

"What Prime Ear are you talking about, man dear?" said Daddy, rather testily.

"Why, the Prime Ear of His Majesty, and no less. Is that satisfaction for you, eh?"

"Well, and who is the Prime Ear?"

"Why, the Prime Ear of His Majesty, I tould you before. You see, he is the one that hears of everything that is to be done for the whole impire in partic'lar; and bekase he *hears* of everything, that's the raison he is called the Prime *Ear*—and a good raison it is."

"Well, but what has that to do with the tithes, I ask you again?" said Daddy, with his usual pertinacity.

Here he was about to be answered by the former speaker, whose definition of "The Premier" had won him golden opinions amongst the bystanders, when he was prevented by a fourth orator, who rushed into the debate with this very elegant opening:

"Arrah! tare-an-ouns, yiz are settin' me mad, so yiz are.

Why, I wondher anyone 'id be sitch a fool as to go arguefy with that crooked ould disciple there."

"Meanin' me?" said Daddy.

"I'd be sorry to contheradict you, sir," said the other, with an admirable mockery of politeness.

"Thank you, sir," said Daddy, with a dignity more comical than the other's buffoonery.

"You're kindly welkim, Daddy," returned the aggressor. "Sure, you niver b'lieved anything yit; and I wondher anyone would throw away their time sthrivin' to rightify you."

"Come, boys," said O'Hara, interrupting the discourse, with a view to prevent further bickering, "there's no use talkin' about the thing now, for whatever way it is, sure, we are met to bury the tithe, and it's proud I am to see you all here to make merry upon the stringth of it, and I think I heerd Honor say this minit that everything is ready in the barn without, so you'll have no difference of opinion about tackling to the breakfast, or I'm mistaken. Come, my hearties, the mate and the praties is crying, 'Who'll ate me?'—away wid you, that's your sort"—and he enforced his summons to the feast by pushing his guests before him towards the scene of action.

This was an ample barn, where tables of all sorts and sizes were spread, loaded with viands of the most substantial character. Wooden forms, three-legged stools, broken-backed chairs, etc., etc., were in requisition for the accommodation of the female portion of the company, and the men attended first to their wants with a politeness which, though deficient in the external graces of polished life, did credit to their natures. The eating part of the business was accompanied with all the clatter that might be expected to attend such an affair; and when the eatables had been tolerably well demolished, O'Hara stood up in the midst of his guests and said he should propose to them a toast which he knew all the boys would fill their glasses for, and that was, to drink the health of the King, and long life to him, for seeing into the rights of the thing, and doing "such a power" for them, and "*more* power to his elbow."

This toast was prefaced by a speech to his friends and neighbours upon the hardships of tithe in particular, spiced with the *laste taste in life* of politics in general; wherein the Repeal of the Union and Daniel O'Connell cut no inconsiderable figure; yet in the midst of the rambling address, certain glimpses of good sense and shrewd observation might be caught; and the many and powerful objections he advanced against the impost that was to be "extinct" so soon, were put forward with a force and distinctness that were worthy of a better speaker, and might have been found difficult to reply to by a more accustomed hand.

He protested that he thought he had lived long enough when he had witnessed in his own life-time two such national benefits as the Catholic Emancipation Bill and the Abolition of Tithes. O'Hara further declared he was the happiest man alive that day only in the regard "of one thing, and that was, that his reverence, Father Hely (the priest) was not there amongst them;" and certainly the absence of the pastor on an occasion of festivity in the house of a snug farmer is of rare occurrence in Ireland. "But you see," said O'Hara, "whin his rivirince heerd what it was we wor goin' to do, he thought it would be *purtier* on his part for to have nothin' whatsomiver to to do with it in hand, act, or part; and indeed, boys, that shows a great deal of good breedin' in Father Hely."

This was quite agreed to by the company; and after many cheers for O'Hara's speech, and some other toasts pertinent to the occasion, the health of O'Hara as the founder of the feast, with the usual addenda of long life, prosperity, etc., to him and his, was drunk, and then preparations were entered into for proceeding with the ceremony of the funeral.

"I b'lieve we have nothin to wait for now," said O'Hara, "since you won't have any more to drink, boys; so let us set about it at once, and make a *clane* day's work of it."

"Oh, we're not quite ready yit," said Larry Lanigan, who seemed to be a sort of master of the ceremonies on the occasion.

"What's the delay?" asked O'Hara.

"Why, the chief *murners* is not arrived yit."

"What murners are you talkin' about, man?" said the other.

"Why, you know, at a *grand* berrin' they have always chief murners, and there's a pair that I ordhered to be brought here for that same."

"Myself doesn't know anything about murners," said O'Hara, "for I niver seen anything finer than the *keeners* at a berrin'; but Larry's up to the ways of the quol'ty, as well as of his own sort."

"But you wouldn't have keeners for the tithe, would you? Sure, the keeners is to say all the good they can of the departed, and more if they can invint it; but sure, the divil a good thing at all they could say of the tithe, barrin' it was lies they wor tellin', and so it would only be throwin' away throuble."

"Thrue for you, Lanigan."

"Besides, it is like a grand berrin' belongin' to the quol'ty to have chief murners, and you know the tithe was aiqual to a lord or king a'most for power."

In a short time the "murners," as Larry called them, arrived in custody of half a dozen of Larry's chosen companions, to whom he had entrusted the execution of the mission. These chief mourners were two tithe proctors, who had been taken forcibly from their homes by the Lanigan party, and threatened with death unless they attended the summons of Larry to be present at "The Berrin'."

Their presence was hailed with a great shout, and the poor devils looked excessively frightened; but they were assured by O'Hara they had nothing to fear.

"I depend an you, Mr. O'Hara, for seeing us safe out of their hands," said one of them, for the other was dumb from terror.

"So you may," was the answer O'Hara returned. "Hurt nor harm shall not be put an you; I give you my word o' that."

"Divil a harm," said Larry. "We'll only put you into a shoot o' clothes that is ready for you, and you may look as melancholy as you plaze, for it is murners you are to be. Well, Honor," said he, addressing O'Hara's daughter, "have you got the mithres and vestments ready, as I tould you?"

"Yes," said Honor; "here comes Biddy Mulligan with them from the house, for Biddy herself helped me to make them."

"And who had a betther right?" said Larry, "when it was herself that laid it all out complate, the whole thing from the beginnin', and sure enough but it was a bright thought of her. Faix, he'll be the *loocky* man that gets Biddy yet."

"You had betther have her yourself, I think," said Honor, with an arch look at Larry, full of meaning.

"An it's that same I've been thinkin' of for some time," said Larry, laughing, and returning Honor's look with one that repaid it with interest. "But where is she at all? Oh, here she comes with the duds, and Mike Nooman afther her. Throth, he's follower' her about all this mornin' like a sucking calf. I'm afeard Mikee is going to *sarcumvint* me wid Biddy; but he'd betther mind what he's at."

Here the conversation was interrupted by the advance of Biddy Mulligan, "and Mikee Nooman afther her," bearing some grotesque imitation of clerical vestments made of coarse sacking, and two enormous head-dresses made of straw in the fashion of mitres. These were decorated with black rags hung fantastically about them, while the vestments were smeared over with black stripes in no very regular order.

"Come here," said Larry to the tithe proctors; "come here, until we put you into your *regimentals.*"

"What are you goin' to do with us, *Mr.* Lanigan?" said the poor, frightened wretch, while his knees knocked together with terror.

"We are just goin' to make a pair o' bishops of you," said Lanigan; "and sure, that's promotion for you."

"Oh, Mr. O'Hara," said the proctor, "sure, you won't let them tie us up in them sacks."

"Do you hear what he calls the iligant vestments we made a' purpose for him? They are sackcloth, to be sure, and why not, seeing as how that you are to be the chief murners? and sackcloth and ashes is what you must be dhressed in, accordin' to raison. Here, my buck," said the rollicking Larry, "I'll be your vally de sham myself," and he proceeded to put the dress on the terrified tithe proctor.

"Oh, Mr. Lanigan dear!" said he, "don't murther me, *if you plaze.*"

"Murther you! Arrah, who's going to murther you? Do you think I'd dirty my hands with killin' a snakin' tithe procthor?"

"Indeed, that's thrue, Mr. Lanigan; it would not be worth your while."

"Here now," said Larry; "hould your head till I put the mithre an you, and make you a bishop complate. But wait a bit; throth, I was nigh forgettin' the ashes, and that would have been a great loss to both o' you, bekase you wouldn't be right murners at all without them, and the people would think you wor only *purtendin'*." This last bit of Larry's waggery produced great merriment amongst the bystanders, for the unfortunate tithe proctors were looking at that moment most doleful examples of wretchedness. A large shovelful of turf ashes was now shaken over their heads, and then they were decorated with their mitres. "Tut, man," said Larry to one of them, "don't thrimble like a dog in a wet sack. Oh, thin, look at him how pale he's turned, the dirty coward that he is. I tell you we're not goin' to do you any hurt, so you needn't be lookin' in sitch mortial dhread. By gor, you're as white as a pen'orth o' curds in a sweep's fist!"

With many such jokes at the expense of the tithe proctors they were attired in their caricature robes and mitres, and presented with a pair of pitchforks, by way of crosiers, and were recommended at the same time to make hay while the sun shone, "bekase the fine weather would be lavin' them soon," with many other bitter sarcasms, conveyed in the language of ridicule.

The procession was now soon arranged, and as they had chief mourners, it was thought a good point of contrast to have their chief rejoicers as well. To this end, in a large cart they put a sow and her litter of pigs, decorated with ribands, a sheaf of wheat standing proudly erect, a bowl of large potatoes, which, at Honor O'Hara's suggestion, were *boiled*, that they might be *laughing* on the occasion, and over these was hung a rude banner, on which was written: "We may stay at home now."

In this cart Hoppy Houligan, the fiddler, with a piper as a

coadjutor, rasped and squeaked their best to the tune of "Go to
the devil and shake yourself," which was meant to convey a
delicate hint to the tithes for the future.

The whole assemblage of people—and it was immense—then
proceeded to the spot where it was decided the tithe was to be
interred, as the most fitting place to receive such a deposit, and
this place was called by what they considered the very appropriate
name of "The Devil's Bit."

In a range of hills, in the neighbourhood where this singular
occurrence took place, there is a sudden gap occurs in the outline
of the ridge, which is stated to have been formed by his sable
majesty taking a bite out of the mountain; whether it was spite or
hunger that had made him do so is not ascertained, but he evidently
did not consider it a very savoury morsel; for, it is said, he spat
it out again, and the rejected *morceau* forms the rock of Cashel.
Such is the wild legend of this wild spot, and here was the interment of the tithe to be achieved, as an appropriate addition to
the Devil's Bit.

The procession now moved onward, and as it proceeded, its
numbers were considerably augmented. Its approach was looked
for by a scout on every successive hill it came within sight of,
and a wild halloo, or the winding of a cow's horn, immediately
succeeded, which called forth scores of fresh attendants upon
"The Berrin'." Thus their numbers were increased every quarter
of a mile they went, until, on their arriving at the foot of the hill
which they were to ascend to reach their final destination, the
multitude assembled presented a most imposing appearance. In
the course of their march, the great point of attraction for the
young men and women was the cart that bore the piper and
fiddler, and the road was rather danced than walked over in this
quarter.

The other distinguished portion of the train was where the two
tithe proctors played their parts of chief mourners. They were
the delight of all the little ragged urchins in the country; the
half-naked young vagabonds hung on their flanks, plucked at
their vestments, made wry faces at them, called them by many
ridiculous names, and an occasional lump of clay was slily flung
at their mitres, which were too tempting a "cock shot" to be
resisted. The multitude now wound up the hill, and the mingling
of laughter, of singing and shouting, produced a wild compound
of sound that rang far and wide. As they doubled an angle in
the road, which opened the Devil's Bit full upon their view, they
saw another crowd assembled there, which consisted of persons
from the other side of the hills, who could not be present at the
breakfast, nor join the procession, but who attended upon the
spot where the interment was to take place. As soon as the

approach of the funeral train was perceived from the top of the hill, the mass of people there sent forth a shout of welcome, which was returned by those from below.

Short space now served to bring both parties together, and the digging of a grave did not take long with such a plenty of able hands for the purpose. "Come, boys," said Larry Lanigan to two or three of his companions, "while they are digging the grave here, we'll go cut some sods to put over it when the thievin' tithe is buried; not for any respect I have for it in partic'lar, but that we may have the place smooth and clane to dance over afterwards; and may I never shuffle the brogue again if myself and Honor O'Hara won't be the first pair that'll set you a patthern."

All was soon ready for the interment; the tithe coffin was lowered into the pit, and the shouting that rent the air was terrific.

As they were about to fill up the grave with earth, their wild hurrah, that had rung out so loudly, was answered by a fierce shout at some distance, and all eyes were turned towards the quarter whence it arose to see from whom it proceeded, for it was evidently a solitary voice that had thus arrested their attention.

Toiling up the hill, supporting himself with a staff, and bearing a heavy load in a wallet slung over his shoulders, appeared an elderly man whose dress proclaimed him at once to be a person who depended on eleemosynary contributions for his subsistence; and many, when they caught the first glimpse of him, proclaimed at once that it was "Tatther the Road" was coming.

"Tatther the Road" was the very descriptive name that had been applied to this poor creature, for he was always travelling about the highways; he never rested even at nights in any of the houses of the peasants, who would have afforded him shelter, but seemed to be possessed by a restless spirit that urged him to constant motion. Of course, the poor creature sometimes slept, but it must have been under such shelter as a hedge, or cave, or gravel-pit might afford, for in the habitation of man he was never seen to sleep; and indeed, I never knew anyone who had seen this strange being in the act of sleep. This fact attached a sort of mysterious character to the wanderer, and many would tell you that "he wasn't right," and firmly believed that he never slept at all. His mind was unsettled, and though he never became offensive in any degree from his mental aberration, yet the nature of his distemper often induced him to do very extraordinary things, and whenever the gift of speech was upon him (for he was habitually taciturn), he would make an outpouring of some rhapsody, in which occasional bursts of very powerful language and striking imagery would occur.   Indeed, the peasants said that "sometimes 'twould make your hair stand an end to hear Tatther the Road make a *noration*."

This poor man's history, as far as I could learn, was a very melancholy one.   In the rebellion of '98 his cabin had been burned over his head by the yeomanry, after every violation that could disgrace his hearth had been committed.   He and his son, then little more than a boy, had attempted to defend their hut, and they were both left for dead.   His wife and his daughter, a girl of sixteen, were also murdered.   The wretched father, unfortunately, recovered his life, but his reason was gone for ever.   Even in the midst of his poverty and madness, there was a sort of respect attached to this singular man.   Though depending on charity for his meat and drink, he could not well be called a beggar, for he never asked for anything—even on the road, when some passenger, ignorant of his wild history, saw the poor wanderer, a piece of money was often bestowed to the silent appeal of his rags, his haggard features, and his grizzly hair and beard.

Thus eternally up and down the country was he moving about, and hence his name of "Tatther the Road."

It was not long until the old man gained the summit of the hill, but while he was approaching, many were the "wonders" what in the name of fortune could have brought Tatther the Road there.   "And by dad," said one, "he's pullin' fut at a great rate, and it's wondherful how an ould cock like him can clamber up the hill so fast."

"Aye," said another; "and with the woight he's carrying too."

"Sure enough," said a third.   "Faix, he's got a fine lob in his wallet to-day."

"Whisht!" said O'Hara.   "Here he comes, and his ears are as sharp as needles."

"And his eyes too," said a woman.   "Lord be good to me, did you ever see poor Tatther's eyes look so terrible bright afore?"

And indeed this remark was not uncalled for, for the eyes of the old man almost gleamed from under the shaggy brows that were darkly bent over them, as, with long strides, he approached the crowd which opened before him, and he stalked up to the side of the grave and threw down the ponderous wallet, which fell to the ground with a heavy crash.

"You were going to close the grave too soon," were the first words he uttered.

"Sure, whin the tithe is wanst buried, what more have we to do?" said one of the bystanders.

"Aye, you have put the tithe in the grave—but will it stay there?"

"Why, indeed," said Larry Lanigan. "I think he'd be a bould resurrection man that would come to rise it."

"I have brought you something here to lie heavy on it, and 'twill never rise more," said the maniac, striking forth his arm fiercely, and clenching his hand firmly.

"And what have you brought us, agrah?" said O'Hara kindly to him.

"Look here!" said the other, unfolding his wallet and displaying five or six large stones.

Some were tempted to laugh, but a mysterious dread of the wild being before them prevented any outbreak of mirth.

"God help the craythur!" said a woman, so loud as to be heard. "He has brought a bag full o' stones to throw a-top o' the tithes to keep them down. O wisha! wisha! poor craythur!"

"Aye, stones!" said the maniac; "but do you know what stones these are? Look, woman—" and his manner became intensely impressive from the excitement, even of madness, under which he was acting. "Look, I say—there's not a stone there that's not a curse—aye, a curse so heavy that nothing can ever rise that falls under it."

"Oh, I don't want to say against it, dear," said the woman.

The maniac did not seem to notice her submissive answer, but pursuing his train of madness, continued his address in his native tongue, whose figurative and poetical construction was heightened in its effect by a manner and action almost theatrically descriptive.

"You all remember the Widow Dempsy. The first choice of her bosom was long gone, but the son she loved was left to her, and her heart was not quite lonely. And at the widow's hearth there was still a welcome for the stranger—and the son of her heart made his choice, like the father before him, and the joy of the widow's house was increased, for the son of her heart was happy. And in due time the widow welcomed the fair-haired child of her son to the world, and a dream of her youth came over her, as she saw the joy of her son and her daughter, when they kissed the fair-haired child. But the hand of God was heavy in the land, and the fever fell hard upon the poor, and the widow was again bereft; for the son of her heart was taken, and the wife of his bosom also, and the fair-haired child was left an orphan. And the widow would have laid down her bones and died, but for the fair-haired child that had none to look to but her. And the widow blessed God's name and bent her head to the blow; and the orphan that was left to her was the pulse of her heart, and often she looked on his pale face with a fearful eye, for health was not on the cheek of the boy; but she cherished him tenderly.

"But the ways of the world grew crooked to the lone woman, when the son that was the staff of her age was gone, and one trouble followed another ; but still the widow was not quite destitute.   And what was it brought the heavy stroke of distress and disgrace to the widow's door ?   The tithe !   The widow's cow was driven and sold to pay a few shillings ; the drop of milk was no longer in the widow's house, and the tender child that needed the nourishment wasted away before the widow's eyes, like snow from the ditch, and died ; and fast the widow followed the son of her heart and his fair-haired boy.

"And now the home of an honest race is a heap of rubbish, and the bleak wind whistles over the hearth where the warm welcome was ever found ; and the cold frog crouches under the ruins.

"These stones are from that desolate place, and the curse of God that follows oppression is on them.   And let them be cast into the grave, and they will lie with the weight of a mountain on the monster that is buried for ever."

So saying, he lifted stone after stone, and flung them fiercely into the pit ; then, after a moment's pause upon its verge, he suddenly strode away with the same noiseless step in which he had approached, and left the scene in silence.

THE WHITE HORSE OF THE PEPPERS

A LEGEND OF THE BOYNE

IT was the night of the 2nd of July, in the year 1690, that a small remnant of a discomfited army was forming its position, in no very good order, on the slope of a wild hill on the borders of the county of Dublin.   In front of a small square tower a sentinel was pacing up and down, darkly brooding over the disastrous fight of the preceding day, and his measured tread was sometimes broken by the fierce stamp of his foot upon the earth, as some bitter thought and muttered curse arose, when the feelings of the man overcame the habit of the soldier.   The hum of the arrival of a small squadron of horse came from the vale below, borne up the hill on the faint breeze that sometimes freshens a summer's night, but neither the laugh nor the song, which so often enlivens a military post, mingled with the sound.   The very trumpet seemed to have lost the inspiring tingle of its tone, and its blast sounded heavily on the ear of the sentinel.

"There come more of our retreating comrades," thought he, as he stalked before the low portal it was his duty to guard. "Retreating.   Curse the word !   Shall we never do anything but fall back and back before this d—d Dutchman and his followers ? And yesterday too, with so fine an opportunity of cutting the rascals to pieces, and all thrown away, and so much hard fighting to go for nothing. Oh, if Sarsefield had led us, we'd have another tale to tell!" And here he struck the heavy heel of his war-boot into the ground, and hurried up and down. But he was roused from his angry musing by the sound of a horse's tramp, which indicated a rapid approach to the tower, and he soon perceived through the gloom a horseman approaching at a gallop. The sentinel challenged the cavalier, who returned the countersign, and was then permitted to ride up to the door of the tower. He was mounted on a superb charger, whose silky coat of milk-white was much travel-stained, and the heaviness of whose breathing told of recent hard riding. The horseman alighted ; his dress was of a mixed character, implying that war was not his profession, though the troubled nature of the times had engaged him in it. His head had no defensive covering ; he wore the slouched hat of a civilian common to the time, but his body was defended by the cuirass of a trooper, and a heavy sword, suspended by a broad cross belt, was at his side—these alone bespoke the soldier, for the large and massively mounted pistols that protruded from the holsters at his saddle-bow were no more than any gentleman, at the time, might have been provided with.

"Will you hold the rein of my horse," said he to the sentry, "while I remain in the castle ? "

"I am a sentinel, sir," answered the soldier, "and cannot."

"I will not remain more than a few minutes."

"I dare not, sir, while I'm on duty—but I suppose you will find some one in the castle who will take charge of your horse."

The stranger now knocked at the door of the tower, and after some questions and answers in token of amity had passed between him and those inside, it was opened.

"Let some one take charge of my horse," said he ; "I do not want him to be stabled, as I shall not remain here long, but I have ridden him hard, and he is warm, so let him be walked up and down until I am ready to get into the saddle again." He then entered the tower, and was ushered into a small and rude apartment, where a man of between fifty and sixty years of age, seated on a broken chair, though habited in a rich *robe de chambre*, was engaged in conversation with a general officer, a man of fewer years, whose finger was indicating certain points upon a map, which, with many other papers, lay on a rude table before them. Extreme dejection was the prevailing expression that overspread the countenance of the elder, while there mingled with the sadness that marked the noble features of the other a tinge of subdued anger, as certain suggestions he offered, when he laid his finger from time to time on the map, were received with coldness, if not with refusal.

"Here at least we can make a bold stand," said the general, and his eye flashed, and his brow knit as he spoke.

"I fear not, Sarsefield," said the king, for it was the unfortunate James the Second who spoke.

Sarsefield withdrew his hand suddenly from the map, and folding his arms, became silent.

"May it please you, my liege," said the horseman, whose entry had not been noticed by either Sarsefield or his sovereign. "I hope I have not intruded on your Majesty."

"Who speaks?" said the king, as he shaded his eyes from the light that burned on the table, and looked into the gloom where the other was standing.

"Your enemies, my liege," said Sarsefield, with some bitterness, "would not be so slow to discover a tried friend of your Majesty—'tis the White Horseman;" and Sarsefield, as he spoke, gave a look full of welcome and joyous recognition towards him.

The horseman felt, with the pride of a gallant spirit, all that the general's look and manner conveyed, and he bowed his head respectfully to the leader, whose boldness and judgment he so often had admired.

"Ha! my faithful White Horseman," said the king.

"Your Majesty's poor and faithful subject, Gerald Pepper," was the answer.

"You have won the name of the White Horseman," said Sarsefield, "and you deserve to wear it."

The horseman bowed.

"The general is right," said the king. "I shall never choose to remember you by any other name. You and your white horse have done good service."

"Would that they could have done more, my liege," was the laconic and modest reply.

"Would that everyone," laying some stress on the word, "had been as true to the cause *yesterday!*" said Sarsefield.

"And what has brought you here?" said the king, anxious perhaps to escape from the thought which his general's last words had suggested.

"I came, my liege, to ask permission to bid your Majesty farewell, and beg the privilege to kiss your royal hand."

"Farewell?" echoed the king, startled at the word. "Are *you*, too, going?—everyone deserts me!" There was intense anguish in the tone of his voice, for as he spoke his eye fell upon a ring he wore, which encircled the portrait of his favourite daughter, Anne, and the remembrance that she, *his own child*, had excited the same remark from the lips of her father—that bitter remembrance came across his soul and smote him to the heart. He was suddenly silent—his brow contracted—he closed his eyes in anguish, and *one* bitter tear sprang from under either lid at the thought. He passed his hand across his face, and wiped away the womanish evidence of his weakness.

"Do not say I desert you, my liege," said Gerald Pepper. "I leave you, 'tis true, for the present, but I do not leave you until I see no way in which I can be longer useful. While in my own immediate district, there were many ways in which my poor services might be made available; my knowledge of the county, of its people and its resources, its passes and its weak points, were of service. But here, or farther southward, where your Majesty is going, I can no longer do anything which might win the distinction that your Majesty and General Sarsefield are pleased to honour me with."

"You have still a stout heart, a clear head, a bold arm, and a noble horse," said Sarsefield.

"I have also a weak woman and helpless children, general," said Gerald Pepper.

The appeal was irresistible—Sarsefield was silent.

"But though I cannot longer aid with my arm, my wishes and my prayers shall follow your Majesty, and whenever I may be thought an agent to be made useful, my king has but to command the willing services of his subject."

"Faithfully promised," said the king.

"The promise shall be faithfully kept," said his follower; "but before I leave, may I beg the favour of a moment's conversation with your Majesty."

"Speak anything you have to communicate before Sarsefield," said the king.

Gerald Pepper hesitated for a moment; he was struggling between his sovereign's command and his own delicacy of feeling; but overcoming the latter, in deference to the former, he said:

"Your Majesty's difficulties with respect to money supplies—"

"I know, I know," said the king somewhat impatiently, "I owe you five hundred pieces."

"Oh, my liege," said the devoted subject, dropping on his knee before him, "deem me not so unworthy as to seek to remind your Majesty of the trifle you did me the honour to allow me to lay at your disposal; I only regret I had not the means of contributing more. It is not that; but I have brought here another hundred pieces, it is all I can raise at present, and if your Majesty will further honour me by the acceptance of so poor a pittance, when the immediate necessities of your army may render every trifle a matter of importance, I shall leave you with a more contented spirit, conscious that I have done all within my power for my king." And as he spoke, he laid on the table a purse containing the gold.

"I cannot deny that we are sorely straitened," said the king, "but I do not like—"

"Pray do not refuse it, my liege," said Gerald, still kneeling— "do not refuse the last poor service your subject may ever have it in his power to do in your cause."

"Well," said the king, "I accept it—but I would not do so if I were not sure of having one day the means of rewarding your loyalty and generosity." And thus allowing himself to be the dupe of his own fallacious hopes, he took from poor Gerald Pepper the last hundred guineas he had in his possession, with that happy facility kings have always exhibited in accepting sacrifices from enthusiastic and self-devoted followers.

"My mission here is ended now," said Gerald. "May I be permitted to kiss my sovereign's hand?"

"Would that all my subjects were as faithful," said James, as he held out his hand to Gerald Pepper, who kissed it respectfully, and then arose.

"What do you propose doing when you leave me?" said the king.

"To return to my home as soon as I may, my liege."

"If it be my fate to be driven from my kingdom by my unnatural son-in-law, I hope he may be merciful to my people, and that none may suffer from their adherence to the cause of their rightful sovereign."

"I wish, my liege," said Gerald, "that he may have half the consideration for his *Irish* subjects which your Majesty had for your *English* ones;" and he shook his head doubtfully as he spoke, and his countenance suddenly fell.

A hard-drawn sigh escaped from Sarsefield, and then, biting his lip, and with knitted brow, he exchanged a look of bitter meaning with Gerald Pepper.

"Adieu then," said the king, "since you will go. See our good friend to his saddle, Sarsefield. Once more, good-night! King James will not forget the White Horseman." So saying, he waved his hand in adieu. Gerald Pepper bowed low to his sovereign, and Sarsefield followed him from the chamber. They were both silent till they arrived at the portal of the tower, and when the door was opened, Sarsefield crossed the threshold with the visitor, and stepped into the fresh air, which he inhaled audibly three or four times, as if it were a relief to him.

"Good-night, General Sarsefield!" said Gerald.

"Good-night, my gallant friend!" said Sarsefield, in a voice that expressed much vexation of spirit.

"Be not so much cast down, general," said Gerald; "better days may come, and fairer fields be fought."

"Never, never!" said Sarsefield. "Never was a fairer field than that of yesterday; never was a surer game if it had been rightly played. But there is a fate, my friend, hangs over our cause, and I fear that destiny throws against us."

"Speak not thus, general—think not thus."

"Would that I could think otherwise—but I fear I speak prophetically."

"Do you then give up the cause?" said Gerald, in surprise.

"No," said Sarsefield firmly, almost fiercely; "never! I *may* die in the cause, but I will never desert it, as long as I have a troop to follow me—but I must not loiter here. Farewell! Where is your horse?"

"I left him in the care of one of the attendants."

"I hope you are well mounted."

"Yes; here comes my charger."

"What!" said Sarsefield, "the white horse!"

"Yes, surely," said Gerald; "you never saw me back any other."

"But after the tremendous fatigue of yesterday," said Sarsefield, in surprise, "is it possible he is still fresh?"

"Fresh enough to serve my turn for to-night," said Gerald, as he mounted into the saddle. The white horse gave a low neigh of seeming satisfaction as his master resumed his seat.

"Noble brute!" said Sarsefield, as he patted the horse on the neck, which was arched into the proud bend of a bold steed who knows a bold rider is on his back.

"And now farewell, general!" said Gerald, extending his hand.

"Farewell, my friend! Fate is unkind to deny the charm of a victorious cause to so gallant a spirit."

"There is more gallantry in remaining unshaken under defeat; and you, general, are a bright example of the fact."

"Good-night, good-night!" said Sarsefield, anxious to escape from hearing his own praise, and wringing the hand that was presented to him with much warmth; he turned towards the portal of the tower, but before he entered, Gerald again addressed him.

"Pray tell me, general, is your regiment here? Before I go, I would wish to take leave of the officers of that gallant corps, in whose ranks I have had the honour to draw a sword."

"They are not yet arrived. They are on the road, perhaps, by this time; but I ordered they should be the last to leave Dublin, for as yesterday they suffered the disgrace of being led the first out of the battle, I took care they should have the honour of being the last in the rear to-night, to cover our retreat."

"Then remember me to them," said Gerald.

"They can never forget the White Horseman," said Sarsefield;

"and they shall hear you left the kind word of remembrance for them. Once more, good-night!"

"Good-night, general! God's blessing be upon you!"

"Amen!" said Sarsefield; "and with you."

They then wrung each other's hand in silence. Sarsefield re-entered the tower, and Gerald Pepper, giving the rein to his steed, the white horse left the spot as rapidly as he had approached it.

For some days Gerald Pepper remained in Dublin, where he had ridden the night after his interview with the king. The house of a friend afforded him shelter, for he did not deem it prudent to be seen in public, as his person was too well known, and his services to King James too notorious not to render such a course dangerous. He therefore was obliged to submit to being cooped up in an attic in his friend's house while he stayed in the city. His sojourn in Dublin originated in his anxiety to hear what was going forward at headquarters; for there was but too much reason to fear, from all former examples in Ireland, that forfeitures to a great extent would take place, and to ascertain whether his name should be amongst the proscribed was the object that detained him from his home. His patience, however, became exhausted, and one morning when his friend came to speak with him previously to going forth into the city to see and hear what was stirring, Gerald said he could bear the restraint of his situation and the separation from his family no longer.

"My poor Magdalene," said he, "can but ill endure the suspense attendant upon my protracted absence, and I fear her gentle nature will sink under so severe a trial; therefore, my excellent, my kind friend, to-morrow morning I will leave you."

"Perhaps a day or two more may set your mind at rest—or, at least, will end your suspense respecting the course about to be pursued with the adherents of the king."

"I wait no longer than to-day," said Gerald; "I am resolved."

His friend sallied forth, with this parting assurance from his guest, and had not been absent more than an hour or two when he returned. A low tap at the door of Gerald's apartment announced his presence; the bolt was drawn, and he entered.

"Gerald!" said his friend, grasping his hand, and remaining silent.

"I understand," said Gerald; "I am a ruined man."

How deeply expressive of meaning mere voice and action become under the influence of feeling! Here the uttering of a name, and the grasping of a hand, were more potent than language; for words could not so soon have expressed the fatal truth, as the electric sympathy that conveyed to Gerald's mind the meaning of his friend. How mysterious the influence between thought and action! I do not mean the action that is the result of mere habit, but the action which we cannot avoid, being a law of Nature, and which everyone indulges in, under the influence of strong affections of the mind. Grief and joy, hope and despair, fear and courage, have each an action to distinguish them, as strongly marked as the distinctions which separate different species.

His friend made no other answer to Gerald's ejaculation than a suppressed groan, and then another fierce grasp of the hand and a melancholy look into each other's eyes passed between them. They then parted palms, and each took a seat, and sat opposite each other for some minutes in perfect silence. In that interval the minds of both were busily engaged. Gerald's thoughts flew back at once to his home—his dear home; he thought of his sweet Magdalene and his darling children. He saw Magdalene deprived of the comforts of life, without a roof to shelter her, and heard his babes cry for food, as they shivered in the cold; the thought overcame him, and he hid his face in his hands. The mind of his friend had been engaged at the moment as to what was the best course Gerald could pursue under existing circumstances, and his case, though hard, seemed not hopeless. Therefore, when he saw Gerald sink as he had done, unconscious of the bitter thought that overcame him, he rose from his seat, and laying his hand kindly on the shoulder of his friend, he said:

"Cheer up; cheer up, man! Matters are not so desperate as to reduce you to despair at once. You are not the man I take you for if such a blow as this, heavy though it be, overcome you."

Gerald looked up; his eye was bright and his countenance serene, as he met the compassionating look that was cast upon him; he had recovered all his self-possession. The voice of his friend had dispelled the terrible vision that fancy had presented him with, and recalled his ideas from home, where his affectionate nature first prompted them to fly.

"I do not despair," he said. "But there was a dreadful thought arose, which quite unmanned me for the moment, but you see I am calm again."

"Yes; you look like yourself now."

"And will not relapse, I promise you. When once I know the worst, I am equal to meet my destiny, whatever it may be: and having said so much, tell me what that fate is. Ruined I know I am; but tell me in what degree. Is my person denounced, as well as my patrimony plundered from me?"

"No. Your life and freedom are not menaced, but your property is forfeited, and in all probability, many days will not elapse until you may be dispossessed by some new master."

"Days!" said Gerald, "hours you mean; these gentry make quick work of such matters. I must hasten home directly."

"Will not to-morrow answer?" asked his friend; "to-day may be profitably spent here, in consulting as to your best mode of proceeding regarding the future."

"The lapse of one day might produce a loss of some consequence to a man who is robbed of every acre he has in the world."

"How?" asked his friend.

"I would like to be beforehand with the plunderers, that I might secure any small articles of value, such as jewels or plate, from their clutches."

"Surely *these* are not included in the forfeiture of a man's lands?"

"The troopers of the Prince of Orange will not be very nice in making such legal distinctions; therefore I will hasten home, and save all I can from the wreck."

"Before you go, one word more," said his friend. "If your property happen to fall to the lot of a trooper, as you say—one of these fellows would rather have a round sum of hard cash than be encumbered with lands—and if you manage matters well, a few hundred pieces may buy off the invader. I have heard of thousands of broad acres being so saved in Cromwell's time."

"That hope of rescue is debarred me," said Gerald; "all the disposable cash I had I gave to the king."

"What! not a rouleau left?"

"The last hundred I could command I gave him."

"That's unfortunate," said his friend; "the more so, as it is beyond my power to supply the want."

"I know it—I know it," said Gerald impatiently; "don't name it. If Heaven be pleased to spare me life and health, I shall be able to weather the storm. I have as much plate and other valuables as, when converted into cash, will enable me to carry my family to France, and still leave something in my purse. At the French Court, I hope I can reckon on a good reception, and I have my sword to offer to the service of the French king, and I doubt not, from the interest I think I can command, that I should find employment in the ranks of gallant Louis."

"You have decided soon on your course of proceeding, Gerald," said his friend, somewhat surprised at the coolness and consideration he exhibited.

"Yes; and you wonder at it," said Gerald, "because you saw me cast down for a moment; but the bitter thought that overcame me is past. I see distinctly the path before me which will save my wife and children from want, and that once secured, I repine not, nor shall cast one regret after the property I have lost in so noble a cause. Farewell, my friend! Thanks and blessings be yours, from me and mine, for all your care for me. Before I leave Ireland you shall see me again, but for the present, farewell!"

In ten minutes more Gerald Pepper was in his saddle, and his trusty steed was bearing him to the home which cost him so much anxiety.

As he pushed his way rapidly along the road, his thoughts were so wholly engrossed by his present calamitous circumstances, that he heeded no outward object, nor even uttered one cheering word, or sound of encouragement, to his favourite horse; and it was not until the noble round tower of Swords rose upon his view that he became conscious of how far he had progressed homewards, and of the speed with which he had been going. He drew the bridle when he had arrived at the summit of the hill that commands the extensive plain which lies at the foot of the mountain range that skirts the counties of Dublin and Kildare, and stretches onward into Meath and Lowth, and the more northern counties. The mountains of Carlingford and Mourne spired upwards in their beautiful forms, where the extreme distance melted into blue haze, and the sea could scarcely be distinguished from the horizon; but nearer, on his right, its level line of blue was distinctly defined, as glimpses of it appeared over the woods of Feltrum and Malahide, occasionally broken by the promontory of Howth, the grotesque pinnacles of Ireland's Eye, and the bold Island of Lambay.

As he was leisurely descending the hill into the village beneath him, a figure suddenly appeared on a bank that overhung the road, and leaped into the highway; he ran over towards Gerald, and clasping his knee with both hands, said, with fervour:

"God save you, Masther Gerald dear! Oh, thin, is that yourself safe and sound agin?"

"What!" said Gerald in surprise. "Rory Oge! by what chance are you here?"

"You may say chance, sure enough. Wait a minit, and I'll tell you, for it's out o' breath I am with the race I made across the field, without, when I seen you powdherin' down the road at the rate of a hunt, and afeard I was you would be gone past and out o' call before I could get to the ditch."

"Is my family well," said Gerald, "can you tell me?"

"They're all hearty."

"Thanks be to God!" said Gerald devoutly.

"Amen!" responded Rory.

"My poor wife, I suppose, has been fretting?"

"Throth, to be sure, an' no wondher; the poor misthriss; but she keeps up wondherful, and I was goin' to Dublin myself to look for you."

"You, Rory!"

"Yis, me; and why not? and very nigh missin' you I was, and would, only for Tareaway here," putting his hand on the neck of the horse; "for you wor so far off when I first got a sight o' you, that I think I wouldn't have minded you, but I knew the proud toss of Tareaway's head, more betoken the white coat of him makes him so noticeable."

"But who sent you to Dublin to look for me?"

"Myself, and nobody else—it was my own notion; for I seen the misthriss was onaisy, and I had a misgivin' somehow that I'd come upon you, and sure enough, I did, for here you are."

"But not in Dublin, Rory," said Gerald, who could not forbear a smile even in his sadness.

"Well, it's all one, sure," said Rory, "for here you are, and I found you, as I said before; and now, Masther Gerald dear, that I see you're safe yourself, will you tell me how matthers goes on wid the king and his cause?"

"Badly enough, I fear, Rory, and worse with his friends," said Gerald, with a heavy sigh.

Rory caught at his meaning with native intelligence, and looking up into his face with the most touching expression of affection and anxiety, said: "God keep uz from harm, Masther Gerald dear, and sure, it's not yourself that is come to throuble, I hope."

"Yes, Rory," said Gerald; "I am a ruined man."

"Oh, Masther Gerald dear, don't say that," said Rory, with much emotion. "Who dar' ruinate you?" said he indignantly; and then, his voice dropping into a tone of tenderness, he added: "Who'd have the heart to ruinate you?"

"Those who have nothing to fear nor love me for, Rory," answered Gerald.

"Is it thim vagabone Williamites—thim thraitors to their king and their God and their counthry—thim outlandish villians! The Peppers o' Ballygarth ruinated! Oh, what will the counthry come to, at all, at all! But how is it they *can* ruinate you, Masther Gerald?"

"By leaving me without house or land."

"You don't want to make me b'live they'll dhrive you out o' Ballygarth?"

"Ballygarth is no longer mine, Rory. I shall not have an acre left me."

"Why, who *dar* for to take it from you?"

"Those who have the power to do so now, Rory; the conquerors at the Boyne."

"Why, bad cess to them. Sure, they won the day there, and more's the pity," said Rory, "and what do they want more? Sure, whin they won the day, that's enough—we don't deny it; and sorry I am to say that same; but sure, that should contint any raisonable faction, without robbin' the people afther. Why, suppose a chap was impident to me, and that I gev him a wallopin' for it, sure, that 'ud be no raison why I should take the clothes aff his back, or rob him iv any thrifle he might have about him; and isn't it *all one?* Sure, instid of havin' a crow over him for bein' the best man, I'd only be a common robber, knockin' a man down for what I could get. And what differ is there betune the cases?"

"That you are only an humble man, Rory, and that the other person is a king."

"Well, and sure if he is a king, shouldn't he behave as *sitch,* and give a good example, instead of doin' a dirty turn like that? Why should a king do what a poor man like me would be ashamed of?"

Here Rory broke out into a mingled strain of indiguation against the oppressor and lament for the oppressed, and wound up by this very argumentative and convincing peroration:

"And so that furrin moroder, they call a king, is goin' to rob and plundher and murdher you intirely—and for what, I'd like to know? Is it bekase you stud up for the rale king, your own king, and your counthry, it is? Bad fortune to him, sure, if he had any honour at all, he'd only like you the betther iv it; and instead of pursuin' you with his blackguard *four-futted* laws, it's plazed he ought to be that you didn't come acrass him yourself when your swoord was in your hand, and the white horse undher you. Oh, the yellow-faced thief! he has no gratitude!"

A good deal more of equally good *reasoning* and abuse was indulged in by Rory, as he walked beside the white horse and his rider. Gerald remained silent until they arrived at the foot of the hill, and were about to enter the village, when he asked his companion what he intended doing, now he had found the object of his search.

"Why, I'll go back, to be sure," said Rory, "and be of any use I can to you; but you had betther make no delay in life, Masther Gerald, but make off to the misthriss as fast as you can, for it's the heart of her will leap for joy when she claps her two good-looking eyes on you."

"I intend doing so, Rory; and I will expect to see you to-morrow."

"It may be a thrifle later nor that, Masther Gerald, for I intind stoppin' in Swoord's to-night; but you'll see me afore long, anyhow."

"Then, good-bye, Rory, for the present," said Gerald, as he put spurs to his horse, and sweeping at a rapid pace round one of the angles of the picturesque castle that formerly commanded the entrance to the village, he was soon lost to the sight of Rory Oge, who sent many an affectionate look and blessing after him.

The appearance of Rory Oge was too sudden to permit any explanation to be given to the reader of who he was, when first introduced into the story ; but now that the horseman's absence gives a little breathing time, a word or two on the subject may not be inapposite.

Rory Oge was foster-brother to Gerald Pepper, and hence the affection and familiarity of address which existed and was permitted between them. In Ireland, as in Scotland, the ties thus originating between two persons who have been nurtured at the same breast are held very dear, and were even more so formerly than now. Rory Oge might thus, as foster-brother to Gerald, have had many advantages in the way of worldly comfort, which he not only did not seek for, but had even shunned. Making use of such advantages must have involved, at the same time, a certain degree of dependence, and this the tone of his character would have rendered unpleasing to him. There was a restlessness in his nature with which a monotonous state of being would have been imcompatible ; an independence of mind also, and a touch of romance, which prompted him to be a free agent. To all these influences was added a passionate love of music ; and it will not, therefore, be wondered at that Rory Oge had determined on becoming an erratic musician. The harp and the bagpipes he had contrived, even in his boyhood, to become tolerably familiar with ; and when he had taken up the resolution of becoming a professed musician, his proficiency upon both instruments increased rapidly, until at length he arrived at a degree of excellence as a performer seldom exceeded. Ultimately, however, the pipes was the instrument he principally practised upon : his intuitive love of sweet sounds would have prompted him to the use of the harp, but the wandering life he led rendered the former instrument so much more convenient, from its portability, that it became his favourite from fitness rather than choice.

In the cool of the evening, Rory Oge was seated at the back of a cottage on the outskirts of a village, and a group of young people of both sexes were dancing on the green sod in the rear of it, to the inspiring music of his pipes. More than an hour had been thus employed, and the twilight was advancing, when a fresh couple stood up to dance, and Rory, after inflating his bag and giving forth the deep hum of his drone, let forth his chanter into one of his best jigs, and was lilting away in his merriest style; but the couple, instead of commencing the dance, joined a group of the bystanders, who seemed to have got their heads together upon some subject of importance, and listened to the conversation, instead of making good use of their own time, the day's declining light, and Rory's incomparable music.

At length they turned from the knot of talkers, and were going to dance, when the girl told her partner she would rather have another jig than the one Rory was playing. The youth begged of Rory to stop.

"For what?" said Rory.

"Aggy would rather have another jig," said her beau, "for she doesn't like the one you're playin'."

"Throth, it's time for her to think iv it," said Rory, "and I playin' away here all this time for nothin', and obleeged now to *put back the tune*. Bad cess to me, but it's too provokin', so it is. And why couldn't you tell me so at wanst?"

"Now, don't be angry, Rory," said Aggy, coming forward herself to appease his anger. "I ax your pardon, but I was just listenin' to the news that they wor tellin'."

"What news?" said the piper. "I suppose they haven't fought another battle?"

"No; but one would think you wor a witch, Rory; for if it's not a battle, there's a sojer in it."

"What sojer?" said Rory, with earnestness.

"Why, a sojer a' horseback rode into the town awhile agon, jist come down from Dublin, and is stoppin' down below at the Public."

A thought at once flashed across Rory's mind that the visit of a soldier at such a time might have some connection with the events he had become acquainted with in the morning, and suddenly rising from his seat, he said: "Faix, and I don't see why I shouldn't see the sojer as well as everybody else, and so I'll go down to the Public myself."

"Sure, you won't go, Rory, until you give us the tune, and we finish our dance?"

"Finish, indeed," said Rory; "why, you didn't begin it yet."

"No; but we will, Rory."

"By my sowl, you won't," said Rory, very sturdily, unyoking his pipes at the same time.

"Oh, Rory," said Aggy, in great dismay—"Rory, if you plaze."

"Well, I don't plaze, and there's an end iv it. I was bellowsing away there for betther nor ten minutes, and the divil a toe you'd dance, but talkin' all the time, and thin you come and want me to put back the tune. Now, the next time you won't let good music be wasted; throth, it's not so plenty."

"Not such as yours, in throth, Rory," said Aggy, in her own little coaxing way. "Ah, now, Rory!"

" 'Twon't do, Aggy. You think to come over me now with the blarney, but you're late, says Boyce," and so saying, off he trudged, leaving the dancers in dudgeon.

He went directly to the Public, where he found an English officer of King William's cavalry had not only arrived, but intended remaining, and to that end was superintending the grooming of his horse, before he was put up for the night in a shabby little shed, which the landlady of the Public chose to call stable. Here Rory Oge proceeded, and entered into conversation with the hostler, as a preliminary to doing the same with the soldier. This he contrived with the address so peculiar to his country and his class, and finding that the stranger intended going northward in the morning, the suspicion which had induced him to leave the dance and visit the Public ripened into uneasiness as to the object of the stranger ; and desirous to arrive closer to the truth, he thought he might test the intentions of the trooper in a way which would not betray his own anxiety on the subject, at the same time that it would sufficiently satisfy him as to the other's proceedings. To this end, in the course of the desultory conversation which may be supposed to take place between three such persons as I have named, Rory ingeniously contrived to introduce the name of " Ballygarth," watching the Englishman closely at the moment, whose attention became at once awakened at the name, and turning quickly to Rory, he said :

" Ballygarth, did you say ? "

" Yis, your honour," said Rory, with the most perfect composure and seeming indifference, though, at the same time, the success of his experiment convinced him that the man who stood before him was he who was selected to expel his beloved foster-brother from his home.

" How far is the place you name from this village ? " asked the soldier.

" Indeed, it's not to say very convaynient," answered Rory.

" How many miles do you reckon it ? "

" Indeed, an' that same would be hard to say."

" I think," said the hostler, " it would be about—"

" Twenty-four or twenty-five," interrupted Rory, giving the hostler a telegraphic kick on the shin at the same time, by way of a hint not to contradict him.

" Aye, something thereaway," said the other, assenting, and rubbing the intelligent spot.

" Why, Drokhē-da is not more than that from Dublin," said the trooper, in some surprise.

" It's Drogheda you mane, I suppose, sir ? " said Rory, noticing the Englishman's false pronunciation, rather than his remark of the *intentional* mistake as to the distance named.

" Aye, Droketty, or whatever you call it."

" Oh, that's no rule in life, your honour; for Ballygarth, you see, does not lie convaynient, and you have to go by so many cruked roads and little boreens to come at it that it is farther off *when you get there* than a body would think.   Faix, I know I wish I was at the ind o' my journey there to-morrow, for it's a *long step* to go."

" Are you going there to-morrow ? " said the trooper.

" Nigh hand it, sir," said Rory, with great composure; and turning to the hostler he said : " That's a fine baste you're clainin', Pether."

" My reason for asking," said the soldier, " is, that I am going in the same direction myself, and as you say the road is intricate, perhaps you will show me the way."

" To be sure I will, your honour," said Rory, endeavouring to conceal his delight at the stranger's falling into his designs so readily.   " At all events, as far as I go your road you're heartily welkim to any sarvice I can do your honour, only I'm afeard I'll delay you an your journey, for indeed the baste I have is not the fastest."

" Shank's mare, I suppose," said Peter, with a wink.

" No ; Teddy Ryan's horse," said Rory.   " An' I suppose your honour will be for startin' in the mornin' ? "

" Yes," said the soldier, and he thereupon arranged with his intended guide as to the hour of their commencing their journey on the morrow ; after which, the piper wished him good-night and retired.

The conjecture of Rory Oge was right as to the identity of the English soldier.   He was one of those English adherents of King William, for whose gratification and emolument an immediate commission had been issued for the enriching a greedy army, inflamed as well by religious animosity as cupidity, at the expense of the community at large.   So indecent was the haste displayed to secure this almost indiscriminate plunder, that "no courts of judicature were opened for proceeding regularly and legally." But a commission was issued, under which extensive forfeitures were made, and there was no delay in making what seizures they could ; but this rapacious spirit defeated its own ends in some instances, for the unsettled state of the country rendered it difficult, if not impossible, to secure the ill-gotten good, from the headlong haste it was necessary to proceed with.

It was in the grey of the succeeding morning that Rory Oge stole softly from the back-door of the house of entertainment where he, as well as the English soldier, slept, and proceeded cautiously across the enclosure, in the rear of the house, to the shed where the horse of the stranger was stabled.   Noiselessly he unhasped the door of rough boards, that swung on one leather hinge, and entering the shed, he shook from his hat some corn into the beast's manger; and while the animal was engaged in despatching his breakfast, Rory lifted his forefoot in a very workmanlike manner into his lap, and commenced, with a rasp, which he had *finessed* from a smith's forge the evening before for the purpose, to loosen the nails of the shoe. As soon as he had accomplished this to his satisfaction, he retired to his sleeping place, and remained there until summoned to arise when the soldier was ready to take the road.

At the skirts of the village, some delay occurred while Rory stopped at the house of one of his friends, who had promised him the loan of a horse for his journey, which arrangement he had contrived to make overnight. It was not long, however, before Rory appeared, leading from behind the low hut of the peasant, by whom he was followed, a very sorry piece of horseflesh. After mounting, he held out his hand, first having passed it across his mouth, and uttered a sharp sound, something resembling "thp." The offered palm was met by that of his friend, after a similar observance on his part, and they shook hands heartily, while exchanging some words in their native tongue. Rory then signified to the Englishman that he was ready to conduct him.

The soldier cast a very discontented eye at the animal on which his guide was mounted, and Rory interpreted the look at once:

"Oh, indeed, he's not the best, sure enough. I tould your honour, last night, I was afeard I might delay you a little for that same; but don't be onaisy, he's like a singed cat, betther nor he looks, and if we can't go in a hand gallop, sure, there's the ould sayin' to comfort us, that 'fair and aisy goes far in a day.'"

"We have a long ride before us, though," said the soldier, "and your horse, I'm afraid, will founder before he goes half-way."

"Oh, don't be afeard av him in the laste," said Rory. "He's ould, to be sure, but an ould friend is preférrable to a new inimy."

Thus, every objection on the part of the Englishman was met by Rory with some old saying, or piece of ingenuity of his own, in answer; and after some few minutes of conversation, they dropped into silence, and jogged along.

In some time, the notice of the stranger was attracted by the singular and picturesque tower of Lusk that arose on their sight, and he questioned Rory as to its history and use.

"It's a church, it is," said his guide.

"It looks more like a place of defence," said the soldier. "It is a square tower with circular flankers."

"To be sure, it is a place of difince," said Rory. "Isn't it a place of difince agin the divil (God bless us!) and all his works; and mighty great people is proud to be berrid in it for that same. There is the Barnewells (the lords of Kingsland, I mane), and they are berrid in it time beyant tellin', and has an iligant monument in it, the lord himself and his lady beside him, an the broad o' their backs, lyin' *dead*, done to the *life*."

There was scarcely any tower or house which came within view of the road they pursued that did not present Rory with an occasion for giving some account of it, or recounting some tale connected with it, and thus many a mile was passed over. It must be confessed, to be sure, that Rory had most of the conversation to himself, as the soldier helped him very little; but as Rory's object was to keep his attention engaged, and while away the time, and delay him on the road as long as he could, he did not relax in his efforts to entertain, however little reciprocity there was on that score between him and his companion.

At last he led him from the high road into every small by-way that could facilitate his purpose of delaying, as well as of tiring the trooper, and his horse too, to say nothing of his plan of having a shoe lost by the charger in a remote spot. Many a wistful glance was thrown on the fore-shoe, and at last he had the pleasure to see it cast, unnoticed by the rider. This Rory said nothing about, until they had advanced a mile or two, and then, looking down for some time as if in anxious observation, he exclaimed: "By dad, I'm afeard your horse's fore-shoe is gone."

The dragoon pulled up immediately and looked down. "I believe it is the off-foot," said he.

"It's the *off*-shoe, anyhow," said Rory, "and that's worse."

The dragoon alighted, and examined the foot thus deprived of its defence, and exhibited a good deal of silent vexation. "It is but a few days since I had him shod," said he.

"Throth, thin, it was a shame for whoever *done* it not to make a betther job iv it," said Rory.

The Englishman then inspected the remaining shoes of his horse, and finding them fast, he noticed the singularity of the loss of one shoe under such circumstances.

"Oh, that's no rule in life," said Rory, "for you may remark that a horse never throws two shoes at a time, but only one, by way of a warnin', as a body may say, to jog your memory that he wants a new set; and indeed, that same is very *cute* of a dumb baste, and I could tell your honour a mighty quare story of a horse I knew wanst, and as reg'lar as the day o' the month kem round—"

"I don't want to hear any of your stories," said the Englishman, rather sullenly; "but can you tell me how I may have this loss speedily repaired?"

"Faix, an' I could tell your honour *two* stories easier nor *that*, for not a forge I know nigher hand to this than one that is in Duleek."

"And how far is Duleek?"

"'Deed, an' it's a good step."

"What do you call a good step?"

"Why, it 'ill take a piece of a day to go there."

"Curse you!" said the dragoon, at last provoked beyond his constitutional phlegm at such evasive replies. "Can't you say how many miles?"

"I ax your honour's pardon," replied his guide, who now saw that trifling would not answer. "To the best o' my knowledge, we are aff o' Duleek about five miles, or thereaway."

"Confound it!" said the soldier. "Five miles, and this barbarous road, and your long miles into the bargain."

"Sure, I don't deny the road is not the best," said Rory; "but if it's not good, sure, we give you good measure, at all events."

It was in vain that the Englishman grumbled. Rory had so ready and so queer an answer to every objection raised by the soldier, that at last he remounted, and was fain to content himself with proceeding at a very slow pace along the vile by-road they travelled, lest he might injure the hoof of his charger.

And now Rory, having effected the first part of his object, set all his wits to work how he could make the rest of the road as little tiresome as possible to the stranger; and he not only succeeded in effecting this, but he managed, in the course of the day, to possess himself of the soldier's secret touching the object of his present journey.

In the doing this, the scene would have been an amusing one to a third person: it was an encounter between phlegm and wit— a trial between English reserve and Irish ingenuity.

By the way, it is not unworthy of observation that a common spring of action influences the higher and the lower animals, under the circumstances of oppression and pursuit. The oppressed and the pursued have only stratagem to encounter force or escape destruction. The fox and other animals of the chase are proverbial for their cunning, and every conquered people have been reduced to the expedient of *finesse* as their last resource.

The slave-driver tells you that every negro is a liar. It is the violation of charity on the one hand that induces the violation of truth on the other; and weakness, in all cases, is thus driven to deceit, as its last defence against power.

The soldier, in the course of his conversation with his guide, thought himself very knowing when he said, in a careless way, that he believed there was someone of the name of Pepper lived at Ballygarth.

"Someone, is it?" said Rory, looking astonished. "Oh! is that all you know about it? *Someone*, indeed! By my conscience, an' it's plenty of them there is. The counthry is overrun with them."

"But I speak of Pepper of Ballygarth," said the other.

"The *Peppers* o' Ballygart, you mane; for they are livin' all over it as thick as rabbits in the back of an ould ditch."

"I mean he who is called Gerald Pepper?"

"Why, thin, indeed, I never heerd him called that-a-way before, and I dunna which o' them at all you mane; for you see, there is so many o' them, as I said before, that we are obleeged to make a differ between them by invintin' names for them; and so we call a smooth-skinned chap that is among them White Pepper, and a dark fellow (another o' the family) Black Pepper; and there's a great long sthreel that is christened Long Pepper; and there is another o' them that is tindher an one of his feet, and we call him Pepper-*corn;* and there is a fine, dashin', well-grown blade, the full of a door he is, long life to him! and he is known by the name of Whole Pepper; and it's quare enough, that he is married to a poor little starved hound of a wife, that has the bittherest tongue ever was in a woman's head, and so they called her Ginger; and I think that is a *highly saisoned* family for you. Now, which o' them is it you mane? Is it White Pepper, or Black Pepper, or Long Pepper, or Whole Pepper, or Pepper-corn?"

"I don't know any of them," said the soldier. "Gerald Pepper is the man I want."

"Oh, you *do* want him, thin," said Rory, with a very peculiar intonation of voice. "Well, av coorse, if you want him, you'll find him; but look forenint you there; there you may see the ould abbey of Duleek"——and he pointed to the object as he spoke.

This was yet a mile or so distant, and the day was pretty well advanced by the time the travellers entered the village. Rory asked the soldier where it was his honour's pleasure to stop while he got his horse shod, and recommended him to go to the abbey, where, of course, the monks would be proud to give "any accommodation in life" to a gentleman like him. But this proposal the soldier did not much relish; for though stout of heart, as most of his countrymen, he was loath to be tempted into any situation where he would have considered himself, to a certain degree, at the mercy of a parcel of Popish monks; and poisoned viands and drugged wine were amongst some of the objections which his Protestant imagination started at the proposal. He inquired if there was not any Public in the village, and being answered in the affirmative, his resolution was taken at once of sheltering and getting some refreshment there while his horse should be under the hands of the blacksmith.

Here again Rory's roguery came into practice; the blacksmith of the village was his relative, and after depositing the fatigued and annoyed soldier at the little *auberge*, Rory went for the avowed purpose of getting the smith to "do the job," but in reality, to send him out of the way; and this was easily done, when the motive for doing so was communicated. On his return to the Public, there was a great deal of well-affected disappointment on Rory's part at the absence of his near relation, the smith, as he told the betrayed trooper how "provoking it was that he wasn't in the forge at that present, but was expected at every hand's-turn, and that the very first instant minute he kem home, Ally (that was his wife) would run up and tell his honour, and the horse should be shod in *no* time."

"In no time?" said the soldier, with a disappointed look. "You know I want to have him shod *in* time."

"Well, sure, that's what I mane," said Rory; "that is, it will be jist *no time at all* antil he *is* shod."

"Indeed, an' you may believe him, your honour," said mine host of the Public, coming to the rescue, "for there's no one he would do a sthroke of work sooner for than Rory Oge here, seein' that he is of his own flesh and blood, his own cousin wance removed."

"Faith, he is farther *removed* than that," replied Rory, unable to contain a joke. "He is a more *distant* relation than you think; but he'll do the work with a heart and a half, for all that, as soon as he comes back; and indeed, I think your honour might as well make yourself comfortable here antil that same time, and the sorra betther enthertainmint you'll meet betune this and the world's end than the same man will give you—Lanty Lalor I mane, and there he is stan'in' forninst you—and it's not to his face I'd say it, but behind his back too, and often did, and will agin, I hope."

"Thank you kindly, Rory," said Lanty, with a bow and scrape.

Some refreshment was accordingly prepared for the soldier, who, after his fatigue, was nothing loath to comfort the inward man; the more particularly as it was not merely the best, but the only thing he could do under existing circumstances; and after gorging profusely on the solids, the fluids were next put under contribution, and acting on the adage that "good eating requires good drinking," he entered into the feeling of the axiom with an earnestness that Sancho Panza himself could not have outdone, either in the spirit or the letter.

Rory was in attendance all the time, and still played his game of engaging the stranger's attention as much as possible, with a view to divert him from his prime object, and make him forget the delays which were accumulated upon him. It was in this spirit that he asked him if he ever "heerd tell of the remarkable place that Duleek was."

"*We* made the place remarkable enough the other day," said the soldier, with the insolence which the habit of domination produces in little minds, "when we drove your flying troops through the pass of Duleek, and your runaway king at the head of them. I was one of the fifty who did it."

Rory, influenced by the dear object he had in view, smothered the indignation he felt rising in his throat; and as he might not exhibit anger, he had recourse to sarcasm, and said:

"In throth, your honour, I don't wondher at all at the brave things you done, in the regard that it was at Duleek; and sure, Duleek was always remarkable for havin' the bowldest things done there and about, ever since the days of the 'Little Waiver.'"

"What little weaver?" said the soldier.

"Why, thin, an' did you never hear of the little waiver of Duleek Gate?"

"Never."

"Well, that's wondherful!" said Rory.

"I don't see how it's wondherful," said the trooper; "for how could I hear of the weaver of Duleek when I have been living in England all my life?"

"Oh, murther!" said Rory, in seeming amazement, "an' don't they know about the little waiver o' Duleek Gate in England?"

"No," said the trooper; "how should they?"

"Oh, thin, what a terrible ignorant place England must be, not for to know about that!!!"

"Is it so *very* wonderful, then?" asked the man whose country was thus aspersed.

"Wondherful!" said Rory. "By my soul, it is *that* that *is* wondherful."

"Well, tell it to me, then," said the soldier.

"Now, suppose I was for to tell you, you see, the divil a one taste you'd b'live a word iv it; and it's callin' me a fool you'd be; and you'd be tired into the bargain before I was half done, for it's a long story, and if you stopped me I'd be lost."

"I won't stop you."

"But you won't b'live it; and that's worse."

"Perhaps I may," said the other, whose curiosity began to waken.

"Well, that same is a promise, anyhow, and so here goes!" and Rory then related, with appropriate voice and gesture, the following legend.

THE LEGEND OF THE
LITTLE WEAVER OF DULEEK GATE

A TALE OF CHIVALRY

You see, there was a waiver lived, wanst upon a time, in Duleek here, hard by the gate, and a very honest, industherous man he was, by all accounts. He had a wife, and av coorse they had childhre—and small blame to them—and plenty of them, so that the poor little waiver was obleeged to work his fingers to the bone a'most, to get them the bit and the sup; but he didn't begridge that, for he was an industherous crayther, as I said before, and it was up airly and down late wid him, and the loom never standin' still. Well, it was one mornin' that his wife called to him, and he sitting very busy throwin' the shuttle, and says she: "Come here," says she, "jewel, and ate your brekquest, now that it's ready." But he never minded her, but wint an workin'. So in a minit or two more, says she, callin' out to him agin: "Arrah! lave off slavin' yourself, my darlin', and ate your bit o' brekquest while it is hot."

"Lave me alone," says he, and he dhruv the shuttle fasther nor before.

Well, in a little time more, she goes over to him where he sot, and says she, coaxin' him like: "Thady dear," says she, "the stirabout will be stone cowld if you don't give over that weary work and come and ate it at wanst."

"I'm busy with a patthern here that is brakin' my heart," says the waiver, "and antil I complate it and masther it intirely, I won't quit."

"Oh, think o' the iligant stirabout, that 'ill be spylte intirely."

"To the divil with the stirabout," says he.

"God forgive you," says she, "for cursin' your good brekquest."

"Aye, and you too," says he.

"Throth, you're as cross as two sticks this blessed morning, Thady," says the poor wife; "and it's a heavy handful I have of you when you are cruked in your temper; but stay there if you like, and let your stirabout grow cowld, and not a one o' me 'ill ax you agin;" and with that off she wint, and the waiver, sure enough, was mighty crabbed, and the more the wife spoke to him the worse he got, which, you know, is only nath'ral. Well, he left the loom at last, and wint over to the stirabout, and what would you think, but whin he looked at it, it was as black as a crow; for, you see, it was in the hoighth o' the summer, and the flies lit upon it to that degree that the stirabout was fairly covered with them.

" Why, thin, bad luck to your impidince," said the waiver. "Would no place sarve you but that? and is it spyling my brekquest yiz are, you dirty bastes?" And with that, bein' altogether cruked-tempered at the time, he lifted his hand, and he made one great slam at the dish o' stirabout, and killed no less than threescore-and-tin flies at the one blow. It was threescore-and-tin exactly, for he counted the carcases one by one, and laid them out an a clane plate for to view them.

Well, he felt a powerful sperit risin' in him when he seen the slaughther he done at one blow, and with that he got as consaited as the very dickens, and not a sthroke more work he'd do that day, but out he wint, and was fractious and impidint to everyone he met, and was squarin' up into their faces and sayin': "Look at that fist! That's the fist that killed threescore-and-tin at one blow—whoo!"

With that all the neighbours thought he was crack'd, and faith, the poor wife herself thought the same when he kem home in the evenin', afther spendin' every rap he had in dhrink, and swaggerin' about the place, and lookin' at his hand every minit.

"Indeed, an' your hand is very dirty, sure enough, Thady jewel," says the poor wife, and thrue for her, for he rowled into a ditch comin' home. "You'd betther wash it, darlin'."

"How dar you say dirty to the greatest hand in Ireland?" says he, going to bate her.

"Well, it's nat dirty," says she.

"It is throwin' away my time I have been all my life," says he, "livin' with you, at all, and stuck at a loom, nothin' but a poor waiver, when it is Saint George or the Dhraggin I ought to be, which is two of the siven champions o' Christendom."

"Well, suppose they christened him twice as much," says the wife, "sure, what's that to uz?"

"Don't put in your prate," says he, "you ignorant sthrap," says he. "You're vulgar, woman—you're vulgar—mighty vulgar; but I'll have nothin' more to say to any dirty, snakin' thrade again—divil a more waivin' I'll do."

"Oh, Thady dear, and what'll the children do thin?"

"Let them go play marvels," says he.

"That would be but poor feedin' for them, Thady."

"They shan't want for feedin'," says he, "for it's a rich man I'll be soon, and a great man too."

"Usha, but I'm glad to hear it, darlin'—though I dunna how it's to be, but I think you had better go to bed, Thady."

"Don't talk to me of any bed, but the bed o' glory, woman," says he, lookin' mortial grand.

"Oh, God send! we'll all be in glory yet," says the wife, crassin' herself; "but go to sleep, Thady, for this present."

"I'll sleep with the brave yit," says he.

"Indeed, an' a brave sleep will do you a power o' good, my darlin'," says she.

"And it's I that will be the knight!" says he.

"All night, if you plaze, Thady," says she.

"None o' your coaxin'," says he. "I'm determined on it, and I'll set off immediantly, and be a knight arriant."

"A what!!!" says she.

"A knight arriant, woman."

"Lord be good to me, what's that?" says she.

"A knight arriant is a rale gintleman," says he, "going round the world for sport, with a swoord by his side, takin' whatever he plazes—for himself; and that's a knight arriant," says he.

("Just a'most like yourself, sir," said Rory, with a sly, sarcastic look at the trooper, who sat listening to him with a sort of half-stupid, half-drunken wonder.)

Well, sure enough, he wint about among his neighbours the next day, and he got an ould kittle from one and a saucepan from another, and he took them to the tailor, and he sewed him up a shuit o' tin clothes like any knight arriant, and he borrowed a pot-lid, and *that* he was very partic'lar about, bekase it was his shield, and he wint to a frind o' his, a painther and glazier, and made him paint an his shield in big letthers:

"I'M THE MAN OF ALL MIN,
THAT KILL'D THREESCORE-AND-TIN,
AT A BLOW."

"When the people sees *that*," says the waiver to himself, "the sorra one will dar for to come near me."

And with that he tould the wife to scour out the small iron pot for him, "for," says he, "it will make an iligant helmet," and when it was done he put it an his head, and his wife said:

"Oh, murther, Thady jewel! is it puttin' a great heavy iron pot an your head you are, by way iv a hat?"

"Sartinly," says he, "for a knight arriant should always have *a woight on his brain.*"

"But, Thady dear," says the wife, "there's a hole in it, and it can't keep out the weather."

"It will be the cooler," says he, puttin' it an him; "besides, if I don't like it, it is aisy to stop it with a wisp o' sthraw, or the like o' that."

"The three legs of it looks mighty quare stickin' up," says she.

"Every helmet has a spike stickin' out o' the top of it," says the weaver, "and if mine has three, it's only the grandher it is."

"Well," says the wife, getting bitther at last, "all I can say is, it isn't the first sheep's head was dhress'd in it."

" *Your sarvant, ma'am,*" says he, and off he set.

Well, he was in want of a horse, and so he wint to a field hard by, where the miller's horse was grazin', that used to carry the ground corn round the counthry. "This is the idintical horse for me," says the waiver. "He is used to carryin' flour and male, and what am I but the *flower* o' shovelry in a coat o' *mail;* so that the horse won't be put out iv his way in the laste."

But as he was ridin' him out o' the field, who should see him but the miller. "Is it stalin' my horse you are, honest man?" says the miller.

"No," says the waiver; "I'm only goin' to *ax*ercise him," says he, "in the cool o' the evenin'. It will be good for his health."

"Thank you kindly," says the miller; "but lave him where he is, and you'll obleege me."

"I can't afford it," says the waiver, runnin' the horse at the ditch.

"Bad luck to your impidince," says the miller. "You've as much tin about you as a thravellin' tinker; but you've more brass. Come back here, you vagabone!" says he.

But he was late. Away galloped the waiver, and took the road to Dublin, for he thought the best thing he could do was to go to the King o' Dublin (for Dublin was a grate place thin, and had a king iv its own), and he thought maybe the King o' Dublin would give him work. Well, he was four days goin' to Dublin, for the baste was not the best, and the roads worse, not all as one was now; but there was no turnpikes thin, glory be to God! Whin he got to Dublin, he wint sthrait to the palace, and whin he got into the coortyard he let his horse go and graze about the place, for the grass was growin' out betune the stones; everything was flourishin' thin, in Dublin, you see. Well, the king was lookin' out of his dhrawin'-room windy for divarshin whin the waiver kem in; but the waiver pretended not to see him, and he wint over to a stone sate undher the windy; for, you see, there was stone sates all round about the place for the accommodation o' the people, for the king was a dacent, obleegin' man. Well, as I said, the waiver wint over and lay down an one o' the sates, just undher the king's windy, and purtended to go asleep; but he took care to turn out the front of his shield that had the letters an it. Well, my dear, with that the king calls out to one of the lords of his coort that was standin' behind him, houldin' up the skirt of his coat, accordin' to raison, and says he: "Look here," says he, "what do you think of a vagabone like that, comin' undher my very nose to go sleep? It is thrue I'm a good king," says he, "and I 'commodate the people by havin' sates for them to sit down and enjoy the raycreation and contimplation of seein' me here lookin' out a' my dhrawin'-room windy for divarshin; but that is no raison they are to *make a hotel* o' the place, and come and sleep here. Who is it at all?" says the king.

"Not a one o me knows, plaze your Majesty."

"I think he must be a furriner," says the king, "bekase his dhress is outlandish."

"And doesn't know manners, more betoken," says the lord.

"I'll go down and *circumspect* him myself," says the king. "Folly me," says he to the lord, wavin' his hand at the same time in the most dignacious manner.

Down he wint accordianly, followed by the lord; and when he wint over to where the waiver was lying, sure, the first thing he seen was his shield with the big letthers an it, and with that says he to the lord: "By dad," says he, "this is the very man I want."

"For what, plaze your Majesty?" says the lord.

"To kill that vagabone dhraggin, to be sure," says the king.

"Sure, do you think he could kill him," says the lord, "when all the stoutest knights in the land wasn't aiquil to it, but never kem back, and was ate up alive by the cruel desaiver."

"Sure, don't you see there," says the king, pointin' at the shield, "that he killed threescore-and-tin at one blow; and the man that done *that*, I think, is a match for anything."

So, with that, he wint over to the waiver and shuck him by the shouldher for to wake him, and the waiver rubbed his eyes as if just wakened, and the king says to him: "God save you," said he.

"God save you kindly," says the waiver, *purtendin'* he was quite onknowst who he was spakin' to.

"Do you know who I am," says the king, "that you make so free, good man?"

"No, indeed," says the waiver; "you have the advantage o' me."

"To be sure I have," says the king, *moighty high;* "sure, ain't I the King o' Dublin?" says he.

The waiver dhropped down an his two knees forninst the king, and says he: "I beg God's pardon and yours for the liberty I tuk. Plaze your holiness, I hope you'll excuse it."

"No offince," says the king. "Get up, good man. And what brings you here?" says he.

"I'm in want o' work, plaze your riverince," says the waiver.

"Well, suppose I give you work?" says the king.

"I'll be proud to sarve you, my lord," says the waiver.

"Very well," says the king. "You killed threescore-and-tin at one blow, I understan'," says the king.

" Yis," says the waiver ; " that was the last thrifle o' work I done, and I'm afeard my hand 'ill go out o' practice if I don't get some job to do at wanst."

" You shall have a job immediantly," says the king. " It is not threescore-and-tin, or any fine thing like that ; it is only a blaguard dhraggin, that is disturbin' the counthry and ruinatin' my tinanthry wid aitin' their powlthry, and I'm lost for want of eggs," says the king.

" Throth, thin, plaze your worship," says the waiver, "you look as yollow as if you swallowed twelve yolks this minit."

" Well, I want this dhraggin to be killed," says the king. " It will be no throuble in life to you ; and I am only sorry that it isn't betther worth your while, for he isn't worth fearin', at all ; only I must tell you that he lives in the county Galway, in the middle of a bog, and he has an advantage in that."

" Oh, I don't value it in the laste," says the waiver ; " for the last threescore-and-tin I killed was in a *soft place*."

" When will you undhertake the job, then ? " says the king.

" Let me at him at wanst," says the waiver.

" That's what I like," says the king. " You're the very man for my money," says he.

" Talkin' of money," says the waiver, " by the same token, I'll want a thrifle o' change from you for my thravellin' charges."

" As much as you plaze," says the king ; and with the word, he brought him into his closet, where there was an ould stockin' in an oak chest, burstin' wid goolden guineas.

" Take as many as you plaze," says the king ; and sure enough, my dear, the little waiver stuffed his tin clothes as full as they could hould with them.

" Now, I'm ready for the road," says the waiver.

" Very well," says the king ; " but you must have a fresh horse," says he.

" With all my heart," says the waiver, who thought he might as well exchange the miller's ould garron for a betther.

And maybe it's wondherin' you are, that the waiver would think of goin' to fight the dhraggin afther what he heerd about him, when he was purtendin' to be asleep ; but he had no sitch notion ; all he intended was—to fob the goold, and ride back again to Duleek with his gains and a good horse. But you see, cute as the waiver was, the king was cuter still ; for these high quolity, you see, is great desaivers ; and so the horse the waiver was put an was larned an purpose ; and sure, the minit he was mounted, away powdhered the horse, and the divil a toe he'd go but right down to Galway. Well, for four days he was goin' evermore, until at last the waiver seen a crowd o' people runnin' as if Ould Nick was at their heels, and they shoutin' a thousand murdhers and cryin': "The dhraggin! the dhraggin!" and he couldn't stop the horse nor make him turn back, but away he pelted right forninst the terrible baste that was comin' up to him, and there was the most *nefaarious* smell o' sulphur, savin' your presence, enough to knock you down; and faith, the waiver seen he had no time to lose, and so he threwn himself off the horse and made to a three that was growin' nigh hand, and away he clambered up into it as nimble as a cat; and not a minit had he to spare, for the dhraggin kem up in a powerful rage, and he devoured the horse, body and bones, in less than no time; and then he began to sniffle and scent about for the waiver, and at last he clapt his eye on him, where he was, up in the three, and says he: "In throth, you might as well come down out o' that," says he, "for I'll have you as sure as eggs is mate."

"Divil a fut I'll go down," says the waiver.

"Sorra care, I care," says the dhraggin, "for you're as good as ready money in my pocket this minit; for I'll lie under this three," says he, "and sooner or later you must fall to my share;" and sure enough he sot down, and began to pick his teeth with his tail, afther the heavy brekquest he made that mornin' (for he ate a whole village, let alone the horse), and he got dhrowsy at last, and fell asleep; but before he wint to sleep, he wound himself all round about the three, all as one, as a lady windin' ribbon round her finger, so that the waiver could not escape.

Well, as soon as the waiver knew he was dead asleep, by the snorin' of him—and every snore he let out of him was like a clap o' thunder—

(Here the trooper began to exhibit some symptoms of following the dragon's example—and perhaps the critics will say, no wonder —but Rory, notwithstanding, pursued the recital of the legend.)

That minit, the waiver began to creep down the three, as cautious as a fox; and he was very nigh-hand the bottom, when, bad cess to it, a thievin' branch he was dipindin an bruk, and down he fell right a-top o' the dhraggin: but if he did, good luck was an his side, for where should he fall but with his two legs right acrass the dhraggin's neck, and, my jew'l, he laid howlt o' the baste's ears, and there he kept his grip, for the dhraggin wakened and endayvoured for to bite him; but, you see, by raison the waiver was behind his ears, he could not come at him, and with that, he endayvoured for to shake him off; but the divil a stir could he stir the waiver; and though he shuk all the scales an his body, he could not turn the scale agin the waiver.

"By the hokey, this is too bad intirely," says the dhraggin; "but if you won't let go," says he, "by the powers o' wildfire, I'll give you a ride that 'ill astonish your sivin small sinses, my

boy;" and with that, away he flew like mad; and where do you
think he did fly? By dad, he flew sthraight for Dublin—divil
a less. But the waiver bein' an his neck was a great disthress to
him, and he would rather have had him an *inside passenger;* but,
anyway, he flew and he flew until he kem *slap* up agin the palace
o' the king; for, bein' blind with the rage, he never seen it, and he
knocked his brains out; that is, the small thrifle he had, and
down he fell spacheless. An' you see, good luck would have it,
the King o' Dublin was lookin' out iv his dhrawin'-room windy
for divarshin that day also, and whin he seen the waiver ridin' an
the fiery dhraggin (for he was blazin' like a tar-barrel), he called
ont to his coortyers to come and see the show. "By the
powdhers o' war, here comes the knight arriant," says the king,
"ridin the dhraggin that's all afire, and if he gets *into the palace*,
yiz must be ready wid the *fire ingines*," says he, "for to *put him
out.*" But when they seen the dhraggin fall outside, they all ran
downstairs and scampered into the palace-yard for to circumspect
the *curiosity;* and by the time they got down, the waiver had got
off o' the dhraggin's neck, and runnin' up to the king, says he:
"Plaze your holiness," says he, "I did not think myself worthy
of killin' this facetious baste, so I brought him to yourself for to do
him the honour of decripitation by your own royal five fingers.
But I tamed him first, before I allowed him the liberty for to *dar*
to appear in your royal prisince, and you'll oblige me if you'll
just make your mark with your own hand upon the onruly
baste's neck." And with that, the king, sure enough, drew out
his swoord and took the head aff the *dirty* brute, as *clane* as a new
pin. Well, there was great rejoicin' in the coort that the
dhraggin was killed; and says the king to the little waiver, says
he: "You are a knight arriant as it is, and so it would be no use
for to knight you over agin; but I will make you a lord," says he.

"Oh, Lord!" says the waiver, thundersthruck like at his own
good luck.

"I will," says the king; "and as you are the first man that I
ever heerd tell of that rode a dhraggin, you shall be called Lord
Mount Dhraggin," says he.

"And where's my estates, plaze your holiness?" says the
waiver, who always had a sharp look-out afther the main chance.

"Oh, I didn't forget that," says the king. "It is my royal
pleasure to provide well for you, and for that raison I make you
a present of all the dhraggins in the world, and give you the
power over them from this out," says he.

"Is that all?" says the waiver.

"All?" says the king. "Why, you ongrateful little vagabone,
was the like ever given to any man before?"

"I b'live not, indeed," says the waiver. "Many thanks to your Majesty."

"But that is not all I'll do for you," says the king. "I'll give you my daughther too, in marriage," says he. Now, you see, that was nothin' more than what he promised the waiver in his first promise; for, by all accounts, the king's daughther was the greatest dhraggin ever was seen, and had the divil's own tongue, and a beard a yard long, which she *purtended* was put an her, by way of a penance, by Father Mulcahy, her confissor; but it was well known was in the family for ages, and no wondher it was so long, by raison of that same.

. . . .

Rory paused. He thought that not only the closed eyes but the heavy breathing of the soldier gave sure evidence of sleep; and in another minute, an audible snore gave notice that he might spare himself any further trouble; and forthwith the chronicler of The Little Weaver stole softly out of the room.

CONCLUSION OF THE WHITE HORSE OF THE PEPPERS

LET the division I have made in my tales serve, in the mind of the reader, as an imaginary boundary between the past day and the ensuing morning. Let him, in his own fancy also, settle how the soldier watched, slept, dreamt or waked through this interval. Rory did not make his appearance, however; he had left the Public on the preceding evening, having made every necessary arrangement for carrying on the affair he had taken in hand; so that the Englishman, on inquiry, found Rory had departed, being "obleeged to lave the place early on his own business, but sure, his honour could have any accommodation in life he wanted, in the regard of a guide, or the like o' that."

Now, for this Rory had provided also, having arranged with the keepers of the Public, to whom he confided everything connected with the affair, that in case the trooper should ask for a guide, they should recommend him a certain young imp, the son of Rory's cousin, the blacksmith, and one of the most mischievous, knowing and daring young vagabonds in the parish.

To such guidance, therefore, did the Englishman commit himself on this, the third day of his search after the lands of the Peppers, which still remained a *Terra Incognita* to him; and the boy, being previously tutored upon the duties he was to perform in his new capacity, was not one likely to enlighten him upon the subject. The system of the preceding day was acted upon, except the casting of the horse's shoe; but by-roads and crooked lanes were put in requisition, and every avenue but the one really leading to his object the trooper was made to traverse.

The boy affected simplicity or ignorance, as best suited his purposes, to escape any inconvenient interrogatory or investigation on the part of the stranger, and at last the young guide turned up a small, rugged lane, down whose gentle slope some water was slowly trickling amongst stones and mud. On arriving at its extremity, he proceeded to throw down some sods, and pull away some brambles, which seemed to be placed there as an artificial barrier to an extensive field that lay beyond the lane.

" What are you doing there ? " said the soldier.

" Makin' a convenience for your honour to get through the gap," said the boy.

" There is no road there," said the other.

" Oh, no, plaze your honour," said the young rascal, looking up in his face with an affectation of simplicity that might have deceived Machiavel himself. " It's not a road, sir, but a short cut."

" Cut it as short, then, as you can, my boy," said the soldier (the only good thing he ever said in his life) ; " for your short cuts in this country are the longest I ever knew—I'd rather go a round."

" So we must go round, by the bottom o' this field, sir, and then, over the hill beyant there, we come out an the road."

" Then there *is* a road beyond the hill ? "

" A fine road, sir," said the boy, who, having cleared a passage for the horseman, proceeded before him at a smart pace, and led him down the slope of the hill to a small valley, intersected by a sluggish stream which ran at its foot. When the boy arrived at this valley, he stepped briskly across it, though the water splashed up about his feet at every bound he gave, and dashing on through the stream, he arrived at the other side by the time the trooper had reached the nearer one. Here the latter was obliged to pull up, for his horse at the first step sank so deep, that the animal instinctively withdrew his foot from the treacherous morass.

The trooper called after his guide, who was proceeding up the opposite acclivity, and the boy turned round.

" I can't pass this, boy," said the soldier.

The boy faced the hill again, without any reply, and commenced his ascent at a rapid pace.

" Come back, you young scoundrel, or I'll shoot you," said the soldier, drawing his pistol from his holster. The boy still continued his flight, and the trooper fired—but ineffectually— upon which the boy stopped, and after making a contemptuous action at the Englishman, rushed up the acclivity, and was soon beyond the reach of small arms, and shortly after out of sight, having passed the summit of the hill.

The Englishman's vexation was excessive at finding himself thus left in such a helpless situation. For a long time he endeavoured to find a spot in the marsh he might make his crossing good upon, but in vain—-and after nearly an hour spent in this useless endeavour, he was forced to turn back and strive to unravel the maze of twisting and twining through which he had been led, for the purpose of getting on some highway, where a chance passenger might direct him in finding his road.

This he failed to accomplish, and darkness at length overtook him, in a wild country to which he was an utter stranger. He still continued, however, cautiously to progress along the road on which he was benighted, and at length the twinkling of a distant light raised some hope of succour in his heart.

Keeping this beacon in view, the benighted traveller made his way as well as he might, until, by favour of the glimmer he so opportunely discovered, he at last found himself in front of the house whence the light proceeded. He knocked at the door, which, after two or three loud summonses, was opened to him, and then, briefly stating the distressing circumstances in which he was placed, he requested shelter for the night.

The domestic who opened the door retired to deliver the stranger's message to the owner of the house, who immediately afterwards made his appearance, and with a reserved courtesy, invited the stranger to enter.

"Allow me first to see my horse stabled," said the soldier.

"He shall be cared for," said the other.

"Excuse me, sir," returned the blunt Englishman, "if I wish to see him in his stall. It has been a hard day for the poor brute, and I fear one of his hoofs is much injured ; how far, I am anxious to see."

"As you please, sir," said the gentleman, who ordered a menial to conduct the stranger to the stable.

There, by the light of a lantern, the soldier examined the extent of injury his charger had sustained, and had good reason to fear that the next day would find him totally unserviceable. After venting many a hearty curse on Irish roads and Irish guides, he was retiring from the stable when his attention was attracted by a superb white horse, and much as he was engrossed by his present annoyance, the noble proportions of the animal were too striking to be overlooked. After admiring all his parts, he said to the attendant : "What a beautiful creature this is ! "

"Troth, you may say that," was the answer.

"What a charger he would make ! "

"Sure enough."

"He must be very fleet ? "

"As the win'."

" An' leaps ? "

" Whoo !—over the moon, if you axed him."

" That horse must trot at least ten miles the hour."

" Tin ! Faix, it wouldn't be convaynient to him to throt undher fourteen ; " and with this assurance on the part of the groom, he left the stable.

On being led into the dwelling-house, the stranger found the table spread for supper, and the owner of the mansion, pointing to a chair, invited him to partake of the evening meal.

The reader need scarcely be told that the invitation came from Gerald Pepper, for I suppose the white horse in the stable has already explained whose house chance had directed the trooper to, though all his endeavours to find it had proved unavailing.

Gerald still maintained the bearing which characterised his first meeting with the Englishman on his threshold—it was that of reserved courtesy. Magdalene, his gentle wife, was seated near the table, with an infant child sleeping upon her lap ; her sweet features were strikingly expressive of sadness ; and as the stranger entered the apartment, her eyes were raised in one timorous glance upon the man whose terrible mission she was too well aware of, and the long lashes sank downwards again upon the pale cheek, which recent sorrow had robbed of its bloom.

" Come, sir," said Gerald, "after such a day of fatigue as yours has been, some refreshment will be welcome;" and the Englishman presently, by deeds, not words, commenced giving ample evidence of the truth of the observation. As the meal proceeded, he recounted some of the mishaps that had befallen him, all of which Gerald knew before, through Rory Oge, who was in the house at that very moment, though, for obvious reasons, he did not make his appearance, and at last the stranger put the question to his host, if he knew anyone in the neighbourhood called Gerald Pepper.

Magdalene felt her blood run cold, but Gerald quietly replied, there was a person of that name thereabouts.

" Is his property a good one ? " said the trooper.

" Very much reduced of late," replied Gerald.

" Ballygarth they call it," said the soldier. " Is that far from here ? "

" It would puzzle me to tell you how to go to it from this place," was the answer.

" It is very provoking," said the trooper. " I have been looking for it these three days, and cannot find it, and nobody seems to know where it is."

Magdalene, at these words, felt a momentary relief, yet still she scarcely dared to breathe.

" The truth is," continued the soldier, "that I am entitled, under the king's last commission, to the property, for all Pepper's possessions have been forfeited."

The baby, as it slept in the mother's lap, smiled as its legalised despoiler uttered these last words, and poor Magdalene, smote to the heart by the incident, melted into tears; but by a powerful effort, she repressed any audible evidence of grief, and shading her eyes with her hand, her tears dropped in silence over her sleeping child.

Gerald observed her emotion, and found it difficult to master his own feelings.

"Now it is rather hard," continued the soldier, "that I have been hunting up and down the country for this confounded place, and can't find it. I thought it a fine thing, but I suppose it's nothing to talk of, or somebody would know of it; and more provoking still, we soldiers have yet our hands so full of work, that I only got four days' leave, and to-morrow night I am bound to return to Dublin, or I shall be guilty of a breach of duty; and how I am to return, with my horse in the disabled state in which this detestable country has left him, I cannot conceive."

"You will be hard run to accomplish it," said Gerald.

"Now will you make a bargain with me?" said the soldier.

"Of what nature?" said Gerald.

"There," said the soldier, throwing down on the table a piece of folded parchment—"there is the debenture entitling the holder thereof to the property I have named. Now, I must give up looking for it, for the present, and I am tired of hunting after it, into the bargain; besides, God knows when I may be able to come here again. You are on the spot, and may make use of this instrument, which empowers you to take full possession of the property whatever it may be; to you it *may* be valuable. At a word, then, if I give you this debenture, will you give me the white horse that is standing in your stable?"

Next to his wife and children, Gerald Pepper loved his white horse; and the favourite animal so suddenly and unexpectedly named startled him, and strange as it may appear, he paused for a moment; but Magdalene, unseen by the soldier, behind whom she was seated, clasped her outstretched hands in the action of supplication to her husband, and met his eye with an imploring look that at once produced his answer.

"Agreed!" said Gerald.

"'Tis a bargain," said the soldier; and he tossed the debenture across the table as the property of the man whom it was intended to leave destitute.

Having thus put his host into possession of his own property, the soldier commenced spending the night pleasantly, and it need

their exultation in his triumphs, had a deeper motive than mere admiration as a warrior. What that motive was, it would be foreign to my pages to touch upon, therefore let me resume.

The conversation amongst these peasant politicians turned upon Buonaparte's imprisonment at St. Helena, and some of the party, unwilling to believe it, doubted the affair altogether.

"By the powdhers o' war," said one, "I'll never b'live that he's a presoner. Tut—who could take him presoner? There's none o' them aiqual to it."

"Oh, I'm afeard it's too thrue it is," said another.

"An' you b'live it, thin?" said a third.

"Faix, I do. Sure, Masther Frank—the captain, I mane—said he seen him there himself."

"Tare-an-ouns, did he see him in airnest?"

"Sure enough, faith, with his own two eyes."

"And was he in chains, like a *rale* presoner?"

"Oh, no, man alive! Sure, they wouldn't go for to put a chain an *him*, like any other housebraker, or the like o' that."

"Well, sure, I heerd them makin' spaches about it at the meetin' was beyant in the town last summer; and a gintleman out o' Dublin, *that kem down an purpose*, had the *hoith* o' fine language all about it, and I remember well he said these very words: 'They will never *blot* the *stain* from their *annuals;* and when he *dies* it will be a *livin'* disgrace to them; for what can he do but die,' says he, '*non compossed* as he is by the wide oceant, chained, undher a burnin' *climax*, to that *salutary* rock? Oh! think o' that!' So you see, he was chained, accordin' to his account."

"But Masther Frank, I tell you, says he *seen* him; and there's no chain an him, at all; but he says he is *there* for sartin."

"Oh, murther, murther! Well, if he's there, sure, he's a pres'ner, and that'll brake his heart."

"Oh, thrue for you! Think o' Bonyparty bein' a presoner like any other man, and him that was able to go over the whole world wherever he plazed, bein' obleeged to live an a rock."

"Aye," said the repeater of the *spache;* "and the villians to have him undher that burnin' climax. I wondher what is it?"

"I didn't hear Masther Frank say a word about that. Oh, what will my poor Bony do, at all, at all!"

"By dad, it is hard for to say."

"By gor!" said Terry Regan, who had been hitherto a silent listener. "I dunna what the divil he'll do wid himself now, *barrin' he takes to dhrink.*"

"Faix, an' there is great comfort in the sup, sure enough," said one of his companions.

"To be sure there is," said Terry. "Musha, thin, Phil," said he to one of the party, "give us 'The Jug o' Punch,' the sorra betther song you have than that same, and sure, it's just the very thing that will be *nate and opprobrious* at this present, as they say in the spaches at the char'ty dinners."

"Well, I'll do my endeavour, if it's plazin' to the company," said Phil.

"That's your sort," said Terry. "Rise it, your sowl!"

Phil then proceeded to sing, after some preliminary hums and hahs and coughing to clear his voice, the following old ballad:

THE JUG OF PUNCH

As I was sitting in my room,
One pleasant evening in the month of June,
I heard a thrush singing in a bush,
And the tune he sung was a jug o' punch.

> Too ra loo! too ra loo! too ra loo! too ra loo!
> A jug o' punch! a jug o' punch!
> The tune he sung was a jug o' punch.

What more divarshin might a man desire
Than to be seated by a nate turf fire,
And by his side a purty wench,
And on the table a jug o' punch?

> Too ra loo, etc.

The Muses twelve and Apollio famed,
In *Castilian* pride dhrinks *pernicious* sthrames;
But I would not grudge them tin times as much,
As long as I had a jug o' punch.

> Too ra loo, etc.

Then the mortial gods dhrinks their necthar wine,
And they tell me claret is very fine;
But I'd give them all, just in a bunch,
For one jolly pull at a jug o' punch.

> Too ra loo, etc.

The docthor fails, with all his art,
To cure an imprission an the heart;
But if life was gone—within an inch—
What would bring it back like a jug o' punch?

> Too ra loo, etc.

But when I *am* dead and in my grave,
No costly tombstone will I crave;
But I'll dig a grave both wide and deep,
With a jug o' punch at my head and feet.

> Too ra loo, too ra loo, too ra loo, fol lol dhe roll;
> A jug o' punch! a jug o' punch!
> Oh! more power to your elbow, my jug o' punch!

Most uproarious applause followed this brilliant lyric, and the thumping of fists and the pewter pots on the table testified the admiration the company entertained for their minstrel.

"My sowl, Phil!" said Terry Regan, "it's betther and betther you're growing every night I hear you; and the real choice sperit is in you that improves with age."

"Faith, an' there's no choicer sperit than this same Mrs. Muldoody has in her house," said one of the party, on whom the liquor had begun to operate, and who did not *take* Terry Regan's allusion.

"Well, fill your glass again with it," said Terry, doing the honours, and then, resuming the conversation and addressing Phil again, he said: "Why, thin, Phil, you have a terrible fine voice."

"Troth, an' you have, Phil," said another of the party. "It's a pity your mother hadn't more of yez—oh, that I may see the woman that deserves you, and that I may dance at your weddin'!"

"Faix, an' I'd rather sing at my own wake," said Phil.

"Och that you may be able!" said Terry Regan; "but I'm afeard there'll be a man hanged the day you die."

"Pray for yourself, Terry, if you plaze," said Phil.

"Well, sing us another song, thin."

"Not a one more I remimber," said Phil.

"Remimber!" said Terry. "Bad cess to me, but you know more songs than would make the fortune of a ballad singer."

"Throth, I can't think of one."

"Ah, don't think at all, man, but let the song out of you. Sure, it'll come of itself if you're willin'."

"Bad cess to me if I remimber one."

"Oh, I'll jog your memory," said Terry. "Sing us the song you deludhered ould Roony's daughter with."

"What's that?" said Phil.

"Oh, you purtind not to know, you desaiver."

"Throth, an' I don't," said Phil.

"Why, bad fortune to you, you know it well—sure, the poor girl was never the same since she heerd it, you kem over her so, with the tindherness."

"Well, what was it; can't you tell me?"

"It was the 'Pig that was in Aughrim.'"

"Oh, that's a beautiful song, sure enough, and it's too thrue, it is. Oh, *them* vagabone staymers that's goin' evermore to England, the divil a pig they'll lave in the counthry, at all."

"Faix, I'm afeard so—but that's no rule why you should not sing the song. Out with it, Phil, my boy."

"Well, here goes," said Phil, and he commenced singing in a most doleful strain the following ballad:

THE PIG THAT WAS IN AUGHRIM.

The pig that was in Aughrim was dhruv to foreign parts,
And when he was goin' an the road it bruk the ould sow's heart.
" Oh," says she, " my counthry's ruin'd and desarted now by all,
And the rise of pigs in England will ensure the counthry's fall,
For the landlords and the pigs are all goin' hand in hand—"

"Oh, stop, Phil jewel," said the fellow who had been doing so much honour to Mrs. Muldoody's liquor—"stop, Phil, my darlin'!" and here he began to cry in a fit of drunken tenderness. "Oh, stop, Phil—that's too much for me—oh, I can't stand it at all. Murther, murther! but it's heart-breakin', so it is."

After some trouble on the part of his companions, this tender-hearted youth was reconciled to hearing the "Pig that was in Aughrim" concluded, though I would not vouch for so much on the part of my readers, and therefore I will quote no more of it. But he was not the only person who began to be influenced by the potent beverage that had been circulating, and the party became louder in their mirth and more diffuse in their conversation, which occasionally was conducted on the good old plan of a Dutch concert, where every man plays his own tune. At last, one of the revellers, who had just sufficient sense left to know it was time to go, yet not sufficient resolution to put his notion in practice, got up and said: "Good-night, boys!"

"Who's that sayin' good-night?" called out Terry Regan, in a tone of indignation.

"Oh, it's only me, and it's time for me to go, you know yourself, Terry," said the deserter; "and the wife will be as mad as a hatter if I stay out longer."

"By the powers o' Moll Kelly, if you had three wives you mustn't go yet," said the president.

"By dad, I must, Terry."

"Ah, thin, why?"

"Bekase I must."

"That's so good a raison, Barny, that I'll say no more—only, mark my words, you'll be sorry."

"*Will* be sorry," said Barny. "Faix, an' it's sorry enough *I am*—and small blame to me; for the company's pleasant and the dhrink's good."

"And why won't you stay, thin?"

"Bekase I must go, as I tould you before."

"Well, be off wid you at wanst, and don't be spylin' good company, if you won't stay. Be off wid you, I tell you, and don't be standin' there with your hat in your hand like an ass betune two bundles o' hay, as you are, but go if you're goin'—and the Curse of Kishogue an you!"

"Well, good-night, boys!" said the departing reveller.

"Faix, you shall have no good-night from uz. You're a bad fellow, Barny Corrigan—so the Curse o' Kishogue an you!"

"Oh, tare-an-ouns," said Barny, pausing at the door, "don't put the curse an a man that is goin' the road, and has to pass by the Rath,[1] more betoken, and no knowin' where the fairies would be."

"Throth, thin, and I will," said Terry Regan, increasing in energy, as he saw Barny was irresolute—"and may the Curse o' Kishogue light on you again and again !"

"Oh, do you hear this ! ! !" exclaimed Barny, in a most comical state of distress.

"Aye !" shouted the whole party, almost at a breath ; "the Curse o' Kishogue an you—and *your health to wear it !* "

"Why, thin, what the dickens do you mane by *that* curse ?" said Barny. "I thought I knew all the curses out, but I never heerd of the Curse o' Kishogue before."

"Oh, you poor, ignorant craythur," said Terry: "Where were you born and bred, at all, at all ? Oh, signs on it, you were always in a hurry to brake up good company, or it's not askin' you'd be for the maynin' of the Curse o' Kishogue."

"Why, thin, what *does* it mane ?" said Barny, thoroughly posed.

"Pull off your caubeen and sit down forninst me there, and tackle to the dhrink like a man, and it is I that will enlighten your benighted undherstandin', and a beautiful warnin' it will be to you all the days o' your life, and all snakin' chaps like you, that would be in a hurry to take to the road and lave a snug house like this, while there was the froth an the pot or the bead an the naggin."

So Barny sat down again, amidst the shouts and laughter of his companions, and after the liquor had passed merrily round the table for some time, Terry, in accordance with his promise, commenced his explanation of the malediction that had brought Barny Corrigan back to his seat ; but before he began, he filled a fresh glass, and profiting by the example, I will proceed with the narrative :—

You see, there was wanst a mighty dacent boy, called Kishogue —and not a complater chap was in the siven parishes nor himself —and for dhrinkin,' or coortin' (and by the same token he was a darlint among the girls, he was so bowld), or cudgellin', or runnin', or wrastlin', or the like o' that, none could come near him ; and at patthern, or fair, or the dance, or the wake, Kishogue was the flower o' the flock.

Well, to be sure, the gintlemen iv the counthry did not belove

[1] Fairies are supposed to haunt all old mounds of earth, such as raths, tumuli, etc., etc.

THE CURSE OF KISHOGUE

him so well as his own sort—that is, the *eldherly* gintlemen, for as to the young 'squires, by gor, they loved him like one of themselves, and betther a'most, for they knew well that Kishogue was the boy to put them up to all sorts and sizes of divilment and divarshin, and that was all they wanted—but the ould, studdy [steady] gintlemen—the responsible people like, didn't give in to his ways at all—and in throth, they used to be thinkin' that if Kishogue was out of the counthry, body and bones, that the counthry would not be the worse iv it, in the laste, and that the deer and the hares and the pattheridges wouldn't be scarcer in the laste, and that the throut and the salmon would lade an aisier life ; but they could get no howlt of him, good or bad, for he was as cute as a fox, and there was no sitch thing as getting him at an amplush, at all, for he was like a weasel a'most— *asleep wid his eyes open.*

Well, that's the way it was for many a long day, and Kishogue was as happy as the day was long, antil, as bad luck id have it, he made a mistake one night, as the story goes, and by dad, how he could make the same mistake was never cleared up yet, barrin' that the night was dark, or that Kishogue had a dhrop o' dhrink in ; but the mistake *was* made, and *this* was the mistake, you see : that he consaived he seen his own mare threspassin' an the man's field by the roadside, and so, with that he cotched the mare—that is, the mare to all appearance, but it was not his own mare, but the Squire's horse, which he tuk for his own mare —all in a mistake, and he thought that she had sthrayed away, and not likin' to see *his* baste threspassin' an another man's field, what does he do, but he dhrives home the horse *in a mistake,* you see, and how he could do the like is hard to say, excep'n that the night was dark, as I said before, or that he had a dhrop too much in ; but howsomever, the mistake was made, and a sore mistake it was for poor Kishogue, for he never persaived it at all, antil three days afther, when the polisman kem to him and tould him he should go along with him.

" For what ? " says Kishogue.

" Oh, you're mighty innocent," says the polisman.

" Thrue for you, sir," says Kishogue, as quite [quiet] as a child. " And where are you goin' to take me, may I make bowld to ax, sir ? " says he.

" To jail," says the peeler.

" For what ? " says Kishogue.

" For staalin' the Squire's horse," says the peeler.

" It's the first I heerd of it," says Kishogue.

" Throth, thin, 'twon't be the last you'll hear of it," says the other.

" Why, tare-an-ouns, sure, it's no housebrakin' for a man to dhrive home his own mare," says Kishogue.

" No," says the peeler; " but it is *burglaarious* to sarcumvint another man's horse," says he.

" But supposin' 'twas a mistake," says Kishogue.

" By gor, it'll be the *dear* mistake to you," says the polisman.

" That's a *poor* case," says Kishogue.

But there was no use in talkin'. He might as well have been whistlin' jigs to a milestone as sthrivin' to invaigle the polisman, and the ind of it was, that he was obleeged to march off to jail, and there he lay in lavendher, like Paddy Ward's pig, antil the 'sizes kem an, and Kishogue, you see, bein' of a high sperrit, did not like the iday at all of bein' undher a complimint to the king for his lodgin'. Besides, to a chap like him, that was used all his life to goin' round the world for sport, the thoughts o' confinement was altogether contagious, though, indeed, his friends endayvoured for to make it as agreeable as they could to him, for he was mightily beloved in the counthry, and they wor goin' to see him mornin', noon, and night—throth, they led the turnkey a busy life lettin' them in and out, for they wor comin' and goin' evermore, like Mulligan's blanket.

Well, at last the 'sizes kem an, and down kem the sheriffs and the judge, and the jury and the witnesses, all book-sworn to tell nothin' but the born thruth; and with that, Kishogue was the first that was put an his thrial for not knowin' the differ betune his own mare and another man's horse, for they wished to give an example to the counthry, and he was bid to hould up his hand at the bar (and a fine big fist he had of his own, by the same token)—and up he held it—no ways danted at all, but as bowld as a ram. Well, thin, a chap in a black coat and a frizzled wig and spectacles gets up, and he reads and reads, and you'd think he'd never have done readin'; and it was all about Kishogue—as we heard afther—but could not make out at the time—and no wondher; and in throth, Kishogue never done the half of what the dirty little ottomy was readin' about him— barrin' he knew lies iv him; and Kishogue himself, poor fellow, got frekened at last, when he heerd him goin' an at that rate about him, but afther a bit, he tuk heart and said :

" By this and by that, I never done the half o' that, anyhow."

" Silence in the coort ! " says the crier—puttin' him down that-a-way. Oh, there's no justice for a poor boy, at all !

" Oh, murther ! " says Kishogue, " is a man's life to be sworn away afther this manner, and mustn't spake a word ? "

" Hould your tongue ! " says my lord the judge. And so, afther some more jabberin' and gibberish, the little man in the spectacles threw down the paper and asked Kishogue if he was guilty or not guilty.

" I never done it, my lord," says Kishogue.

"Answer as you are bid, sir," says the spectacle man.

"I'm innocent, my lord!" says Kishogue.

"Bad cess to you, can't you say what you're bid," says my lord the judge. "*Guilty* or *not* guilty."

"*Not* guilty," says Kishogue.

"I don't believe you," says the judge.

"Small blame to you," says Kishogue. "You're ped for hangin' people, and you must do something for your wages."

'You've too much prate, sir," says my lord.

"Faix, thin, I'm thinking' it's yourself and your friend, the hangman, will cure me o' that very soon," says Kishogue.

And thrue for him, faith, he wasn't far out in sayin' that same, for they murthered him intirely. They brought a terrible sight o' witnesses agin him, that swore away his life an the cross-examination; and indeed, sure enough, it *was* the crossest examination altogether I ever seen. Oh, they wor the bowld witnesses, that would *sware a hole in an iron pot* any day in the year. Not but that Kishogue's friends done their duty by him. Oh, they stud to him like men, and swore a power for him, and sthrove to make out a *lullaby* for him—maynin,' by that same, that he was asleep in another place at the time—but it wouldn't do, they could not make it *plazin'* to the judge and the jury; and my poor Kishogue was condimned for to die; and the judge put an his black cap—and indeed, it is not becomin'—and discoorsed the hoighth of fine language, and gev Kishogue a power o' good advice, that it was a mortial pity Kishogue didn't get sooner; and the last words the judge said was: "The Lord have marcy an your sowl!"

"Thank'ee, my lord," says Kishogue; "though, indeed, it is few has luck or grace afther your prayers."

And sure enough, faith; for the next Sathurday Kishogue was ordhered out to be hanged, and the sthreets through which he was to pass was mighty throng; for in them days, you see, the people used to be hanged outside o' the town, not all as one, as now, when we're hanged genteelly out o' the front o' the jail; but in them days they did not attind to the comforts o' the people at all, but put them into a cart, all as one a conthrairy pig goin' to market, and stravaiged them through the town to the gallows, that was full half a mile beyant it; but to be sure, whin they kem to the corner of the crass streets, where the Widdy Houlaghan's public-house was then, afore them dirty swaddlers knocked it down and built a meetin'-house there—bad cess to them, sure, they're spylin' divarshin wherever they go—when they kem there, as I was tellin' you, the purcesshin was always stopped, and they had a fiddler and mulled wine for the divarshin of the presoner, for to rise his heart for what he was to go through; for, by all accounts, it is not plazin' to be goin' to be hanged, supposin' you die in a good cause itself, as my Uncle Jim tould me whin he suffer'd for killin' the gauger.

Well, you see, they always stopped tin minutes at the public-house, not to hurry a man with his dhrink, and besides, to give the presoner an opportunity for sayin' an odd word or so to a frind in the crowd, to say nothin' of its bein' mighty improvin to the throng, to see the man lookin' pale at the thoughts o' death, and maybe an idification and warnin' to thim that was inclined to sthray. But however, it happened, and the like never happened afore nor sence; but as bad luck would have it, that day the divil a fiddler was there whin Kishogue dhruv up in the cart, no ways danted, at all; but the minit the cart stopped rowlin' he called out as stout as a ram : "Sind me out Tim Riley here"—Tim Riley was the fiddler's name—"sind me out Tim Riley here," says he, "that he may rise my heart wid 'The Rakes o' Mallow';" for he was a Mallow man, by all accounts, and mighty proud of his town. Well, av coorse, the tune was not to be had, bekase Tim Riley was not there, but was lyin' dhrunk in a ditch at the same time comin' home from confission; and when poor Kishogue heerd that he could not have his favourite tune, it wint to his heart to that degree that he'd hear of no comfort in life, and he bid them dhrive him an, and put him out o' pain at wanst.

"Oh, take the dhrink anyhow, aroon," says the Widdy Houlaghan, who was mighty tindher-hearted, and always attinded the man that was goin' to be hanged with the dhrink herself, if he was ever so grate a sthranger; but if he was a frind of her own, she'd go every fut to the gallows wid him and see him suffer. Oh, she was a darlint! Well—"Take the dhrink, Kishogue, my jewel," says she, handin' him up a brave big mug o' mulled wine, fit for a lord—but he wouldn't touch it. "Take it out o' my sight," says he, "for my heart is low because Tim Riley desaived me, whin I expected to die game, like one of the Rakes o' Mallow! Take it out o' my sight," says he, puttin' it away wid his hand, and sure, 'twas the first time Kishogue was ever known to refuse the dhrop o' dhrink, and many remarked that it was *the change before death* was comin' over him.

Well, away they rowled to the gallows, where there was no delay in life for the presoner, and the sheriff asked him if he had anything to say to him before he suffered; but Kishogue hadn't a word to throw to a dog, and av coorse, he said nothin' to the sheriff, and wouldn't say a word that might be improvin', even to the crowd, by way of an idification; and indeed, a sore disappointment it was to the throng, for they thought he would make an iligant dyin' speech; and the prenthers there, and the ballad-singers, all ready for to take it down complate, and thought it was a dirty turn of Kishogue to chate them out o' their honest penny, like; but they owed him no spite, for all that, for they considhered his heart was low an account of the disappointment, and he was lookin' mighty pale while they wor makin matthers tidy for him; and indeed, the last words he said himself was: "Put me out o' pain at wanst, for my heart is low bekase Tim Riley desaived me, whin I thought he would rise it, that I might die like a rale Rake o' Mallow!" And so, to make a long story short, my jewel, they done the business for him—it was soon over wid him; it was just one step wid him, aff o' the laddher into glory; and to do him justice, though he was lookin pale, he died bowld, and put his best leg foremost.

Well, what would you think, but just as all was over wid him, there was a shout o' the crowd, and a shilloo that you'd think would split the sky; and what should we see gallopin' up to the gallows, but a man covered with dust an a white horse, to all appearance, but it wasn't a white horse but a black horse, only white wid the foam, he was dhruv to that degree; and the man hadn't a breath to dhraw, and couldn't spake, but dhrew a piece o' paper out of the breast of his coat and handed it up to the sheriff; and, my jewel, the sheriff grewn as white as the paper itself, when he clapt his eyes an it; and says he:

"Cut him down—cut him down this minute!" says he; and the dhragoons made a slash at the messenger, but he ducked his head and sarcumvinted them. And then the sheriff shouted out: "Stop, you villians, and bad luck to yiz, you murtherin' vagabones," says he to the sojers; "is it goin' to murther the man you wor? It isn't him at all I mane, but the man that's hangin'. Cut *him* down," says he; and they cut him down; but it was no use. It was all over wid poor Kishogue; he was as dead as small-beer, and as stiff as a crutch.

"Oh, tare-an-ouns," says the sheriff, tarin' the hair aff his head at the same time, with the fair rage. "Isn't it a poor case that he's dead, and here is a reprieve that is come for him; but, bad cess to him," says he, "it's his own fault, he wouldn't take it aisy."

"Oh, millia murther! millia murther!" cried out the Widdy Houlaghan, in the crowd. "Oh, Kishogue, my darlint, why did you refuse my mull'd wine? Oh, if you stopped wid me to take your dhrop o' dhrink, you'd be alive and merry now!"

So that is the maynin' of the Curse o' Kishogue; for, you see, Kishogue was hanged *for lavin' his liquor behind him.*

THE FAIRY FINDER

" Finding a fortune " is a phrase often heard amongst the peasantry of Ireland. If any man from small beginnings arrives at wealth, in a reasonable course of time, the fact is scarcely ever considered as the result of perseverance, superior intelligence or industry; it passes as a by-word through the country that " he found a fortin' " ; whether by digging up " a crock o' goold " in the ruins of an old abbey, or by catching a Leprechaun and forcing him to " deliver or die," or discovering it behind an old wainscot, is quite immaterial ; the *when* or the *where* is equally unimportant, and the thousand are satisfied with the rumour: " He found a fortin'." Besides, going into particulars destroys romance—and the Irish are essentially romantic—and their love of wonder is more gratified in considering the change from poverty to wealth as the result of superhuman aid, than in attributing it to the mere mortal causes of industry and prudence.

The crone of every village has plenty of stories to make her hearers wonder how fortunes have been arrived at by extraordinary short cuts ; and as it has been laid down as an axiom, " That there never was a fool who had not a greater fool to admire him," so there never was an old woman who told such stories without plenty of listeners.

Now, Darby Kelleher was one of the latter class, and there was a certain collioch[1] who was an extensive dealer in the marvellous, and could supply " wholesale, retail, and for exportation," any customer such as Darby Kelleher, who not only was a devoted listener, but also made an occasional offering at the cave of the sibyl, in return for her oracular communications. This tribute generally was tobacco, as the collioch was partial to chewing the weed ; and thus Darby returned a *quid pro quo*, without having any idea that he was giving a practical instance of the foregoing well-known pun.

Another constant attendant at the hut of the hag was Oonah Lenehan, equally prone to the marvellous with Darby Kelleher, and quite his equal in idleness. A day never passed without Darby and Oonah paying the old woman a visit. She was sure to be " at home," for age and decrepitude rendered it impossible for her to be otherwise, the utmost limit of her ramble from her own chimney-corner being the seat of sods outside the door of her hut, where, in the summer-time, she was to be found, so soon as the sunbeams fell on the front of her abode, and made the seat habitable for one whose accustomed vicinity to the fire rendered heat indispensable to comfort.

[1] Old woman.

THE FAIRY FINDER

Here she would sit and rock herself to and fro in the hot noons of July and August, her own appearance and that of her wretched cabin being in admirable keeping. To a fanciful beholder the question might have suggested itself, whether the hag was made for the hovel or it for her; or whether they had grown into a likeness of one another, as man and wife are said to do, for there were many points of resemblance between them. The tattered thatch of the hut was like the straggling hair of its mistress, and Time, that had grizzled the latter, had covered the former with grey lichens. To its mud walls, a strong likeness was to be found in the tint of the old woman's shrivelled skin; they were both seriously out of the perpendicular; and the rude mud and wicker chimney of the edifice having toppled over the gable, stuck out, something in the fashion of the doodeen, or short pipe, that projected from the old woman's upper storey; and so they both were smoking away from morning till night; and to complete the similitude sadly, both were poor, both lonely, both fast falling to decay.

Here were Darby Kelleher and Oonah Lenehan sure to meet every day. Darby might make his appearance thus:

" Good morrow, kindly, granny."

" The same to you, avic," mumbled out the crone.

" Here's some 'baccy for you, granny."

" Many thanks to you, Darby. I didn't lay it out for seeing you so airly the day."

" No, nor you wouldn't neither, only I was passin' this-a-way, runnin' an arrand for the Squire, and I thought I might as well step in and ax you how you wor."

" Good boy, Darby."

" Throth, an' it's a hot day that's in it, this blessed day. Phew! Faix, it's out o' breath I am, and mighty hot intirely; for I was runnin' a'most half the way, bekase it's an arrand, you see, and the Squire tould me to make haste, and so I did, and wint across the fields by the short cut; and as I was passin' by the ould castle, I remimbered what you tould me a while agon, granny, about the crock o' goold that is there *for sartin*, if anyone could come upon it."

" An' that's thrue indeed, Darby avick—and never heerd any other the longest day I can remimber."

" Well, well! think o' that! Oh, thin, it's he that 'ill be the lucky fellow that finds it."

" Thrue for you, Darby; but that won't be *antil it is laid out* for some one to rise it."

" Sure, that's what I said to myself often; and why mightn't it be my chance to be the man that it was laid out for to find it."

" There's no knowin'," mumbled the crone mysteriously, as she shook the ashes out of her tobacco-pipe, and replenished the *doodeen* with some of the fresh stock Darby had presented.

"Faix, an' that's thrue, sure enough. Oh, but you've a power o' knowledge, granny! Sure enough, indeed, there's no knowin'; but they say there's great virtue in dhrames."

"That's ondeniable, Darby," said the hag; "and by the same token maybe you'd step into the house and bring me out a bit o' live turf to light my pipe."

"To be sure, granny;" and away went Darby to execute the commission.

While he was raking from amongst the embers on the hearth a piece of turf sufficiently "alive" for the purpose, Oonah made her appearance outside the hut, and gave the usual cordial salutation to the old woman. Just as she had done her civility, out came Darby, holding the bit of turf between the two extremities of an osier twig, bent double for the purpose of forming a rustic tongs.

"Musha, an' is that you, Darby?" said Oonah.

"Who else would it be?" said Darby.

"Why, you tould me over an hour agone, down there in the big field, that you wor in a hurry."

"And so I am in a hurry, and wouldn't be here, only I jist stepped in to say 'God save you!' to the mother here, and to light her pipe for her, the craythur."

"Well, don't be standin' there lettin' the coal go black out, Darby," said the old woman; "but let me light my pipe at wanst."

"To be sure, granny," said Darby, applying the morsel of lighted ember to the bowl of her pipe until the process of ignition had been effected. "And now, Oonah, my darlint, if you're so sharp an other people, what the dickens brings you here, when it is mindin' the geese in the stubbles you ought to be, and not here? What would the misthriss say to that, I wondher?"

"Oh, I left them safe enough, and they're able to take care of themselves for a bit, and I wanted to ax the granny about a dhrame I had.'

"Sure, so do I," said Darby; "and you know *first come first sarved* is a good ould sayin'. And so, granny, you own to it that there's a power o' vartue in dhrames?"

A long-drawn whiff of the pipe was all the hag vouchsafed in return.

"Oh, thin, but that's the iligant tabaccy! Musha, but it's fine an' sthrong, and takes the breath from one a'most, it's so good. Long life to you, Darby—paugh!"

"You're kindly welkim, granny. An' as I was sayin' about the dhrames—you say there's a power o' vartue in them."

"Who says agin it?" said the hag authoritatively, and looking with severity on Darby.

"Sure, an' it's not me you'd suspect o' the like? I was only goin' to say that *myself* had a mighty sharp dhrame last night, and sure, I kem to ax you about the maynin' av it."

"Well, avic, tell us your dhrame," said the hag, sucking her pipe with increased energy.

"Well, you see," said Darby, "I dhremt I was goin' along a road, and that all of a suddint I kem to *crass* roads, and, you know, there's grate vartue in crass roads."

"That's thrue, avourneen! Paugh! go an."

"Well, as I was sayin', I kem to the crass roads, and soon afther I seen four walls. Now, I think the four walls *manes* the ould castle."

"Likely enough, avic."

"Oh," said Oonah, who was listening with her mouth as wide open as if the faculty of hearing lay there, instead of in her ears, "sure, you know the ould castle has only *three* walls, and how could that be it?"

"No matther for that," said the crone, "it *ought* to have four, and that's the same thing."

"Well, well! I never thought o' that," said Oonah, lifting her hands in wonder. "Sure enough, so it ought!"

"Go on, Darby," said the hag.

"Well, I thought the greatest sight o' crows ever I seen flew out o' the castle, and I think *that* must mane the goold there is in it!"

"Did you count how many there was?" said the hag, with great solemnity.

"Faith, I never thought o' that," said Darby, with an air of vexation,

"Could you tell me itself, wor they odd or even, avic?"

"Faix, an' I could not say for *sartin*."

"Ah, that's it!" said the crone, shaking her head in token of disappointment. "How can I tell the mayin' o' your dhrame, if you don't know how it kem out exactly?"

"Well, granny, but don't you think the crows was *likely* for goold?"

"Yis—if they flew heavy."

"Throth, thin, an' now I remimber, they did fly heavy, and I said to myself there would be rain soon, the crows was flyin' so heavy."

"I wish you didn't dhrame o' rain, Darby."

"Why, granny? What harm is it?"

"Oh, nothin'; only it comes in a crass place there."

"But it doesn't spile the dhrame, I hope?"

"Oh no. Go an."

"Well, with that, I thought I was passin' by Doolins the miller's, and says he to me: 'Will you carry home this sack o' male for me?' Now, you know, male is money, every fool knows."

"Right, avic."

"And so I tuk the sack o' male an my shouldher, and I thought the woight iv it was killin' me, just as if it *was* a sack o' goold."

"Go an, Darby."

"And with that I thought I met with a cat, and that, you know, manes an ill-nathur'd woman."

"Right, Darby."

"And says she to me: 'Darby Kelleher,' says she, 'you're mighty yollow. God bless you! is it the jandhers you have?' says she. Now wasn't that mighty sharp? I think the jandhers manes goold?"

"Yis; if it was the yollow jandhers you dhremt iv, but not the black jandhers."

"Well, it *was* the yollow jandhers."

"Very good, avic; that's makin' a fair offer at it."

"I thought so myself," said Darby, "more by token when there was a dog in my dhrame next; and that's a frind, you know."

"Right, avic."

"And he had a silver collar an him."

"Oh, bad luck to that silver collar, Darby. What made you dhrame o' silver at all?"

"Why, what harm?"

"Oh, I thought you knew better nor to dhrame o' silver. Why, cushla machree, sure, silver is a disappointment, all the world over."

"Oh, murther!" said Darby, in horror, "and is my dhrame spylte [spoiled] by that blackguard collar?"

"Nigh hand, indeed, but not all out. It would be spylte only for the dog, but the dog is a frind, and so it will be only a frindly disappointment, or maybe a fallin' out with an acquaintance."

"Oh, what matther," said Darby. "So the dhrame is to the good still?"

"The dhrame *is* to the good still; but tell me if you dhremt o' three sprigs o' *spare*mint at the ind iv it?"

"Why, thin, now I could not say for sartin, bekase I was nigh wakin' at the time, and the dhrame was not so clear to me."

"I wish you could be sartin o' that."

"Why, I have it an my mind that there *was* sparemint in it, bekase I thought there was a garden in part iv it, and the sparemint was *likely* to be there."

"Sure enough, and so you did dhrame o' the three sprigs o' sparemint.

"Indeed, I could a'most make my book-oath that I dhremt iv it. I'm partly sartin, if not all out."

"Well, that's raysonable. It's a good dhrame, Darby."

"Do you tell me so!"

"'Deed an' it is, Darby. Now wait till the next quarther o' the new moon, and dhrame agaiu *then*, and you'll see what'll come of it."

"By dad, an' I will, granny. Oh, but it's you *has* taken the maynin' out of it beyant everything; and faix, if I find the crock, it's yourself won't be the worse iv it; but I must be goin', granny, for the Squire bid me to hurry, or else I would stay longer wid you. Good mornin' to you—good mornin', Oonah! I'll see you to-morrow sometime, granny." And off went Darby, leisurely enough.

The foregoing dialogue shows the ready credulity of poor Darby; but it was not in his belief of the "vartue of dhrames" that his weakness only lay. He likewise had a most extensive creed as regarded fairies of all sorts and sizes, and was always on the look-out for a Leprechaun. Now, a Leprechaun is a fairy of peculiar tastes, properties and powers, which it is necessary to acquaint the reader with. His taste as to occupation is very humble, for he employs himself in making shoes, and he loves retirement, being fond of shady nooks where he can sit alone and pursue his avocation undisturbed. He is quite a hermit in this respect, for there is no instance on record of two Leprechauns being seen together.

But he is quite a beau in his dress, notwithstanding, for he wears a red square-cut coat, richly laced with gold, waistcoat and inexpressibles of the same, cocked hat, shoes and buckles. He has the property of deceiving, in so great a degree, those who chance to discover him, that none has ever yet been known whom he has not overreached in the "keen encounter of the wits," which his meeting with mortals always produces. This is occasioned by his possessing the power of bestowing unbounded wealth on whoever can keep him within sight until he is weary of the *surveillance*, and gives the ransom demanded; and to this end the object of the mortal who is so fortunate as to surprise one is to seize him, and never withdraw his eye from him, until the threat of destruction forces the Leprechaun to produce the treasure; but the sprite is too many for us clumsy-witted earthlings, and is sure, by some device, to make us avert our eyes, when he vanishes at once.

This Enchanted Cobbler of the meadows Darby Kelleher was always on the look-out for. But though so constantly on the watch for a Leprechaun, he never had got even within sight of one, and the name of the Fairy Finder was bestowed upon him in derision. Many a trick, too, was played on him. Sometimes a twig stuck amongst long grass, with a red rag hanging upon it, has betrayed Darby into cautious observance and approach, until a nearer inspection, and a laugh from behind some neighbouring hedge, have dispelled the illusion. But this, though often repeated, did not cure him, and no turkey-cock had a quicker eye for a bit of red, or flew at it with greater eagerness, than Darby Kelleher; and he entertained the belief that one day or other he would reap the reward of all his watching, by finding a Leprechaun in good earnest.

But that was all in the hands of Fate, and must be waited for. In the meantime, there was the castle and the "crock o' goold" for a certainty, and under the good omens of the "sharp dhrame" he had, he determined on taking that affair in hand at once. For his companion in the labour of digging, and pulling the ponderous walls of the castle to pieces, he selected Oonah, who was, in the parlance of her own class, "a brave, two-handed, long-sided jack," and as great a believer in dreams and omens as Darby himself; besides, she promised profound secrecy, and agreed to take a small share of the treasure for her reward in assisting to discover it.

For about two months Darby and Oonah laboured in vain; but at last, something came of their exertions. In the course of their work, when they occasionally got tired, they would sit down to rest themselves and talk over their past disappointments and future hopes. Now it was during one of these intervals of repose that Darby, as he was resting himself on one of the coign-stones of the ruin, suddenly discovered—that he was in love with Oonah.

Now Oonah happened to be thinking much in the same sort of way about Darby at that very moment, and the end of the affair was, that Darby and Oonah were married the Sunday following.

The calculating Englishman will ask, Did he find the treasure before he married the girl? The unsophisticated boys of the sod never calculate on these occasions; and the story goes that Oonah Lenehan was the only treasure Darby discovered in the old castle. Darby's acquaintances were in high glee on the occasion, and swore he got *a great lob*—for Oonah, be it remembered, was on the grenadier scale, or what in Ireland is called "the full of a door," and the news spread over the country in some such fashion as this—

"Arrah, an' did you hear the news?"

"What news?"

"About Darby Kelleher."

"What of him?"

"Sure, he found a fairy at last."

" Tare-an-ounty ! "

"Thruth I'm tellin' you. He's married to Oonah Lenehan."

" Ha ! ha ! ha ! by the powers, it's she that is the rale fairy! Musha, more power to you, Darby, but you've cotched it in airnest now ! "

But the fairy he had caught did not satisfy Darby so far as to make him give up the pursuit for the future. He was still on the watch for a Leprechaun ; and one morning as he was going to his work, he stopped suddenly on his path, which lay through a field of standing corn, and his eye became riveted on some object with the most eager expression. He crouched and crawled, and was making his way with great caution towards the point of his attraction, when he was visited on the back of the head with a thump that considerably disturbed his visual powers, and the voice of his mother, a vigorous old beldame, saluted his ear at the same time with a hearty " Bad luck to you, you lazy thief ; what are you slindging there for, when it's mindin' your work you ought to be ? "

"Whist ! whist ! mother," said Darby, holding up his hand in token of silence.

" What do you mane, you omadhaun ? "

" Mother, be quiet, I bid you ! Whist ! I see it."

"What do you see ? "

"Stoop down here. Straight forninst you, don't you see it as plain as a pikestaff ? "

"See what ? "

"That little red thing."

"Well, what of it ? "

"See there, how it stirs. Oh, murther ! it's goin' to be off afore I can catch it. Oh, murther ! why did you come here at all, makin' a noise and frightenin' it away ? "

"Frightenin' what, you big fool ? "

"The Leprechaun there. Whisht ! it is quiet agin."

"May the d—l run a-huntin' wid you for a big omadhaun. Why, you born nath'ral, is it that red thing over there you mane ? "

" Yis ; to be sure it is. Don't spake so loud, I tell you."

" Why, bad scran to you, you fool, it's a poppy, it is, and nothin' else ; " and the old woman went over to the spot where it grew, and plucking it up by the roots, threw it at Darby, with a great deal of abuse into the bargain, and bade him go mind his work, instead of being a " slindging vagabone, as he was."

It was some time after this occurrence that Darby Kelleher had a meeting with a certain Doctor Dionysius MacFinn, whose name became much more famous than it had hitherto been, from the wonderful events that ensued in consequence.

Of the doctor himself it becomes necessary to say something. His father was one Paddy Finn, and had been so prosperous in the capacity of a cow doctor, that his son Denis, seeing the dignity of a professor in the healing art must increase in proportion to the nobleness of the animal he operates upon, determined to make the human, instead of the brute creation, the object of his care. To this end he was assisted by his father, who had scraped some money together in his humble calling, and having a spice of ambition in him, as well as his aspiring son, he set him up in the neighbouring village as an apothecary. Here Denny enjoyed the reputation of being an "iligant bone-setter"; and cracked skulls — the result of *fair* fighting and whisky fevers — were treated by him on the most approved principles. But Denny's father was gathered unto *his* fathers, and the son came into the enjoyment of all the old man's money. This, considering his condition, was considerable, and the possession of a few hundred pounds so inflated the apothecary, that he determined on becoming a "doctor" at once. For this purpose he gave up his apothecary's shop, and set off—where do you think?—to Spain.

Here he remained for some time, and returned to Ireland, declaring himself a full physician of one of the Spanish universities; his name of Denny Finn transformed into Doctor Dionysius MacFinn, or, as his neighbours chose to call it, MacFun, and fun enough the doctor certainly gave birth to. The little money he once had was spent in his pursuit of professional honours, and he returned to his native place with a full title and an empty purse, and his practice did not tend to fill it. At the same time, there was a struggle to keep up appearances. He kept a horse, or what he intended to be considered as such, but 'twas only a pony, and if he had but occasion to go to the end of the village on a visit, the pony was ordered on service.

He was glad to accept an invitation to dinner whenever he had the luck to get one, and the offer of a bed even was sure to be accepted, because that insured breakfast the next morning. Thus poor Doctor Dionysius made out the cause. Often asked to dinner from mingled motives of kindness and fun, for while a good dinner was a welcome novelty to the doctor, the absurdities of his pretension and manner rendered him a subject of unfailing diversion to his entertainers. Now, he had gone the round of all the snug farmers and country gentlemen in the district, but at last he had the honour to receive an invitation from *the* Squire himself, and on the appointed day Doctor Dionysius bestrode his pony, attired in the full dress of a Spanish physician, which happens to be *red* from head to foot, and presented himself at "The Hall."

When a groom appeared to take his "horse" to the stable, the doctor requested that his steed might be turned loose into the lawn, declaring it to be more wholesome for the animal than being cooped up in a house. The saddle and bridle were accordingly removed, and his desire complied with.

The doctor's appearance in the drawing-room, attired as he was, caused no small diversion, but attention was speedily called off from him by the announcement of dinner, that electric sound that stimulates a company at the same instant, and supersedes every other consideration whatsoever. Moreover, the Squire's dinners were notoriously good, and the doctor profited largely by the same that day, and lost no opportunity of filling his glass with the choice wines that surrounded him. This he did to so much purpose, that the poor little man was very far gone when the guests were about to separate.

At the doctor's request the bell was rung, and his horse ordered, as the last remaining few of the company were about to separate, but everyone of them had departed, and still there was no announcement of the steed being at the door. At length a servant made his appearance, and said it was impossible to catch the doctor's pony.

"What do you mean by 'catch'?" said the Squire. "Is it not in the stable?"

"No, sir."

Here an explanation ensued, and the Squire ordered a fresh attempt to be made to take the fugitive ; but though many fresh hands were employed in the attempt, the pony baffled all their efforts—every manœuvre usually resorted to on such occasions was vainly put in practice. He was screwed up into corners, but no sooner was he there than, squealing and flinging up his heels, he broke through the blockade. Again his flank was turned by nimble runners, but the pony was nimbler still ; a sieve full of oats was presented as an inducement, but the pony was above such vulgar tricks, and defied all attempts at being captured.

This was the mode by which the doctor generally secured the offer of a bed, and he might have been successful in this instance but for a knowing old coachman who was up to the trick, and out of pure fun, chose to expose it ; so, bringing out a huge blunder-buss, he said : "Never mind ; just let me at him, and I'll engage I'll make him stand."

"Oh, my good man," said the doctor, "pray don' take so much trouble—just let me go with you ;" and proceeding to the spot where the pony was still luxuriating on the rich grass of the Squire's lawn, he gave a low whistle, and the little animal walked up to his owner with as much tractability as a dog. The saddling and bridling did not take much time, and the doctor was obliged to renounce his hopes of a bed and the morrow's breakfast, and ride home—or homewards, I should say—for it was as little his destiny as his wish to sleep at home that night, for he was so overpowered with his potations that he could not guide the pony, and the pony's palate was so tickled by the fresh herbage that he wished for more of it, and finding a gate that led to a meadow, open by the roadside, he turned into the field, where he very soon turned the doctor into a ditch, so that they had bed and board between them to their heart's content.

The doctor and his horse slept and ate profoundly all night, and even the " rosy-fingered morn," as the poets have it, found them in the continuance of their enjoyment. Now it happened that Darby Kelleher was passing along the path that lay by the side of the ditch where the doctor was sleeping, and on perceiving him, Darby made as dead a set as ever pointer did at game.

The doctor, be it remembered, was dressed in red. Moreover, he was a little man, and his gold-laced hat and ponderous shoe-buckles completed the resemblance to the being that Darby took him for. Darby was at last certain that he had discovered a Leprechaun, and amaze so riveted him to the spot, and anxiety made his pulse beat so fast, that he could not move nor breathe for some seconds. At last he recovered himself, and stealing stealthily to the spot where the doctor slept, every inch of his approach made him more certain of the reality of his prize ; and when he found himself within reach of it, he made one furious spring, and flung himself on the unfortunate little man, fastening his tremendous fist on his throat, at the same time exclaiming in triumph : "Hurrah ! By the hoky, I have you at last ! "

The poor little doctor, thus rudely and suddenly aroused from his tipsy sleep, looked excessively bewildered when he opened his eyes, and met the glare of ferocious delight that Darby Kelleher cast upon him, and he gurgled out : "What's the matter ? " as well as the grip of Darby's hand upon his throat would permit him.

"Goold's the matther," shouted Darby. "Goold ! goold ! goold ! "

"What about goold ? " says the doctor.

"Goold—yollow goold—that's the matther."

"Is it Paddy Goold that's taken ill again ? " said the doctor, rubbing his eyes. "Don't choke me, my good man. I'll go immediately," said he, endeavouring to rise.

"By my sowl, you won't," said Darby, tightening his hold.

"For mercy's sake, let me go ! " said the doctor.

"Let you go, indeed !—ow ! ow ! "

"For the tender mercy—"

"Goold ! goold ! you little vagabone ! "

"Well, I'm going, if you let me."

"Divil a step;" and here he nearly choked him.

"Oh, murder! For God's sake!"

"Whisht, you thief! How *dar* you say God, you divil's imp!"

The poor little man, between the suddenness of his waking and the roughness of the treatment he was under, was in such a state of bewilderment, that for the first time he now perceived he was lying amongst grass and under bushes, and rolling his eyes about, he exclaimed:

"Where am I? God bless me!"

"Whisht! you little cruked ottomy—by the holy farmer, if you say God agin, I'll cut your throat."

"What do you hold me so tight for?"

"Just for fear you'd vanish, you see. Oh, I know you well."

"Then, my good man, if you know me so well, treat me with proper respect, if you please."

"Divil send you respect. Respect, indeed! that's a good thing. Musha, bad luck to your impidence, you thievin' ould rogue."

"Who taught you to call such names to your betters, fellow? How dare you use a professional gentleman so rudely?"

"Oh, do you hear this!—a profissionil gintleman! Arrah, do you think I don't know you, you little ould cobbler?"

"Cobbler! Zounds, what do you mean, you ruffian? Let me go, sirrah!" and he struggled violently to rise.

"Not a taste, 'scure, to the step you'll go out o' this till you give me what I want."

"What do you want, then?"

"Goold—goold!"

"Ho! ho! so you're a robber, sir. You want to rob me, do you?"

"Oh, what robbery it is! Throth, that won't do, as cunnin' as you think yourself; you won't frighten me that way. Come, give it at wanst—you may as well. I'll never let go my grip o' you antil you hand me out the goold."

"'Pon the honour of a gentleman, gold nor silver is not in my company. I have fourpence-halfpenny in my breeches' pocket, which you are welcome to if you let go my throat."

"Fourpence-ha'pny! Why, thin, do you think me sitch a *gom*, all out, as to put me off wid fourpence-hap'ny. Throth, for three straws, this minit I'd thrash you within an inch o' your life for your impidence. Come, no humbuggin'; out with the goold!"

"I have no gold. Don't choke me. If you murder me, remember there's law in the land. You'd better let me go."

"Not a fut. Gi' me the goold, I tell you, you little vagabone!" said Darby, shaking him violently.

" Don't murder me, for Heaven's sake ! "

" I will murdher you if you don't give me a hatful o' goold this minit."

" A hatful of gold ! Why, who do you take me for ? "

" Sure, I know you're a Leprechaun, you desaiver o' the world ! "

" A Leprechaun ! " said the doctor, in mingled indignation and amazement. " My good man, you mistake."

" Oh, how soft I am ! 'Twon't do, I tell you. I have you, and I'll hould you ; long I've been lookin' for you, and I cotch you at last, and by the 'tarnal o' war, I'll have your life or the goold."

" My good man, be merciful — you mistake — I'm no Leprechaun—I'm Doctor MacFinn."

" That won't do either ! You think to desaive me, but 'twon't do—just as if I didn't know a docthor from a Leprechaun. Gi' me the goold, you ould chate ! "

" I tell you, I'm Doctor Dionysius MacFinn. Take care what you're about—there's law in the land ; and I think I begin to know you. Your name is Kelleher ! "

" Oh, you cunnin' ould thief ! Oh, thin you are the complate ould rogue ; only I'm too able for you. You want to freken me, do you ? Oh, you little scrap o' deception, but you are deep ! "

" Your name is Kelleher—I remember. My good fellow, take care ; don't you know I'm Doctor MacFinn—don't you see I am ? "

" Why, thin, but you have the dirty yollow pinched look iv him, sure enough ; but don't I know you've only put in an you to desaive me ; besides, the docthor has dirty ould tatthers o' black clothes an him, and isn't as red as a sojer like you."

" That's an accident, my good man."

" Gi' me the goold this minit, and no more prate wid you."

" I tell you, Kelleher—"

" Hould your tongue, and gi' me the goold."

" By all that's—"

" Will you give it ? "

" How can I ? "

" Very well. You'll see what the ind of it 'ill be," said Darby, rising, but still keeping his iron grip of the doctor. " Now, for the last time, I ask you, will you gi' me the goold ? or by the powers o' wildfire, I'll put you where you'll never see daylight antil you make me a rich man."

" I have no gold, I tell you."

" Faix, thin, I'll keep you till you find it," said Darby, who tucked the little man under his arm, and ran home with him as fast as he could.

He kicked at his cabin door for admittance when he reached home, exclaiming :

"Let me in! let me in! Make haste; I have him."

"Who have you?" said Oonah, as she opened the door.

"Look at that!" said Darby in triumph. "I cotch him at last!"

"Weira, thin, it is a Leprechaun, it is?" said Oonah.

"Divil a less," said Darby, throwing down the doctor on the bed, and still holding him fast. "Open the big chest, Oonah, and we'll lock him up in it, and keep him antil he gives us the goold."

"Murder! murder!" shouted the doctor. "Lock me up in a chest!"

"Gi' me the goold, thin, and I won't."

"My good man, you know I have not gold to give."

"Don't b'live him, Darby jewel," said Oonah. "Them Leprechauns is the biggest liars in the world."

"Sure, I know that!" said Darby, "as well as you. Oh, all the throuble I've had wid him; throth, only I'm aiqual to a counsellor for knowledge, he'd have namplushed me long ago."

"Long life to you, Darby dear!"

"Mrs. Kelleher," said the doctor.

"Oh, Lord!" said Oonah, in surprise, "did you ever hear the likes o' that—how he knows my name!"

"To be sure he does," said Darby; "and why not? Sure, he's a fairy, you know."

"I'm no fairy, Mrs. Kelleher. I'm a doctor — Doctor MacFinn."

"Don't b'live him, darlin'," said Darby. "Make haste and open the chest."

"Darby Kelleher," said the doctor, "let me go, and I'll cure you whenever you want my assistance."

"Well, I want your assistance now," said Darby, "for I'm very bad this minit wid poverty; and if you cure me o' that, I'll let you go."

"What will become of me?" said the doctor in despair, as Darby carried him towards the big chest which Oonah had opened.

"I'll tell you what'll become o' you," said Darby, seizing a hatchet that lay within his reach. "By the seven blessed candles, if you don't consint before night to fill me that big chest full o' goold, I'll chop you as small as aribs [herbs] for the pot." And Darby crammed him into the box.

"Oh, Mrs. Kelleher, be merciful to me," said the doctor, "and whenever you're sick I'll attend you."

"God forbid!" said Oonah; "it's not the likes o' you I want when I'm sick. Attind me, indeed! bad luck to you, you little imp, maybe you'd run away with my babby, or it's a *Banshee* you'd turn yourself into, and sing for my death. Shut him up, Darby; it's not loocky to be houldin' discoorse wid the likes iv him."

"Oh!" roared the doctor, as his cries were stifled by the lid of the chest being closed on him. The key was turned, and Oonah sprinkled some holy water she had in a little bottle that hung in one corner of the cabin over the lock, to prevent the fairy having any power upon it.

Darby and Oonah now sat down in consultation on their affairs, and began forming their plans on an extensive scale, as to what they were to do with their money—for have it they must—now that the Leprechaun was fairly in their power. Now and then Darby would rise and go over to the chest, very much as one goes to the door of a room where a naughty child has been locked up, to know "if it be good yet," and giving a thump on the lid, would exclaim: "Well, you little vagabone, will you gi' me the goold yet?"

A groan and a faint answer of denial was all the reply he received.

"Very well, stay there; but remimber, if you don't consint before night, I'll chop you to pieces." He then got his bill-hook, and began to sharpen it close by the chest, that the Leprechaun might hear him; and when the poor doctor heard this process going forward, he felt more dead than alive; the horrid scraping of the iron against the stone being interspersed with occasional interjectional passages from Darby, such as: "Do you hear that, you thief? I'm gettin' ready for you." Then away he'd rasp at the grindstone again, and as he paused to feel the edge of the weapon, exclaim: "By the powers, I'll have it as sharp as a razhir."

In the meantime, it was well for the prisoner that there were many large chinks in the chest, or suffocation from his confinement would have anticipated Darby's pious intentions upon him; and when he found matters likely to go so hard with him, the thought struck him at last of affecting to be what Darby mistook him for, and regaining his freedom by stratagem.

To this end, when Darby had done sharpening his bill-hook, the doctor replied, in answer to one of Darby's summonses for gold, that he saw it was in vain longer to deny giving it, that Darby was too cunning for him, and that he was ready to make him the richest man in the country.

"I'll take no less than the full o' that chest," said Darby.

"You'll have ten times the full of it, Darby," said the doctor, "if you'll only do what I bid you."

"Sure, I'll do anything."

"Well, you must first prepare the mystificandherumbrandherum."

"Tare-an-ouns, how do I know what that is?"

"Silence, Darby Kelleher, and attend to me: that's a magical ointment, which I will show you how to make; and whenever you want gold, all you have to do is to rub a little of it on the point of a pick-axe or your spade, and dig wherever you please, and you will be sure to find treasure."

"Oh, think o' that! Faix, an I'll make plenty of it when you show me. How is it made?"

"You must go into the town, Darby, and get me three things, and fold them three times in three rags torn out of the left side of a petticoat that has not known water for a year."

"Faith, I can do that much, anyhow," said Oonah, who began tearing the prescribed pieces out of her under-garment.

"And what three things am I to get you?"

"First bring me a grain of salt from a house that stands at cross roads."

"Crass roads!" said Darby, looking significantly at Oonah. "By my sowl, but it's my dhrame's comin' out!"

"Silence, Darby Kelleher," said the doctor, with solemnity. "Mark me, Darby Kelleher;" and then he proceeded to repeat a parcel of gibberish to Darby, which he enjoined him to remember and repeat again; but as Darby could not, the doctor said he should only write it down for him, and tearing a leaf from his pocket-book, he wrote in pencil a few words, stating the condition he was in, and requesting assistance. This slip of paper he desired Darby to deliver to the apothecary in the town, who would give him a drug that would complete the making of the ointment.

Darby went to the apothecary's as he was desired, and it happened to be dinner-time when he arrived. The apothecary had a few friends dining with him, and Darby was detained until they chose to leave the table and go in a body to liberate the poor little doctor. He was pulled out of the chest amidst the laughter of his liberators and the fury of Darby and Oonah, who both made considerable fight against being robbed of their prize. At last the doctor's friends got him out of the house, and proceeded to the town to supper, where the whole party kept getting magnificently drunk, until sleep plunged them into dizzy dreams of Leprechauns and Fairy Finders.

The doctor for some days swore vengeance against Darby, and threatened a prosecution; but his friends recommended him to let the matter rest, as it would only tend to make the affair more public, and get him nothing but laughter for damages.

As for Darby Kelleher, nothing could ever persuade him that it was not a *real* Leprechaun he had caught, which by some villainous contrivance on the Fairy's part changed itself into the semblance of the doctor ; and he often said the great mistake he made was "givin' the little vagabone so much time, for that if he done right he'd have set about cutting his throat at wanst."

LITTLE FAIRLY

THE words great and little are sometimes contradictory terms to their own meaning. This is stating the case rather confusedly, but as I am an Irishman, and writing an Irish story, it is the more in character. I might do, perhaps, like a very clever and agreeable friend of mine, who, when he deals in some extravagance which you don't quite understand, says : "Well, you know what I mean." But I will not take that for granted, so what I mean is this : that your great man, as far as size is concerned, is often a nobody ; and your little man is often a *great* man. The works of fiction abound with instances, that the author does not consider it necessary his hero shall be an eligible candidate for the "grenadier corps" ; the earlier works of fiction in particular : Fairy-tales, universally, dedicate some *giant* to destruction at the hands of some "clever little fellow," "Tom Thumb," "Jack and the Bean Stalk," and fifty other such, for instance, and I am now going to add another to the list, a brilliant example, I trust, of the unfailing rule that your *little* man is always a *great* man.

There is a proverb also, that "*little* said is soon mended," and with all my preaching, I fear I have been forgetting the wholesome adage. So I shall conclude this little introduction, which I only thought a becoming flourish of trumpets for introducing my hero, by placing *Little Fairly* before my readers, and I hope they will not think, in the words of another adage, that I have given them *great* cry and *little* wool.

You see, ould Fairly was a mighty dacent man, that lived, as the story goes, out over the back o' the hills beyant there, and was a thrivin' man ever afther he married little Shan Ruadh's daughter, and she was little, like her father before her, a dawnshee craythur, but mighty cute, and industhered a power always, and a fine wife she was to a sthrivin' man, up early and down late ; and sure, if she was doin' nothin' else, the bit iv a stocking was never out iv her hand, and the knittin' needles goin' like mad. Well, sure, they thruv like a flag or a bulrush, and the snuggest cabin in the counthryside was ould Fairly's. And in due coorse, she brought him a son—throth, she lost no time about it either, for she was never given to loitherin'—and he was the picthur o' the mother, the little ottomy that he was, as slim as a ferret and as red as a fox, but a hardy craythur.

LITTLE FAIRLY

Well, ould Fairly didn't like the thoughts of havin' sitch a bit
iv a brat for a son, and besides, he thought he got on so well and
prospered in the world with one wife, that, by gor, he detarmined
to improve his luck and get another. So with that, he ups and
goes to one Doody, who had a big daughter—a wopper, by my
sowl, throth, she was the full of a door, and was called by the
neighbours *garran more*, for in throth, she was a garran, the
dirty dhrop was in her; a nasty stag that never done a good
turn for anyone but herself, the long-sided jack that she was,
but her father had a power o' money, and above a hundher head
o' cattle, and divil a chick nor child he had but herself; so that
she was a great catch for whoever could get her, as far as the
fortin' wint; but throth, the boys did not like the looks iv her,
and let herself and her fortin' alone. Well, as I was sayin', ould
Fairly ups and he goes to Doody and puts his *comether* an the
girl, and faix, she was glad to be ax'd, and so matthers was soon
settled, and the ind of it was they wor married.

Now, maybe it's axin' you'd be, how he could marry two wives
at wanst; but I tould you before, it was long ago, in the good
ould ancient times, whin a man could have plinty of everything.
So home he brought the dirty garran, and sorra long was she in
the place whin she began to breed (arrah, lave off and don't be
laughin' now; I don't mane that at all)—whin she began to breed
ructions in the fam'ly, and to kick up *antagions* from mornin' till
night, and *put betune* ould Fairly and his first wife. Well, she
had a son of her own soon, and he was a big boss iv a divil, like
his mother—a great, fat lob, that had no life in him at all; and
while the little dawnshee craythur would laugh in your face and
play wid you if you cherrup'd to him, or would amuse himself,
the craythur, crawlin' about the flure and playin' wid the sthraws,
and atein' the gravel, the jewel, the other bosthoon was roarin'
from mornin' till night, barrin' he was crammed wid stirabout and
dhrownded a'most wid milk.

Well, up they grew, and the big chap turned out a *gommoch*,
and the little chap was as knowin' as a jailor; and though the
big mother was always puttin' up her lob to malthrate and abuse
little Fairly, the dickens a one but the little chap used to
sarcumvint him, and gev him no pace, but led him the life iv a
dog wid the cunnin' thricks he played an him. Now, while all
the neighbours a'most loved the ground that little Fairly throd
on, they cudn't abide the garran more's foal, good, bad, or
indifferent, and many's the sly *malavoguein'* he got behind a
hedge from one or another, when his father or mother wasn't
near to purtect him, for ould Fairly was as great a fool about
him as the mother, and would give him his eyes a'most to play
marvels, while he didn't care three *thraneens* for the darlint little

chap. And 'twas the one thing as long as he lived; and at last he fell sick, and sure, many thought it was a judgment an him for his unnath'ral doin's to his own flesh and blood, and the sayin' through the parish was, from one and all:

"There's ould Fairly is obleeged *to take to his bed with the weight of his sins.*"

And sure enough, off o' that same bed he never riz, but grew weaker and weaker every day, and sint for the priest to make his sowl, the wicked ould sinner, God forgive me for sayin' the word, and sure, the priest done whatever he could for him; but afther the priest wint away he called his two wives beside his bed, and the two sons, and says he:

"I'm goin' to lave yiz now," says he, "and sorry I am," says he, "for I'd rather stay in ould Ireland than go anywhere else," says he, "for a raison I have — heigh! heigh! heigh! Oh, murther! this cough is smotherin' me, so it is. Oh, wurra! wurra! but it's sick and sore I am. Well, come here, yiz both," says he to the women. "You wor good wives, both o' ye; I have nothin' to say agin it (Molly, don't forget the whate is to be winny'd the first fine day)—and ready you wor to make and to mind (Judy, there's a hole in the foot of my left stockin'), and—"

"Don't be thinkin' o' your footin' here," says little Judy, the knowledgable craythur as she was, " but endayvour to make your footin' in heaven," says she, "mavourneen."

"Don't put in your prate till you're ax'd," says the ould savage, no ways obleeged that his trusty little ould woman was wantin' to give him a helpin' hands tow'rds puttin' his poor sinful sowl in the way o' glory.

"Lord look down an you!" says she.

"Tuck the blanket round my feet," says he, "for I'm gettin' very cowld." So the big old hag of a wife tucked the blankets round him.

"Ah, you were always a comfort to me," says ould Fairly.

"Well, remember my son for that same," says she, "for it's time, I think, you'd be dividin' what you have bechuxt uz," says she.

"Well, I suppose I must do it at last," says the ould chap, "though—heigh! heigh! heigh! oh, this thievin' cough—though it's hard to be obleeged to lave one's hard airnin's and comforts this-a-way," says he, the unfort'nate ould thief, thinkin' o' this world instead of his own poor sinful sowl.

"Come here, big Fairly," says he, "my own bully boy, that's not a starved poor ferret, but worth while lookin' at. I lave you this house," says he.

"Ha!" says the big ould sthrap, makin' a face over the bed

at the poor little woman that was cryin', the craythur, although the ould villian was usin' her so bad.

"And I lave you all my farms," says he.

"Ha!" says the big ould sthreel again.

"And my farmin' *ingraydients*," says he.

"Ha!" says she again, takin' a pinch o' snuff.

"And *all* my cattle," says he.

"Did you hear that, ma'am?" says the garran more, stickin' her arms akimbo, and lookin' as if she was goin' to bate the woman.

"All my cattle," says the ould fellow; "every head," says he, "barrin' one, and that one is for that poor scarecrow there," says he, "little Fairly."

"And is it only one you lave my poor boy?" says the poor little woman.

"If you say much," says the ould dyin' vagabone, "the divil resave the taste of anything I'll lave him or you," says he.

"Don't say divil, darlin'."

"Hould your prate, I tell you, and listen to me. I say, you little Fairly."

"Well, daddy," says the little chap.

"Go over to that corner cupboard," says he, "and in the top shelf," says he, "in the bottom of a crack'd taypot, you'll find a piece of an ould rag, and bring it here to me."

With that little Fairly wint to do as he was bid, but he could not reach up so high as the corner cupboard, and he run into the next room for a stool to stand upon to come at the crack'd taypot, and he got the ould piece iv a rag and brought it to his father.

"Open it," says the father.

"I have it open now," says little Fairly.

"What's in it?" says the ould boy.

"Six shillin's in silver, and three farthin's," says little Fairly.

"That was your mother's fortune," says the father, "and I am going to behave like the hoighth of a gintleman, as I am," says he; "and I hope you won't squandher it," says he, "the way that every blackguard now thinks he has a right to squandher any dacent man's money he is the heir to," say he; "but be careful of it," says he, "as I was, for I never touched a rap iv it, but let it lie gotherin' in that taypot ever since the day I got it from Shan Ruadh, the day we sthruck the bargain about Judy, over beyant at the 'Cat and Bagpipes,' comin' from the fair; and I lave you that *six* shillin's, and *five* stone o' mouldy oats that's no use to me, and *four* broken plates, and that *three*-legged stool you stood upon to get at the cupboard, you poor *nharrough* that you are, and the *two* spoons without handles, and the *one* cow that's gone back of her milk."

"What use is the cow, daddy," says little Fairly, "widout land to feed her an?"

"Maybe it's land you want, you pinkeen," says the big brother.

"Right, my bully boy," says the mother; "stand up for your own."

"Well, well," says the ould chap. "I tell you what, big Fairly," says he; "you may as well do a dacent turn for the little chap, and give him grass for his cow. I lave you all the land," says he, "but you'll never miss grass for one cow," says he, "and you'll have the satisfaction of bein' bountiful to your little brother, bad cess to him for a starved hound as he is."

But to make a long story short, the ould chap soon had the puff out iv him; and whin the wake was over and that, they put him out to grass—laid him asleep, snug, with a *daisy quilt over him*—throth, that minit the poor little woman and her *little offsprig* was turned out, body and bones, and forced to seek shelter anyway they could.

Well, little Fairly was a cute chap, and so he made a little snug place out of the back iv a ditch, and wid moss and rishes and laves and brambles, made his ould mother snug enough antil he got a little mud cabin built for her, and the cow gev them milk, and the craythurs got on purty well, antil the big dirty vagabone of a brother began to grudge the cow the bit o' grass, and he ups and says he to little Fairly one day:

"What's the raison," says he, "your cow does be thresspassin' an my fields?"

"Sure, and wasn't it the last dyin' words o' my father to you," says little Fairly, "that you would let me have grass for my cow?"

"I don't remember it," says big Fairly—the dirty naygur, who was put up to all by the garran more, his mother.

"Yiv a short memory," says little Fairly.

"Yis; but I've a long stick," says the big chap, shakin' it at him at the same time, "and I'd rekimmind you to keep a civil tongue in your head," says he.

"You're mighty ready to bate your little brother, but would you fight your match?" says little Fairly.

"Match or no match," says big Fairly, "I'll brake your bones if you give me more o' your prate," says he; "and I tell you again, don't let your cow be thresspassin' an my land, or I warn you that you'll be sorry," and off he wint.

Well, little Fairly kept never mindin' him, and brought his cow to graze every day on big Fairly's land; and the big fellow used to come and *hish* her off the land, but the cow was as little and cute as her masther—she was a Kerry cow, and there's a power o' cuteness comes out o' Kerry. Well, as I was sayin', the cow used to go off as *quite* as a lamb; but the minit the big bosthoon

used to turn his back—*whoo!* my jewel, she used to leap the
ditch as clever as a hunter, and back wid her again to graze; and
faix, good use she made of her time, for she got brave and hearty,
and gev a power o' milk, though she was goin' back of it shortly
before, but there was a blessin' over Fairly, and all belongin' to
him, and all that he put his hand to thruv with him. Well, now
I must tell you what big Fairly done—and the dirty turn it was;
but the dirt was in him ever and always, and kind mother it
was for him. Well, what did he do but he dug big pits all
through the field where little Fairly's cow used to graze, and he
covers them up with branches o' threes and sods, makin' it look
fair and even, and all as one as the rest o' the field, and with that
he goes to little Fairly, and says he:

"I tould you before," says he, "not to be sendin' your little
blackguard cow to threspass on my fields," says he; "and mind
I tell you now, that it won't be good for her health to let her go
there again, for I tell you, she'll come to harm, and it's dead she'll
be before long."

"Well, she may as well die one way as another," says little
Fairly; "for sure, if she doesn't get grass she must die, and I tell
you again, divil an off your land I'll take my cow."

"Can't you let your dirty cow graze along the roadside?"
says big Fairly.

"Why, thin, do you think," says little Fairly, answering him
mighty smart—"do you think I have so little respect for my
father's cow as to turn her out a beggar an the road to get her
dinner off the common highway? Throth, I'll do no sitch
thing."

"Well, you'll soon see the ind iv it," says big Fairly; and off
he wint in great delight, thinkin' how poor little Fairly's cow
would be killed. And now wasn't he the dirty, threacherous,
black-hearted villian, to take advantage of a poor cow, and lay a
thrap for the dumb baste?—but whin the dirty dhrop is in, it
must come out. Well, poor Fairly sent his cow to graze next
mornin', but the poor little darlin' craythur fell into one o' the
pits and was kilt; and when little Fairly kem for her in the
evenin', there she was, cowld and stiff, and all he had to do
now was to sing *drimmin dhu dheelish* over her, and dhrag her
home as well as he could, wid the help of some neighbours that
pitied the craythur, and cursed the big bosthoon that done such
a threacherous turn.

Well, little Fairly was the fellow to put the best face upon
everything; and so, instead of givin' in to fret, and makin'
lamentations that would do him no good, by dad, he began to
think how he could make the best of what happened, and the
little craythur sharpened a knife immediantly and began to shkin

the cow. "And anyhow," says he, "the cow is good mate, and my ould mother and me 'ill have beef for the winther."

"Thrue for you, little Fairly," said one of the neighbours that was helpin' him ; "and besides, the hide 'ill be good to make soles for your brogues for many a long day."

"Oh, I'll do betther with the hide nor that," says little Fairly.

"Why, what better can you do nor that wid it?" says the neighbour.

"Oh, I know myself," says little Fairly, for he was as cute as a fox, as I said before, and wouldn't tell his saycrets to a stone wall, let alone a companion. And what do you think he done with the hide? Guess now ; throth, I'd let you guess from this to Christmas, and you'd never come inside it. Faix, it was the complatest thing ever you heerd. What would you think, but he tuk the hide and cut six little holes an partic'lar places he knew av himself, and thin he goes and he gets his mother's fortin— the six shillin's I tould you about—and he hides the six shillin's in the six holes, and away he wint to a fair was that convenient, about three days afther, where there was a great sight o' people, and a power o' sellin' and buyin', and dhrinkin' and fightin', by coorse, *and why nat ?*

Well, Fairly ups and he goes right into the very heart o' the fair, an' he spread out his hide to the greatest advantage, and he began to cry out (and by the same token, though he was little, he had a mighty sharp voice, and could be hard farther nor a bigger man)—well he began to cry out : "Who wants to buy a hide—the *rale* hide—the ould original goolden bull's hide that kem from furrin parts—who wants to make their fortin now ?"

"What do you ax for your hide ?" says a man to him.

"Oh, I only want a thrifle for it," says Fairly, "seein' I'm disthressed for money at this present writin'," says he ; "and by fair or foul manes, I must rise the money," says he, "at wanst, for if I could wait, it's not the thrifle I'm axin' now I'd take for the hide."

"By gor, you talk," says the man, "as if the hide was worth the King's ransom ; and I'm thinkin' you must have a great want of a few shillin's," says he, "whin the hide is all you have to the fore to dipind an."

"Oh, that's all *you* know about it," says Fairly. "Shillin's, indeed ! by gor, it's handfuls o' money the hide is worth. Who'll buy a hide—the rale goolden bull's hide ?"

"What do you ax for your hide ?" says another man.

"Only a hundher guineas," says little Fairly.

"A hundher what ?" says the man.

"A hundher guineas," says Fairly.

"Is it takin' lave of your siven smallsinses you are?" says the man.

"Why, thin, indeed I b'live I am takin' lave o' my sinses sure enough," says Fairly, "to sell my hide so chape."

"Chape!" says the man. "Arrah, thin, listen to the little mad vagabone," says he to the crowd that was gother about by this time; "listen to him askin' a hundher guineas for a hide."

"Aye," says Fairly; "and the well-laid-out money it' ill be to whoever has the luck to buy it. This is none o' your common hides—it's the goolden bull's hide—the Pope's goolden bull's hide, that kem from furrin parts, and it's a fortin to whoever 'ill have patience to bate his money out iv it."

"How do you mane?" says a snug ould chap, that was always poachin' about for bargains. "I never heard of batin' money out of a hide," says he.

"Well, thin, I'll show you," says . Fairly; "and only I'm disthressed for a hundher guineas, that I must have before Monday next," says he, "I wouldn't part wid this hide; for every day in the week you may thrash a fistful o' shillin's out iv it, if you take pains, as you may see." And wid that, my jewel, he ups wid a cudgel he had in his hand, and he began leatherin' away at the hide; and he hits it *in the places he knew himself*, and out jump'd one o' the shillin's he hid there. "Hurroo!" says little Fairly, "darlint you wor, you never desaived me yet!" and away he thrashed agin, and out jumped another shillin'. "That's your sort!" says Fairly, "the divil a sitch wages any o' yiz ever got for thrashin' as this"—and then another whack, and away wid another shillin'.

"Stop, stop!" says the ould cravin' chap. "I'll give you the money for the hide," says he, "if you'll let me see can I bate money out iv it." And wid that he began to thrash the hide, and by course, another shillin' jumped out.

"Oh, it's yourself has the rale twist in your elbow for it," says Fairly; "and I see by that same that you're above the common, and desarvin' o' my favour."

Well, my dear, at the word, *desarvin' o' my favour*, the people that was gother round (for by this time all the fair a'most was there) began to look into the rights o' the thing, and, one and all, they agreed that little Fairly was one o' the *good people*; for if he wasn't a fairy, how could he do the like? and besides, he was sitch a dawnshee craythur they thought what else could he be? and says they to themselves: "That ould divil, Mulligan, it's the likes iv him id have the luck iv it; and let alone all his gains in *this* world, and his scrapin' and screwin', and it's the fairies themselves must come to help him, as if he wasn't rich enough before." Well, the ould chap paid down a hundher guineas in hard goold to little Fairly, and off he wint wid his bargain.

"The divil do you good wid it," says one, grudgin' it to him.

"What business has he wid a hide?" says another, jealous of the old fellow's luck.

"Why nat?" says another. "Sure, he'd shkin a flint any day, and why wouldn't he shkin a cow?"

Well, the ould codger wint home as plazed as Punch wid his bargain; and indeed, little Fairly had no raison not to be satisfied, for in throth, he got a good price for the hide, considherin' the markets wasn't so high thin as they are now, by raison of the staymers, that *makes gintlemen av the pigs,* sendin' them an their thravels to furrin parts, so that a rasher o' bacon in poor Ireland is gettin' scarce even an a Aisther Sunday.

You may be sure the poor ould mother of little Fairly was proud enough whin she seen him tumble out the hard goold an the table forninst her, and "my darlint you wor," says she, "an' how did you come by that sight o' goold?"

"I'll tell you another time," says little Fairly; "but you must set off to my brother's now, and ax him to lind me the loan av his scales."

"Why, what do you want wid a scales, honey?" says the ould mother.

"Oh, I'll tell you *that* another time too," says little Fairly; "but be aff now, and don't let the grass grow undher your feet."

Well, off wint the ould woman, and maybe you'd want to know yourself what it was Fairly wanted wid the scales. Why, thin, he only wanted thim just for to make big Fairly curious about the matther, that he might play him a thrick, as you'll see by-and-by.

Well, the little ould woman wasn't long in bringin' back the scales, and whin she gave them to little Fairly:

"There now," says he, "sit down beside the fire, and there's a new pipe for you and a quarther o' tobaccy that I brought home for you from the fair, and do you make yourself comfortable," says he, "till I come back;" and out he wint and sat down behind a ditch, to watch if big Fairly was comin' to the house, for he thought the curosity o' the big gommoch and the garran more would make them come down to spy about the place, and see what he wanted wid the scales; and sure enough, he wasn't there long when he seen them both crassin' a stile hard by, and in he jumped into the gripe o' the ditch, and run along under the shelter o' the back av it, and whipped into the house, and spread all his goold out an the table, and began to weigh it in the scales.

But he wasn't well in, whin the cord o' the latch was dhrawn, and in marched big Fairly, and the garran more, his mother, without "by your lave," or "God save you," for they had no breedin' at all. Well, my jewel, the minit they clapped their eyes an the goold, you'd think the sight id lave their eyes; and indeed, not only their eyes, let alone, but their tongues in their heads was no use to thim, for the divil a word either o' thim could spake for beyant a good five minutes. So, all that time little Fairly kept never mindin' thim, but wint an a-weighin' the goold as busy as a nailor, and at last, when the big brute kem to his speech:

"Why, thin," says he; "what's that I see you doin'?" says he.

"Oh, it's only divartin' myself I am," says little Fairly, "thryin' what woight o' goold I got for my goods at the fair," says he.

"Your goods, indeed," says the big chap. "I suppose you robbed some honest man an the road, you little vagabone," says he.

"Oh, I'm too little to rob anyone," says little Fairly. "I'm not a fine, big, able fellow *like you*, to *do that same*."

"Thin, how did you come by the goold?" says the big savage.

"I tould you before, by sellin' my goods," says the little fellow.

"Why, what goods have *you*, you poor unsignified little brat?" says big Fairly. "You never had anything but your poor beggarly cow, and she's dead."

"Throth, thin, she is dead; and, more by token, 'twas yourself done for her complate, anyhow; and I'm beholden to you for that same the longest day I have to live, for it was the makin' o' me. You wor ever and always *the good brother to me;* and never more than whin you killed my cow, for it's the makin' o' me. The divil a rap you see here I'd have had if my cow was alive, for I wint to the fair to sell her hide, brakin' my heart to think that it was only a poor hide I had to sell, and wishin' it was a cow was to the fore; but, my dear, whin I got there, there was no ind to the demand for hides, and the divil a one, good, bad, or indifferent, was there but my own, and there was any money for hides, and so I got a hundher guineas for it, and there they are."

"Why, thin, do you tell me so?" says the big chap.

"Divil a lie in it," says little Fairly. "I got a hundher guineas for the hide. Oh, I wish I had another cow for you to kill for me—throth, would I!"

"Come home, mother," says big Fairly, without sayin' another word, and away he wint home, and what do you think he done but he killed every individyal cow he had, and, "By gor," says he, "it's the rich man I'll be whin I get a hundher guineas apiece for all their hides," and accordingly, off he wint to the next fair, hard by, and he brought a car-load o' hides, and began to call out in the fair:

"Who wants the hides? Here's the chape hides — only a hundher guineas apiece!"

"Oh, do you hear that vagabone that has the assurance to come chatin' the counthry again?" says some people that was convaynient, and that heerd o' the doin's at the other fair, and how the man was chated by a *sleeveen* vagabone—"and think of him to have the impidence to come *here*, so nigh the place, to take in *uz* now ! But we'll be even wid him," says they ; and so they went up to him, and says they to the thievin' rogue : " Honest man," says they, " what's that you have to sell ? "

" Hides," says he.

" What do you ax for them ? " says they.

" A hundher and ten guineas apiece," says he—for he was a greedy craythur, and thought he never could have enough.

" Why, you riz the price on them since the last time," says they.

" Oh, these are better," says big Fairly ; " but I don't mind if I sell them for a hundher apiece, if you give me the money down," says he.

" *You shall be ped on the spot*," says they—and with that they fell on him, and thrash'd him like a *shafe*, till they didn't lave a *spark* o' sinse in him, and then they left him sayin' : " *Are you ped now, my boy ?* Faix, you'll be a warnin' to all rogues for the futhur, how they come to fairs, chatin' honest min out o' their money, wid cock-and-bull stories about their hides ; but in throth, I think your own hide isn't much the better of the tannin' it got to-day—faix, an it was the rale *oak bark* was put to it, and that's the finest tan stuff in the world, and I think it'll sarve you for the rest of your life." And with that they left him for dead.

But you may remark its hardher to kill a dirty, noxious craythur than any thing good—and so by big Fairly—he contrived to get home, and his vagabone mother sawdhered him up afther a manner, and the minit he was come to his strength at all, he detarmint to be revinged on little Fairly for what he had done, and so off he set to catch him while he'd be at brekquest, and he boulted into the cabin wid a murtherin' shillely in his fist—and :

" Oh," says he, " you little mischievious miscrayant," says he, " what made you ruinate me by makin' me kill my cows ? " says he.

" Sure, I didn't bid you kill your cows," says little Fairly—and that was all thrue, for you see, *there* was the cuteness o' the little chap, for he didn't *bid* him kill them, sure enough, but he *let an* in that manner, that deludhered the big fool, and sure, divil mind him.

" Yes, you did bid me," says big Fairly, " or all as one as bid me, and I haven't a cow left ; and my bones is bruck all along o' your little jackeen *manyewvers*, you onloocky sprat that you are ; but by this and that, I'll have my revinge o' you now," and with that he fell an him, and was goin' to murthur poor little Fairly, only he run undher a stool, and kept tiggin' about from one place to th' other, that the big botch couldn't get a right offer at him, at all, at all; and at last the little ould mother got up to put a stop to the ruction, but if she did, my jewel, it was the unloocky miuit for her, for by dad, she kem in for a chance tap o' the cudgel that big Fairly was weltin' away with, and you know, there's an ould sayin', "a chance shot may kill the divil," and why not an ould woman?

Well, that put an end to the *skrimmage*, for the phillilew that little Fairly set up whin he seen his ould mother kilt would ha' waked the dead, and the big chap got frekened himself, and says little Fairly:

"By gor, if there's law to be had," says he—"and I think *I have* a chance o' justice, *now that I have money to spare*—and if there's law in the land, I'll have you in the body o' the jail afore to-morrow," says he; and wid that the big chap got cowed, and wint off like a dog without his tail, and so poor little Fairly escaped bein' murthered that offer, and was left to cry over his mother; an' indeed, the craythur was sorry enough, and he brought in the neighbours and gev the ould woman a dacent wake, and there was few pleasanther evenin's that night in the county than the same wake, for Fairly was mighty fond of his mother, and faix, he done the thing ginteelly by her, and good raison he had, for she was the good mother to him while she was alive, and by dad, by his own cuteness, he conthrived she should be the useful mother to him afther she was dead too. For what do you think he done?

Oh! by the Piper o' Blessin'town, you'd never guess, if you wor guessin' from this to Saint Tib's eve, and that falls neither before nor afther Christmas, we all know. Well, there's no use guessin', so I must tell you. You see, the ould mother was a nurse to the Squire that lived hard by, and so, by coorse, she had a footin' in the house any day in the week she plazed, and used often to go over and see the Squire's childher, for she was as fond o' thim a'most as if she nursed *thim* too; and so what does Fairly do, but he carried over the ould mother stiff as she was, and dhressed in her best, and he stole in, *unknownst*, into the Squire's gardin, and he propped up the dead ould woman standin' hard by a well was in the gardin, wid her face forninst the gate, and her back to the well, and wid that he wint into the house, and made out the childher, and says he:

"God save you, Masther Tommy," says he. "God save you, Masther Jimmy, Miss Matty and Miss Molshee," says he, "an' I'm glad to see you well. And sure, there's the old mammy nurse come to see yiz, childher," says he, "and she's down by the well in the gardin, and she has gingerbread for yiz," says he, "and who-ever o' yiz runs to her first 'ill get the most gingerbread; and I'd rekimmind yiz to lose no time, but run a race and sthrive who'll win the gingerbread."

Well, my dear, to be sure, off set the young imps, runnin' and screechin' : "Here I am, mammy nurse, here I am," and they wor brakin' their necks a'most, to see who'd be there first, and wid that, they run wid sitch *voylence* that the first o' thim run whack up agin the poor ould woman's corps, and threwn it over plump into the middle o' the well. To be sure, the childher was frekened, as well they might, and back agin they ran as fast as they kem, roarin' murdher, and they riz the house in no time, and little Fairly was among the first to go see what was the matther (by the way), and he set up a *hullagone*, my jewel, that ud split the heart of a stone ; and out kem the Squire and his wife, and :

"What's the matther ?" says they.

"Is it what's the matther ?" says Fairly. "Don't yiz see my lovely ould mother is dhrowned by these divil's imps o' childher ?" says he. "Oh, Masther Jimmy, is that the way you thrated the poor ould mammy nurse, to go dhrowned her like a *rot* afther that manner ?"

"Oh, the childher didn't intind it," said the Squire. "I'm sorry fcr your mother, Fairly, but—"

"But what ?" says little Fairly. "Sorry—in throth, and I'll make you sorry, for I'll rise the counthry, or I'll get justice for such an unnath'ral murther ; and whoever done it must go to jail, if it was even Miss Molshee herself."

Well, the Squire did not like the matther to go to that, and so says he :

"Oh, I'll make it worth your while to say nothing about it, Fairly, and here's twenty goolden guineas for you," says he.

"Why, thin, do you think me such a poor-blooded craythur, as to sell my darlin' ould mother's life for twenty guineas ? No, in throth, tho' if you wor to make it fifty I might be talkin' to you."

Well, the Squire thought it was a dear mornin's work, and that he had very little for his money in a dead ould woman, but sooner than have the childher get into trouble, and have the matther made *a blowin' horn* of, he gev him the fifty guineas, and the ould mother was dhried and waked over agin, so that she had greather respect ped to her than a lord or a lady. So you see what cleverness and a *janius* for cuteness does.

Well, away he wint home afther the ould woman was buried, wid his fifty guineas snug in his pocket, and so he wint to big Fairly to ax for the loan of the scales once more, and the brother ax'd him for what ?

"Oh, it's only a small thrifle more o' goold I have," says the little chap, "that I want to weigh."

"Is it *more* goold ?" says big Fairly. "Why, it's a folly to talk ; but you must be either a robber or a coiner to come by money so fast."

" Oh, this is only a thrifle I kem by at the death o' my mother," says little Fairly.

" Why, bad luck to the rap *she* had to lave you, anyway," says the big chap.

" I didn't say she left me a fortin," says little Fairly.

" You said you kem by the money by your mother's death," says the big brother.

" Well, an' that's thrue," says the little fellow; " and I'll tell you how it was. You see, afther you killed her, I thought I might as well make the most I could of her, and says I to myself, faix, and I had great good luck wid the cow he killed for me, and why wouldn't I get more for my mother nor a cow? and so away I wint to the town, and I offered her to the docthor there, and he was greatly taken wid her, and, by dad, he wouldn't let me lave the house without sellin' her to him, and faix, he gev me fifty guineas for her."

" Is it fifty guineas for a corps?"

" It's thruth I'm tellin' you, and was much obleeged into the bargain; and the raison is, you see, that there's no sitch thing to be had for love or money as a dead ould woman—there's no killin' them, at all, at all, so that a dead ould woman is quite a curosity."

" Well, there's the scales for you," says big Fairly, and away the little chap wint to weigh his goold (as he let on) as he did before. But what would you think, my dear—throth, you'll hardly b'live me whin I tell you. Little Fairly hadn't well turned his back whin the big savage wint into the house where his ould mother was, and tuck up a rapin' hook, and kilt her an the spot— divil a lie in it.

Oh, no wondher you look cruked at the thoughts of it; but it's morially thrue—faix, he cut the life out iv her, and he detarmined to turn in his harvist for that same as soon as he could, and so away he wint to the docthor in the town hard by, where little Fairly tould him he sould *his* mother, and he knocked at the door and walked into the hall with a sack on his shouldher, and settin· down the sack, he said he wanted to spake to the docthor. Well, whin the docthor kem, and heerd the vagabone talkin' o' fifty guineas for an old woman, he began to laugh at him; but whin he opened the sack, and seen how the poor ould craythur was murthered, he set up a shout:

" Oh, you vagabone," says he ; " you sack-im up villian," says he, " you've Burked the woman," says he, " and now you come to *rape* the fruits o' your *murdher*."

Well, the minit big Fairly heerd the word *murdher*, and *rapin'* the reward, he thought the docthor was up to the way of it, and he got frekened, and with that the docthor opened the hall-door and called the watch, but Fairly bruk loose from him, and ran away home ; and when once he was gone, *the docthor thought there would be no use in rising a ruction* about it, and so he shut the door and never minded the police.   Big Fairly, to be sure, was so frekened he never cried stop until he got clean outside the town, and with that, the first place he wint to was little Fairly's house, and burstin' in the door, he said, in a tarin' passion : "What work is this you have been at now, you onloocky miscrayant ?" says he.

"I haven't been at any work," says little Fairly.   "See yourself," says he, "*my sleeves is new,*" says he, houldin' out the cuffs av his coat to him at the same time, to show him.

"Don't think to put me aff that-a-way with your little kimmeens and your divartin' capers," says the big chap, "for I tell you I'm in airnest, and it's no jokin' matther it 'ill be to you, for, by this an' that, I'll have the life o' you, you little *spidhogue* of an abortion as you are, you made me kill my cows.   Don't say a word, for you know it's thrue."

"I never made you kill your cows," says little Fairly, no ways daunted by the fierce looks o' the big bosthcon.

"Whist, you vagabone !" says the big chap.   "You didn't bid me do it out o' the face in plain words, but you made me sinsible."

"*Faix, an' that was doin' a wondher,*" says little Fairly, who couldn't help having the laugh at him, though he was sore afeard.

"Bad luck to you, you little sneerin' vagabone," says the big chap again.   "I know what you mane, you long-headed schkamer, that you are ; but, by my sowl, your capers 'ill soon be cut short, as you'll see to your cost.   But before I kill you, I'll show you to your face, the villian that you are, and it is no use your endayvourin' to consale your bad manners to me, for if you had a veil as thick as the shield of A—jax, which was made o' siv'n bull hides, it would not sarve for to cover the half o' your inni—quitties."

"Whoo ! that's the ould schoolmasther's speech you're puttin' an us now," says little Fairly.   "And faith, it's the only thing you iver larned, I b'live, from him."

"Yis ; I larned how fine a thing it is to bate a little chap less than myself, and you'll see, with a blessin', how good a scholar I am at that same ; and you desarve it, for I tould you just now before you intherrupted me, how you made me kill all my cows (and that was the sore loss), and afther that, whin you could do no more, you made me kill my mother, and divil a good it done me, but nighhand got me into the watch-house ; and so now I'm detarmint you won't play me any more thricks, for I'll hide you snug, in the deepest bog-hole in the Bog of Allen; and if you throuble me afther that, faix, I think it'll be the wondher," and with that he made a grab at the little chap, and while you'd be sayin' "thrap stick," he cotch him and put him, body and bones, into a sack, and he threwn the sack over the back of a horse was at the door, and away he wint in a tarin' rage, straight for the Bog of Allen.

Well, to be sure, he couldn't help stoppin' at a public-house by the roadside, *for he was dhry with the rage;* an' he tuk the sack where little Fairly was tied up, an' he lifted it aff o' the horse, an' put it standin' up beside the door goin' into the public-house. An' he wasn't well gone in, whin a farmer was comin' by too, and he was as dhry wid the dust as ever big Fairly was wid the rage (an' indeed, it's wondherful how aisy it is to make a man dhry); and so, as he was goin' by, he sthruck agin the sack that little Fairly was in, and little Fairly gev a groan that you'd think kem from the grave; and says he (from inside o' the sack): "God forgive you!" says he.

"Who's there?" says the farmer, startin'; and no wondher.

"It's me!" says little Fairly. "And may the Lord forgive you," says he, "for you have disturbed me, and I *half-way to heaven.*"

"Why, who are you, at all?" says the farmer. "Are you a man?" says he.

"I am a man now," says little Fairly; "though if you didn't disturb me, I'd have been an angel of glory in less than no time," says he.

"How do you make that out, honest man?" says the farmer.

"I can't explain it to you," says little Fairly, "*for it's a mysthery;* but what I tell you is thruth," says he, "and I tell you that whoever is in this sack at this present," says he, "is as good as half-way to heaven; and indeed, I thought I was there a'most, only you sthruck agin me an' disturbed me."

"An' do you mane for to say," says the farmer, "that whoiver is in that sack will go to heaven?"

"Faix, they are on their road there, at all events," says little Fairly; "and if they lose their way, it's their own fault."

"Oh, thin," says the farmer, "maybe you'd let me get into the sack along wid you, for to go to heaven too?"

"Oh, the horse that's to bring us *doesn't carry double,*" says little Fairly.

"Well, will you let me get into the sack instead iv you?" says the farmer.

"Why, thin, do you think I'd let anyone take sitch a dirty advantage o' me as to go to heaven afore me?" says little Fairly.

"Oh, I'll make it worth your while," says the farmer.

"Why, thin, will you ontie the sack," says little Fairly, "and just let me see who it is that has the impidence to ax me to do the like." And with that the farmer ontied the sack, and little Fairly popped out his head. "Why, thin, do you think," says he, "that a hangin'-bone lookin' thief *like you* has a right to go to heaven afore me?"

"Oh," says the farmer, "I've been a wicked sinner in my time, and I haven't much longer to live; and, to tell you the thruth, I'd be glad to get to heaven in that sack, if it's thrue what you tell me."

"Why," says little Fairly, "don't you know it is by *sackcloth and ashes* that the faithful see the light o' glory?"

"Thrue for you, indeed," says the farmer. "Oh, murther! let me get in there, and I'll make it worth your while."

"How do you make that out?" says little Fairly.

"Why, I'll give you five hundher guineas," says the farmer; "and I think that's a power o' money."

"But what's a power o' money compared to heaven?" says little Fairly. "And do you think I'd sell my sowl for five hundher guineas?"

"Well, there's five hundher more in an ould stockin' in the oak box, in the cabin by the crass roads, at Dhrumsnookie; for I am ould Tims o' Dhrumsnookie, and you'll inherit all I have, if you consint."

"But what's a thousand guineas compared to heaven?" says little Fairly.

"Well, do you see all them heads o' cattle there?" says the farmer. "I have just dhruv them here from Ballinasloe," says he, "and every head o' cattle you see here shall be yours also, if you let me into that sack, that I may go to heaven instead o' you."

"Oh, think o' my poor little sowl!" says Fairly.

"Tut, man!" says the farmer; "I've twice as big a sowl as you; and besides, I'm ould and you're young, and I have no time to spare, and you may get absolution aisy, and make your pace in good time."

"Well," says little Fairly, "I feel for you," says he; "an' I'm half inclined to let you overpersuade me to have your will o' me."

"That's a jewel," says the farmer.

"But make haste," says little Fairly, "for I don't know how soon you might get a refusal."

"Let me in at wanst," says the farmer. So, my dear, Fairly got out and the farmer got in, and the little chap tied him up, and says he to the farmer:

"There will be great *norations* made agin you all the way you're goin' along; and you'll hear o' your sins over and over

agin, and you'll hear o' things you never done at all," says little
Fairly. "But never say a word, or you won't go where I was
goin'. Oh, why did I let you persuade me ? "

" Lord reward you ! " says the poor farmer.

" And your conscience will be sthrekin' you all the time," says
little Fairly; "and you'll think a'most it's a stick is sthrekin'
you, but you mustn't let an, nor say a word, but pray *inwardly*
in the sack."

" I'll not forget," says the farmer.

" Oh, you'll be reminded of it," says Fairly, "for you've a bad
conscience, I know ; and the seven deadly sins will be goin' your
road and keepin' you company, and every now and then they'll
be *puttin' their comether* an you, and callin' you 'brother,' but
don't let on to know them at all, for they'll be mislaydin' you, and
just do you keep quite [quiet] and *you'll see the ind iv it.*"

Well, just at that minit little Fairly heerd big Fairly comin',
and away he run and hid inside iv a churn that was dhryin' at the
ind o' the house ; and big Fairly lifted the sack that was standin' at
the door, and feelin' it was more weighty nor it was before, he said :

" Throth, I think you're growin' heavy with grief; but here
goes, anyhow," and with that he hoist it up on the horse's back,
an' away he wint to the Bog iv Allen.

Now, you see, big Fairly, like every blackguard that has the
bad blood in him, the minit he had the sup o' dhrink in, the dirty
turn kem out ; and so, as he wint along he began to wollop the
poor baste, and the sack where his little brother was (as he
thought, the big fool), and to jibe and jeer him for his divarshin.
But the poor farmer did as little Fairly tould him, and never a
word he said at all, though he could not help roaring out every
now and thin when he felt the soft ind of big Fairly's shillelah
across his backbone ; and sure, the poor fool thought it was his
bad conscience and the seven deadly sins was tazin' him ; but he
wouldn't answer a word for all that, though the big savage was
aggravatin' him every fut o' the road antil they kem to the bog ;
and whin he had him there, faix, he wasn't long in choosin' a bog-
hole for him—and, my jewel, in he popped the poor farmer, neck
and heels, sack and all, and as the soft bog stuff and muddy
wather closed over him :

" I wish you a safe journey to the bottom, young man," says
the big brute, grinnin' like a cat at a cheese ; " and as clever a
chap as you are, I don't think you'll come back out o' that in a
hurry ; and it's throubled I was with you long enough, you little
go-the-round schkamer, but I'll have a quiet life for the futhur."

And with that he got up an his horse, and away he wint home ;
but he had not gone over a mile, or thereaway, whin who should
he see but little Fairly mounted on the farmer's horse, dhrivin'

the biggest dhrove o' black cattle you ever seen; and, by dad, big
Fairly grewn as white as a sheet whin he clapt his eyes an him,
for he thought it was not himself at all was in it, but his ghost;
and he was goin' to turn and gallop off, whin little Fairly called
out to him to stay, for that he wanted to see him. So whin he
seen it was himself, he wondhered, to be sure, and small blame to
him, and says he:

"Well, as cute as I know you wor, by gor, this last turn o'
yours bates Bannagher—and how the divil are you here at all,
whin I thought you wor cuttin' turf wid your sharp little nose in
the Bog of Allen? for I'll take my affidowndavy, I put you into the
deepest hole in it, head foremost, not half an hour agon."

"Throth, you did, sure enough," says little Fairly, "and you
wor ever and always the good brother to me, as I often said before,
but, by dad, you never done rightly for me until to-day, but you
made me up now in airnest."

"How do you mane?" says big Fairly.

"Why, do you see all this cattle here I'm dhrivin'?" says little
Fairly.

"Yes, I do; and whose cattle are they?"

"They're all my own, every head o' them."

"And how did you come by them?"

"Why, you see, when you thrown me into the bog-hole, I felt
it mighty cowld at first, and it was mortial dark, and I felt myself
goin' down and down, that I thought I'd never stop sinking, and
wondhered if there was any bottom to it at all, and at last I began
to feel it growin' warm and pleasant and light, and whin I kem
to the bottom there was the loveliest green field you ever clapped
your eyes on, and thousands upon thousands o' cattle feedin', and
the grass so heavy that they wor up to their ears in it—its thruth
I'm tellin' you—oh, divil sitch meadows I ever seen, and whin I
kem to myself, for indeed I was rather surprised, and thought it
was dhramin' I was—whin I kem to myself, I was welkimed by a
very ginteel-spoken little man, the dawnshiest craythur you ever
seen—by dad, I'd have made six iv him myself—and says
he:

"'You're welkim to the undher story o' the Bog iv Allen,
Fairly.' 'Thank you kindly, sir,' says I. 'And how is all wid
you?' says he. 'Hearty, indeed,' says I. 'And what brought
you here?' says he. 'My big brother,' says I. 'That was very
good iv him,' says he. 'Thrue for you, sir,' says I. 'He is
always doin' me a good turn,' says I. 'Oh, thin, he never done
you half so good a turn as this,' says he, 'for you'll be the richest
man in Ireland soon.' 'Thank you, sir,' says I; 'but I don't see
how.' 'Do you see all them cattle grazin' there?' says he. 'To
be sure I do,' says I. 'Well,' says he, 'take as many o' them as

your heart desires, and bring them home wid you.' ' Why, sure,' says I, 'how could I get back myself up out of the bog-hole, let alone dhraggin' bullocks afther me?'

" ' Oh,' says he, ' the way is aisy enough, for you have nothin' to do but dhrive them out the back way over there,' says he, pointin' to a gate. And sure enough, my darlint, I got all the bastes you see here, and dhruv them out, and here I'm goin' home wid' em, and maybe I won't be the rich man—av coorse I gev the best o' thanks to the little ould man, and gev him the hoighth o' good language for his behavor. And with that, says he : ' You may come back again, and take the rest o' them,' says he—and faix, sure enough, I'll go back the minit I get these bastes home, and have another turn out o' the bog-hole."

"Faix, and I'll be beforehand wid you," says big Fairly.

"Oh, but you shan't," says little Fairly. "It was I discovered the place, and why shouldn't I have the good iv it?"

"You greedy little hound," says the big fellow. " I'll have my share o' them as well as you."

And with that he turned about his horse, and away he galloped to the bog-hole, and the little fellow galloped afther him, purtendin' to be in a desperate fright afeard the other would get there first, and he cried : " Stop the robber," afther him, and whin he came to the soft place in the bog, they both lit, and little Fairly got before the big fellow, and purtended to be makin' for the bog-hole in a powerful hurry, cryin' out as he passed him :

" I'll win the day ! I'll win the day !"

And the big fellow pulled fut afther him as hard as he could, and hardly a puff left in him he run to that degree, and he was afeard that little Fairly would bate him and get all the cattle, and he was wishin' for a gun that he might shoot him, whin the cute little divil, just as he kem close to the edge o' the bog-hole, *let an* that his fut slipped, and he fell down, cryin' out :

" Fair play ! fair play !—wait till I rise !" but the words wasn't well out of his mouth when the big fellow kem up.

" Oh, the divil a wait," says he, and he made one desperate dart at the bog-hole and jumped into the middle of it.

" Hurroo !" says little Fairly, gettin' an his legs agin and runnin' over to the edge of the bog-hole, and just as he seen the great splaw feet o' the big savage sinkin' into the sludge, he called afther him, and says he : " I say, big Fairly, don't take all the cattle, but lave a thrifle for me. *I'll wait, however, till you come back*," says the little rogue, laughin' at his own cute conthrivance, "and I think now I'll lade a quiet life," says he ; and with that he wint home, and from that day out he grewn richer and richer every day, and was the greatest man in the whole counthryside ; and all the neighbours gev in to him that he was the most knowledgable man in thim parts, but they all thought it was quare that his name should be *Fairly*, for it was agreed, one and all, *that he was the biggest rogue out*—barrin' Balfe, the robber.

Thomas Crofton Croker's
Fairy Legends
of the
SOUTH OF IRELAND

Legends of the Shefro

I

THE LEGEND OF KNOCKSHEOGOWNA

In Tipperary is one of the most singularly shaped hills in the world. It has got a peak at the top like a conical nightcap thrown carelessly over your head as you awake in the morning. On the very point is built a sort of lodge, where, in the summer, the lady who built it and her friends used to go on parties of pleasure; but that was long after the days of the fairies, and it is, I believe, now deserted.

But before lodge was built, or acre sown, there was close to the head of this hill a large pasturage, where a herdsman spent his days and nights among the herd. The spot had been an old fairy ground, and the good people were angry that the scene of their light and airy gambols should be trampled by the rude hoofs of bulls and cows. The lowing of the cattle sounded sad in their ears, and the chief of the fairies of the hill determined in person to drive away the new-comers; and the way she thought of was this: When the harvest nights came on, and the moon shone bright and brilliant over the hill, and the cattle were lying down hushed and quiet, and the herdsman, wrapt in his mantle, was musing with his heart gladdened by the glorious company of the stars twinkling above him, she would come and dance before him—now in one shape, now in another—but all ugly and frightful to behold. One time she would be a great horse, with the wings of an eagle and a tail like a dragon, hissing loud and spitting fire. Then, in a moment, she would change into a little man lame of a leg, with a bull's head, and a lambent flame playing round it. Then into a great ape, with duck's feet and a turkey-cock's tail. But I should be all day about it were I to tell you all the shapes she took. And then she would roar, or neigh, or hiss, or bellow, or howl, or hoot, as never yet was roaring, neighing, hissing, bellowing, howling, or hooting heard in this world before or since. The poor herdsman would cover his face, and call on all the saints for help, but it was no use. With one puff of her breath she would blow away the fold of his great-coat, let him

271

hold it ever so tightly over his eyes, and not a saint in heaven paid him the slightest attention. And to make matters worse, he never could stir; no, nor even shut his eyes, but there was obliged to stay, held by what power he knew not, gazing at these terrible sights until the hair of his head would lift his hat half a foot over his crown, and his teeth would be ready to fall out from chattering. But the cattle would scamper about mad, as if they were bitten by the fly; and this would last until the sun rose over the hill.

The poor cattle, from want of rest, were pining away, and food did them no good; besides, they met with accidents without end. Never a night passed that some of them did not fall into a pit, and get maimed, or maybe killed. Some would tumble into a river and be drowned; in a word, there seemed never to be an end of the accidents. But what made the matter worse, there could not be a herdsman got to tend the cattle by night. One visit from the fairy drove the stoutest-hearted almost mad. The owner of the ground did not know what to do. He offered double, treble, quadruple wages, but not a man could be found for the sake of money to go through the horror of facing the fairy. She rejoiced at the successful issue of her project, and continued her pranks. The herd gradually thinning, and no man daring to remain on the ground, the fairies came back in numbers, and gambolled as merrily as before, quaffing dew-drops from acorns, and spreading their feast on the heads of capacious mushrooms.

What was to be done? The puzzled farmer thought in vain. He found that his substance was daily diminishing, his people terrified, and his rent-day coming round. It is no wonder that he looked gloomy, and walked mournfully down the road. Now in that part of the world dwelt a man of the name of Larry Hoolahan, who played on the pipes better than any other player within fifteen parishes. A roving, dashing blade was Larry, and feared nothing. Give him plenty of liquor, and he would defy the devil. He would face a mad bull, or fight single-handed against a fair. In one of his gloomy walks, the farmer met him, and on Larry's asking the cause of his down looks, he told him all his misfortunes.

"If that is all ails you," said Larry, "make your mind easy. Were there as many fairies on Knocksheogowna as there are potato-blossoms in Eliogurty, I would face them. It would be a queer thing, indeed, if I, who never was afraid of a proper man, should turn my back upon a brat of a fairy not the bigness of one's thumb."

"Larry," said the farmer, "do not talk so bold, for you know not who is hearing you; but if you make your words good, and watch my herds for a week on the top of the mountain, your hand shall be free of my dish till the sun has burnt itself down to the bigness of a farthing rushlight."

The bargain was struck, and Larry went to the hill-top, when the moon began to peep over the brow. He had been regaled at the farmer's house, and was bold with the extract of barley-corn. So he took his seat on a big stone under a hollow of the hill, with his back to the wind, and pulled out his pipes. He had not played long when the voice of the fairies was heard upon the blast, like a slow stream of music. Presently they burst out into a loud laugh, and Larry could plainly hear one say: "What! another man upon the fairies' ring? Go to him, queen, and make him repent his rashness;" and they flew away. Larry felt them pass by his face as they flew, like a swarm of midgies; and looking up hastily, he saw, between the moon and him, a great black cat, standing on the very tip of its claws, with its back up, and mewing with the voice of a water-mill. Presently it swelled up towards the sky, and turning round on its left hind-leg, whirled till it fell to the ground, from which it started up in the shape of a salmon, with a cravat round its neck, and a pair of new top-boots.

"Go on, jewel," said Larry. "If you dance, I'll pipe," and he struck up. So she turned into this and that and the other, but still Larry played on, as he well knew how. At last she lost patience, as ladies will do when you do not mind their scolding, and changed herself into a calf, milk-white as the cream of Cork, and with eyes as mild as those of the girl I love. She came up gentle and fawning, in hopes to throw him off his guard by quietness, and then to work him some wrong. But Larry was not so deceived; for when she came up, he, dropping his pipes, leaped upon her back.

Now from the top of Knocksheogowna, as you look westward to the broad Atlantic, you will see the Shannon, queen of rivers, "spreading like a sea," and running on in gentle course to mingle with the ocean through the fair city of Limerick. It on this night shone under the moon, and looked beautiful from the distant hill. Fifty boats were gliding up and down on the sweet current, and the song of the fishermen rose gaily from the shore. Larry, as I said before, leaped upon the back of the fairy, and she, rejoiced at the opportunity, sprung from the hill-top, and bounded clear, at one jump, over the Shannon, flowing as it was just ten miles from the mountain's base. It was done in a second, and when she alighted on the distant bank, kicking up her heels, she flung Larry on the soft turf. No sooner was he thus planted, than he looked her straight in the face, and scratching his head, cried out: "By my word, well done! That was not a bad leap *for a calf!*"

She looked at him for a moment, and then assumed her own shape. "Laurence," said she, "you are a bold fellow. Will you come back the way you went?"

"And that's what I will," said he, "if you let me." So changing to a calf again, again Larry got on her back, and at another bound, they were again upon the top of Knocksheogowna. The fairy, once more resuming her figure, addressed him:

"You have shown so much courage, Laurence," said she, "that while you keep herds on this hill you never shall be molested by me or mine. The day dawns; go down to the farmer and tell him this, and if anything I can do may be of service to you, ask, and you shall have it."

She vanished accordingly, and kept her word in never visiting the hill during Larry's life; but he never troubled her with requests. He piped and drank at the farmer's expense, and roosted in his chimney-corner, occasionally casting an eye to the flock. He died at last, and is buried in a green valley of pleasant Tipperary; but whether the fairies returned to the hill of Knocksheogowna after his death, is more than I can say.

II

THE LEGEND OF KNOCKFIERNA

IT is a very good thing not to be any way in dread of the fairies, for without doubt they have then less power over a person; but to make too free with them, or to disbelieve in them altogether, is as foolish a thing as man, woman, or child can do.

It has been truly said that "good manners are no burthen," and that "civility costs nothing"; but there are some people foolhardy enough to disregard doing a civil thing, which, whatever they may think, can never harm themselves or anyone else, and who, at the same time, will go out of their way for a bit of mischief which never can serve them; but sooner or later they will come to know better, as you shall hear of Carroll O'Daly, a strapping young fellow up out of Connaught, whom they used to call in his own country "Devil Daly."

Carroll O'Daly used to go roving about from one place to another, and the fear of nothing stopped him; he would as soon pass an old churchyard or a regular fairy ground at any hour of the night as go from one room into another without ever making the sign of the cross, or saying, "Good luck attend you, gentlemen."

It so happened that he was once journeying in the county of Limerick towards "the Balbec of Ireland," the venerable town of Kilmallock, and just at the foot of Knockfierna he overtook a respectable-looking man jogging along upon a white pony. The night was coming on, and they rode side by side for some time, without much conversation passing between them, further than saluting each other very kindly. At last Carroll O'Daly asked his companion how far he was going.

"Not far your way," said the farmer, for such his appearance bespoke him. "I'm only going to the top of this hill here."

"And what might take you there," said O'Daly, "at this time of the night?"

"Why, then," replied the farmer, "if you want to know, 'tis the *good people*."

"The fairies, you mean," said O'Daly.

"Whist! whist!" said his fellow-traveller, "or you may be sorry for it," and he turned his pony off the road they were going, towards a little path which led up the side of the mountain, wishing Carroll O'Daly good-night and a safe journey.

"That fellow," thought Carroll, "is about no good this blessed night, and I would have no fear of swearing wrong if I took my Bible oath that it is something else beside the fairies, or the good people, as he calls them, that is taking him up the mountain at this hour. The fairies!" he repeated. "Is it for a well-shaped man like him to be going after little chaps like the fairies! To be sure some say there are such things, and more say not; but I know this, that never afraid would I be of a dozen of them—ay, of two dozen, for that matter, if they are no bigger than what I hear tell of."

Carroll O'Daly, whilst these thoughts were passing in his mind, had fixed his eyes steadfastly on the mountain, behind which the full moon was rising majestically. Upon an elevated point that appeared darkly against the moon's disk, he beheld the figure of a man leading a pony, and he had no doubt it was that of the farmer with whom he had just parted company.

A sudden resolve to follow flashed across the mind of O'Daly with the speed of lightning: both his courage and curiosity had been worked up by his cogitations to a pitch of chivalry; and muttering, "Here's after you, old boy!" he dismounted from his horse, bound him to an old thorn-tree, and then commenced vigorously ascending the mountain.

Following as well as he could the direction taken by the figures of the man and pony, he pursued his way, occasionally guided by their partial appearance; and, after toiling nearly three hours over a rugged and sometimes swampy path, came to a green spot on the top of the mountain, where he saw the white pony at full liberty grazing as quietly as may be. O'Daly looked around for the rider, but he was nowhere to be seen; he, however, soon discovered, close to where the pony stood, an opening in the mountain like the mouth of a pit, and he remembered having heard, when a child, many a tale about the "Poul-duve," or Black Hole of Knockfierna; how it was the entrance to the fairy castle which was within the mountain; and how a man whose name was Ahern, a land surveyor in that part of the country, had once attempted to fathom it with a line, and had been drawn down into it and was never again heard of; with many other tales of the like nature.

"But," thought O'Daly, "these are old women's stories; and since I've come up so far, I'll just knock at the castle door and see if the fairies are at home."

No sooner said than done; for, seizing a large stone, as big, aye, bigger than his two hands, he flung it with all his strength down into the Poul-duve of Knockfierna. He heard it bounding and tumbling about from one rock to another with a terrible noise, and he leant his head over to try and hear when it would reach the bottom—and what should the very stone he had thrown in do but come up again with as much force as it had gone down, and gave him such a blow full in the face, that it sent him rolling down the side of Knockfierna, head over heels, tumbling from one crag to another, much faster than he came up. And in the morning Carroll O'Daly was found lying beside his horse; the bridge of his nose broken, which disfigured him for life; his head all cut and bruised, and both his eyes closed up, and as black as if Sir Daniel Donnelly had painted them for him.

Carroll O'Daly was never bold again in riding alone near the haunts of the fairies after dusk; but small blame to him for that; and if ever he happened to be benighted in a lonesome place, he would make the best of his way to his journey's end, without asking questions, or turning to the right or to the left, to seek after the good people, or any who kept company with them.

III

THE LEGEND OF KNOCKGRAFTON

THERE was once a poor man who lived in the fertile glen of Aherlow, at the foot of the gloomy Galtee Mountains, and he had a great hump on his back: he looked just as if his body had been rolled up and placed upon his shoulders; and his head was pressed down with the weight so much, that his chin, when he was sitting, used to rest upon his knees for support. The country people were rather shy of meeting him in any lonesome place, for though, poor creature, he was as harmless and as inoffensive as a new-born infant, yet his deformity was so great, that he scarcely appeared to be a human being, and some ill-minded persons had set strange stories about him afloat. He was said to have a great knowledge of herbs and charms; but certain it was that he had a mighty skilful hand in plaiting straw and rushes into hats and baskets, which was the way he made his livelihood.

Lusmore—for that was the nickname put upon him by reason of his always wearing a sprig of the fairy-cap, or lusmore, in his little straw hat—would ever get a higher penny for his plaited-work than anyone else, and perhaps that was the reason why some-one, out of envy, had circulated the strange stories about him. Be that as it may, it happened that he was returning one evening from the pretty town of Cahir towards Cappagh; and as little Lusmore walked very slowly, on account of the great hump upon his back, it was quite dark when he came to the old moat of Knockgrafton, which stood on the right-hand side of his road. Tired and weary was he, and noways comfortable in his own mind at thinking how much farther he had to travel, and that he should be walking all the night; so he sat down under the moat to rest himself, and began looking mournfully enough upon the moon, which,

> " Rising in clouded majesty, at length,
> Apparent Queen, unveil'd her peerless light,
> And o'er the dark her silver mantle threw."

Presently there rose a wild strain of unearthly melody upon the ear of little Lusmore. He listened, and he thought that he had never heard such ravishing music before. It was like the sound of many voices, each mingling and blending with the other so strangely that they seemed to be one, though all singing different strains, and the words of the song were these :

Da Luan, Da Mort, Da Luan, Da Mort, Da Luan, Da Mort;
when there would be a moment's pause, and then the round of melody went on again.

Lusmore listened attentively, scarcely drawing his breath, lest he might lose the slightest note. He now plainly perceived that the singing was within the moat; and though at first it had charmed him so much, he began to get tired of hearing the same round sung over and over so often without any change. So, availing himself of the pause when the *Da Luan, Da Mort* had been sung three times, he took up the tune and raised it with the words *augus Da Cadine*, and then went on singing with the voices inside of the moat, *Da Luan, Da Mort,* finishing the melody, when the pause again came, with *augus Da Cadine.*[1]

[1] Correctly written, *Dia Luain, Dia Mairt, agus Dia Ceadaoine, i.e.,* Monday, Tuesday and Wednesday.

The fairies within Knockgrafton—for the song was a fairy melody—when they heard this addition to their tune, were so much delighted that, with instant resolve, it was determined to bring the mortal among them, whose musical skill so far exceeded theirs, and little Lusmore was conveyed into their company with the eddying speed of a whirlwind.

Glorious to behold was the sight that burst upon him as he came down through the moat, twirling round and round and round with the lightness of a straw, to the sweetest music that kept time to his motion. The greatest honour was then paid him, for he was put up above all the musicians, and he had servants tending upon him, and everything to his heart's content, and a hearty welcome to all; and in short, he was made as much of as if he had been the first man in the land.

Presently Lusmore saw a great consultation going forward among the fairies, and, notwithstanding all their civility, he felt very much frightened, until one, stepping out from the rest, came up to him and said:

> " Lusmore ! Lusmore !
> Doubt not, nor deplore,
> For the hump which you bore
> On your back is no more !—
> Look down on the floor,
> And view it, Lusmore ! "

When these words were said, poor little Lusmore felt himself so light and so happy, that he thought he could have bounded at one jump over the moon, like the cow in the history of the cat and the fiddle; and he saw, with inexpressible pleasure, his hump tumble down upon the ground from his shoulders. He then tried to lift up his head, and he did so with becoming caution, fearing that he might knock it against the ceiling of the grand hall, where he was. He looked round and round again with the greatest wonder and delight upon everything, which appeared more and more beautiful; and, overpowered at beholding such a resplendent scene, his head grew dizzy, and his eyesight became dim. At last he fell into a sound sleep, and when he awoke he found that it was broad daylight, the sun shining brightly, the birds singing sweetly; and that he was lying just at the foot of the moat of Knockgrafton, with the cows and sheep grazing peaceably round about him. The first thing Lusmore did, after saying his prayers, was to put his hand behind to feel for his hump; but no sign of one was there on his back, and he looked at himself with great pride, for he had now become a well-shaped, dapper little fellow; and more than that, he found himself in a full suit of new clothes, which, he concluded, the fairies had made for him.

Towards Cappagh he went, stepping out as lightly, and springing up at every step, as if he had been all his life a dancing-master. Not a creature who met Lusmore knew him without his hump, and he had great work to persuade everyone that he was the same man—in truth, he was not, so far as outward appearance went.

Of course, it was not long before the story of Lusmore's hump got about, and a great wonder was made of it. Through the country, for miles round, it was the talk of everyone high and low.

One morning, as Lusmore was sitting contented enough at his cabin door, up came an old woman to him, and asked if he could direct her to Cappagh.

"I need give you no directions, my good woman," said Lusmore, "for this is Cappagh. And who do you want here?"

"I have come," said the woman, "out of Decie's country, in the county of Waterford, looking after one Lusmore, who, I have heard tell, had his hump taken off by the fairies; for there is a son of a gossip of mine has got a hump on him that will be his death; and maybe, if he could use the same charm as Lusmore, the hump may be taken off him. And now I have told you the reason of my coming so far: 'tis to find out about this charm, if I can."

Lusmore, who was ever a good-natured little fellow, told the woman all the particulars, how he had raised the tune for the fairies at Knockgrafton, how his hump had been removed from his shoulders, and how he had got a new suit of clothes into the bargain.

The woman thanked him very much, and then went away quite happy, and easy in her own mind. When she came back to her gossip's house, in the county Waterford, she told her everything that Lusmore had said, and they put the little hump-backed man, who was a peevish and cunning creature from his birth, upon a car, and took him all the way across the country. It was a long journey, but they did not care for that, so the hump was taken from off him; and they brought him just at nightfall, and left him under the old moat of Knockgrafton.

Jack Madden—for that was the humpy man's name—had not been sitting there long when he heard the tune going on within the moat much sweeter than before; for the fairies were singing in the way Lusmore had settled their music for them, and the song was going on: *Da Luan, Da Mort, Da Luan, Da Mort, Da Luan, Da Mort, augus Da Cadine*, without ever stopping. Jack Madden, who was in a great hurry to get quit of his hump, never thought of waiting until the fairies had done, or watching for a fit opportunity to raise the tune higher again than Lusmore had;

so having heard them sing it over seven times without stopping, out he bawls, never minding the time or the humour of the tune, or how he could bring his words in properly, *augus da Cadine, augus Da Hena*, thinking that if one day was good, two were better ; and that if Lusmore had one new suit of clothes given to him, he should have two.

No sooner had the words passed his lips than he was taken up and whisked into the moat with prodigious force ; and the fairies came crowding round about him with great anger, screeching and screaming, and roaring out : " Who spoiled our tune ? who spoiled our tune ? " and one stepped up to him above all the rest, and said :

> " Jack Madden ! Jack Madden !
> Your words came so bad in
> The tune we feel glad in ;
> This castle you're had in,
> That your life we may sadden ;
> Here's two humps for Jack Madden ! "

And twenty of the strongest fairies brought Lusmore's hump and put it down upon poor Jack's back, over his own, where it became fixed as firmly as if it was nailed on with twelvepenny nails, by the best carpenter that ever drove one. Out of their castle they then kicked him ; and in the morning when Jack Madden's mother and her gossip came to look after their little man, they found him half dead, lying at the foot of the moat, with the other hump upon his back. Well, to be sure, how they did look at each other ; but they were afraid to say anything, lest a hump might be put upon their shoulders. Home they brought the unlucky Jack Madden with them, as downcast in their hearts and their looks as ever two gossips were ; and what through the weight of his other hump, and the long journey, he died soon after, leaving, they say, his heavy curse to anyone who would go to listen to fairy tunes again.

IV

THE PRIEST'S SUPPER

IT is said by those who ought to understand such things, that the good people, or the fairies, are some of the angels who were turned out of heaven, and who landed on their feet in this world, while the rest of their companions, who had more sin to sink them, went down further to a worse place. Be this as it may, there was a merry troop of the fairies, dancing and playing all manner of wild pranks on a bright moonlight evening towards the end of September. The scene of their merriment was not far

distant from Inchegeela, in the west of the county Cork—a poor
village, although it had a barrack for soldiers; but great
mountains and barren rocks, like those round about it, are
enough to strike poverty into any place. However, as the fairies
can have everything they want for wishing, poverty does not
trouble them much, and all their care is to seek out unfrequented
nooks and places where it is not likely anyone will come to
spoil their sport.

On a nice green sod by the river's side were the little fellows
dancing in a ring as gaily as may be, with their red caps wagging
about at every bound in the moonshine; and so light were these
bounds, that the lobes of dew, although they trembled under
their feet, were not disturbed by their capering. Thus did they
carry on their gambols, spinning round and round, and twirling
and bobbing, and diving and going through all manner of figures,
until one of them chirped out:

> " Cease, cease, with your drumming,
> Here's an end to our mumming.
> By my smell
> I can tell
> A priest this way is coming !"

And away every one of the fairies scampered off as hard as they
could, concealing themselves under the green leaves of the lusmore,
where, if their little red caps should happen to peep out, they
would only look like its crimson bells; and more hid themselves
in the hollow of stones, or at the shady side of brambles, and
others under the bank of the river, and in holes and crannies of
one kind or another.

The fairy speaker was not mistaken; for along the road, which
was within view of the river, came Father Horrigan on his pony,
thinking to himself that as it was so late he would make an end
of his journey at the first cabin he came to. According to this
determination, he stopped at the dwelling of Dermod Leary,
lifted the latch, and entered with "My blessing on all here."

I need not say that Father Horrigan was a welcome guest
wherever he went, for no man was more pious or better beloved
in the country. Now it was a great trouble to Dermod that he
had nothing to offer his reverence for supper as a relish to the
potatoes which "the old woman"—for so Dermod called his
wife, though she was not much past twenty—had down boiling
in the pot over the fire. He thought of the net which he had
set in the river, but as it had been there only a short time, the
chances were against his finding a fish in it. "No matter,"
thought Dermod; "there can be no harm in stepping down to
try, and maybe as I want the fish for the priest's supper, that one
will be there before me."

Down to the river-side went Dermod, and he found in the net as fine a salmon as ever jumped in the bright waters of "the spreading Lee"; but as he was going to take it out, the net was pulled from him—he could not tell how or by whom—and away got the salmon, and went swimming along with the current as gaily as if nothing had happened.

Dermod looked sorrowfully at the wake which the fish had left upon the water, shining like a line of silver in the moonlight, and then, with an angry motion of his right hand and a stamp of his foot, gave vent to his feelings by muttering: "May bitter bad luck attend you night and day for a blackguard schemer of a salmon, wherever you go! You ought to be ashamed of yourself, if there's any shame in you, to give me the slip after this fashion. And I'm clear in my own mind you'll come to no good, for some kind of evil thing or other helped you. Did I not feel it pull the net against me as strong as the devil himself?"

"That's not true for you," said one of the little fairies, who had scampered off at the approach of the priest coming up to Dermod Leary, with a whole throng of companions at his heels; "there was only a dozen and a half of us pulling against you."

Dermod gazed on the tiny speaker with wonder, who continued: "Make yourself noways uneasy about the priest's supper, for if you will go back and ask him one question from us, there will be as fine a supper as ever was put on a table, spread out before him in less than no time."

"I'll have nothing at all to do with you," replied Dermod, in a tone of determination, and after a pause, he added: "I'm much obliged to you for your offer, sir, but I know better than to sell myself to you or the like of you for a supper; and more than that, I know Father Horrigan has more regard for my soul than to wish me to pledge it for ever, out of regard to anything you could put before him, so there's an end of the matter."

The little speaker, with a pertinacity not to be repulsed by Dermod's manner, continued: "Will you ask the priest one civil question for us?"

Dermod considered for some time, and he was right in doing so, but he thought that no one could come to harm out of asking a civil question. "I see no objection to do that same, gentlemen," said Dermod: "but I will have nothing in life to do with your supper; mind that."

"Then," said the little speaking fairy, whilst the rest came crowding after him from all parts, "go and ask Father Horrigan to tell us whether our souls will be saved at the last day, like the souls of good Christians; and if you wish us well, bring back word what he says without delay."

Away went Dermod to his cabin, where he found the potatoes

thrown out on the table, and his good wife handing the biggest of them all—a beautiful, laughing, red apple, smoking like a hard-ridden horse on a frosty night—over to Father Horrigan.

" Please your reverence," said Dermod, after some hesitation, "may I make bold to ask your honour one question ? "

" What may that be ? " said Father Horrigan.

" Why, then, begging your reverence's pardon for my freedom, it is, if the souls of the good people are to be saved at the last day ? "

" Who bid you ask me that question, Leary ? " said the priest, fixing his eyes upon him very sternly, which Dermod could not stand before at all.

" I'll tell no lies about the matter, and nothing in life but the truth," said Dermod. " It was the good people themselves who sent me to ask the question, and there they are in thousands down on the bank of the river waiting for me to go back with the answer."

" Go back, by all means," said the priest, " and tell them if they want to know to come here to me themselves, and I'll answer that or any other question they are pleased to ask, with the greatest pleasure in life."

Dermod accordingly returned to the fairies, who came swarming round about him to hear what the priest had said in reply, and Dermod spoke out among them like a bold man as he was ; but when they heard that they must go to the priest, away they fled, some here and more there, and some this way and more that, whisking by poor Dermod so fast, and in such numbers, that he was quite bewildered.

When he came to himself, which was not for a long time, back he went to his cabin and ate his dry potatoes along with Father Horrigan, who made quite light of the thing ; but Dermod could not help thinking it a mighty hard case that his reverence, whose words had the power to banish the fairies at such a rate, should have no sort of relish to his supper, and that the fine salmon he had in the net should have been got away from him in such a manner.

V

THE BREWERY OF EGG-SHELLS

It may be considered impertinent were I to explain what is meant by a changeling ; both Shakespeare and Spenser have already done so, and who is there unacquainted with the Midsummer's Night's Dream and the Fairy Queen?

Now Mrs. Sullivan fancied that her youngest child had been

changed by "fairies' theft," to use Spenser's words, and certainly appearances warranted such a conclusion; for in one night her healthy, blue-eyed boy had become shrivelled up into almost nothing, and never ceased squalling and crying. This naturally made poor Mrs. Sullivan very unhappy; and all the neighbours, by way of comforting her, said that her own child was, beyond any kind of doubt, with the good people, and that one of themselves had been put in his place.

Mrs. Sullivan, of course, could not disbelieve what everyone told her, but she did not wish to hurt the thing; for although its face was so withered, and its body wasted away to a mere skeleton, it had still a strong resemblance to her own boy; she therefore could not find it in her heart to roast it alive on the griddle, or to burn its nose off with the red-hot tongs, or to throw it out in the snow on the roadside, notwithstanding these, and several like proceedings, were strongly recommended to her for the recovery of her child.

One day who should Mrs. Sullivan meet but a cunning woman, well known about the country by the name of Ellen Leah (or Grey Ellen). She had the gift, however she got it, of telling where the dead were, and what was good for the rest of their souls; and could charm away warts and wens, and do a great many wonderful things of the same nature.

"You're in grief this morning, Mrs. Sullivan," were the first words of Ellen Leah to her.

"You may say that, Ellen," said Mrs. Sullivan; "and good cause I have to be in grief, for there was my own fine child whipped off from me out of his cradle, without as much as by your leave or ask your pardon, and an ugly dony bit of a shrivelled-up fairy put in his place. No wonder, then, that you see me in grief, Ellen."

"Small blame to you, Mrs. Sullivan," said Ellen Leah; "but are you sure 'tis a fairy?"

"Sure!" echoed Mrs. Sullivan. "Sure enough am I to my sorrow, and can I doubt my own two eyes? Every mother's soul must feel for me!"

"Will you take an old woman's advice?" said Ellen Leah, fixing her wild and mysterious gaze upon the unhappy mother; and, after a pause, she added: "But maybe you'll call it foolish?"

"Can you get me back my child—my own child, Ellen?" said Mrs. Sullivan, with great energy.

"If you do as I bid you," returned Ellen Leah, "you'll know." Mrs. Sullivan was silent in expectation, and Ellen continued: "Put down the big pot, full of water, on the fire, and make it boil like mad; then get a dozen new-laid eggs, break them, and keep the shells, but throw away the rest. When that is done, put the shells in the pot of boiling water, and you will soon know whether it is your own boy or a fairy. If you find that it is a fairy in the cradle, take the red-hot poker and cram it down his ugly throat, and you will not have much trouble with him after that, I promise you."

Home went Mrs. Sullivan, and did as Ellen Leah desired. She put the pot in the fire, and plenty of turf under it, and set the water boiling at such a rate that if ever water was red hot, it surely was.

The child was lying for a wonder quite easy and quiet in the cradle, every now and then cocking his eye, that would twinkle as keen as a star in a frosty night, over at the great fire, and the big pot upon it; and he looked on with great attention at Mrs. Sullivan breaking the eggs, and putting down the egg-shells to boil. At last he asked, with the voice of a very old man: "What are you doing, mammy?"

Mrs. Sullivan's heart, as she said herself, was up in her mouth ready to choke her, at hearing the child speak. But she contrived to put the poker in the fire, and to answer, without making any wonder at the words: "I'm brewing, *a vick* [my son]."

"And what are you brewing, mammy?" said the little imp, whose supernatural gift of speech now proved beyond question that he was a fairy substitute.

"I wish the poker was red," thought Mrs. Sullivan; but it was a large one, and took a long time heating; so she determined to keep him in talk until the poker was in a proper state to thrust down his throat, and therefore repeated the question:

"Is it what I'm brewing, *a vick*," said she, "you want to know?"

"Yes, mammy. What are you brewing?" returned the fairy.

"Egg-shells, *a vick*," said Mrs. Sullivan.

"Oh," shrieked the imp, starting up in the cradle and clapping his hands together, "I'm fifteen hundred years in the world, and I never saw a brewery of egg-shells before!" The poker was by this time quite red, and Mrs. Sullivan, seizing it, ran furiously towards the cradle; but somehow or other her foot slipped, and she fell flat on the floor, and the poker flew out of her hand to the other end of the house. However, she got up, without much loss of time, and went to the cradle intending to pitch the wicked thing that was in it into the pot of boiling water, when there she saw her own child in a sweet sleep; one of his soft round arms rested upon the pillow; his features were as placid as if their repose had never been disturbed, save the rosy mouth which moved with a gentle and regular breathing.

Who can tell the feelings of a mother when she looks upon her sleeping child? Why should I, therefore, endeavour to describe those of Mrs. Sullivan at again beholding her long-lost boy? The fountain of her heart overflowed with the excess of joy—and she wept!—tears trickled silently down her cheeks, nor did she strive to check them—they were tears not of sorrow, but of happiness.

VI

LEGEND OF BOTTLE HILL

IT was in the good days, when the little people, most impudently called fairies, were more frequently seen than they are in these unbelieving times, that a farmer, named Mick Purcell, rented a few acres of barren ground in the neighbourhood of the once celebrated preceptory of Mourne, situated about three miles from Mallow and thirteen from "the beautiful city called Cork." Mick had a wife and family: they all did what they could, and that was but little, for the poor man had no child grown up big enough to help him in his work; and all the poor woman could do was to mind the children, and to milk the one cow, and to boil the potatoes, and to carry the eggs to market to Mallow; but with all they could do, 'twas hard enough on them to pay the rent. Well, they did manage it for a good while; but at last came a bad year, and the little grain of oats was all spoiled, and the chickens died of the pip, and the pig got the measles—*she* was sold in Mallow and brought almost nothing; and poor Mick found that he hadn't enough to half pay his rent, and two gales were due.

"Why, then, Molly," says he, "what'll we do?"

"Wisha, then, mavourneen, what would you do but take the cow to the fair of Cork and sell her?" says she. "And Monday is fair day, and so you must go to-morrow, that the poor beast may be rested *again* the fair."

"And what'll we do when she's gone?" says Mick sorrowfully.

"Never a know I know, Mick; but sure, God won't leave us without Him, Mick; and you know how good He was to us when poor little Billy was sick, and we had nothing at all for him to take, that good doctor gentleman at Ballydahin come riding and asking for a drink of milk; and how he gave us two shillings; and how he sent the things and bottles for the child, and gave me my breakfast when I went over to ask a question, so he did; and how he came to see Billy, and never left off his goodness till he was quite well?"

"Oh, you are always that way, Molly, and I believe you are right, after all, so I won't be sorry for selling the cow; but I'll go to-morrow, and you must put a needle and thread through my coat, for you know 'tis ripped under the arm."

Molly told him he should have everything right; and about twelve o'clock next day he left her, getting a charge not to sell his cow except for the highest penny. Mick promised to mind it, and went his way along the road. He drove his cow slowly through the little stream which crosses it, and runs by the old walls of Mourne. As he passed he glanced his eye upon the towers and one of the old elder trees, which were only then little bits of switches.

"Oh, then, if I only had half the money that's buried in you, 'tisn't driving this poor cow I'd be now! Why, then, isn't it too bad that it should be there covered over with earth, and many a one besides me wanting? Well, if it's God's will, I'll have some money myself coming back."

So saying, he moved on after his beast. 'Twas a fine day, and the sun shone brightly on the walls of the old abbey as he passed under them; he then crossed an extensive mountain track, and after six long miles, he came to the top of that hill—Bottle Hill 'tis called now, but that was not the name of it then, and just there a man overtook him. "Good morrow!" says he.

"Good morrow!" kindly says Mick, looking at the stranger, who was a little man, you'd almost call him a dwarf, only he wasn't quite so little neither; he had a bit of an old, wrinkled, yellow face, for all the world like a dried cauliflower, only he had a sharp little nose, and red eyes and white hair, and his lips were not red, but all his face was one colour, and his eyes never were quiet, but looking at everything, and although they were red, they made Mick feel quite cold when he looked at them. In truth, he did not much like the little man's company; and he couldn't see one bit of his legs nor his body; for, though the day was warm, he was all wrapped up in a big great-coat. Mick drove his cow something faster, but the little man kept up with him. Mick didn't know how he walked, for he was almost afraid to look at him, and to cross himself, for fear the old man would be angry. Yet he thought his fellow-traveller did not seem to walk like other men, nor to put one foot before the other, but to glide over the rough road—and rough enough it was—like a shadow, without noise and without effort. Mick's heart trembled within him, and he said a prayer to himself, wishing he hadn't come out 'that day, or that he was on Fair Hill, or that he hadn't the cow to mind, that he might run away from the bad thing—when, in the midst of his fears, he was again addressed by his companion.

"Where are you going with the cow, honest man?"

"To the fair of Cork, then," says Mick, trembling at the shrill and piercing tones of the voice.

"Are you going to sell her?" said the stranger.

"Why, then, what else am I going for but to sell her?"

"Will you sell her to me?"

Mick started—he was afraid to have anything to do with the little man, and he was more afraid to say no.

"What'll you give for her?" at last says he.

"I'll tell you what, I'll give you this bottle," said the little one, pulling a bottle from under his coat.

Mick looked at him and the bottle, and in spite of his terror, he could not help bursting into a loud fit of laughter.

"Laugh if you will," said the little man; "but I tell you this bottle is better for you than all the money you will get for the cow in Cork—ay, than ten thousand times as much."

Mick laughed again. "Why, then," says he, "do you think I am such a fool as to give my good cow for a bottle—and an empty one too? Indeed, then, I won't."

"You had better give me the cow, and take the bottle—you'll not be sorry for it."

"Why, then, and what would Molly say? I'd never hear the end of it; and how would I pay the rent? and what would we all do without a penny of money?"

"I tell you this bottle is better to you than money; take it, and give me the cow. I ask you for the last time, Mick Purcell."

Mick started.

"How does he know my name?" thought he.

The stranger proceeded: "Mick Purcell, I know you, and I have a regard for you; therefore, do as I warn you, or you may be sorry for it. How do you know but your cow will die before you get to Cork?"

Mick was going to say "God forbid!" but the little man went on (and he was too attentive to say anything to stop him; for Mick was a very civil man, and he knew better than to interrupt a gentleman, and that's what many people that hold their heads higher don't mind now).

"And how do you know but there will be much cattle at the fair, and you will get a bad price, or maybe you might be robbed when you are coming home? But what need I talk more to you, when you are determined to throw away your luck, Mick Purcell?"

"Oh, no! I would not throw away my luck, sir," said Mick. "And if I was sure the bottle was as good as you say—though I never liked an empty bottle, although I had drank what was in it—I'd give you the cow in the name—"

"Never mind names," said the stranger, "but give me the cow; I would not tell you a lie. Here, take the bottle, and when you go home do what I direct exactly."

Mick hesitated.

"Well, then, good-bye ! I can stay no longer. Once more, take it, and be rich; refuse it, and beg for your life, and see your children in poverty and your wife dying for want; that will happen to you, Mick Purcell !" said the little man, with a malicious grin, which made him look ten times more ugly than ever.

"Maybe 'tis true," said Mick, still hesitating; he did not know what to do—he could hardly help believing the old man, and at length, in a fit of desperation, he seized the bottle. "Take the cow," said he, "and if you are telling a lie, the curse of the poor will be on you."

"I care neither for your curses nor your blessings, but I have spoken truth, Mick Purcell, and that you will find to-night, if you do what I tell you."

"And what's that ?" says Mick.

"When you go home, never mind if your wife is angry, but be quiet yourself, and make her sweep the room clean, set the table out right, and spread a clean cloth over it ; then put the bottle on the ground, saying these words, 'Bottle, do your duty,' and you will see the end of it."

"And is this all ?" says Mick.

"No more," said the stranger. "Good-bye, Mick Purcell ! you are a rich man."

"God grant it !" said Mick, as the old man moved after the cow, and Mick retraced the road towards his cabin ; but he could not help turning back his head to look after the purchaser of his cow, who was nowhere to be seen.

"Lord between us and harm !" said Mick. "*He* can't belong to this earth ; but where is the cow ?" She, too, was gone, and Mick went homeward muttering prayers, and holding fast the bottle.

"And what would I do if it broke ?" thought he. "Oh, but I'll take care of that." So he put it into his bosom, and went on, anxious to prove his bottle, and doubting of the reception he should meet from his wife. Balancing his anxieties with his expectation, his fears with his hopes, he reached home in the evening, and surprised his wife sitting over the turf fire in the big chimney.

"Oh, Mick, are you come back ? Sure, you weren't at Cork all the way ? What has happened to you ? Where is the cow ? Did you sell her ? How much money did you get for her ? What news have you ? Tell us everything about it."

"Why, then, Molly, if you'll give me time, I'll tell you all about it. If you want to know where the cow is, 'tisn't Mick can tell you, for the never a know does he know where she is now."

" Oh, then, you sold her. And where's the money ? "

" Arrah ! stop a while, Molly, and I'll tell you all about it."

" But what is that bottle under your waistcoat ? " said Molly, spying its neck sticking out.

" Why, then, be easy now, can't you," says Mick, " till I tell it to you ? " and putting the bottle on the table : " That's all I got for the cow."

His poor wife was thunderstruck. " All you got ! And what good is that, Mick ? Oh, I never thought you were such a fool ? and what'll we do for the rent, and what— "

" Now, Molly," says Mick, " can't you hearken to reason. Didn't I tell you how the old man, or whatsomever he was, met me—no, he did not meet me neither, but he was there with me— on the big hill, and how he made me sell him the cow, and told me the bottle was the only thing for me ? "

" Yes, indeed ; the only thing for you, you fool ! " said Molly, seizing the bottle to hurl it at her poor husband's head ; but Mick caught it, and quietly (for he minded the old man's advice) loosened his wife's grasp, and placed the bottle again in his bosom. Poor Molly sat down crying, while Mick told her his story, with many a crossing and blessing between him and harm. His wife could not help believing him, particularly as she had as much faith in fairies as she had in the priest, who indeed never discouraged her belief in the fairies ; maybe he didn't know she believed in them, and maybe he believed in them himself. She got up, however, without saying one word, and began to sweep the earthen floor with a bunch of heath ; then she tidied up everything, and put out the long table, and spread the clean cloth, for she had only one, upon it, and Mick, placing the bottle on the ground, looked at it, and said : " Bottle, do your duty."

" Look there ! look there, mammy ! " said his chubby eldest son, a boy about five years old—" look there ! look there ! " and he sprang to his mother's side, as two tiny little fellows rose like light from the bottle, and in an instant covered the table with dishes and plates of gold and silver, full of the finest victuals that ever were seen, and when all was done, went into the bottle again. Mick and his wife looked at everything with astonishment ; they had never seen such plates and dishes before, and didn't think they could ever admire them enough ; the very sight almost took away their appetites ; but at length Molly said : " Come and sit down, Mick, and try and eat a bit ; sure, you ought to be hungry after such a good day's work."

" Why, then, the man told no lie about the bottle."

Mick sat down, after putting the children to the table, and they made a hearty meal, though they couldn't taste half the dishes.

"Now," says Molly, "I wonder will those two good little gentlemen carry away these fine things again?" They waited, but no one came; so Molly put up the dishes and plates very carefully, saying: "Why, then, Mick, that was no lie, sure enough; but you'll be a rich man yet, Mick Purcell."

Mick and his wife and children went to their bed, not to sleep, but to settle about selling the fine things they did not want, and to take more land. Mick went to Cork and sold his plate, and bought a horse and cart, and began to show that he was making money; and they did all they could to keep the bottle a secret; but for all that, their landlord found it out, for he came to Mick one day, and asked him where he got all his money—sure, it was not by the farm; and he bothered him so much, that at last Mick told him of the bottle. His landlord offered him a deal of money for it; but Mick would not give it, till at last he offered to give him all his farm for ever; so Mick, who was very rich, thought he'd never want any more money, and gave him the bottle; but Mick was mistaken—he and his family spent money as if there was no end of it; and to make the story short, they became poorer and poorer, till at last they had nothing but one cow; and Mick once more drove his cow before him to sell her at Cork Fair, hoping to meet the old man and get another bottle. It was hardly daybreak when he left home, and he walked on at a good pace till he reached the big hill; the mists were sleeping in the valleys, and curling like smoke-wreaths upon the brown heath around him. The sun rose on his left, and just at his feet a lark sprang from its grassy couch and poured forth its joyous matin song, ascending into the clear blue sky—

> "Till its form like a speck in the airiness blending,
> And thrilling with music, was melting in light."

Mick crossed himself, listening as he advanced to the sweet song of the lark, but thinking, notwithstanding, all the time of the little old man; when, just as he reached the summit of the hill, and cast his eyes over the extensive prospect before and around him, he was startled and rejoiced by the same well-known voice: "Well, Mick Purcell, I told you you would be a rich man."

"Indeed, then, sure enough I was; that's no lie for you, sir. Good morning to you; but it is not rich I am now—but have you another bottle, for I want it now as much as I did long ago; so if you have it, sir, here is the cow for it."

"And here is the bottle," said the old man, smiling. "You know what to do with it."

"Oh, then, sure I do, as good right I have."

"Well, farewell for ever, Mick Purcell! I told you you would be a rich man."

"And good-bye to you, sir," said Mick, as he turned back; "and good luck to you, and good luck to the big hill—it wants a name—Bottle Hill. Good-bye, sir, good-bye!" so Mick walked back as fast as he could, never looking after the white-faced little gentleman and the cow, so anxious was he to bring home the bottle. Well, he arrived with it safely enough, and called out, as soon as he saw Molly: "Oh, sure, I've another bottle!"

"Arrah! then, have you? Why, then, you're a lucky man, Mick Purcell, that's what you are."

In an instant she put everything right; and Mick, looking at his bottle, exultingly cried out: "Bottle, do your duty." In a twinkling, two great stout men with big cudgels issued from the bottle (I do not know how they got room in it), and belaboured poor Mick and his wife and all his family, till they lay on the floor, when in they went again. Mick, as soon as he recovered, got up and looked about him; he thought and thought, and at last he took up his wife and his children; and leaving them to recover as well as they could, he took the bottle under his coat, and went to his landlord, who had a great company. He got a servant to tell him he wanted to speak to him, and at last he came out to Mick.

"Well, what do you want now?"

"Nothing, sir; only I have another bottle."

"Oh, ho! is it as good as the first?"

"Yes, sir, and better; if you like, I will show it to you before all the ladies and gentlemen."

"Come along, then." So saying, Mick was brought into the great hall, where he saw his old bottle standing high up on a shelf; "Ah, ha!" says he to himself; "maybe I won't have you by-and-by."

"Now," says his landlord, "show us your bottle." Mick set it on the floor, and uttered the words. In a moment, the landlord was tumbled on the floor; ladies and gentlemen, servants and all, were running and roaring, and sprawling and kicking and shrieking. Wine-cups and salvers were knocked about in every direction, until the landlord called out: "Stop those two devils, Mick Purcell, or I'll have you hanged!"

"They never shall stop," said Mick, "till I get my own bottle that I see up there at top of that shelf."

"Give it down to him, give it down to him, before we are all killed!" says the landlord.

Mick put the bottle in his bosom; in jumped the two men into the new bottle, and he carried the bottles home. I need not lengthen my story by telling how he got richer than ever, how his son married his landlord's only daughter, how he and his wife died when they were very old, and how some of the servants, fighting at their wake, broke the bottles; but still the hill has the name upon it—ay, and so 'twill be always Bottle Hill to the end of the world, and so it ought, for it is a strange story.

VII

THE CONFESSIONS OF TOM BOURKE

Tom Bourke lives in a low, long farm-house, resembling in outward appearance a large barn, placed at the bottom of the hill, just where the new road strikes off from the old one, leading from the town of Kilworth to that of Lismore. He is of a class of persons who are a sort of black swans in Ireland; he is a wealthy farmer. Tom's father had, in the good old times, when a hundred pounds were no inconsiderable treasure, either to lend or spend, accommodated his landlord with that sum, at interest; and obtained, as a return for the civility, a long lease, about half-a-dozen times more valuable than the loan which procured it. The old man died worth several hundred pounds, the greater part of which, with his farm, he bequeathed to his son Tom. But besides all this, Tom received from his father, upon his death-bed, another gift, far more valuable than worldly riches, greatly as he prized, and is still known to prize them. He was invested with the privilege, enjoyed by few of the sons of men, of communicating with those mysterious beings called "the good people."

Tom Bourke is a little, stout, healthy, active man, about fifty-five years of age. His hair is perfectly white, short and bushy behind, but rising in front erect and thick above his forehead, like a new clothes'-brush. His eyes are of that kind which I have often observed with persons of a quick but limited intellect—they are small, grey and lively. The large and projecting eyebrows under, or rather within, which they twinkle, give them an expression of shrewdness and intelligence, if not of cunning. And this is very much the character of the man. If you want to make a bargain with Tom Bourke, you must act as if you were a general besieging a town, and make your advances a long time before you can hope to obtain possession; if you march up boldly, and tell him at once your object, you are for the most part sure to have the gates closed in your teeth. Tom does not wish to part with what you wish to obtain, or another person has been speaking to him for the whole of the last week. Or, it may be, your proposal seems to meet the most favourable reception. "Very well, sir;" "That's true, sir;" "I'm very thankful to your honour," and other expressions of kindness and confidence, greet you in reply to every sentence; and you part from him wondering how he can have obtained the character which he universally bears, of being a man whom no one can make anything of in a bargain. But when you next meet him, the flattering illusion is dissolved; you find you are a great deal farther from your object than you were when you thought you had almost succeeded; his eye and his tongue express a total forgetfulness of what the mind within never lost sight of for an instant; and you have to begin operations afresh, with the disadvantage of having put your adversary completely upon his guard.

Yet, although Tom Bourke is, whether from supernatural revealings, or (as many will think more probable) from the tell-truth experience, so distrustful of mankind, and so close in his dealings with them, he is no misanthrope. No man loves better the pleasures of the genial board. The love of money, indeed, which is with him (and who will blame him?) a very ruling propensity, and the gratification which it has received from habits of industry, sustained throughout a pretty long and successful life, have taught him the value of sobriety, during those seasons, at least, when a man's business requires him to keep possession of his senses. He has, therefore, a general rule never to get drunk but on Sundays. But in order that it should be a general one to all intents and purposes, he takes a method which, according to better logicians than he is, always proves the rule. He has many exceptions: among these, of course, are the evenings of all the fair and market days that happen in his neighbourhood; so also all the days on which funerals, marriages, and christenings take place among his friends within many miles of him. As to this last class of exceptions, it may appear at first very singular, that he is much more punctual in his attendance at the funerals than at the baptisms or weddings of his friends. This may be construed as an instance of disinterested affection for departed worth, very uncommon in this selfish world. But I am afraid that the motives which lead Tom Bourke to pay more court to the dead than the living are precisely those which lead to the opposite conduct in the generality of mankind—a hope of future benefit and a fear of future evil. For the good people, who are a race as powerful as they are capricious, have their favourites among those who inhabit this world; often show their affection, by easing the objects of it from the load of this burdensome life; and frequently reward or punish the living, according to the degree of reverence paid to the obsequies and the memory of the elected dead.

It is not easy to prevail on Tom to speak of those good people, with whom he is said to hold frequent and intimate communications. To the faithful, who believe in their power, and their occasional delegation of it to him, he seldom refuses, if properly asked, to exercise his high prerogative, when any unfortunate being is *struck* in his neighbourhood. Still, he will not be won unsued; he is at first difficult of persuasion, and must be overcome by a little gentle violence. On these occasions he is unusually solemn and mysterious, and if one word of reward be mentioned, he at once abandons the unhappy patient, such a proposition being a direct insult to his supernatural superiors. It is true, that as the labourer is worthy of his hire, most persons, gifted as he is, do not scruple to receive a token of gratitude from the patients or their friends *after* their recovery.

To do Tom Bourke justice, he is on these occasions, as I have heard from many competent authorities, perfectly disinterested. Not many months since, he recovered a young woman (the sister of a tradesman living near him), who had been struck speechless after returning from a funeral, and had continued so for several days. He steadfastly refused receiving any compensation, saying, that even if he had not as much as would buy him his supper, he could take nothing in this case, because the girl had offended at the funeral one of the *good people* belonging to his own family, and though he would do her a kindness, he could take none from her.

About the time this last remarkable affair took place, my friend, Mr. Martin, who is a neighbour of Tom's, had some business to transact with him, which it was exceedingly difficult to bring to a conclusion. At last Mr. Martin, having tried all quiet means, had recourse to a legal process, which brought Tom to reason, and the matter was arranged to their mutual satisfaction, and with perfect good-humour between the parties. The accommodation took place after dinner at Mr. Martin's house, and he invited Tom to walk into the parlour and take a glass of punch, made of some excellent *potteen*, which was on the table. He had long wished to draw out his highly-endowed neighbour on the subject of his supernatural powers, and as Mrs. Martin, who was in the room, was rather a favourite of Tom's, this seemed a good opportunity.

"Well, Tom," said Mr. Martin, "that was a curious business of Molly Dwyer's, who recovered her speech so suddenly the other day."

"You may say that, sir," replied Tom Bourke; "but I had to travel far for it: no matter for that, now. Your health, ma'am," said he, turning to Mrs. Martin.

"Thank you, Tom. But I am told you had some trouble once in that way in your own family," said Mrs. Martin.

"So I had, ma'am; trouble enough; but you were only a child at that time."

"Come, Tom," said the hospitable Mr. Martin, interrupting him, "take another tumbler;" and he then added: "I wish you would tell us something of the manner in which so many of your children died. I am told they dropped off, one after another, by the same disorder, and that your eldest son was cured in a most extraordinary way, when the physicians had given over."

"'Tis true for you, sir," returned Tom. "Your father, the doctor (God be good to him, I won't belie him in his grave), told me, when my fourth little boy was a week sick, that himself and Dr. Barry did all that man could do for him; but they could not keep him from going after the rest. No more they could, if the people that took away the rest wished to take him too. But they left him; and sorry to the heart I am I did not know before why they were taking my boys from me; if I did, I would not be left trusting to two of 'em now."

"And how did you find it out, Tom?" inquired Mr. Martin.

"Why, then, I'll tell you, sir," said Bourke. "When your father said what I told you, I did not know very well what to do. I walked down the little *bohereen*, you know, sir, that goes to the river-side near Dick Heafy's ground; for 'twas a lonesome place, and I wanted to think of myself. I was heavy, sir, and my heart got weak in me, when I thought I was to lose my little boy; and I did not know well how to face his mother with the news, for she doted down upon him. Beside, she never got the better of all she cried at his brother's berrin' [burying] the week before. As I was going down the bohereen, I met an old bocough, that used to come about the place once or twice a year, and used always sleep in our barn while he stayed in the neighbourhood. So he asked me how I was. 'Bad enough, Shamous [James],' says I. 'I'm sorry for your trouble,' says he; 'but you're a foolish man, Mr. Bourke. Your son would be well enough if you would only do what you ought with him.' 'What more can I do with him, Shamous?' says I: 'the doctors give him over.' 'The doctors know no more what ails him than they do what ails a cow when she stops her milk,' says Shamous; 'but go to such a one,' says he, telling me his name, 'and try what he'll say to you.'"

"And who was that, Tom?" asked Mr. Martin.

"I could not tell you that, sir," said Bourke, with a mysterious look; "howsoever, you often saw him, and he does not live far from this. But I had a trial of him before; and if I went to him at first, maybe I'd have now some of them that's gone, and so Shamous often told me. Well, sir, I went to this man, and he came with me to the house. By course, I did everything as he bid me. According to his order, I took the little boy out of the dwelling-house immediately, sick as he was, and made a bed for him and myself in the cow-house. Well, sir, I lay down by his side in the bed, between two of the cows, and he fell asleep. He got into a perspiration, saving your presence, as if he was drawn through the river, and breathed hard, with a great *impression* [oppression] on his chest, and was very bad—very bad entirely, through the night. I thought about twelve o'clock he was going at last, and I was just getting up to go call the man I told you of; but there was no occasion. My friends were getting the better of them that wanted to take him away from me. There was nobody in the cow-house but the child and myself. There was only one halfpenny candle lighting, and that was stuck in the wall at the far end of the house. I had just enough of light where we were laying to see a person walking or standing near us; and there was no more noise than if it was a churchyard, except the cows chewing the fodder in the stalls. Just as I was thinking of getting up, as I told you—I won't belie my father, sir, he was a good father to me—I saw him standing at the bedside holding out his right hand to me, and leaning his other hand on the stick he used to carry when he was alive, and looking pleasant and smiling at me, all as if he was telling me not to be afeard, for I would not lose the child. 'Is that you, father?' says I. He said nothing. 'If that's you,' says I again, 'for the love of them that's gone, let me catch your hand.' And so he did, sir; and his hand was as soft as a child's. He stayed about as long as you'd be going from this to the gate below at the end of the avenue, and then went away. In less than a week the child was as well as if nothing ever ailed him; and there isn't to-night a healthier boy of nineteen, from this blessed house to the town of Ballyporeen, across the Kilworth mountains."

"But I think, Tom," said Mr. Martin, "it appears as if you are more indebted to your father than to the man recommended to you by Shamous; or do you suppose it was he who made favour with your enemies among the good people, and that then your father—"

"I beg your pardon, sir," said Bourke, interrupting him; "but don't call them my enemies. 'Twould not be wishing to me for a good deal to sit by when they are called so. No offence to you, sir. Here's wishing you a good health and long life."

"I assure you," returned Mr. Martin, "I meant no offence, Tom; but was it not as I say?"

"I can't tell you that, sir," said Bourke. "I'm bound down, sir. Howsoever, you may be sure the man I spoke of and my father, and those they know, settled it between them."

There was a pause, of which Mrs. Martin took advantage to inquire of Tom whether something remarkable had not happened about a goat and a pair of pigeons at the time of his son's illness —circumstances often mysteriously hinted at by Tom.

"See that, now," said he, returning to Mr. Martin; "how well she remembers it! True for you, ma'am. The goat I gave the mistress, your mother, when the doctors ordered her goats' whey."

Mrs. Martin nodded assent, and Tom Bourke continued: "Why, then, I'll tell you how that was. The goat was as well as e'er a goat ever was for a month after she was sent to Killaan to your father's. The morning after the night I just told you of, before the child woke, his mother was standing at the gap leading out of the barn-yard into the road, and she saw two pigeons flying from the town of Kilworth, off the church down towards her. Well, they never stopped, you see, till they came to the house on the hill at the other side of the river, facing our farm. They pitched upon the chimney of that house, and after looking about them for a minute or two, they flew straight across the river, and stopped on the ridge of the cow-house where the child and I were lying. Do you think they came there for nothing, sir?"

"Certainly not, Tom!" returned Mr. Martin.

"Well, the woman came in to me, frightened, and told me. She began to cry. 'Whisht, you fool!' says I; ''tis all for the better.' 'Twas true for me. What do you think, ma'am: the goat that I gave your mother, that was seen feeding at sunrise that morning by Jack Cronin, as merry as a bee, dropped down dead, without anybody knowing why, before Jack's face; and at that very moment he saw two pigeons fly from the top of the house out of the town towards the Lismore road. 'Twas at the same time my woman saw them, as I just told you."

"'Twas very strange indeed, Tom," said Mr. Martin. "I wish you could give us some explanation of it."

"I wish I could, sir," was Tom Bourke's answer; "but I'm bound down. I can't tell but what I'm allowed to tell, any more than a sentry is let walk more than his rounds."

"I think you said something of having had some former knowledge of the man that assisted in the cure of your son," said Mr. Martin.

"So I had, sir," returned Bourke. "I had a trial of that man. But that's neither here nor there. I can't tell you anything about that, sir. But would you like to know how he got his skill?"

"Oh, very much indeed," said Mr. Martin.

"But you can tell us his Christian name, that we may know him the better through the story," added Mrs. Martin. Tom Bourke paused for a minute to consider this proposition.

"Well, I believe I may tell you that, anyhow; his name is Patrick. He was always a smart, active, cute boy, and would be a great clerk if he stuck to it. The first time I knew him, sir, was at my mother's wake. I was in great trouble, for I did not know where to bury her. Her people and my father's people—I mean their friends, sir, among the *good people*—had the greatest battle that was known for many a year, at Dunmanwaycross, to see to whose churchyard she'd be taken. They fought for three nights, one after another, without being able to settle it. The neighbours wondered how long I was before I buried my mother; but I had my reasons, though I could not tell them at that time. Well, sir, to make my story short, Patrick came on the fourth morning and told me he settled the business, and that day we buried her in Kilcrumper Churchyard, with my father's people."

"He was a valuable friend, Tom," said Mrs. Martin, with difficulty suppressing a smile. "But you were about to tell us how he became so skilful."

"So I will, and welcome," replied Bourke. "Your health, ma'am. I am drinking too much of this punch, sir; but to tell the truth, I never tasted the like of it: it goes down one's throat like sweet oil. But what was I going to say? Yes— well, Patrick, many a long year ago, was coming home from a *berrin'* late in the evening, and walking by the side of the river, opposite the big inch, near Ballyhefaan ford. He had taken a drop, to be sure; but he was only a little merry, as you may say, and knew very well what he was doing. The moon was shining—for it was in the month of August—and the river was as smooth and as bright as a looking-glass. He heard nothing for a long time but the fall of the water at the mill weir about a mile down the river, and now and then the crying of the lambs on the other side of the river. All at once, there was a noise of a great number of people, laughing as if they'd break their hearts, and of a piper playing among them. It came from the inch at the other side of the ford, and he saw, through the mist that hung over the river, a whole crowd of people dancing on the inch. Patrick was as fond of a dance as he was of a glass, and that's saying enough for him; so he whipped off his shoes and stockings, and away with him across the ford. After putting on his shoes and stockings at the other side of the river, he walked over to the crowd, and mixed with them for some time without being minded. He thought, sir, that he'd show them better dancing than any of themselves, for he was proud of his feet, sir, and good right he had, for there was not a boy in the same parish could foot a double or treble with him. But, pwah!—his dancing was no more to theirs than mine would be to the mistress there. They did not seem as if they had a bone in their bodies, and they kept it up as if nothing could tire them. Patrick was 'shamed within himself, for he thought he had not his fellow in all the country round; and was going away, when a little old man, that was looking at the company for some time bitterly, as if he did not like what was going on, came up to him. 'Patrick,' says he. Patrick started, for he did not think anybody there knew him. 'Patrick,' says he, 'you're discouraged, and no wonder for you. But you have a friend near you. I'm your friend, and your father's friend, and I think worse [more] of your little finger than I do of all that are here, though they think no one is as good as themselves. Go into the ring and call for a lilt. Don't be afeard. I tell you the best of them did not do as well as you shall, if you will do as I bid you.' Patrick felt something within him as if he ought not to gainsay the old man. He went into the ring, and called the piper to play up the best double he had. And sure enough, all that the others were able for was nothing to him. He bounded like an eel, now here and now there, as light as a feather, although the people could hear the music answered by his steps, that beat time to every turn of it, like the left foot of the piper. He first danced a hornpipe on the ground. Then they got a table, and he danced a treble on it that drew down shouts from the whole company. At last he called for a trencher; and when they saw him, all as if he was spinning on it like a top, they did not know what to make of him. Some praised him for the best dancer that ever entered a ring; others hated him because he was better than themselves, although they had good right to think themselves better than him or any other man that never went the long journey."

"And what was the cause of his great success?" inquired Mr. Martin.

"He could not help it, sir," replied Tom Bourke. "They that could make him do more than that made him do it. Howsomever, when he had done, they wanted him to dance again, but he was tired, and they could not persuade him. At last he got angry, and swore a big oath, saving your presence, that he could not dance a step more; and the word was hardly out of his mouth, when he found himself all alone, with nothing but a white cow grazing by his side."

"Did he ever discover why he was gifted with these extraordinary powers in the dance, Tom?" said Mr. Martin.

"I'll tell you that too, sir," answered Bourke, "when I come to it. When he went home, sir, he was taken with a shivering, and went to bed; and the next day they found he got the fever, or something like it, for he raved like as if he was mad. But they couldn't make out what it was he was saying, though he talked constant. The doctors gave him over. But it's little they know what ailed him. When he was, as you may say, about ten days sick, and everybody thought he was going, one of the neighbours came in to him with a man, a friend of his, from Ballinlacken, that was keeping with him some time before. I can't tell you his name either, only it was Darby. The minute Darby saw Patrick, he took a little bottle, with the juice of herbs in it, out of his pocket, and gave Patrick a drink of it. He did the same every day for three weeks, and then Patrick was able to walk about, as stout and as hearty as ever he was in his life. But he was a long time before he came to him self; and he used to walk the whole day sometimes by the ditch-side, talking to himself, like as if there was someone along with him. And so there was, surely, or he wouldn't be the man he is to-day."

"I suppose it was from some such companion he learned his skill," said Mr. Martin.

"You have it all now, sir," replied Bourke. "Darby told him his friends were satisfied with what he did the night of the dance, and though they couldn't hinder the fever, they'd bring him over it, and teach him more than many knew beside him. And so they did. For, you see, all the people he met on the inch that night were friends of a different faction; only the old man that spoke to him, he was a friend of Patrick's family, and it went again' his heart, you see, that the others were so light and active, and he was bitter in himself to hear 'em boasting how they'd dance with any set in the whole country round. So he gave Patrick the gift that night, and afterwards gave him the skill that makes him the wonder of all that know him. And to be sure, it was only learning he was that time when he was wandering in his mind after the fever."

"I have heard many strange stories about that inch near Ballyhefaan ford," said Mr. Martin. "'Tis a great place for the good people, isn't it, Tom?"

"You may say that, sir," returned Bourke. "I could tell you a great deal about it. Many a time I sat for as good as two hours by moonlight, at th' other side of the river, looking at 'em playing goal as if they'd break their hearts over it, with their coats and waistcoats off, and white handkerchiefs on the heads of one party, and red ones on th' other, just as you'd see on a Sunday in Mr. Simming's big field. I saw 'em one night play till the moon set, without one party being able to take the ball from th' other. I'm sure they were going to fight, only 'twas near morning. I'm told your grandfather, ma'am, used to see 'em there too," said Bourke, turning to Mrs. Martin.

"So I have been told, Tom," replied Mrs. Martin. "But don't they say that the churchyard of Kilcrumper is just as favourite a place with the good people as Ballyhefaan Inch?"

"Why, then, maybe you never heard, ma'am, what happened to Davy Roche in that same churchyard," said Bourke; and turning to Mr. Martin, added: "'Twas a long time before he went into your service, sir. He was walking home, of an evening, from the fair of Kilcummer, a little merry, to be sure, after the day, and he came up with a berrin'. So he walked along with it, and thought it very queer that he did not know a mother's soul in the crowd, but one man, and he was sure that man was dead many years afore. Howsomever, he went on with the berrin', till they came to Kilcrumper Churchyard, and faith, he went in and stayed with the rest, to see the corpse buried. As soon as the grave was covered, what should they do but gather about a piper that *come* along with 'em, and fall to dancing as if it was a wedding. Davy longed to be among 'em (for he hadn't a bad foot of his own that time, whatever he may now); but he was loath to begin, because they all seemed strange to him, only the man I told you that he thought was dead. Well, at last this man saw what Davy wanted, and came up to him. 'Davy,' says he, 'take out a partner, and show what you can do, but take care and don't offer to kiss her.' 'That I won't,' says Davy, 'although her lips were made of honey.' And with that he made his bow to the *purtiest* girl in the ring, and he and she began to dance. 'Twas a jig they danced, and they did it to th' admiration, do you see, of all that were there. 'Twas all very well till the jig was over; but just as they had done, Davy—for he had a drop in, and was warm with the dancing—forgot himself, and kissed his partner, according to custom. The smack was no sooner off of his lips, you see, than he was left alone in the churchyard, without a creature near him, and all he could see was the tall tombstones. Davy said they seemed as if they were dancing too, but I suppose that was only the wonder that happened him, and he being a little in drink. Howsomever, he found it was a great many hours later than he thought it; 'twas near morning when he came home; but they couldn't get a word out of him till the next day, when he 'woke out of a dead sleep about twelve o'clock."

When Tom had finished the account of Davy Roche and the berrin', it became quite evident that spirits of some sort were working too strong within him to admit of his telling many more tales of the good people. Tom seemed conscious of this. He muttered for a few minutes broken sentences concerning churchyards, river-sides, leprechauns and *dina magh*, which were quite unintelligible, perhaps to himself, certainly to Mr. Martin and his lady. At length he made a slight motion of the head upwards, as if he would say, "I can talk no more;" stretched his arm on the table, upon which he placed the empty tumbler

slowly, and with the most knowing and cautious air, and rising
from his chair, walked, or rather rolled, to the parlour-door.
Here he turned round to face his host and hostess ; but after
various ineffectual attempts to bid them good-night—the words
as they rose being always choked by a violent hiccup, while the
door, which he held by the handle, swung to and fro, carrying
his unyielding body along with it—he was obliged to depart in
silence.   The cow-boy, sent by Tom's wife, who knew well what
sort of allurement detained him when he remained out after a
certain hour, was in attendance to conduct his master home.   I
have no doubt that he returned without meeting any material
injury, as I know that within the last month he was, to use his
own words, " as stout and hearty a man as any of his age in the
county Cork."

VIII

FAIRIES OR NO FAIRIES

JOHN MULLIGAN was as fine an old fellow as ever threw a Carlow
spur into the sides of a horse.   He was, besides, as jolly a boon
companion over a jug of punch as you would meet from Carnsore
Point to Bloody Farland.   And a good horse he used to ride ; and
a stiffer jug of punch than his was not in nineteen baronies.
Maybe he stuck more to it than he ought to have done ; but
that is nothing whatever to the story I am going to tell.

John believed devoutly in fairies, and an angry man was he if
you doubted them.   He had more fairy stories than would make,
if properly printed in a rivulet of print running down a meadow
of margin, two thick quartos for Mr. Murray of Albemarle Street ;
all of which he used to tell on all occasions that he could find
listeners.   Many believed his stories—many more did not believe
them—but nobody, in process of time, used to contradict the old
gentleman, for it was a pity to vex him.   But he had a couple of
young neighbours who were just come down from their first
vacation in Trinity College to spend the summer months with
an uncle of theirs, Mr. Whaley, an old Cromwellian, who lived
at Ballybegmullinahone, and they were too full of logic to let the
old man have his own way undisputed.

Every story he told they laughed at, and said that it was
impossible—that it was merely old woman's gabble, and other
such things.   When he would insist that all his stories were
derived from the most credible sources—nay, that some of them
had been told him by his own grandmother, a very respectable
old lady, but slightly affected in her faculties, as things that
came under her own knowledge—they cut the matter short by

declaring that she was in her dotage, and at the best of times had a strong propensity to pulling a long bow.

"But," said they, "Jack Mulligan, did you ever see a fairy yourself?"

"Never," was the reply—"never, as I am a man of honour and credit."

"Well, then," they answered, "until you do, do not be bothering us with any more tales of my grandmother."

Jack was particularly nettled at this, and took up the cudgels for his grandmother; but the younkers were too sharp for him, and finally he got into a passion, as people generally do who have the worst of an argument. This evening—it was at their uncle's, an old crony of his, with whom he had dined—he had taken a large portion of his usual beverage, and was quite riotous. He at last got up in a passion, ordered his horse, and in spite of his host's entreaties, galloped off, although he had intended to have slept there, declaring that he would not have anything more to do with a pair of jackanapes' puppies who, because they had learned how to read good-for-nothing books in cramp writing, and were taught by a parcel of wiggy, red-snouted, prating prigs ("not," added he, "however, that I say a man may not be a good man and have a red nose"), they imagined they knew more than a man who had held buckle and tongue together facing the wind of the world for five dozen years.

He rode off in a fret, and galloped as hard as his horse Shaunbuie could powder away over the limestone. "Damn it!" hiccuped he; "Lord pardon me for swearing! the brats had me in one thing—I never did see a fairy; and I would give up five as good acres as ever grew apple-potatoes to get a glimpse of one—and by the powers! what is that?"

He looked, and saw a gallant spectacle. His road lay by a noble demesne, gracefully sprinkled with trees, not thickly planted as in a dark forest, but disposed, now in clumps of five or six, now standing singly, towering over the plain of verdure around them as a beautiful promontory arising out of the sea. He had come right opposite the glory of the wood. It was an oak, which in the oldest title-deeds of the county—and they were at least five hundred years old—was called the old oak of Ballinghassig. Age had hollowed its centre, but its massy boughs still waved with their dark serrated foliage. The moon was shining on it brightly. If I were a poet, like Mr. Wordsworth, I should tell you how the beautiful light was broken into a thousand different fragments—and how it filled the entire tree with a glorious flood, bathing every particular leaf, and showing forth every particular bough; but as I am not a poet, I shall go on with my story. By this light Jack saw a brilliant company of lovely little forms dancing under the oak with an unsteady and rolling motion. The company was large. Some spread out far beyond the furthest boundary of the shadow of the oak's branches—some were seen glancing through the flashes of light shining through its leaves—some were barely visible, nestling under the trunk—some no doubt were entirely concealed from his eyes.

Never did man see anything more beautiful. They were not three inches in height, but they were white as the driven snow, and beyond number numberless. Jack threw the bridle over his horse's neck, and drew up to the low wall which bounded the demesne, and leaning over it, surveyed, with infinite delight, their diversified gambols. By looking long at them, he soon saw objects which had not struck him at first; in particular, that in the middle was a chief of superior stature, round whom the group appeared to move. He gazed so long that he was quite overcome with joy, and could not help shouting out. "Bravo! little fellow," said he; "well kicked and strong." But the instant he uttered the words the night was darkened, and the fairies vanished with the speed of lightning.

"I wish," said Jack, "I had held my tongue; but no matter now. I shall just turn bridle about and go back to Bally-begmullinahone Castle, and beat the young Master Whaleys, fine reasoners as they think themselves, out of the field clean."

No sooner said than done; and Jack was back again as if upon the wings of the wind. He rapped fiercely at the door, and called aloud for the two collegians.

"Halloo!" said he, "young Flatcaps, come down now, if you dare. Come down, if you dare, and I shall give you *oc-oc*-ocular demonstration of the truth of what I was saying."

Old Whaley put his head out of the window, and said: "Jack Mulligan, what brings you back so soon?"

"The fairies," shouted Jack; "the fairies!"

"I am afraid," muttered the Lord of Ballybegmullinahone, "the last glass you took was too little watered. But no matter; come in and cool yourself over a tumbler of punch."

He came in, and sat down again at table. In great spirits he told his story: how he had seen thousands and tens of thousands of fairies dancing about the old oak of Ballinghassig. He described their beautiful dresses of shining silver; their flat-crowned hats, glittering in the moonbeams; and the princely stature and demeanour of the central figure. He added that he heard them singing and playing the most enchanting music; but this was merely imagination. The young men laughed, but Jack held his ground. "Suppose," said one of the lads, "we join company with you on the road, and ride along to the place where you saw that fine company of fairies?"

" Done ! " cried Jack. " But I will not promise that you will find them there, for I saw them scudding up in the sky like a flight of bees, and heard their wings whizzing through the air." This, you know, was a bounce ; for Jack had heard no such thing.

Off rode the three, and came to the demesne of Oakwood. They arrived at the wall flanking the field where stood the great oak ; and the moon, by this time, having again emerged from the clouds, shone bright as when Jack had passed. " Look there ! " he cried exultingly, for the same spectacle again caught his eyes, and he pointed to it with his horse-whip. " Look ! and deny if you can."

"Why," said one of the lads, pausing, "true it is that we do see a company of white creatures; but were they fairies ten times over, I shall go among them," and he dismounted to climb over the wall.

"Ah, Tom ! Tom !" cried Jack. " Stop, man, stop ! What are you doing ? The fairies—the good people, I mean—hate to be meddled with. You will be pinched or blinded ; or your horse will cast its shoe ; or—look ! a wilful man will have his way. Oh, oh ! he is almost at the oak. God help him ! for he is past the help of man."

By this time Tom was under the tree, and burst out laughing. "Jack," said he, "keep your prayers to yourself. Your fairies are not bad at all. I believe they will make tolerably good catsup."

" Catsup ! " said Jack, who, when he found that the two lads (for the second had followed his brother) were both laughing in the middle of the fairies, had dismounted and advanced slowly. "What do you mean by catsup ? "

" Nothing," replied Tom, " but that they are mushrooms " (as indeed they were), " and your Oberon is merely this overgrown puff-ball."

Poor Mulligan gave a long whistle of amazement, staggered back to his horse without saying a word, and rode home in a hard gallop, never looking behind him. Many a long day was it before he ventured to face the laughers at Ballybegmullinahone ; and to the day of his death the people of the parish—aye, and five parishes round—called him nothing but Musharoon Jack, such being their pronunciation of mushroom.

I should be sorry if all my fairy stories ended with so little dignity ; but—

> " These our actors,
> As I foretold you, were all spirits, and
> Are melted into air—into thin air."

Note.—The name SHEFRO, by which the foregoing section is distinguished, literally signifies a fairy house or mansion, and is adopted as a general name for the Elves, who are supposed to live in troops or communities, and were popularly supposed to have castles or mansions of their own.

LEGENDS OF THE CLURICAUNE

I

THE HAUNTED CELLAR

THERE are few people who have not heard of the MacCarthies— one of the real old Irish families, with the true Milesian blood running in their veins, as thick as buttermilk. Many were the clans of this family in the south; as the MacCarthy-more—and the MacCarthy-reagh—and the MacCarthy of Muskerry; and all of them were noted for their hospitality to strangers, gentle and simple.

But not one of that name, or of any other, exceeded Justin MacCarthy of Ballinacarthy at putting plenty to eat and drink upon his table; and there was a right hearty welcome for every-one who would share it with him. Many a wine-cellar would be ashamed of the name if that at Ballinacarthy was the proper pattern for one; large as that cellar was, it was crowded with bins of wine, and long rows of pipes, and hogsheads, and casks, that it would take more time to count than any sober man could spare in such a place, with plenty to drink about him, and a hearty welcome to do so.

There are many, no doubt, who will think that the butler would have little to complain of in such a house; and the whole country round would have agreed with them, if a man could be found to remain as Mr. MacCarthy's butler for any length of time worth speaking of; yet not one who had been in his service gave him a bad word.

"We have no fault," they would say, "to find with the master; and if he could but get anyone to fetch his wine from the cellar, we might every one of us have grown grey in the house, and have lived quiet and contented enough in his service until the end of our days."

"'Tis a queer thing that, surely," thought young Jack Leary, a lad who had been brought up from a mere child in the stables of Ballinacarthy to assist in taking care of the horses, and had occasionally lent a hand in the butler's pantry—"'tis a mighty queer thing, surely, that one man after another cannot content himself with the best place in the house of a good master, but that every one of them must quit, all through the means, as they say, of the wine-cellar. If the master, long life to him! would but make me his butler, I warrant never the word more would be heard of grumbling at his bidding to go to the wine-cellar."

Young Leary accordingly watched for what he conceived to be a favourable opportunity of presenting himself to the notice of his master.

A few mornings after, Mr. MacCarthy went into his stable-yard rather earlier than usual, and called loudly for the groom to saddle his horse, as he intended going out with the hounds. But there was no groom to answer, and young Jack Leary led Rainbow out of the stable.

"Where is William?" inquired Mr. MacCarthy.

"Sir?" said Jack; and Mr. MacCarthy repeated the question.

"Is it William, please your honour?" returned Jack. "Why, then, to tell the truth, he had just *one* drop too much last night."

"Where did he get it?" said Mr. MacCarthy; "for since Thomas went away, the key of the wine-cellar has been in my pocket, and I have been obliged to fetch what was drank myself."

"Sorrow a know I know," said Leary, "unless the cook might have given him the *least taste* in life of whisky. But," continued he, performing a low bow by seizing with his right hand a lock of hair, and pulling down his head by it, whilst his left leg, which had been put forward, was scraped back against the ground, "may I make so bold as just to ask your honour one question?"

"Speak out, Jack," said Mr. MacCarthy.

"Why, then, does your honour want a butler?"

"Can you recommend me one," returned his master, with the smile of good-humour upon his countenance, "and one who will not be afraid of going to my wine-cellar?"

"Is the wine-cellar all the matter?" said young Leary. "Devil a doubt I have of myself then for that."

"So you mean to offer me your services in the capacity of butler?" said Mr. MacCarthy, with some surprise.

"Exactly so!" answered Leary, now for the first time looking up from the ground.

"Well, I believe you to be a good lad, and have no objection to give you a trial."

"Long may your honour reign over us, and the Lord spare you to us!" ejaculated Leary, with another national bow, as his master rode off; and he continued for some time to gaze after him with a vacant stare, which slowly and gradually assumed a look of importance.

"Jack Leary," said he at length, "Jack—is it Jack?" in a tone of wonder. "Faith, 'tis not Jack now, but Mr. John, the butler;" and with an air of becoming consequence, he strode out of the stable-yard towards the kitchen.

It is of little purport to my story, although it may afford an instructive lesson to the reader, to depict the sudden transition of nobody into somebody. Jack's former stable companion, a poor superannuated hound named Bran, who had been accustomed to receive many an affectionate pat on the head, was spurned from him with a kick and an "Out of the way, sirrah." Indeed, poor Jack's memory seemed sadly affected by this sudden change of situation. What established the point beyond all doubt was his almost forgetting the pretty face of Peggy, the kitchen wench, whose heart he had assailed but the preceding week by the offer of purchasing a gold ring for the fourth finger of her right hand, and a lusty imprint of good-will upon her lips.

When Mr. MacCarthy returned from hunting, he sent for Jack Leary—so he still continued to call his new butler. "Jack," said he, "I believe you are a trustworthy lad, and here are the keys of my cellar. I have asked the gentlemen with whom I hunted to-day to dine with me, and I hope they may be satisfied at the way in which you will wait on them at table; but above all, let there be no want of wine after dinner."

Mr. John having a tolerably quick eye for such things, and being naturally a handy lad, spread his cloth accordingly, laid his plates and knives and forks in the same manner he had seen his predecessors in office perform these mysteries, and really, for the first time, got through attendance on dinner very well.

It must not be forgotten, however, that it was at the house of an Irish country squire, who was entertaining a company of booted and spurred fox-hunters, not very particular about what are considered matters of infinite importance under other circumstances and in other societies.

For instance, few of Mr. MacCarthy's guests (though all excellent and worthy men in their way) cared much whether the punch produced after soup was made of Jamaica or Antigua rum; some even would not have been inclined to question the correctness of good old Irish whisky; and, with the exception of their liberal host himself, everyone in company preferred the port which Mr. MacCarthy put on his table to the less ardent flavour of claret—a choice rather at variance with modern sentiment.

It was waxing near midnight when Mr. MacCarthy rang the bell three times. This was a signal for more wine; and Jack proceeded to the cellar to procure a fresh supply, but it must be confessed not without some little hesitation.

The luxury of ice was then unknown in the south of Ireland; but the superiority of cool wine had been acknowledged by all men of sound judgment and true taste.

The grandfather of Mr. MacCarthy, who had built the mansion of Ballinacarthy upon the site of an old castle which had belonged to his ancestors, was fully aware of this important fact; and in the construction of his magnificent wine-cellar, had availed himself of a deep vault, excavated out of the solid rock in former times as a place of retreat and security. The descent to this vault was by a flight of steep stone stairs, and here and there in the wall were narrow passages—I ought rather to call them crevices; and also certain projections which cast deep shadows, and looked very frightful when anyone went down the cellar stairs with a single light; indeed, two lights did not much improve the matter, for though the breadth of the shadows became less, the narrow crevices remained as dark and darker than ever.

Summoning up all his resolution, down went the new butler, bearing in his right hand a lantern and the key of the cellar, and in his left a basket, which he considered sufficiently capacious to contain an adequate stock for the remainder of the evening. He arrived at the door without any interruption whatever; but when he put the key, which was of an ancient and clumsy kind— for it was before the days of Bramah's patent—and turned it in the lock, he thought he heard a strange kind of laughing within the cellar, to which some empty bottles that stood upon the floor outside vibrated so violently, that they struck against each other: in this he could not be mistaken, although he may have been deceived in the laugh, for the bottles were just at his feet, and he saw them in motion.

Leary paused for a moment, and looked about him with becoming caution. He then boldly seized the handle of the key, and turned it with all his strength in the lock, as if he doubted his own power of doing so; and the door flew open with a most tremendous crash, that, if the house had not been built upon the solid rock, would have shook it from the foundation.

To recount what the poor fellow saw would be impossible, for he seems not to know very clearly himself; but what he told the cook the next morning was, that he heard a roaring and bellowing like a mad bull, and that all the pipes and hogsheads and casks in the cellar went rocking backwards and forwards with so much force, that he thought everyone would have been staved in, and that he should have been drowned or smothered in wine.

When Leary recovered, he made his way back as well as he could to the dining-room, where he found his master and the company very impatient for his return.

"What kept you?" said Mr. MacCarthy, in an angry voice; "and where is the wine? I rung for it half an hour since."

"The wine is in the cellar, I hope, sir," said Jack, trembling violently. "I hope 'tis not all lost."

"What do you mean, fool?" exclaimed Mr. MacCarthy, in a still more angry tone. "Why did you not fetch some with you?"

Jack looked wildly about him, and only uttered a deep groan.

"Gentlemen," said Mr. MacCarthy to his guests, "this is too much. When I next see you to dinner, I hope it will be in another house, for it is impossible I can remain longer in this, where a man has no command over his own wine-cellar, and cannot get a butler to do his duty. I have long thought of moving from Ballinacarthy; and I am now determined, with the blessing of God, to leave it to-morrow. But wine shall you have, were I to go myself to the cellar for it." So saying, he rose from the table, took the key and lantern from his half-stupefied servant, who regarded him with a look of vacancy, and descended the narrow stairs, already described, which led to his cellar.

When he arrived at the door, which he found open, he thought he heard a noise, as if of rats or mice scrambling over the casks, and on advancing perceived a little figure, about six inches in height, seated astride upon the pipe of the oldest port in the place, and bearing a spigot upon his shoulder. Raising the lantern, Mr. MacCarthy contemplated the little fellow with wonder: he wore a red nightcap on his head; before him was a short leather apron, which now, from his attitude, fell rather on one side; and he had stockings of a light blue colour, so long as nearly to cover the entire of his legs; with shoes having huge silver buckles in them, and with high heels (perhaps out of vanity to make him appear taller). His face was like a withered winter apple; and his nose, which was of a bright crimson colour, about the tip wore a delicate purple bloom, like that of a plum: yet his eyes twinkled

"like those mites
Of candied dew in moony nights—"

and his mouth twitched up at one side with an arch grin.

"Ha, scoundrel!" exclaimed Mr. MacCarthy, "have I found you at last? Disturber of my cellar—what are you doing there?"

"Sure, and master," returned the little fellow, looking up at him with one eye, and with the other throwing a sly glance towards the spigot on his shoulder, "ain't we going to move to-morrow? and sure, you would not leave your own little Cluricaune Naggeneen behind you?"

"Oh!" thought Mr. MacCarthy, "if you are to follow me, Master Naggeneen, I don't see much use in quitting Ballina-carthy." So filling with wine the basket which young Leary in his fright had left behind him, and locking the cellar door, he rejoined his guests.

For some years after, Mr. MacCarthy had always to fetch the wine for his table himself, as the little Naggeneen seemed to feel a personal respect towards him. Notwithstanding the labour of these journeys, the worthy lord of Ballinacarthy lived in his paternal mansion to a good round age, and was famous to the last for the excellence of his wine and the conviviality of his company; but at the time of his death that same conviviality had nearly emptied his wine-cellar; and as it was never so well filled again, nor so often visited, the revels of Master Naggeneen became less celebrated, and are now only spoken of amongst the legendary lore of the country. It is even said that the poor little fellow took the declension of the cellar so to heart that he became negligent and careless of himself, and that he has been sometimes seen going about with hardly a skreed to cover him.

Some, however, believe that he turned brogue - maker, and assert that they have seen him at his work, and heard him whistling as merry as a blackbird on a May morning, under the shadow of a brown jug of foaming ale, bigger—aye, bigger than himself; decently dressed enough, they say—only looking mighty old. But still 'tis clear he has his wits about him, since no one ever had the luck to catch him, or to get hold of the purse he has with him, which they call *spré-na-skillinagh*, and 'tis said is never without a shilling in it.

II

MASTER AND MAN

BILLY MACDANIEL was once as likely a young man as ever shook his brogue at a patron, emptied a quart, or handled a shillelagh: fearing for nothing but the want of drink; caring for nothing but who should pay for it; and thinking of nothing but how to make fun over it: drunk or sober, a word and a blow was ever the way with Billy MacDaniel; and a mighty easy way it is of either getting into or ending a dispute. More is the pity that, through the means of his drinking and fearing and caring for nothing, this same Billy MacDaniel fell into bad company; for surely the good people are the worst of all company anyone could come across.

It so happened that Billy was going home one clear frosty night not long after Christmas. The moon was round and bright; but although it was as fine a night as heart could wish for, he felt pinched with the cold. "By my word," chattered Billy, "a drop of good liquor would be no bad thing to keep a man's soul from freezing in him; and I wish I had a full measure of the best."

"Never wish it twice, Billy," said a little man in a three-cornered hat, bound all about with gold lace, and with great silver buckles in his shoes—so big that it was a wonder how he could carry them—and he held out a glass as big as himself, filled with as good liquor as ever eye looked on or lip tasted.

"Success, my little fellow," said Billy MacDaniel, nothing daunted, though well he knew the little man to belong to the *good people;* "here's your health, anyway, and thank you kindly, no matter who pays for the drink;" and he took the glass and drained it to the very bottom, without ever taking a second breath to it.

"Success," said the little man; "and you're heartily welcome, Billy; but don't think to cheat me as you have done others. Out with your purse, and pay me like a gentleman."

"Is it I pay you?" said Billy. "Could I not just take you up and put you in my pocket as easily as a blackberry?"

"Billy MacDaniel," said the little man, getting very angry, "you shall be my servant for seven years and a day, and that is the way I will be paid; so make ready to follow me."

When Billy heard this, he began to be very sorry for having used such bold words towards the little man; and he felt himself, yet could not tell how, obliged to follow the little man the live-long night about the country, up and down, and over hedge and ditch, and through bog and brake, without any rest.

When morning began to dawn, the little man turned round to him, and said: "You may now go home, Billy, but on your peril, don't fail to meet me in the Fort-field to-night; or if you do, it may be the worse for you in the long run. If I find you a good servant, you will find me an indulgent master."

Home went Billy MacDaniel; and though he was tired and weary enough, never a wink of sleep could he get for thinking of the little man; but he was afraid not to do his bidding, so up he got in the evening, and away he went to the Fort-field. He was not long there before the little man came towards him and said: "Billy, I want to go a long journey to-night; so saddle one of my horses, and you may saddle another for yourself, as you are to go along with me, and may be tired after your walk last night."

Billy thought this very considerate of his master, and thanked him accordingly. "But," said he, "if I may be so bold, sir, I would ask which is the way to your stable; for never a thing do I see but the fort here, and the old thorn-tree in the corner of the field, and the stream running at the bottom of the hill, with the bit of bog over against us."

"Ask no questions, Billy," said the little man, "but go over to that bit of bog, and bring me two of the strongest rushes you can find."

Billy did accordingly, wondering what the little man would be at; and he picked out two of the stoutest rushes he could find, with a little bunch of brown blossom stuck at the side of each, and brought them back to his master.

"Get up, Billy!" said the little man, taking one of the rushes from him and striding across it.

"Where will I get up, please your honour?" said Billy.

"Why, upon horseback, like me, to be sure," said the little man.

"Is it after making a fool of me you'd be," said Billy, "bidding me get a-horseback upon that bit of a rush? Maybe you want to persuade me that the rush I pulled but while ago out of the bog over there is a horse?"

"Up! up! and no words," said the little man, looking very vexed. "The best horse you ever rode was but a fool to it." So Billy, thinking all this was in joke, and fearing to vex his master, straddled across the rush. "Borram! Borram! Borram!" cried the little man three times (which, in English, means to become great), and Billy did the same after him. Presently the rushes swelled up into fine horses, and away they went full speed; but Billy, who had put the rush between his legs, without much minding how he did it, found himself sitting on horseback the wrong way, which was rather awkward, with his face to the horse's tail; and so quickly had his steed started off with him, that he had no power to turn round, and there was therefore nothing for it but to hold on by the tail.

At last they came to their journey's end, and stopped at the gate of a fine house. "Now, Billy," said the little man, "do as you see me do, and follow me close; but as you did not know your horse's head from his tail, mind that your own head does not spin round until you can't tell whether you are standing on it or on your heels; for remember that old liquor, though able to make a cat speak, can make a man dumb."

The little man then said some queer kind of words, out of which Billy could make no meaning; but he contrived to say them after him for all that, and in they both went through the keyhole of the door, and through one keyhole after another, until they got into the wine-cellar, which was well stored with all kinds of wine.

The little man fell to drinking as hard as he could, and Billy, noway disliking the example, did the same. "The best of masters are you, surely," said Billy to him, "no matter who is the next; and well pleased will I be with your service, if you continue to give me plenty to drink."

"I have made no bargain with you," said the little man, "and will make none; but up and follow me!" Away they went, through keyhole after keyhole; and each mounting upon the rush which he had left at the hall-door, scampered off, kicking the clouds before them like snowballs, as soon as the words "Borram, Borram, Borram" had passed their lips.

When they came back to the Fort-field, the little man dismissed Billy, bidding him to be there the next night at the same hour. Thus did they go on, night after night, shaping their course one night here, and another night there—sometimes north, and sometimes east, and sometimes south—until there was not a gentleman's wine-cellar in all Ireland they had not visited, and could tell the flavour of every wine in it as well—aye, better than the butler himself.

One night, when Billy MacDaniel met the little man as usual in the Fort-field, and was going to the bog to fetch the horses for their journey, his master said to him: "Billy, I shall want another horse to-night, for maybe we may bring back more company with us than we take." So Billy, who now knew better than to question any order given to him by his master, brought a third rush, much wondering who it might be that would travel back in their company, and whether he was about to have a fellow-servant. "If I have," thought Billy, "he shall go and fetch the horses from the bog every night; for I don't see why I am not, every inch of me, as good a gentleman as my master."

Well, away they went, Billy leading the third horse, and never stopped until they came to a snug farmer's house in the county Limerick, close under the old castle of Carrigogunniel, that was built, they say, by the great Brian Boru. Within the house there was great carousing going forward, and the little man stopped outside for some time to listen; then turning round all of a sudden, said: "Billy, I will be a thousand years old to-morrow!"

"God bless you, sir!" said Billy, "will you?"

"Don't say these words again, Billy," said the little man, "or you will be my ruin for ever. Now, Billy, as I will be a thousand years in the world to-morrow, I think it is full time for me to get married."

"I think so too, without any kind of doubt at all," said Billy, "if ever you mean to marry."

"And to that purpose," said the little man, "have I come all the way to Carrigogunniel; for in this house, this very night, is young Darby Riley going to be married to Bridget Rooney; and as she is a tall and comely girl, and has come of decent people, I think of marrying her myself, and taking her off with me."

"And what will Darby Riley say to that?" said Billy.

"Silence!" said the little man, putting on a mighty severe look. "I did not bring you here with me to ask questions;" and without holding further argument, he began saying the queer

words which hadt he power of passing him through the keyhole
as free as air, and which Billy thought himself mighty clever to be
able to say after him.

In they both went ; and for the better viewing the company,
the little man perched himself up as nimbly as a cock-sparrow
upon one of the big beams which went across the house over all
their heads, and Billy did the same upon another facing him ; but
not being much accustomed to roosting in such a place, his legs
hung down as untidy as may be, and it was quite clear he had
not taken pattern after the way in which the little man had
bundled himself up together. If the little man had been a tailor
all his life, he could not have sat more contentedly upon his
haunches.

There they were, both master and man, looking down upon the
fun that was going forward—and under them were the priest and
piper—and the father of Darby Riley, with Darby's two brothers
and his uncle's son—and there were both the father and the
mother of Bridget Rooney, and proud enough the old couple were
that night of their daughter, as good right they had—and her
four sisters with brand new ribands in their caps, and her three
brothers, all looking as clean and as clever as any three boys in
Munster—and there were uncles and aunts, and gossips and
cousins enough besides to make a full house of it—and plenty
was there to eat and drink on the table for every one of them, if
they had been double the number.

Now it happened, just as Mrs. Rooney had helped his Reverence
to the first cut of the pig's head which was placed before her,
beautifully bolstered up with white savoys, that the bride gave a
sneeze which made everyone at table start, but not a soul said
" God bless us ! " all thinking that the priest would have done so,
as he ought, if he had done his duty ; no one wished to take the
word out of his mouth, which, unfortunately, was preoccupied with
pig's head and greens. And, after a moment's pause, the fun
and merriment of the bridal feast went on without the pious
benediction.

Of this circumstance both Billy and his master were no in-
attentive spectators from their exalted stations. "Ha !" exclaimed
the little man, throwing one leg from under him with a joyous
flourish, and his eye twinkled with a strange light, whilst his eyebrows became elevated into the curvature of Gothic arches—
" Ha ! " said he, leering down at the bride, and then up at Billy,
" I have half of her now, surely. Let her sneeze but twice
more, and she is mine, in spite of priest, mass-book, and Darby
Riley."

Again the fair Bridget sneezed ; but it was so gently, and she
blushed so much, that few except the little man took, or seemed

to take, any notice; and no one thought of saying "God bless us!"

Billy all this time regarded the poor girl with a most rueful expression of countenance; for he could not help thinking what a terrible thing it was for a nice young girl of nineteen, with large blue eyes, transparent skin, and dimpled cheeks, suffused with health and joy, to be obliged to marry an ugly little bit of a man who was a thousand years old, barring a day.

At this critical moment the bride gave a third sneeze, and Billy roared out with all his might: "God save us!" Whether this exclamation resulted from his soliloquy, or from the mere force of habit, he never could tell exactly himself; but no sooner was it uttered than the little man, his face glowing with rage and disappointment, sprung from the beam on which he had perched himself, and shrieking out in the shrill voice of a cracked bagpipe, "I discharge you my service, Billy MacDaniel—take *that* for your wages," gave poor Billy a most furious kick in the back, which sent his unfortunate servant sprawling upon his face and hands right in the middle of the supper-table.

If Billy was astonished, how much more so was everyone of the company into which he was thrown with so little ceremony; but when they heard his story, Father Cooney laid down his knife and fork, and married the young couple out of hand with all speed; and Billy MacDaniel danced the Rinka at their wedding, and plenty did he drink at it too, which was what he thought more of than dancing.

III

THE LITTLE SHOE

"Now, tell me, Molly," said Mr. Coote to Molly Cogan, as he met her on the road one day, close to one of the old gateways of Kilmallock,[1] "did you ever hear of the Cluricaune?"

"Is it the Cluricaune? Why, then, sure I did, often and often; many's the time I heard my father—rest his soul!—tell about 'em."

"But did you ever see one, Molly, yourself?"

"Och! no, I never *see* one in my life; but my grandfather, that's my father's father, you know, he *see* one, one time, and caught him too."

"Caught him! Oh, Molly, tell me how?"

"Why, then, I'll tell you. My grandfather, you see, was out there above in the bog, drawing home turf, and the poor old mare

[1] "Kilmallock seemed to me like the Court of the Queen of Silence."— "O'Keefe's Recollections."

was tired after her day's work, and the old man went out to the stable to look after her, and to see if she was eating her hay; and when he came to the stable door there, my dear, he heard something hammering, hammering, hammering, just for all the world like a shoemaker making a shoe, and whistling all the time the prettiest tune he ever heard in his whole life before. Well, my grandfather, he thought it was the Cluricaune, and he said to himself, says he, 'I'll catch you, if I can, and then I'll have money enough always.' So he opened the door very quietly, and didn't make a bit of noise in the world that ever was heard, and looked all about, but the never a bit of the little man he could see anywhere, but he heard him hammering and whistling, and so he looked and looked, till at last he *see* the little fellow; and where was he, do you think, but in the girth under the mare, and there he was with his little bit of an apron on him, and hammer in his hand, and a little red nightcap on his head, and he making a shoe, and he was so busy with his work, and he was hammering and whistling so loud, that he never minded my grandfather till he caught him fast in his hand. 'Faith, I have you now,' says he, 'and I'll never let you go till I get your purse, that's what I won't, so give it here to me at once now.' 'Stop, stop,' says the Cluricaune; 'stop, stop,' says he, 'till I get it for you.' So my grandfather, like a fool, you see, opened his hand a little, and the little fellow jumped away laughing, and he never saw him any more, and the never the bit of the purse did he get, only the Cluricaune left his little shoe that he was making, and my grandfather was mad enough angry with himself for letting him go; but he had the shoe all his life, and my own mother told me she often *see* it, and had it in her hand, and 'twas the prettiest little shoe she ever saw."

"And did you see it yourself, Molly?"

"Oh, no, my dear! It was lost long afore I was born; but my mother told me about it often and often enough."

NOTE.—The main point of distinction between the Cluricaune and the Shefro arises from the sottish and solitary habits of the former, who are rarely found in troops or communities. The Cluricaune of the county of Cork, the Luricaune of Kerry, and the Lurigadaune of Tipperary, appear to be the same as the Leprechaun or Leprochaune of Leinster and the Logherry-man of Ulster. "Old German and Northern poems contain numerous accounts of the skill of the dwarfs in curious smiths'-work." "The Irish Cluricaune is heard hammering. He is particularly fond of making shoes, but these were in ancient times made of metal (in the old Northern language a shoemaker is called a *shoe-smith*); and, singularly enough, the wights in a German tradition manifest the same propensity, for, whatever work the same shoemaker has been able to cut out in the day, they finish with incredible quickness during the night."—THE BROTHERS' GRIMM.

LEGENDS OF THE BANSHEE

I

THE Reverend Charles Bunworth was rector of Buttevant, in the county of Cork, about the middle of the last century. He was a man of unaffected piety and of sound learning, pure in heart and benevolent in intention. By the rich he was respected, and by the poor beloved ; nor did a difference of creed prevent their looking up to "*the minister*" (so was Mr. Bunworth called by them) in matters of difficulty and in seasons of distress, confident of receiving from him the advice and assistance that a father would afford to his children. He was the friend and the bene- factor of the surrounding country ; to him, from the neighbouring town of Newmarket, came both Curran and Yelverton for advice and instruction, previous to their entrance at Dublin College. Young, indigent and inexperienced, these afterwards eminent men received from him, in addition to the advice they sought, pecuniary aid, and the brilliant career which was theirs justified the discrimination of the giver.

But what extended the fame of Mr. Bunworth far beyond the limits of the parishes adjacent to his own was his performance on the Irish harp, and his hospitable reception and entertainment of the poor harpers who travelled from house to house about the country. Grateful to their patron, these itinerant minstrels sang his praises to the tingling accompaniment of their harps, invoking in return for his bounty abundant blessings on his white head, and celebrating in their rude verses the blooming charms of his daughters, Elizabeth and Mary. It was all these poor fellows could do ; but who can doubt that their gratitude was sincere when, at the time of Mr. Bunworth's death, no less than fifteen harps were deposited on the loft of his granary, bequeathed to him by the last members of a race which has now ceased to exist. Trifling, no doubt, in intrinsic value were these relics, yet there is something in gifts of the heart that merits preservation, and it is to be regretted that, when he died, these harps were broken up one after the other, and used as firewood by an ignorant follower of the family, who, on their removal to Cork for a temporary change of scene, was left in charge of the house.

The circumstances attending the death of Mr. Bunworth may be doubted by some ; but there are still living credible witnesses who declare their authenticity, and who can be produced to attest most, if not all, of the following particulars.

About a week previous to his dissolution, and early in the evening, a noise was heard at the hall door resembling the shearing of sheep ; but at the time no particular attention was paid to it. It was nearly eleven o'clock the same night when Kavanagh, the herdsman, returned from Mallow, whither he had been sent in the afternoon for some medicine, and was observed by Miss Bunworth, to whom he delivered the parcel, to be much agitated. At this time, it must be observed, her father was by no means considered in danger.

"What is the matter, Kavanagh ? " asked Miss Bunworth ; but the poor fellow, with a bewildered look, only uttered : " The master, miss — the master—he is going from us ; " and overcome with real grief, he burst into a flood of tears.

Miss Bunworth, who was a woman of strong nerve, inquired if anything he had learned in Mallow induced him to suppose that her father was worse.

"No, miss," said Kavanagh ; " it was not in Mallow—"

"Kavanagh," said Miss Bunworth, with that stateliness of manner for which she is said to have been remarkable, " I fear you have been drinking, which, I must say, I did not expect at such a time as the present, when it was your duty to have kept yourself sober ; I thought you might have been trusted. What should we have done if you had broken the medicine bottle or lost it ? For the doctor said it was of the greatest consequence that your master should take the medicine to-night. But I will speak to you in the morning, when you are in a fitter state to understand what I say."

Kavanagh looked up with a stupidity of aspect which did not serve to remove the impression of his being drunk, as his eyes appeared heavy and dull after the flood of tears ; but his voice was not that of an intoxicated person.

"Miss," said he, " as I hope to receive mercy hereafter, neither bit nor sup has passed my lips since I left this house ; but the master—"

"Speak softly," said Miss Bunworth ; " he sleeps, and is going on as well as we could expect."

"Praise be to God for that, anyway," replied Kavanagh ; "but oh ! miss, he is going from us surely—we will lose him— the master—we will lose him, we will lose him ! " and he wrung his hands together.

"What is it you mean, Kavanagh ? " asked Miss Bunworth.

"Is it mean ? " said Kavanagh ; " the Banshee has come for him, miss ; and 'tis not I alone who have heard her."

" 'Tis an idle superstition," said Miss Bunworth.

"Maybe so," replied Kavanagh, as if the words " idle superstition " only sounded upon his ear without reaching his mind—

"Maybe so," he continued ; "but as I came through the glen of Ballybeg, she was along with me keening and screeching, and clapping her hands by my side, every step of the way, with her long white hair falling about her shoulders, and I could hear her repeat the master's name every now and then, as plain as ever I heard it. When I came to the old abbey, she parted from me there, and turned into the pigeon-field next the *berrin'* ground, and folding her cloak about her, down she sat under the tree that was struck by the lightning, and began keening so bitterly, that it went through one's heart to hear it."

"Kavanagh," said Miss Bunworth, who had, however, listened attentively to this remarkable relation, "my father is, I believe, better ; and I hope will himself soon be up and able to convince you that all this is but your own fancy ; nevertheless, I charge you not to mention what you have told me, for there is no occasion to frighten your fellow-servants with the story."

Mr. Bunworth gradually declined ; but nothing particular occurred until the night previous to his death : that night both his daughters, exhausted with continued attendance and watching, were prevailed upon to seek some repose ; and an elderly lady, a near relative and friend of the family, remained by the bedside of their father. The old gentleman then lay in the parlour, where he had been in the morning removed at his own request, fancying the change would afford him relief ; and the head of his bed was placed close to the window. In a room adjoining sat some male friends, and, as usual on like occasions of illness, in the kitchen many of the followers of the family had assembled.

The night was serene and moonlit—the sick man slept—and nothing broke the stillness of their melancholy watch, when the little party in the room adjoining the parlour, the door of which stood open, was suddenly roused by a sound at the window near the bed. A rose-tree grew outside the window, so close as to touch the glass ; this was forced aside with some noise, and a low moaning was heard, accompanied by clapping of hands, as if of a female in deep affliction. It seemed as if the sound proceeded from a person holding her mouth close to the window. The lady who sat by the bedside of Mr. Bunworth went into the adjoining room, and in a tone of alarm inquired of the gentlemen there if they had heard the Banshee? Sceptical of supernatural appearances, two of them rose hastily and went out to discover the cause of these sounds, which they also had distinctly heard. They walked all round the house, examining every spot of ground, particularly near the window from whence the voice had proceeded ; the bed of earth beneath, in which the rose-tree was planted, had been recently dug, and the print of a footstep—if the tree had been forced aside by mortal hand—would have inevitably remained; but they could perceive no such impression; and an unbroken stillness reigned without. Hoping to dispel the mystery, they continued their search anxiously along the road, from the straightness of which, and the lightness of the night, they were enabled to see some distance around them; but all was silent and deserted, and they returned surprised and disappointed. How much more, then, were they astonished at learning that the whole time of their absence, those who remained within the house had heard the moaning and clapping of hands even louder and more distinct than before they had gone out; and no sooner was the door of the room closed on them, than they again heard the same mournful sounds! Every succeeding hour the sick man became worse, and as the first glimpse of the morning appeared, Mr. Bunworth expired.

II

THE family of MacCarthy have for some generations possessed a small estate in the county of Tipperary. They are the descendants of a race, once numerous and powerful in the south of Ireland; and though it is probable that the property they at present hold is no part of the large possessions of their ancestors, yet the district in which they live is so connected with the name of MacCarthy by those associations which are never forgotten in Ireland, that they have preserved with all ranks a sort of influence much greater than that which their fortune or connections could otherwise give them. They are, like most of this class, of the Roman Catholic persuasion, to which they adhere with somewhat of the pride of ancestry, blended with a something, call it what you will, whether bigotry, or a sense of wrong, arising out of repeated diminutions of their family possessions, during the more rigorous periods of the penal laws. Being an old family, and especially being an old Catholic family, they have of course their Banshee; and the circumstances under which the appearance, which I shall relate, of this mysterious harbinger of death, took place, were told me by an old lady, a near connection of theirs, who knew many of the parties concerned, and who, though not deficient in understanding or education, cannot to this day be brought to give a decisive opinion as to the truth or authenticity of the story. The plain inference to be drawn from this is, that she believes it, though she does not own it; and as she was a contemporary of the persons concerned—as she heard the account from many persons about the same period, all concurring in the important particulars —as some of her authorities were themselves actors in the scene

—and as none of the parties were interested in speaking what was false, I think we have about as good evidence that the whole is undeniably true as we have of many narratives of modern history, which I could name, and which many grave and sober-minded people would deem it very great pyrrhonism to question. This, however, is a point which it is not my province te determine. People who deal out stories of this sort must be content to act like certain young politicians, who tell very freely to their friends what they hear at a great man's table ; not guilty of the impertinence of weighing the doctrines, and leaving it to their hearers to understand them in any sense, or in no sense, just as they may please.

Charles MacCarthy was, in the year 1749, the only surviving son of a very numerous family. His father died when he was little more than twenty, leaving him the MacCarthy estate, not much encumbered, considering that it was an Irish one. Charles was gay, handsome, unfettered either by poverty, a father or guardians, and therefore was not, at the age of one-and-twenty, a pattern of regularity and virtue. In plain terms, he was an exceedingly dissipated—I fear I may say debauched young man. His companions were, as may be supposed, of the higher classes of youth in his neighbourhood, and, in general, of those whose fortunes were larger than his own, whose dispositions to pleasure were therefore under still less restrictions, and in whose example he found at once an incentive and an apology for his irregularities. Besides, Ireland, a place to this day not very remarkable for the coolness and steadiness of its youth, was then one of the cheapest countries in the world in most of those articles which money supplies for the indulgence of the passions. The odious excise-man, with his portentous book in one hand, his unrelenting pen held in the other, or stuck beneath his hat-band, and the ink-bottle ("black emblem of the informer") dangling from his waistcoat-button—went not then from ale-house to ale-house, denouncing all those patriotic dealers in spirit, who preferred selling whisky, which had nothing to do with English laws (but to elude them), to retailing that poisonous liquor, which derived its name from the British "Parliament," that compelled its circulation among a reluctant people. Or if the gauger — recording angel of the law—wrote down the peccadillo of a publican, he dropped a tear upon the word, and blotted it out for ever !

For, welcome to the tables of their hospitable neighbours, the guardians of the excise, where they existed at all, scrupled to abridge those luxuries which they freely shared ; and thus the competition in the market between the smuggler, who incurred little hazard, and the personage yclept fair trader, who enjoyed little protection, made Ireland a land flowing, not merely with milk and honey, but with whisky and wine.   In the enjoyments supplied by these, and in the many kindred pleasures to which frail youth is but too prone, Charles MacCarthy indulged to such a degree, that just about the time when he had completed his four-and-twentieth year, after a week of great excesses, he was seized with a violent fever, which, from its malignity, and the weakness of his frame, left scarcely a hope of his recovery.   His mother, who had at first made many efforts to check his vices, and at last had been obliged to look on at his rapid progress to ruin in silent despair, watched day and night at his pillow.   The anguish of parental feeling was blended with that still deeper misery which those only know who have striven hard to rear in virtue and piety a beloved and favourite child ; have found him grow up all that their hearts could desire, until he reached manhood ; and then, when their pride was highest, and their hopes almost ended in the fulfilment of their fondest expectations, have seen this idol of their affections plunge headlong into a course of reckless profligacy, and, after a rapid career of vice, hang upon the verge of eternity, without the leisure for, or the power of, repentance.   Fervently she prayed that, if his life could not be spared, at least the delirium, which continued with increasing violence from the first few hours of his disorder, might vanish before death, and leave enough of light and of calm for making his peace with offended Heaven.

After several days, however, Nature seemed quite exhausted, and he sank into a state too like death to be mistaken for the repose of sleep.   His face had that pale, glossy, marble look, which is in general so sure a symptom that life has left its tenement of clay.   His eyes were closed and sunk, the lids having that compressed and stiffened appearance which seemed to indicate that some friendly hand had done its last office.   The lips, half-closed and perfectly ashy, discovered just so much of the teeth as to give to the features of death their most ghastly, but most impressive look.   He lay upon his back, with his hands stretched beside him, quite motionless ; and his distracted mother, after repeated trials, could discover not the least symptom of animation.   The medical man who attended, having tried the usual modes for ascertaining the presence of life, declared at last his opinion that it was flown, and prepared to depart from the house of mourning.   His horse was seen to come to the door.

A crowd of people who were collected before the windows, or scattered in groups on the lawn in front, gathered round when the door opened.   These were tenants, fosterers, and poor relations of the family, with others attracted by affection, or by that interest which partakes of curiosity, but is something more, and which collects the lower ranks round a house where a human being is in his passage to another world. They saw the professional man come out from the hall door and approach his horse, and while slowly, and with a melancholy air, he prepared to mount, they clustered round him with inquiring and wishful looks. Not a word was spoken; but their meaning could not be misunderstood; and the physician, when he had got into his saddle, and while the servant was still holding the bridle as if to delay him, and was looking anxiously at his face as if expecting that he would relieve the general suspense, shook his head, and said in a low voice: "It's all over, James;" and moved slowly away.

The moment he had spoken, the women present, who were very numerous, uttered a shrill cry, which, having been sustained for about half a minute, fell suddenly into a full, loud, continued and discordant but plaintive wailing, above which occasionally were heard the deep sounds of a man's voice, sometimes in broken sobs, sometimes in more distinct exclamations of sorrow. This was Charles's foster-brother, who moved about in the crowd, now clapping his hands, now rubbing them together in an agony of grief. The poor fellow had been Charles's playmate and companion when a boy, and afterwards his servant; had always been distinguished by his peculiar regard, and loved his young master, as much, at least, as he did his own life.

When Mrs. MacCarthy became convinced that the blow was indeed struck, and that her beloved son was sent to his last account, even in the blossoms of his sin, she remained for some time gazing with fixedness upon his cold features; then, as if something had suddenly touched the string of her tenderest affections, tear after tear trickled down her cheeks, pale with anxiety and watching. Still she continued looking at her son, apparently unconscious that she was weeping, without once lifting her handkerchief to her eyes, until reminded of the sad duties which the custom of the country imposed upon her by the crowd of females belonging to the better class of the peasantry, who now, crying audibly, nearly filled the apartment. She then withdrew, to give directions for the ceremony of waking, and for supplying the numerous visitors of all ranks with the refreshments usual on these melancholy occasions. Though her voice was scarcely heard, and though no one saw her but the servants and one or two old followers of the family, who assisted her in the necessary arrangements, everything was conducted with the greatest regularity; and though she made no effort to check her sorrows, they never once suspended her attention, now more than ever required to preserve order in her household, which, in this season of calamity, but for her would have been all confusion.

The night was pretty far advanced; the boisterous lamentations which had prevailed during part of the day in and about the house had given place to a solemn and mournful stillness; and Mrs. MacCarthy, whose heart, notwithstanding her long fatigue and watching, was yet too sore for sleep, was kneeling in fervent prayer in a chamber adjoining that of her son, when suddenly her devotions were disturbed by an unusual noise, proceeding from the persons who were watching round the body.   First, there was a low murmur—then all was silent, as if the movements of those in the chamber were checked by a sudden panic—and then a loud cry of terror burst from all within—the door of the chamber was thrown open, and all who were not overturned in the press rushed wildly into the passage which led to the stairs, and into which Mrs. MacCarthy's room opened.   Mrs. MacCarthy made her way through the crowd into her son's chamber, where she found him sitting up in the bed, and looking vacantly around like one risen from the grave.   The glare thrown upon his sunk features and thin, lathy frame gave an unearthly horror to his whole aspect.   Mrs. MacCarthy was a woman of some firmness; but she was a woman, and not quite free from the superstitions of her country.   She dropped on her knees, and clasping her hands, began to pray aloud.   The form before her moved only its lips, and barely uttered: "Mother;" but though the pale lips moved, as if there was a design to finish the sentence, the tongue refused its office.   Mrs. MacCarthy sprang forward, and catching the arm of her son, exclaimed: "Speak! in the name of God and His saints, speak! Are you alive?"

He turned to her slowly, and said, speaking still with apparent difficulty: "Yes, my mother, alive, and— But sit down and collect yourself; I have that to tell which will astonish you still more than what you have seen."   He leaned back upon his pillow, and while his mother remained kneeling by the bedside, holding one of his hands clasped in hers, and gazing on him with the look of one who distrusted all her senses, he proceeded:

"Do not interrupt me until I have done.   I wish to speak while the excitement of returning life is upon me, as I know I shall soon need much repose.   Of the commencement of my illness I have only a confused recollection; but within the last twelve hours, I have been before the judgment-seat of God.   Do not stare incredulously on me—'tis as true as have been my crimes, and, as I trust, shall be my repentance.   I saw the awful Judge arrayed in all the terrors which invest Him when mercy gives place to justice.   The dreadful pomp of offended Omnipotence, I saw—I remember.   It is fixed here; printed on my brain in characters indelible; but it passeth human language.   What I *can* describe I *will*—I may speak it briefly.   It is enough to say, I was weighed in the balance and found wanting.   The irrevocable sentence was upon the point of being pronounced; the eye of my Almighty Judge, which had already glanced upon me, half spoke my doom; when I observed the guardian saint, to whom you so often directed my prayers when I was a child, looking at me with an expression of benevolence and compassion. I stretched forth my hands to him, and besought his intercession; I implored that one year, one month might be given to me on earth, to do penance and atonement for my transgressions. He threw himself at the feet of my Judge, and supplicated for mercy. Oh, never—not if I should pass through ten thousand successive states of being—never, for eternity, shall I forget the horrors of that moment, when my fate hung suspended—when an instant was to decide whether torments unutterable were to be my portion for endless ages! But Justice suspended its decree, and Mercy spoke in accents of firmness, but mildness: 'Return to that world in which thou hast lived but to outrage the laws of Him who made that world and thee. Three years are given thee for repentance; when these are ended, thou shalt again stand here, to be saved or lost for ever.' I heard no more; I saw no more, until I awoke to life, the moment before you entered."

Charles's strength continued just long enough to finish these last words, and on uttering them he closed his eyes, and lay quite exhausted. His mother, though, as was before said, some-what disposed to give credit to supernatural visitations, yet hesitated whether or not she should believe that, although awakened from a swoon, which might have been the crisis of his disease, he was still under the influence of delirium. Repose, however, was at all events necessary, and she took immediate measures that he should enjoy it undisturbed. After some hours' sleep, he awoke refreshed, and thenceforward gradually but steadily recovered.

Still he persisted in his account of the vision, as he had at first related it; and his persuasion of its reality had an obvious and decided influence on his habits and conduct. He did not altogether abandon the society of his former associates, for his temper was not soured by his reformation; but he never joined in their excesses, and often endeavoured to reclaim them. How his pious exertions succeeded, I have never learnt; but of himself it is recorded, that he was religious without ostentation, and temperate without austerity; giving a practical proof that vice may be exchanged for virtue, without a loss of respectability, popularity or happiness.

Time rolled on, and long before the three years were ended, the story of his vision was forgotten, or, when spoken of, was usually mentioned as an instance proving the folly of believing in such things. Charles's health, from the temperance and regularity of his habits, became more robust than ever. His friends, indeed, had often occasion to rally him upon a seriousness and abstractedness of demeanour, which grew upon him as he approached the completion of his seven-and-twentieth year, but for the most part his manner exhibited the same animation and cheerfulness for which he had always been remarkable. In company, he evaded every endeavour to draw from him a distinct opinion on the subject of the supposed prediction; but among his own family it was well known that he still firmly believed it. However, when the day had nearly arrived on which the prophecy was, if at all, to be fulfilled, his whole appearance gave such promise of a long and healthy life, that he was persuaded by his friends to ask a large party to an entertainment at Spring House to celebrate his birthday. But the occasion of this party, and the circumstances which attended it, will be best learned from a perusal of the following letters, which have been carefully preserved by some relations of his family. The first is from Mrs. MacCarthy to a lady, a very near connexion and valued friend of hers, who lived in the county of Cork, at about fifty miles' distance from Spring House.

"*To Mrs. Barry, Castle Barry.*

" Spring House, Tuesday Morning,
" *15th October, 1752.*

"My dearest Mary,—I am afraid I am going to put your affection for your old friend and kinswoman to a severe trial. A two days' journey at this season, over bad roads and through a troubled country, it will indeed require friendship such as yours to persuade a sober woman to encounter. But the truth is, I have, or fancy I have, more than usual cause for wishing you near me. You know my son's story. I can't tell how it is, but as next Sunday approaches, when the prediction of his dream or his vision will be proved false or true, I feel a sickening of the heart, which I cannot suppress, but which your presence, my dear Mary, will soften, as it has done so many of my sorrows. My nephew, James Ryan, is to be married to Jane Osborne (who, you know, is my son's ward), and the bridal entertainment will take place here on Sunday next, though Charles pleaded hard to have it postponed a day or two longer. Would to God—but no more of this till we meet. Do prevail upon yourself to leave your good man for *one* week, if his farming concerns will not admit of his accompanying you; and come to us, with the girls, as soon before Sunday as you can.

" Ever my dear Mary's attached cousin and friend,

" Ann MacCarthy."

Although this letter reached Castle Barry early on Wednesday, the messenger having travelled on foot, over bog and moor, by paths impassable to horse or carriage, Mrs. Barry, who at once determined on going, had so many arrangements to make for the regulation of her domestic affairs (which in Ireland, among the middle orders of the gentry, fall soon into confusion when the mistress of the family is away), that she and her two younger daughters were unable to leave home until late on the morning of Friday. The eldest daughter remained to keep her father company, and superintend the concerns of the household. As the travellers were to journey in an open one-horse vehicle, called a jaunting-car (still used in Ireland), and as the roads, bad at all times, were rendered still worse by the heavy rains, it was their design to make two easy stages; to stop about midway the first night, and reach Spring House early on Saturday evening. This arrangement was now altered, as they found that from the lateness of their departure they could proceed, at the utmost, no further than twenty miles on the first day; and they therefore purposed sleeping at the house of a Mr. Bourke, a friend of theirs, who lived at somewhat less than that distance from Castle Barry. They reached Mr. Bourke's in safety, after rather a disagreeable drive. What befel them on their journey the next day to Spring House, and after their arrival there, is fully related in a letter from the second Miss Barry to her eldest sister.

"SPRING HOUSE, SUNDAY EVENING,
20th October, 1752.

"DEAR ELLEN,—As my mother's letter, which encloses this, will announce to you briefly the sad intelligence which I shall here relate more fully, I think it better to go regularly through the recital of the extraordinary events of the last two days.

"The Bourkes kept us up so late on Friday night that yesterday was pretty far advanced before we could begin our journey, and the day closed when we were nearly fifteen miles distant from this place. The roads were excessively deep, from the heavy rains of the last week, and we proceeded so slowly that at last my mother resolved on passing the night at the house of Mr. Bourke's brother (who lives about a quarter of a mile off the road), and coming here to breakfast in the morning. The day had been windy and showery, and the sky looked fitful, gloomy and uncertain. The moon was full, and at times shone clear and bright; at others, it was wholly concealed behind the thick, black and rugged masses of clouds, that rolled rapidly along, and were every moment becoming larger and collecting together, as if gathering strength for a coming storm. The wind, which blew in our faces, whistled bleakly along the low hedges of the

narrow road, on which we proceeded with difficulty from the
number of deep sloughs, and which afforded not the least
shelter, no plantation being within some miles of us.   My
mother, therefore, asked Leary, who drove the jaunting-car, how
far we were from Mr. Bourke's.   ''Tis about ten spades from this
to the cross, and we have then only to turn to the left into the
avenue, ma'am.'   'Very well, Leary ; turn up to Mr. Bourke's
as soon as you reach the cross roads.'   My mother had scarcely
spoken these words, when a shriek that made us thrill as if our
very hearts were pierced by it burst from the hedge to the right
of our way.   If it resembled anything earthly, it seemed the cry
of a female, struck by a sudden and mortal blow, and giving out
her life in one long, deep pang of expiring agony.   'Heaven
defend us !' exclaimed my mother.   'Go you over the hedge,
Leary, and save that woman, if she is not yet dead, while we
run back to the hut we just passed, and alarm the village near
it.'   'Woman !' said Leary, beating the horse violently, while
his voice trembled—'that's no woman : the sooner we get on,
ma'am, the better ;' and he continued his efforts to quicken the
horse's pace.   We saw nothing.   The moon was hid.   It was
quite dark, and we had been for some time expecting a heavy
fall of rain.   But just as Leary had spoken, and had succeeded
in making the horse trot briskly forward, we distinctly heard a
loud clapping of hands, followed by a succession of screams, that
seemed to denote the last excess of despair and anguish, and to
issue from a person running forward inside the hedge, to keep
pace with our progress.   Still we saw nothing ; until, when we
were within about ten yards of the place where an avenue
branched off to Mr. Bourke's to the left, and the road turned to
Spring House on the right, the moon started suddenly from
behind a cloud, and enabled us to see, as plainly as I now see
this paper, the figure of a tall, thin woman, with uncovered
head, and long hair that floated round her shoulders, attired in
something which seemed either a loose white cloak or a sheet
thrown hastily about her.   She stood on the corner hedge, where
the road on which we were met that which leads to Spring
House, with her face towards us, her left hand pointing to this
place, and her right arm waving rapidly and violently, as if to
draw us on in that direction.   The horse had stopped, apparently
frightened at the sudden presence of the figure, which stood in
the manner I have described, still uttering the same piercing
cries, for about half a minute.   It then leaped upon the road,
disappeared from our view for one instant, and the next was
seen standing upon a high wall a little way up the avenue, on
which we purposed going, still pointing towards the road to
Spring House, but in an attitude of defiance and command, as

if prepared to oppose our passage up the avenue. The figure was now quite silent, and its garments, which had before flown loosely in the wind, were closely wrapped around it. 'Go on, Leary, to Spring House, in God's name,' said my mother; 'whatever world it belongs to, we will provoke it no longer.' ''Tis the Banshee, ma'am,' said Leary; 'and I would not, for what my life is worth, go anywhere this blessed night but to Spring House. But I'm afraid there's something bad going forward, or *she* would not send us there.' So saying, he drove forward; and as we turned on the road to the right, the moon suddenly withdrew its light, and we saw the apparition no more; but we heard plainly a prolonged clapping of hands, gradually dying away, as if it issued from a person rapidly retreating. We proceeded as quickly as the badness of the roads and the fatigue of the poor animal that drew us would allow, and arrived here about eleven o'clock last night. The scene which awaited us you have learned from my mother's letter. To explain it fully, I must recount to you some of the transactions which took place here during the last week.

" You are aware that Jane Osborne was to have been married this day to James Ryan, and that they and their friends have been here for the last week. On Tuesday last, the very day on the morning of which cousin MacCarthy despatched the letter inviting us here, the whole of the company were walking about the grounds a little before dinner. It seems that an unfortunate creature, who had been seduced by James Ryan, was seen prowling in the neighbourhood in a moody, melancholy state for some days previous. He had separated from her for several months, and, they say, had provided for her rather handsomely; but she had been seduced by the promise of his marrying her; and the shame of her unhappy condition, uniting with disappointment and jealousy, had disordered her intellects. During the whole fore-noon of this Tuesday she had been walking in the plantations near Spring House, with her cloak folded tight round her, the hood nearly covering her face; and she had avoided conversing with or even meeting any of the family.

" Charles MacCarthy, at the time I mentioned, was walking between James Ryan and another, at a little distance from the rest, on a gravel path, skirting the shrubbery. The whole party were thrown into the utmost consternation by the report of a pistol, fired from a thickly planted part of the shrubbery, which Charles and his companions had just passed. He fell instantly, and it was found that he had been wounded in the leg. One of the party was a medical man. His assistance was immediately given; and on examining, he declared that the injury was very slight, that no bone was broken, that it was merely a flesh wound, and that it would certainly be well in a few days. 'We shall know more by Sunday,' said Charles, as he was carried to his chamber. His wound was immediately dressed, and so slight was the inconvenience which it gave, that several of his friends spent a portion of the evening in his apartment.

"On inquiry, it was found that the unlucky shot was fired by the poor girl I just mentioned. It was also manifest that she had aimed, not at Charles, but at the destroyer of her innocence and happiness, who was walking beside him. After a fruitless search for her through the grounds, she walked into the house of her own accord, laughing and dancing and singing wildly, and every moment exclaiming that she had at last killed Mr. Ryan. When she heard that it was Charles, and not Mr. Ryan, who was shot, she fell into a violent fit, out of which, after working convulsively for some time, she sprang to the door, escaped from the crowd that pursued her, and could never be taken until last night, when she was brought here, perfectly frantic, a little before our arrival.

"Charles's wound was thought of such little consequence, that the preparations went forward, as usual, for the wedding entertainment on Sunday. But on Friday night he grew restless and feverish, and on Saturday (yesterday) morning felt so ill that it was deemed necessary to obtain additional medical advice. Two physicians and a surgeon met in consultation about twelve o'clock in the day, and the dreadful intelligence was announced that unless a change, hardly hoped for, took place before night, death must happen within twenty-four hours after. The wound, it seems, had been too tightly bandaged, and otherwise injudiciously treated. The physicians were right in their anticipations. No favourable symptom appeared, and long before we reached Spring House every ray of hope had vanished. The scene we witnessed on our arrival would have wrung the heart of a demon. We heard briefly at the gate that Mr. Charles was upon his death-bed. When we reached the house, the information was confirmed by the servant who opened the door. But just as we entered, we were horrified by the most appalling screams issuing from the staircase. My mother thought she heard the voice of poor Mrs. MacCarthy, and sprang forward. We followed, and on ascending a few steps of the stairs we found a young woman, in a state of frantic passion, struggling furiously with two men-servants, whose united strength was hardly sufficient to prevent her rushing upstairs over the body of Mrs. MacCarthy, who was lying in strong hysterics upon the steps. This, I afterwards discovered, was the unhappy girl I before described, who was attempting to gain access to Charles's room, to 'get his forgiveness,' as she said, 'before he went away to accuse her for having killed him.'

This wild idea was mingled with another, which seemed to dispute with the former possession of her mind. In one sentence she called on Charles to forgive her; in the next she would denounce James Ryan as the murderer both of Charles and her. At length she was torn away; and the last words I heard her scream were: 'James Ryan, 'twas you killed him, and not I— 'twas you killed him, and not I.'

"Mrs. MacCarthy, on recovering, fell into the arms of my mother, whose presence seemed a great relief to her. She wept —the first tears, I was told, that she had shed since the fatal accident. She conducted us to Charles's room, who, she said, had desired to see us the moment of our arrival, as he found his end approaching, and wished to devote the last hours of his existence to uninterrupted prayer and meditation. We found him perfectly calm, resigned, and even cheerful. He spoke of the awful event which was at hand with courage and confidence, and treated it as a doom for which he had been preparing ever since his former remarkable illness, and which he never once doubted was truly foretold to him. He bade us farewell with the air of one who was about to travel a short and easy journey; and we left him with impressions which, notwithstanding all their anguish, will, I trust, never entirely forsake us.

"Poor Mrs. MacCarthy—but I am just called away. There seems a slight stir in the family; perhaps—"

The above letter was never finished. The enclosure to which it more than once alludes told the sequel briefly, and it is all that I have further learned of this branch of the MacCarthy family. Before the sun had gone down upon Charles's seven-and-twentieth birthday, his soul had gone to render its last account to its Creator.

NOTE.—"BANSHEE, plural she-fairies or women fairies, credulously supposed by the common people to be so affected to certain families that they are heard to sing mournful lamentations about their houses at night, whenever any of the family labours under a sickness which is to end in death. But no families which are not of an ancient and noble stock are believed to be honoured with this fairy privilege."—O'Brien's "Irish Dictionary."

LEGENDS OF THE FHOOKA

I

THE SPIRIT HORSE

THE history of Morty Sullivan ought to be a warning to all young men to stay at home, and to live decently and soberly if they can, and not to go roving about the world. Morty, when he had just turned fourteen, ran away from his father and mother, who were a mighty respectable old couple, and many and many a tear they shed on his account. It is said they both died heart-broken for his loss; all they ever learned about him was, that he went on board of a ship bound to America.

Thirty years after the old couple had been laid peacefully in their graves, there came a stranger to Beerhaven inquiring after them; it was their son Morty. And, to speak the truth of him, his heart did seem full of sorrow when he heard that his parents were dead and gone. But what else could he expect to hear? Repentance generally comes when it is too late.

Morty Sullivan, however, as an atonement for his sins, was recommended to perform a pilgrimage to the blessed chapel of Saint Gobnate, which is in a wild place called Ballyvourney.

This he readily undertook, and willing to lose no time, commenced his journey the same afternoon. He had not proceeded many miles before the evening came on. There was no moon, and the starlight was obscured by a thick fog, which ascended from the valleys. His way was through a mountainous country, with many cross-paths and by-ways, so that it was difficult for a stranger like Morty to travel without a guide. He was anxious to reach his destination, and exerted himself to do so; but the fog grew thicker and thicker, and at last he became doubtful if the track he was in led to the blessed chapel of Saint Gobnate. But seeing a light which he imagined not to be far off, he went towards it, and when he thought himself close to it, the light suddenly seemed at a great distance, twinkling dimly through the fog. Though Morty felt some surprise at this, he was not disheartened, for he thought that it was a light sent by the holy Saint Gobnate to guide his feet through the mountains to her chapel.

And thus did he travel for many a mile, continually, as he believed, approaching the light, which would suddenly start off to a great distance. At length he came so close as to perceive that the light came from a fire, seated beside which he plainly saw an old woman; then, indeed, his faith was a little shaken, and much did he wonder that both the fire and the old woman should travel before him so many weary miles and over such uneven roads.

"In the holy names of the pious Gobnate, and of her preceptor Saint Abban," said Morty, "how can that burning fire move on so fast before me, and who can that old woman be sitting beside the moving fire?"

These words had no sooner passed Morty's lips than he found himself, without taking another step, close to this wonderful fire, beside which the old woman was sitting munching her supper.

With every wag of the old woman's jaw her eyes would roll
fiercely upon Morty, as if she was angry at being disturbed ; and
he saw with more astonishment than ever that her eyes were
neither black nor blue, nor grey nor hazel, like the human eye,
but of a wild red colour, like the eye of a ferret. If before he
wondered at the fire, much greater was his wonder at the old
woman's appearance ; and stout-hearted as he was, he could not
but look upon her with fear—judging, and judging rightly, that
it was for no good purpose her supping in so unfrequented a place,
and at so late an hour, for it was near midnight. She said not
one word, but munched and munched away, while Morty looked
at her in silence. "What's your name?" at last demanded the
old hag, a sulphureous puff coming out of her mouth, her nostrils
distending, and her eyes growing redder than ever, when she had
finished her question.

Plucking up all his courage, "Morty Sullivan," replied he, "at
your service ; " meaning the latter words only in civility.

"*Ubbubbo !*" said the old woman, "we'll soon see that ; " and
the red fire of her eyes turned into a pale green colour. Bold
and fearless as Morty was, yet much did he tremble at hearing
this dreadful exclamation : he would have fallen down on his
knees and prayed to Saint Gobnate, or any other saint, for he
was not particular ; but he was so petrified with horror, that he
could not move in the slightest way, much less go down on his
knees.

"Take hold of my hand, Morty," said the old woman. "I'll
give you a horse to ride that will soon carry you to your journey's
end." So saying, she led the way, the fire going before them—
it is beyond mortal knowledge to say how, but on it went,
shooting out bright tongues of flame, and flickering fiercely.

Presently they came to a natural cavern in the side of the
mountain, and the old hag called aloud in a most discordant
voice for her horse. In a moment a jet-black steed started from
its gloomy stable, the rocky floor whereof rung with a sepulchral
echo to the clanging hoofs.

"Mount, Morty, mount ! " cried she, seizing him with supernatural strength, and forcing him upon the back of the horse.
Morty, finding human power of no avail, muttered : "Oh, that I
had spurs ! " and tried to grasp the horse's mane ; but he caught
at a shadow ; it nevertheless bore him up and bounded forward
with him, now springing down a fearful precipice, now clearing the
rugged bed of a torrent, and rushing like the dark midnight
storm through the mountains.

The following morning Morty Sullivan was discovered by some
pilgrims (who came that way after taking their rounds at
Gougane Barra) lying on the flat of his back, under a steep

cliff, down which he had been flung by the Phooka. Morty was severely bruised by the fall, and he is said to have sworn on the spot, by the hand of O'Sullivan (and that is no small oath), never again to take a full quart bottle of whisky with him on a pilgrimage.

II

DANIEL O'ROURKE

PEOPLE may have heard of the renowned adventures of Daniel O'Rourke, but how few are there who know that the cause of all his perils, above and below, was neither more nor less than his having slept under the walls of the Phooka's tower. I knew the man well; he lived at the bottom of Hungry Hill, just at the right-hand side of the road as you go towards Bantry. An old man was he at the time that he told me the story, with grey hair and a red nose; and it was on the 25th of June, 1813, that I heard it from his own lips, as he sat smoking his pipe under the old poplar tree, on as fine an evening as ever shone from the sky. I was going to visit the caves in Dursey Island, having spent the morning at Glengariff.

"I am often *axed* to tell it, sir," said he, "so that this is not the first time. The master's son, you see, had come from beyond foreign parts in France and Spain, as young gentlemen used to go, before Buonaparte or any such was heard of; and sure enough, there was a dinner given to all the people on the ground, gentle and simple, high and low, rich and poor. The *ould* gentlemen were the gentlemen, after all, saving your honour's presence. They'd swear at a body a little, to be sure, and maybe give one cut of a whip now and then, but we were no losers by it in the end; and they were so easy and civil, and kept such rattling houses, and thousands of welcomes; and there was no grinding for rent, and few agents; and there was hardly a tenant on the estate that did not taste of his landlord's bounty often and often in the year; but now it's another thing: no matter for that, sir, for I'd better be telling you my story.

"Well, we had everything of the best, and plenty of it; and we ate, and we drank, and we danced, and the young master, by the same token, danced with Peggy Barry, from the Bohereen— a lovely young couple they were, though they are both low enough now. To make a long story short, I got, as a body may say, the same thing as tipsy almost, for I can't remember ever at all, no ways, how it was I left the place: only I did leave it, that's certain. Well, I thought, for all that, in myself, I'd just step to Molly Cronohan's, the fairy woman, to speak a word about the bracket heifer that was bewitched; and so as I was crossing the stepping-stones of the ford of Ballyasheenough, and was looking up at the stars and blessing myself—for why? it was Lady Day— I missed my foot, and souse I fell into the water. 'Death alive!' thought I, 'I'll be drowned now!' However, I began swimming, swimming, swimming away for the dear life, till at last I got ashore, somehow or other, but never the one of me can tell how, upon a *dissolute* island.

"I wandered and wandered about there, without knowing where I wandered, until at last I got into a big bog. The moon was shining as bright as day, or your fair lady's eyes, sir (with your pardon for mentioning her), and I looked east and west, and north and south, and every way, and nothing did I see but bog, bog, bog. I could never find out how I got into it; and my heart grew cold with fear, for sure and certain I was that it would be my *berrin'*-place. So I sat down upon a stone which, as good luck would have it, was close by me, and I began to scratch my head and sing the *Ullagone*—when all of a sudden the moon grew black, and I looked up, and saw something for all the world as if it was moving down between me and it, and I could not tell what it was. Down it came with a pounce, and looked at me full in the face; and what was it but an eagle? as fine a one as ever flew from the kingdom of Kerry. So he looked at me in the face, and says he to me: 'Daniel O'Rourke,' says he 'how do you do?' 'Very well, I thank you, sir,' says I. 'I hope you're well;' wondering out of my senses all the time how an eagle came to speak like a Christian. 'What brings you here, Dan?' says he. 'Nothing at all, sir,' says I; 'only I wish I was safe home again.' 'Is it out of the island you want to go, Dan?' says he. ''Tis, sir,' says I; so I up and told him how I had taken a drop too much, and fell into the water; how I swam to the island; and how I got into the bog, and did not know my way out of it. 'Dan,' says he, after a minute's thought, 'though it is very improper for you to get drunk on Lady Day, yet as you are a decent, sober man, who 'tends mass well, and never flings stones at me nor mine, nor cries out after us in the fields—my life for yours,' says he; 'so get up on my back, and grip me well for fear you'd fall off, and I'll fly you out of the bog.' 'I am afraid,' says I, 'your honour's making game of me; for who ever heard of riding a-horseback on an eagle before?' ''Pon the honour of a gentleman,' says he, putting his right foot on his breast, 'I am quite in earnest; and so now either take my offer or starve in the bog—besides, I see that your weight is sinking the stone.'

"It was true enough as he said, for I found the stone every minute going from under me. I had no choice; so thinks I to myself, faint heart never won fair lady, and this is fair per- suadance. 'I thank your honour,' says I, 'for the loan of your civility; and I'll take your kind offer.' I therefore mounted upon the back of the eagle, and held him tight enough by the throat, and up he flew in the air like a lark. Little I knew the trick he was going to serve me. Up—up—up—God knows how far up he flew. 'Why, then,' said I to him—thinking he did not know the right road home—very civilly, because why?—I was in his power entirely; 'sir,' says I, 'please your honour's glory, and with humble submission to your better judgment, if you'd fly down a bit, you're now just over my cabin, and I could be put down there, and many thanks to your worship.'

" '*Arrah*, Dan,' said he, ' do you think me a fool? Look down in the next field, and don't you see two men and a gun? By my word, it would be no joke to be shot this way, to oblige a drunken blackguard that I picked up off a *cowld* stone in a bog.' ' Bother you,' said I to myself, but I did not speak out, for where was the use? Well, sir, up he kept, flying, flying, and I asking him every minute to fly down, and all to no use. ' Where in the world are you going, sir?' says I to him. ' Hold your tongue, Dan,' says he. 'Mind your own business, and don't be interfering with the business of other people.' ' Faith, this is my business, I think,' says I. ' Be quiet, Dan,' says he ; so I said no more.

"At last, where should we come to but to the moon itself. Now you can't see it from this, but there is, or there was in my time, a reaping-hook sticking out of the side of the moon, this way (drawing the figure thus **O̅** on the ground with the end of his stick).

" ' Dan,' said the eagle, ' I'm tired with this long fly ; I had no notion 'twas so far.' ' And, my lord, sir,' said I, ' who in the world *axed* you to fly so far—was it I? Did not I beg and pray, and beseech you to stop half an hour ago?' ' There's no use talking, Dan,' said he ; ' I'm tired bad enough, so you must get off, and sit down on the moon until I rest myself.' ' Is it sit down on the moon?' said I; ' is it upon that little round thing, then? why, then, sure I'd fall off in a minute, and be *kilt* and split, and smashed all to bits. You are a vile deceiver—so you are.' ' Not at all, Dan,' said he ; ' you can catch fast hold of the reaping-hook that's sticking out of the side of the moon, and 'twill keep you up.' ' I won't, then,' said I. ' Maybe not,' said he, quite quiet. ' If you don't, my man, I shall just give you a shake, and one slap of my wing, and send you down to the ground, where every bone in your body will be smashed as small as a drop of dew on a cabbage-leaf in the morning.' ' Why, then, I'm in a fine way,' said I to myself, ' ever to have come along with the likes of you ;' and so giving him a hearty curse in Irish, for fear he'd know what I said, I got off his back with a heavy heart, took a hold of the reaping-hook, and sat down upon the moon; and a mighty cowld seat it was, I can tell you that.

"When he had me there fairly landed, he turned about on me, and said : ' Good morning to you, Daniel O'Rourke,' said he ; ' I think I've nicked you fairly now. You robbed my nest last year' ('twas true enough for him, but how he found it out is hard to say), ' and in return you are freely welcome to cool your heels dangling upon the moon like a cockthrow.'

" ' Is that all, and is this the way you leave me, you brute, you ?' says I. ' You ugly unnatural *baste*, and is this the way you serve me at last ? Bad luck to yourself, with your hooked nose, and to all your breed, you blackguard.' 'Twas all to no manner of use : he spread out his great big wings, burst out a-laughing, and flew away like lightning. I bawled after him to stop ; but I might have called and bawled for ever, without his minding me. Away he went, and I never saw him from that day to this—sorrow fly away with him ! You may be sure I was in a disconsolate condition, and kept roaring out for the bare grief, when all at once a door opened right in the middle of the moon, creaking on its hinges as if it had not been opened for a month before. I suppose they never thought of greasing 'em, and out there walks—who do you think but the man in the moon himself ? I knew him by his bush.

" ' Good morrow to you, Daniel O'Rourke,' said he. ' How do you do ?' ' Very well, thank your honour,' said I. ' I hope your honour's well.' ' What brought you here, Dan ?' said he. So I told him how I was a little overtaken in liquor at the master's, and how I was cast on a *dissolute* island, and how I lost my way in the bog, and how the thief of an eagle promised to fly me out of it, and how instead of that he had fled me up to the moon.

" ' Dan,' said the man in the moon, taking a pinch of snuff when I was done, ' you must not stay here.' ' Indeed, sir,' says I, ' 'tis much against my will I'm here at all ; but how am I to go back ?' ' That's your business,' said he. ' Dan, mine is to tell you that here you must not stay, so be off in less than no time.' ' I'm doing no harm,' says I, ' only holding on hard by the reaping-hook, lest I fall off.' ' That's what you must not do, Dan,' says he. ' Pray, sir,' says I, ' may I ask how many you are in family, that you would not give a poor traveller lodging ? I'm sure 'tis not so often you're troubled with strangers coming to see you, for 'tis a long way.' ' I'm by myself, Dan,' says he ; ' but you'd better let go the reaping-hook.' ' Faith, and with your leave,' says I, ' I'll not let go the grip, and the more you bids me, the more I won't let go—so I will.' ' You had better, Dan,' says he again. ' Why, then, my little

fellow,' says I, taking the whole weight of him with my eye
from head to foot, 'there are two words to that bargain; and
I'll not budge, but you may if you like.' 'We'll see how that is
to be,' says he ; and back he went, giving the door such a great
bang after him (for it was plain he was huffed) that I thought
the moon and all would fall down with it.

"Well, I was preparing myself to try strength with him, when
back again he comes, with the kitchen cleaver in his hand, and
without saying a word, he gives two bangs to the handle of the
reaping-hook that was keeping me up, and *whap !* it came in two.
'Good morning to you, Dan,' says the spiteful little old blackguard, when he saw me cleanly falling down with a bit of the
handle in my hand; 'I thank you for your visit, and fair weather
after you, Daniel.' I had not time to make any answer to him,
for I was tumbling over and over, and rolling and rolling at the
rate of a fox-hunt. 'God help me,' says I, 'but this is a pretty
pickle for a decent man to be seen in at this time of night ; I am
now sold fairly.' The word was not out of my mouth, when
whiz! what should fly by close to my ear but a flock of wild
geese ; all the way from my own bog of Ballyasheenough, else
how should they know *me ?* The *ould* gander, who was their
general, turning about his head, cried out to me : 'Is that you,
Dan ?' 'The same,' said I, not a bit daunted now at what he
said, for I was by this time used to all kinds of *bedevilment,* and
besides, I knew him of *ould.* 'Good morrow to you,' says he,
'Daniel O'Rourke. How are you in health this morning ?' 'Very
well, sir,' says I, 'I thank you kindly,' drawing my breath, for I
was mightily in want of some. 'I hope your honour's the same.'
'I think 'tis falling you are, Daniel,' says he. 'You may say
that, sir,' says I. 'And where are you going all the way so
fast ?' said the gander. So I told him how I had taken the drop,
and how I came on the island, and how I lost my way in the
bog, and how the thief of an eagle flew me up to the moon, and
how the man in the moon turned me out. 'Dan,' said he, 'I'll
save you : put out your hand and catch me by the leg, and I'll
fly you home.' 'Sweet is your hand in a pitcher of honey, my
jewel,' says I, though all the time I thought in myself that I
don't much trust you ; but there was no help, so I caught the
gander by the leg, and away I and the other geese flew after him
as fast as hops.

"We flew and we flew and we flew, until we came right over
the wide ocean. I knew it well, for I saw Cape Clear to my right
hand, sticking up out of the water. 'Ah ! my lord,' said I to
the goose, for I thought it best to keep a civil tongue in my head,
anyway, 'fly to land, if you please.' 'It is impossible, you see,
Dan,' said he, 'for a while, because you see we are going to

Arabia.' 'To Arabia!' said I; 'that's surely some place in foreign parts far away. Oh, Mr. Goose; why, then, to be sure, I'm a man to be pitied among you.' 'Whist, whist, you fool,' said he, 'hold your tongue; I tell you Arabia is a very decent sort of place, as like West Carbery as one egg is like another, only there is a little more sand there.'

"Just as we were talking, a ship hove in sight, scudding so beautiful before the wind. 'Ah, then, sir,' said I, 'will you drop me on the ship, if you please?' 'We are not fair over it,' said he. 'We are,' said I. 'We are not,' said he. 'If I dropped you now, you would go splash into the sea.' 'I would not,' says I; 'I know better than that, for it's just clean under us, so let me drop now at once.'

"'If you must, you must,' said he. 'There, take your own way;' and he opened his claw, and faith, he was right—sure enough I came down plump into the very bottom of the salt sea! Down to the very bottom I went, and I gave myself up then for ever, when a whale walked up to me, scratching himself after his night's sleep, and looked me full in the face, and never the word did he say, but lifting up his tail, he splashed me all over again with the cold salt water, till there wasn't a dry stitch upon my whole carcass; and I heard somebody saying—'twas a voice I knew too: 'Get up, you drunken brute, off of that;' and with that I woke up, and there was Judy with a tub full of water, which she was splashing all over me; for, rest her soul! though she was a good wife, she never could bear to see me in drink, and had a bitter hand of her own.

"'Get up,' said she again; 'and of all places in the parish, would no place *sarve* your turn to lie down upon but under the *ould* walls of Carrigaphooka? An uneasy resting I am sure you had of it.' And sure enough I had; for I was fairly bothered out of my senses with eagles and men of the moon, and flying ganders and whales, driving me through bogs, and up to the moon, and down to the bottom of the green ocean. If I was in drink ten times over, long would it be before I'd lie down in the same spot again, I know that."

III

THE CROOKENED BACK

PEGGY BARRETT was once tall, well-shaped and comely. She was in her youth remarkable for two qualities, not often found together —of being the most thrifty housewife and the best dancer in her native village of Ballyhooley. But she is now upwards of sixty years old, and during the last ten years of her life she has never been able to stand upright. Her back is bent nearly to a level, yet she has the freest use of all her limbs that can be enjoyed in such a posture ; her health is good, and her mind vigorous, and in the family of her eldest son, with whom she has lived since the death of her husband, she performs all the domestic services which her age and the infirmity just mentioned allow. She washes the potatoes, makes the fire, sweeps the house (labours in which she good-humouredly says "she finds her crooked back mighty convenient"), plays with the children, and tells stories to the family and their neighbouring friends, who often collect round her son's fireside to hear them during the long winter evenings. Her powers of conversation are highly extolled, both for humour and in narration, and anecdotes of droll or awkward incidents connected with the posture in which she has been so long fixed, as well as the history of the occurrence to which she owes that misfortune, are favourite topics of her discourse. Among other matters, she is fond of relating how, on a certain day, at the close of a bad harvest, when several tenants of the estate on which she lived concerted in a field a petition for an abatement of rent, they placed the paper on which they wrote upon her back, which was found no very inconvenient substitute for a table.

Peggy, like all experienced story-tellers, suited her tales, both in length and subject, to the audience and the occasion. She knew that, in broad daylight, when the sun shines brightly, and the trees are budding, and the birds singing around us—when men and women, like ourselves, are moving and speaking, employed variously in business or amusement—she knew, in short (though certainly without knowing or much caring wherefore), that when we are engaged about the realities of life and Nature, we want that spirit of credulity, without which tales of the deepest interest will lose their power. At such times Peggy was brief, very particular as to facts, and never dealt in the marvellous. But round the blazing hearth of a Christmas evening, when infidelity is banished from all companies, at least, in low and simple life, as a quality, to say the least of it, out of season—when the winds of "dark December" whistled bleakly round the walls, and almost through the doors of the little mansion, reminding its inmates that as the world is vexed by elements superior to human power, so it may be visited by beings of a superior nature—at such times would Peggy Barrett give full scope to her memory, or her imagination, or both, and upon one of these occasions she gave the following circumstantial account of the "crookening of her back."

"It was, of all days in the year, the day before May Day that I went out to the garden to weed the potatoes. I would not have gone out that day, but I was dull in myself and sorrowful, and wanted to be alone ; all the boys and girls were laughing and joking in the house, making goaling - balls, and dressing out ribands for the mummers next day. I couldn't bear it. 'Twas only at the Easter that was then past (and that's ten years last Easter ; I won't forget the time) that I buried my poor man, and I thought how gay and joyful I was, many a long year before that, at the May Eve before our wedding, when, with Robin by my side, I sat cutting and sewing the ribands for the goaling-ball I was to give the boys on the next day, proud to be preferred above all the other girls of the banks of the Blackwater by the handsomest boy and the best hurler in the village ; so I left the house and went to the garden.

"I stayed there all the day, and didn't come home to dinner. I don't know how it was, but somehow I continued on, weeding, and thinking sorrowfully enough, and singing over some of the old songs that I sung many and many a time in the days that are gone, and for them that never will come back to me to hear them. The truth is, I hated to go and sit silent and mournful among the people in the house, that were merry and young, and had the best of their days before them. 'Twas late before I thought of returning home, and I did not leave the garden till some time after sunset. The moon was up ; but though there wasn't a cloud to be seen, and though a star was winking here and there in the sky, the day wasn't long enough gone to have it clear moonlight. Still, it shone enough to make everything on one side of the heavens look pale and silvery-like, and the thin white mist was just beginning to creep along the fields. On the other side, near where the sun was set, there was more of daylight, and the sky looked angry, red and fiery through the trees, like as if it was lighted up by a great town burning below.

"Everything was as silent as a churchyard ; only now and then one could hear far off a dog barking, or a cow lowing after being milked. There wasn't a creature to be seen on the road or in the fields. I wondered at this first, but then I remembered it was May Eve, and that many a thing, both good and bad, would be wandering about that night, and that I ought to shun danger as well as others. So I walked on as quick as I could, and soon came to the end of the demesne wall, where the trees rise high and thick at each side of the road, and almost meet at the top. My heart misgave me when I got under the shade. There was so much light let down from the opening above that I could see about a stone-throw before me. All of a sudden I heard a rustling among the branches on the right side of the road, and saw something like a small black goat, only with long wide horns turned out instead of being bent backwards, standing upon its hind-legs upon the top of the wall, and looking down on me.

"My breath was stopped, and I couldn't move for near a minute. I couldn't help, somehow, keeping my eyes fixed on it; and it never stirred, but kept looking in the same fixed way down at me. At last I made a rush, and went on; but I didn't go ten steps when I saw the very same sight, on the wall to the left of me, standing in exactly the same manner, but three or four times as high, and almost as tall as the tallest man. The horns looked frightful; it gazed upon me as before; my legs shook, and my teeth chattered, and I thought I would drop down dead every moment. At last I felt as if I was obliged to go on; and on I went; but it was without feeling how I moved, or whether my legs carried me. Just as I passed the spot where this frightful thing was standing, I heard a noise as if something sprung from the wall, and felt like as if a heavy animal plumped down upon me, and held with the fore-feet clinging to my shoulder, and the hind ones fixed in my gown, that was folded and pinned up behind me.

"'Tis the wonder of my life ever since how I bore the shock; but so it was, I neither fell, nor even staggered with the weight, but walked on as if I had the strength of ten men, though I felt as if I couldn't help moving, and couldn't stand still if I wished it. Though I gasped with fear, I knew as well as I do now what I was doing. I tried to cry out, but couldn't; I tried to run, but wasn't able; I tried to look back, but my head and neck were as if they were screwed in a vice. I could barely roll my eyes on each side, and then I could see, as clearly and plainly as if it was in the broad light of the blessed sun, a black and cloven foot planted upon each of my shoulders. I heard a low breathing in my ear; I felt, at every step I took, my leg strike back against the feet of the creature that was on my back. Still I could do nothing but walk straight on. At last I came within sight of the house, and a welcome sight it was to me, for I thought I would be released when I reached it.

"I soon came close to the door, but it was shut; I looked at the little window, but it was shut too, for they were more cautious about May Eve than I was; I saw the light inside, through the chinks of the door; I heard 'em talking and laughing within; I felt myself at three yards' distance from them that would die to save me—and may the Lord save me from ever again feeling what I did that night, when I found myself held by what couldn't be good nor friendly, but without the power to help myself, or to call my friends, or to put out my hand to knock, or even to lift my leg to strike the door, and let them know that I was outside it! 'Twas as if my hands grew to my sides, and my feet were glued to the ground, or had the weight of a rock fixed to them. At last I thought of blessing myself; and my right hand, that would do nothing else, did that for me. Still the weight remained on my back, and all was as before. I blessed myself again : 'twas still all the same. I then gave myself up for lost : but I blessed myself a third time, and my hand no sooner finished the sign than all at once I felt the burthen spring off my back; the door flew open as if a clap of thunder burst it, and I was pitched forward on my forehead, in upon the middle of the floor. When I got up my back was crookened, and I never stood straight from that night to this blessed hour."

There was a pause when Peggy Barrett finished. Those who had heard the story before had listened with a look of half-satisfied interest, blended, however, with an expression of that serious and solemn feeling which always attends a tale of super-natural wonders, how often soever told. They moved upon their seats out of the posture in which they had remained fixed during the narrative, and sat in an attitude which denoted that their curiosity as to the cause of this strange occurrence had been long since allayed. Those to whom it was before unknown still retained their look and posture of strained attention, and anxious but solemn expectation. A grandson of Peggy's, about nine years old (not the child of the son with whom she lived), had never before heard the story. As it grew in interest, he was observed to cling closer and closer to the old woman's side ; and at the close he was gazing steadfastly at her, with his body bent back across her knees, and his face turned up to hers, with a look through which a disposition to weep seemed contending with curiosity. After a moment's pause, he could no longer restrain his impatience ; and catching her grey locks in one hand, while the tear of dread and wonder was just dropping from his eyelash, he cried : "Granny, what was it ?"

The old woman smiled, first at the elder part of her audience, and then at her grandson, and patting him on the forehead, she said : "It was the Phooka."

NOTE.—The *Pouke* or *Phooka*, as the word is pronounced, means, in plain terms, the Evil One. "Playing the puck," a common Anglo-Irish phrase, is equivalent to "playing the devil." Much learning has been displayed in tracing this word through various languages, *vide Quarterly Review* (vol. xxii.), etc. The commentators on Shakespeare derive the beautiful and frolicsome Puck of the "Midsummer Night's Dream" from this mischievous Pouke.— *Vide* Drayton's "Nymphidia."

"The Irish Phooka, in its nature, perfectly resembles the *Mahr ;* and we have only to observe that there is a particular German tradition of a spirit which sits among reeds and alder bushes, and which, like the Phooka, leaps upon the back of those who pass by in the night, and does not leave them till they faint and fall to the earth."—THE BROTHERS GRIMM.

LEGENDS OF THE THIERNA NA OGE

I

FIOR USGA

A LITTLE way beyond the Gallows Green of Cork, and just outside the town, there is a great lough of water, where people in the winter go and skate for the sake of diversion; but the sport above the water is nothing to what is under it, for at the very bottom of this lough there are buildings and gardens far more beautiful than any now to be seen; and how they came there was in this manner:

Long before Saxon foot pressed Irish ground there was a great king called Corc, whose palace stood where the lough now is, in a round green valley, that was just a mile about. In the middle of the courtyard was a spring of fair water, so pure and so clear that it was the wonder of all the world. Much did the king rejoice at having so great a curiosity within his palace; but as people came in crowds from far and near to draw the precious water of this spring, he was sorely afraid that in time it might become dry; so he caused a high wall to be built up round it, and would allow nobody to have the water, which was a very great loss to the poor people living about the palace. Whenever he wanted any for himself, he would send his daughter to get it, not liking to trust his servants with the key of the well-door, fearing that they might give some away.

One night the King gave a grand entertainment, and there were many great princes present, and lords and nobles without end; and there were wonderful doings throughout the palace: there were bonfires, whose blaze reached up to the very sky; and dancing was there, to such sweet music that it ought to have waked up the dead out of their graves; and feasting was there in the greatest of plenty for all who came; nor was anyone turned away from the palace gates, but "You're welcome—you're welcome, heartily," was the porter's salute for all.

Now, it happened at this grand entertainment there was one young prince above all the rest mighty comely to behold, and as tall and as straight as ever eye would wish to look on. Right merrily did he dance that night with the old king's daughter, wheeling here and wheeling there, as light as a feather, and footing it away to the admiration of everyone. The musicians played the better for seeing their dancing; and they danced as if their lives depended upon it. After all this dancing came the supper, and the young prince was seated at table by the side of his beautiful partner, who smiled upon him as often as he spoke to her; and that was by no means so often as he wished, for he had constantly to turn to the company and thank them for the many compliments passed upon his fair partner and himself.

In the midst of the banquet, one of the great lords said to King Corc : "May it please your Majesty, here is everything in abundance that heart can wish for, both to eat and drink, except water."

"Water!" said the King, mightily pleased at someone calling for that of which purposely there was a want. "Water shall you have, my lord, speedily, and that of such a delicious kind, that I challenge all the world to equal it. Daughter," said he, "go fetch some in the golden vessel which I caused to be made for the purpose."

The King's daughter, who was called Fior Usga (which signifies, in English, Spring Water), did not much like to be told to perform so menial a service before so many people, and though she did not venture to refuse the commands of her father, yet hesitated to obey him, and looked down upon the ground. The King, who loved his daughter very much, seeing this, was sorry for what he had desired her to do, but having said the word, he was never known to recall it ; he therefore thought of a way to make his daughter go speedily and fetch the water, and it was by proposing that the young prince her partner should go along with her. Accordingly, with a loud voice, he said : "Daughter, I wonder not at your fearing to go alone so late at night; but I doubt not the young prince at your side will go with you." The prince was not displeased at hearing this ; and taking the golden vessel in one hand, with the other led the king's daughter out of the hall so gracefully that all present gazed after them with delight.

When they came to the spring of water in the courtyard of the palace, the fair Usga unlocked the door with the greatest care, and stooping down with the golden vessel to take some of the water out of the well, found the vessel so heavy that she lost her balance and fell in. The young prince tried in vain to save her, for the water rose and rose so fast that the entire courtyard was speedily covered with it, and he hastened back almost in a state of distraction to the King.

The door of the well being left open, the water, which had been so long confined, rejoiced at obtaining its liberty, rushed forth incessantly, every moment rising higher and higher, and was in the hall of the entertainment sooner than the young prince himself, so that when he attempted to speak to the king he was up to his neck in water. At length the water rose to such a height that it filled the whole of the green valley in which the king's palace stood, and so the present lough of Cork was formed.

Yet the King and his guests were not drowned, as would now happen if such an awful inundation were to take place; neither was his daughter, the fair Usga, who returned to the banquet-hall the very next night after this dreadful event; and every night since the same entertainment and dancing goes on in the palace at the bottom of the lough, and will last until someone has the luck to bring up out of it the golden vessel which was the cause of all this mischief.

Nobody can doubt that it was a judgment upon the King for his shutting up the well in the courtyard from the poor people; and if there are any who do not credit my story, they may go and see the lough of Cork, for there it is to be seen to this day; the road to Kinsale passes at one side of it; and when its waters are low and clear, the tops of towers and stately buildings may be plainly viewed in the bottom by those who have good eyesight, without the help of spectacles.

II

CORMAC AND MARY

"She is not dead—she has no grave—she lives beneath Lough Corrib's water; and in the murmur of each wave, methinks I catch the songs I taught her."

Thus many an evening on the shore sat Cormac raving wild and lowly; still idly muttering o'er and o'er: "She lives, detain'd by spells unholy.

"Death claims her not, too fair for earth, her spirit lives—alien of heaven; nor will it know a second birth when sinful mortals are forgiven.

"Cold is this rock—the wind comes chill, and mists the gloomy waters cover; but oh! her soul is colder still—to lose her God—to leave her lover!"

The lake was in profound repose, yet one white wave came gently curling, and as it reach'd the shore, arose dim figures—banners gay unfurling.

Onward they move, an airy crowd: through each thin form a moonlight ray shone; while spear and helm, in pageant proud, appear in liquid undulation.

Bright barbed steeds, curvetting, tread their trackless way with antic capers; and curtain clouds hang overhead, festoon'd by rainbow-colour'd vapours.

And when a breath of air would stir that drapery of Heaven's own wreathing, light wings of prismy gossamer just moved and sparkled to the breathing.

Nor wanting was the choral song, swelling in silvery chimes of sweetness; to sound of which this subtile throng advanced in playful grace and fleetness.

With music's strain, all came and went upon poor Cormac's doubting vision; now rising in wild merriment, now softly fading in derision.

"Christ, save her soul," he boldly cried; and when that blessed name was spoken, fierce yells and fiendish shrieks replied, and vanished all—the spell was broken.

And now on Corrib's lonely shore, freed by his word from power of faëry, to life, to love restored once more, young Cormac welcomes back his Mary.

III

THE LEGEND OF LOUGH GUR

LARRY COTTER had a farm on one side of Lough Gur, and was thriving in it, for he was an industrious, proper sort of man, who would have lived quietly and soberly to the end of his days but for the misfortune that came upon him, and you shall hear how that was. He had as nice a bit of meadow-land, down by the water-side, as ever a man would wish for; but its growth was spoiled entirely on him, and no one could tell how.

One year after the other it was all ruined just in the same way: the bounds were well made up, and not a stone of them was disturbed; neither could his neighbours' cattle have been guilty of the trespass, for they were spancelled; but however it was done, the grass of the meadow was destroyed, which was a great loss to Larry.

"What in the wide world will I do?" said Larry Cotter to his neighbour, Tom Welsh, who was a very decent sort of man himself; "that bit of meadow-land, which I am paying the great rent for, is doing nothing at all to make it for me; and the times are bitter bad, without the help of that to make them worse."

"'Tis true for you, Larry," replied Welsh; "the times are bitter bad—no doubt of that; but maybe if you were to watch by night you might make out all about it; sure, there's Mick and Terry, my two boys, will watch with you; for 'tis a thousand pities any honest man like you should be ruined in such a scheming way."

Accordingly, the following night, Larry Cotter, with Welsh's two sons, took their station in a corner of the meadow. It was just at the full of the moon, which was shining beautifully down upon the lake, that was as calm all over as the sky itself; not a cloud was there to be seen anywhere, nor a sound to be heard, but the cry of the corncrakes answering one another across the water.

"Boys! boys!" said Larry, "look there! look there! but for your lives don't make a bit of noise, nor stir a step till I say the word."

They looked, and saw a great fat cow, followed by seven milk-white heifers, moving on the smooth surface of the lake towards the meadow.

"'Tis not Tim Dwyer the piper's cow, anyway, that danced all the flesh off her bones," whispered Mick to his brother.

"Now, boys!" said Larry Cotter, when he saw the fine cow and her seven white heifers fairly in the meadow, "get between them and the lake if you can, and, no matter who they belong to, we'll just put them into the pound."

But the cow must have overheard Larry speaking, for down she went in a great hurry to the shore of the lake, and into it with her, before all their eyes: away made the seven heifers after her, but the boys got down to the bank before them, and work enough they had to drive them up from the lake to Larry Cotter.

Larry drove the seven heifers, and beautiful beasts they were, to the pound; but after he had them there for three days, and could hear of no owner, he took them out, and put them up in a field of his own. There he kept them, and they were thriving mighty well with him, until one night the gate of the field was left open, and in the morning the seven heifers were gone. Larry could not get any account of them after; and, beyond all doubt, it was back into the lake they went. Wherever they came from, or to whatever world they belonged, Larry Cotter never had a crop of grass off the meadow through their means. So he took to drink, fairly out of the grief; and it was the drink that killed him, they say.

IV

THE ENCHANTED LAKE

In the west of Ireland there was a lake, and no doubt it is there still, in which many young men had been at various times drowned. What made the circumstance remarkable was that the bodies of the drowned persons were never found. People naturally wondered at this, and at length the lake came to have a bad repute. Many dreadful stories were told about that lake. Some would affirm that on a dark night its waters appeared like fire; others would speak of horrid forms which were seen to glide over it; and everyone agreed that a strange, sulphureous smell issued from out of it.

There lived not far distant from this lake a young farmer, named Roderick Keating, who was about to be married to one of the prettiest girls in that part of the country. On his return from Limerick, where he had been to purchase the wedding-ring, he came up with two or three of his acquaintances, who were standing on the shore, and they began to joke with him about Peggy Honan. One said that young Delaney, his rival, had in his absence contrived to win the affection of his mistress. But Roderick's confidence in his intended bride was too great to be disturbed at this tale; and putting his hand in his pocket, he produced and held up with a significant look the wedding-ring. As he was turning it between his fore-finger and thumb, in token of triumph, somehow or other the ring fell from his hand and rolled into the lake. Roderick looked after it with the greatest sorrow; it was not so much for its value, though it had cost him half-a-guinea, as for the ill-luck of the thing; and the water was so deep that there was little chance of recovering it. His companions laughed at him, and he in vain endeavoured to tempt any of them by the offer of a handsome reward to dive after the ring. They were all as little inclined to venture as Roderick Keating himself; for the tales which they had heard when children were strongly impressed on their memories, and a superstitious dread filled the mind of each.

"Must I, then, go back to Limerick to buy another ring?" exclaimed the farmer. "Will not ten times what the ring cost tempt anyone of you to venture after it?"

There was within hearing a man who was considered to be a poor, crazy, half-witted fellow, but he was as harmless as a child, and used to go wandering up and down through the country from one place to another. When he heard of so great a reward, Paddeen—for that was his name—spoke out, and said that if Roderick Keating would give him encouragement equal to what he had offered to others, he was ready to venture after the ring into the lake; and Paddeen, all the while he spoke, looked as covetous after the sport as the money.

"I'll take you at your word," said Keating. So Paddeen pulled off his coat, and, without a single syllable more, down he plunged, head foremost, into the lake. What depth he went to, no one can tell exactly; but he was going, going, going down through the water, until the water parted from him, and he came upon the dry land. The sky, and the light, and everything, was there just as it is here; and he saw fine pleasure-grounds, with an elegant avenue through them, and a grand house, with a power of steps going up to the door. When he had recovered from his wonder at finding the land so dry and comfortable under the water, he looked about him, and what should he see but all

the young men that were drowned working away in the pleasure-
grounds as if nothing had ever happened to them ! Some of
them were mowing down the grass, and more were settling out
the gravel walks, and doing all manner of nice work, as neat
and as clever as if they had never been drowned ; and they were
singing away with high glee :

> " She is fair as Cappoquin ;
> Have you courage her to win ?
> And her wealth it far outshines
> Cullen's bog and Silvermines.
> She exceeds all heart can wish ;
> Not brawling like the Foherish,
> But as the brightly flowing Lee,
> Graceful, mild, and pure is she ! "

Well, Paddeen could not but look at the young men, for he
knew some of them before they were lost in the lake ; but he
said nothing, though he thought a great deal more, for all that,
like an oyster—no, not the wind of a word passed his lips ; so on
he went towards the big house, bold enough, as if he had seen
nothing to speak of, yet all the time mightily wishing to know
who the young woman could be that the young men were singing
the song about.

When he had nearly reached the door of the great house, out
walks from the kitchen a powerful fat woman, moving along like
a beer-barrel on two legs, with teeth as big as horses' teeth, and
up she made towards him.

" Good morrow, Paddeen ! " said she.

" Good morrow, ma'am ! " said he.

" What brought you here ? " said she.

" 'Tis after Rory Keating's gold ring," said he, " I'm come."

" Here it is for you," said Paddeen's fat friend, with a smile
on her face that moved like boiling stirabout [gruel].

" Thank you, ma'am," replied Paddeen, taking it from her.
" I need not say the Lord increase you, for you're fat enough
already. Will you tell me, if you please, am I to go back the
same way I came ? "

" Then you did not come to marry me ? " cried the corpulent
woman, in a desperate fury.

" Just wait till I come back again, my darling," said Paddeen.
" I'm to be paid for my message, and I must return with the
answer, or else they'll wonder what has become of me."

" Never mind the money," said the fat woman. " If you marry
me, you shall live for ever and a day in that house, and want
for nothing."

Paddeen saw clearly that, having got possession of the ring, the
fat woman had no power to detain him ; so without minding

anything she said, he kept moving and moving down the avenue, quite quietly, and looking about him ; for, to tell the truth, he had no particular inclination to marry a fat fairy. When he came to the gate, without ever saying good-bye, out he bolted, and he found the water coming all about him again. Up he plunged through it, and wonder enough there was when Paddeen was seen swimming away at the opposite side of the lake ; but he soon made the shore, and told Roderick Keating and the other boys that were standing there looking out for him all that had happened. Roderick paid him the five guineas for the ring on the spot ; and Paddeen thought himself so rich with such a sum of money in his pocket that he did not go back to marry the fat lady with the fine house at the bottom of the lake, knowing she had plenty of young men to choose a husband from, if she pleased to be married.

V

THE LEGEND OF O'DONOGHUE

In an age so distant that the precise period is unknown, a chieftain named O'Donoghue ruled over the country which surrounds the romantic Lough Lean, now called the Lake of Killarney. Wisdom, beneficence and justice distinguished his reign, and the prosperity and happiness of his subjects were their natural results. He is said to have been as renowned for his warlike exploits as for his pacific virtues ; and as a proof that his domestic administration was not the less rigorous because it was mild, a rocky island is pointed out to strangers, called " O'Donoghue's Prison," in which this prince once confined his own son for some act of disorder and disobedience.

His end—for it cannot correctly be called his death—was singular and mysterious. At one of those splendid feasts for which his court was celebrated, surrounded by the most distinguished of his subjects, he was engaged in a prophetic relation of the events which were to happen in ages yet to come. His auditors listened, now wrapt in wonder, now fired with indignation, burning with shame, or melted into sorrow, as he faithfully detailed the heroism, the injuries, the crimes and the miseries of their descendants. In the midst of his predictions he rose slowly from his seat, advanced with a solemn, measured, and majestic tread to the shore of the lake, and walked forward composedly upon its unyielding surface. When he had nearly reached the centre, he paused for a moment, then turning slowly round, looked towards his friends, and waving his arms to them with the cheerful air of one taking a short farewell, disappeared from their view.

The memory of the good O'Donoghue has been cherished by successive generations with affectionate reverence: and it is believed that at sunrise, on every May - dew morning—the anniversary of his departure—he revisits his ancient domains. A favoured few only are in general permitted to see him, and this distinction is always an omen of good fortune to the beholders: when it is granted to many, it is a sure token of an abundant harvest—a blessing, the want of which during this prince's reign was never felt by his people.

Some years have elapsed since the last appearance of O'Donoghue. The April of that year had been remarkably wild and stormy; but on May morning the fury of the elements had altogether subsided. The air was hushed and still; and the sky, which was reflected in the serene lake, resembled a beautiful but deceitful countenance, whose smiles, after the most tempestuous emotions, tempt the stranger to believe that it belongs to a soul which no passion has ever ruffled.

The first beams of the rising sun were just gilding the lofty summit of Glenaa, when the waters near the eastern shores of the lake became suddenly and violently agitated, though all the rest of its surface lay smooth and still as a tomb of polished marble; the next moment a foaming wave darted forward, and, like a proud, high-crested war-horse, exulting in his strength, rushed across the lake towards Toomies Mountain. Behind this wave appeared a stately warrior fully armed, mounted upon a milk-white steed; his snowy plume waved gracefully from a helmet of polished steel, and at his back fluttered a light blue scarf. The horse, apparently exulting in his noble burden, sprang after the wave along the water, which bore him up like firm earth, while showers of spray that glittered brightly in the morning sun were dashed up at every bound.

The warrior was O'Donoghue; he was followed by numberless youths and maidens who moved lightly and unconstrained over the watery plain, as the moonlight fairies glide through the fields of air; they were linked together by garlands of delicious spring flowers, and they timed their movements to strains of enchanting melody. When O'Donoghue had nearly reached the western side of the lake, he suddenly turned his steed, and directed his course along the wood-fringed shore of Glenaa, preceded by the huge wave that curled and foamed up as high as the horse's neck, whose fiery nostrils snorted above it. The long train of attendants followed with playful deviations the track of their leader, and moved on with unabated fleetness to their celestial music, till gradually, as they entered the narrow strait between Glenaa and Dinis, they became involved in the mists which still partially floated over the lakes, and faded from the view of the wondering beholders; but the sound of their music still fell upon the ear, and echo, catching up the harmonious strains, fondly repeated and prolonged them in soft and softer tones, till the last faint repetition died away, and the hearers awoke as from a dream of bliss.

NOTE.—*Thierna na Oge*, or the Country of Youth, is the name given to the foregoing section, from the belief that those who dwell in regions of enchantment beneath the water are not affected by the movements of time.

LEGENDS OF THE MERROW

I

THE LADY OF GOLLERUS

ON the shore of Smerwick Harbour, one fine summer's morning, just at daybreak, stood Dick Fitzgerald "shoghing the dudeen," which may be translated, smoking his pipe. The sun was gradually rising behind the lofty Brandon, the dark sea was getting green in the light, and the mists, clearing away out of the valleys, went rolling and curling like the smoke from the corner of Dick's mouth.

"'Tis just the pattern of a pretty morning," said Dick, taking the pipe from between his lips, and looking towards the distant ocean, which lay as still and tranquil as a tomb of polished marble. "Well, to be sure," continued he, after a pause, "'tis mighty lonesome to be talking to one's self by way of company, and not to have another soul to answer one—nothing but the child of one's own voice, the echo! I know this, that if I had the luck, or maybe the misfortune," said Dick, with a melancholy smile, "to have the woman, it would not be this way with me!— and what in the wide world is a man without a wife? He's no more surely than a bottle without a drop of drink in it, or dancing without music, or the left leg of a scissors, or a fishing-line without a hook, or any other matter that is no ways complete. Is it not so?" said Dick Fitzgerald, casting his eyes towards a rock upon the strand, which, though it could not speak, stood up as firm and looked as bold as ever Kerry witness did.

But what was his astonishment at beholding, just at the foot of that bare rock, a beautiful young creature combing her hair, which was of a sea-green colour; and now the salt water shining on it appeared, in the morning light, like melted butter upon cabbage.

Dick guessed at once that she was a Merrow, although he had never seen one before, for he spied the *cohuleen driuth*, or little enchanted cap, which the sea people use for diving down into the ocean, lying upon the strand, near her; and he had heard that if once he could possess himself of the cap, she would lose the power of going away into the water; so he seized it with all speed, and she, hearing the noise, turned her head about as natural as any Christian.

When the Merrow saw that her little diving-cap was gone, the salt tears—doubly salt, no doubt, from her—came trickling down her cheeks, and she began a low, mournful cry with just the tender voice of a new-born infant. Dick, although he knew well enough what she was crying for, determined to keep the *cohuleen driuth*, let her cry ever so much, to see what luck would come out of it. Yet he could not help pitying her, and when the dumb thing looked up in his face, and her cheeks all moist with tears, 'twas enough to make anyone feel, let alone Dick, who had ever and always, like most of his countrymen, a mighty tender heart of his own.

"Don't cry, my darling," said Dick Fitzgerald; but the Merrow, like any bold child, only cried the more for that.

Dick sat himself down by her side, and took hold of her hand, by way of comforting her. 'Twas in no particular an ugly hand, only there was a small web between the fingers, as there is in a duck's foot, but 'twas as thin and as white as the skin between egg and shell.

"What's your name, my darling?" says Dick, thinking to make her conversant with him; but he got no answer, and he was certain sure now either that she could not speak, or did not understand him. He therefore squeezed her hand in his, as the only way he had of talking to her. It's the universal language, and there's not a woman in the world, be she fish or lady, that does not understand it.

The Merrow did not seem much displeased at this mode of conversation, and making an end of her whining all at once, "Man," says she, looking up in Dick Fitzgerald's face—"man, will you eat me?"

"By all the red petticoats and check aprons between Dingle and Tralee," cried Dick, jumping up in amazement, "I'd as soon eat myself, my jewel! Is it I eat you, my pet? Now, 'twas some ugly, ill-looking thief of a fish put that notion into your own pretty head, with the nice green hair down upon it, that is so cleanly combed out this morning."

"Man," said the Merrow, "what will you do with me if you won't eat me?"

Dick's thoughts were running on a wife. He saw at the first glimpse that she was handsome; but since she spoke, and spoke, too, like any real woman, he was fairly in love with her. 'Twas the neat way she called him man that settled the matter entirely.

"Fish," says Dick, trying to speak to her after her own short fashion—"fish," says he, "here's my word, fresh and fasting, for you this blessed morning, that I'll make you Mistress Fitzgerald before all the world, and that's what I'll do."

"Never say the word twice," says she. "I'm ready and willing to be yours, Mister Fitzgerald; but stop, if you please, till I twist up my hair."

It was some time before she had settled it entirely to her liking; for she guessed, I suppose, that she was going among strangers, where she would be looked at. When that was done, the Merrow put the comb in her pocket, and then bent down her head and whispered some words to the water that was close to the foot of the rock.

Dick saw the murmur of the words upon the top of the sea, going out towards the wide ocean just like a breath of wind rippling along, and says he, in the greatest wonder: "Is it speaking you are, my darling, to the salt water?"

"It's nothing else," says she, quite carelessly. "I'm just sending word home to my father not to be waiting breakfast for me, just to keep him from being uneasy in his mind."

"And who's your father, my duck?" says Dick.

"What!" said the Merrow. "Did you never hear of my father? He's the king of the waves, to be sure."

"And yourself, then, is a real king's daughter?" said Dick, opening his two eyes to take a full and true survey of his wife that was to be. "Oh, I'm nothing else but a made man with you, and a king your father. To be sure, he has all the money that's down in the bottom of the sea."

"Money," repeated the Merrow; "what's money?"

"'Tis no bad thing to have when one wants it," replied Dick. "And maybe now the fishes have the understanding to bring up whatever you bid them?"

"Oh, yes," said the Merrow; "they bring me what I want."

"To speak the truth, then," said Dick, "'tis a straw bed I have at home before you, and that, I'm thinking, is no ways fitting for a king's daughter; so if 'twould not be displeasing to you just to mention a nice feather-bed, with a pair of new blankets. But what am I talking about? Maybe you have not such things as beds down under the water?"

"By all means," said she, "Mr. Fitzgerald; plenty of beds at your service. I've fourteen oyster-beds of my own, not to mention one just planting for the rearing of young ones."

"You have?" says Dick, scratching his head and looking a little puzzled. "'Tis a feather-bed I was speaking of; but clearly, yours is the very cut of a decent plan, to have bed and supper so handy to each other that a person, when they'd have the one, need never ask for the other."

However, bed or no bed, money or no money, Dick Fitzgerald determined to marry the Merrow, and the Merrow had given her consent. Away they went, therefore, across the strand, from Gollerus to Ballinrunnig, where Father Fitzgibbon happened to be that morning.

"There are two words to this bargain, Dick Fitzgerald," said his Reverence, looking mighty glum. "And is it a fishy woman you'd marry? The Lord preserve us! Send the scaly creature home to her own people, that's my advice to you, wherever she came from."

Dick had the *cohuleen driuth* in his hand, and was about to give it back to the Merrow, who looked covetously at it, but he thought for a moment, and then says he:

"Please, your Reverence, she's a king's daughter."

"If she was the daughter of fifty kings," said Father Fitzgibbon, "I tell you you can't marry her, she being a fish."

"Please, your Reverence," said Dick again, in an undertone, "she is as mild and as beautiful as the moon."

"If she was as mild and as beautiful as the sun, moon and stars all put together, I tell you, Dick Fitzgerald," said the priest, stamping his right foot, "you can't marry her, she being a fish."

"But she has all the gold that's down in the sea only for the asking, and I'm a made man if I marry her; and," said Dick, looking up slily, "I can make it worth anyone's while to do the job."

"Oh, that alters the case entirely," replied the priest. "Why, there's some reason now in what you say; why didn't you tell me this before? Marry her, by all means, if she was ten times a fish. Money, you know, is not to be refused in these bad times, and I may as well have the hansel of it as another, that maybe would not take half the pains in counselling you as I have done."

So Father Fitzgibbon married Dick Fitzgerald to the Merrow, and like any loving couple, they returned to Gollerus well pleased with each other. Everything prospered with Dick— he was at the sunny side of the world; the Merrow made the best of wives, and they lived together in the greatest contentment.

It was wonderful to see, considering where she had been brought up, how she would busy herself about the house, and how well she nursed the children; for at the end of three years, there were as many young Fitzgeralds—two boys and a girl.

In short, Dick was a happy man, and so he might have continued to the end of his days, if he had only the sense to take proper care of what he had got; many another man, however, beside Dick, has not had wit enough to do that.

One day, when Dick was obliged to go to Tralee, he left his

wife minding the children at home after him, and thinking she had plenty to do without disturbing his fishing tackle.

Dick was no sooner gone than Mrs. Fitzgerald set about cleaning up the house, and chancing to pull down a fishing-net, what should she find behind it in a hole in the wall but her own *cohuleen driuth.*

She took it out and looked at it, and then she thought of her father the king, and her mother the queen, and her brothers and sisters, and she felt a longing to go back to them.

She sat down on a little stool and thought over the happy days she had spent under the sea; then she looked at her children, and thought on the love and affection of poor Dick, and how it would break his heart to lose her. "But," says she, "he won't lose me entirely, for I'll come back to him again; and who can blame me for going to see my father and my mother, after being so long away from them."

She got up and went towards the door, but came back again to look once more at the child that was sleeping in the cradle. She kissed it gently, and as she kissed it, a tear trembled for an instant in her eye and then fell on its rosy cheek. She wiped away the tear, and turning to the eldest little girl, told her to take good care of her brothers, and to be a good child herself, until she came back. The Merrow then went down to the strand. The sea was lying calm and smooth, just heaving and glittering in the sun, and she thought she heard a faint sweet singing, inviting her to come down. All her old ideas and feelings came flooding over her mind, Dick and her children were at the instant forgotten, and placing the *cohuleen driuth* on her head, she plunged in.

Dick came home in the evening, and missing his wife, he asked Kathelin, his little girl, what had become of her mother, but she could not tell him. He then inquired of the neighbours, and he learned that she was seen going towards the strand with a strange-looking thing like a cocked hat in her hand. He returned to his cabin to search for the *cohuleen driuth.* It was gone, and the truth now flashed upon him.

Year after year did Dick Fitzgerald wait, expecting the return of his wife, but he never saw her more. Dick never married again, always thinking that the Merrow would sooner or later return to him, and nothing could ever persuade him but that her father the king kept her below by main force. "For," said Dick, "she surely would not of herself give up her husband and her children."

While she was with him, she was so good a wife in every respect, that to this day she is spoken of in the tradition of the country as the pattern for one, under the name of THE LADY OF GOLLERUS.

II

FLORY CANTILLON'S FUNERAL

THE ancient burial-place of the Cantillon family was on an island in Ballyheigh Bay. This island was situated at no great distance from the shore, and at a remote period was overflowed in one of the encroachments which the Atlantic has made on that part of the coast of Kerry. The fishermen declare they have often seen the ruined walls of an old chapel beneath them in the water, as they sailed over the clear green sea, of a sunny afternoon. However this may be, it is well known that the Cantillons were, like most other Irish families, strongly attached to their ancient burial-place ; and this attachment led to the custom, when any of the family died, of carrying the corpse to the seaside, where the coffin was left on the shore within reach of the tide. In the morning it had disappeared, being, as was traditionally believed, conveyed away by the ancestors of the deceased to their family tomb.

Connor Crowe, a County Clare man, was related to the Cantillons by marriage. "Connor Mac in Cruagh, of the seven quarters of Breintragh," as he was commonly called, and a proud man he was of the name. Connor, be it known, would drink a quart of salt water, for its medicinal virtues, before breakfast ; and for the same reason, I suppose, double that quantity of raw whisky between breakfast and night, which last he did with as little inconvenience to himself as any man in the barony of Moyferta ; and were I to add Clanderalaw and Ibrickan, I don't think I should say wrong.

On the death of Florence Cantillon, Connor Crowe was determined to satisfy himself about the truth of this story of the old church under the sea : so when he heard the news of the old fellow's death, away with him to Ardfert, where Flory was laid out in high style, and a beautiful corpse he made.

Flory had been as jolly and as rollicking a boy in his day as ever was stretched, and his wake was in every respect worthy of him. There was all kind of entertainment and all sort of diversion at it, and no less than three girls got husbands there— more luck to them. Everything was as it should be : all that side of the country, from Dingle to Tarbert, was at the funeral. The Keen was sung long and bitterly ; and, according to the family custom, the coffin was carried to Ballyheigh strand, where it was laid upon the shore, with a prayer for the repose of the dead.

The mourners departed, one group after another, and at last Connor Crowe was left alone : he then pulled out his whisky bottle, his drop of comfort, as he called it, which he required, being in grief; and down he sat upon a big stone that was sheltered by a projecting rock, and partly concealed from view, to await with patience the appearance of the ghostly undertakers.

The evening came on mild and beautiful; he whistled an old air which he had heard in his childhood, hoping to keep idle fears out of his head; but the wild strain of that melody brought a thousand recollections with it, which only made the twilight appear more pensive.

"If 'twas near the gloomy tower of Dunmore, in my own sweet county, I was," said Connor Crowe, with a sigh, "one might well believe that the prisoners, who were murdered long ago, there in the vaults under the castle, would be the hands to carry off the coffin out of envy, for never a one of them was buried decently, nor had as much as a coffin amongst them all. 'Tis often, sure enough, I have heard lamentations and great mourning coming from the vaults of Dunmore Castle; but," continued he, after fondly pressing his lips to the mouth of his companion and silent comforter, the whisky bottle, "didn't I know all the time well enough 'twas the dismal sounding waves working through the cliffs and hollows of the rocks, and fretting themselves to foam. Oh, then, Dunmore Castle, it is you that are the gloomy-looking tower on a gloomy day, with the gloomy hills behind you; when one has gloomy thoughts on their heart, and sees you like a ghost rising out of the smoke made by the kelp-burners on the strand, there is, the Lord save us! as fearful a look about you as about the Blue Man's Lake at midnight. Well, then, anyhow," said Connor, after a pause, "is it not a blessed night, though surely the moon looks mighty pale in the face? St. Senan himself between us and all kinds of harm!"

It was, in truth, a lovely moonlight night; nothing was to be seen around but the dark rocks and the white pebbly beach, upon which the sea broke with a hoarse and melancholy murmur. Connor, notwithstanding his frequent draughts, felt rather queerish, and almost began to repent his curiosity. It was certainly a solemn sight to behold the black coffin resting upon the white strand. His imagination gradually converted the deep moaning of old ocean into a mournful wail for the dead, and from the shadowy recesses of the rocks he imaged forth strange and visionary forms.

As the night advanced, Connor became weary with watching; he caught himself more than once in the act of nodding, when suddenly giving his head a shake, he would look towards the black coffin. But the narrow house of death remained unmoved before him.

It was long past midnight, and the moon was sinking into the sea, when he heard the sound of many voices, which gradually became stronger, above the heavy and monotonous roll of the sea. He listened, and presently could distinguish a Keen, of exquisite sweetness, the notes of which rose and fell with the heaving of the waves, whose deep murmur mingled with and supported the strain!

The Keen grew louder and louder, and seemed to approach the beach, and then fell into a low, plaintive wail. As it ended, Connor beheld a number of strange, and in the dim light mysterious-looking, figures emerge from the sea and surround the coffin, which they prepared to launch into the water.

"This comes of marrying with the creatures of earth," said one of the figures, in a clear yet hollow tone.

"True," replied another, with a voice still more fearful, "our king would never have commanded his gnawing white-toothed waves to devour the rocky roots of the island cemetery, had not his daughter, Durfulla, been buried there by her mortal husband!"

"But the time will come," said a third, bending over the coffin,

> "When mortal eye—our work shall spy,
> And mortal ear—our dirge shall hear."

"Then," said a fourth, "our burial of the Cantillons is at an end for ever!"

As this was spoken, the coffin was borne from the beach by a retiring wave, and the company of sea people prepared to follow it; but at the moment, one chanced to discover Connor Crowe, as fixed with wonder and as motionless with fear as the stone on which he sat.

"The time is come," cried the unearthly being; "the time is come: a human eye looks on the forms of ocean, a human ear has heard their voices! Farewell to the Cantillons; the sons of the sea are no longer doomed to bury the dust of the earth!"

One after the other turned slowly round, and regarded Connor Crowe, who still remained as if bound by a spell. Again arose their funeral song; and on the next wave they followed the coffin. The sound of the lamentation died away, and at length nothing was heard but the rush of waters. The coffin and the train of sea people sank over the old churchyard, and never, since the funeral of old Flory Cantillon, have any of the family been carried to the strand of Ballyheigh, for conveyance to their rightful burial-place, beneath the waves of the Atlantic.

III

THE LORD OF DUNKERRON

THE lord of Dunkerron [1]—O'Sullivan More, why seeks he at midnight the sea-beaten shore? His bark lies in haven, his hounds are asleep; no foes are abroad on the land or the deep.

Yet nightly the lord of Dunkerron is known on the wild shore to watch and to wander alone; for a beautiful spirit of ocean, 'tis said, the lord of Dunkerron would win to his bed.

When, by moonlight, the waters were hush'd to repose, that beautiful spirit of ocean arose; her hair, full of lustre, just floated and fell o'er her bosom, that heaved with a billowy swell.

Long, long had he loved her—long vainly essay'd to lure from her dwelling the coy ocean maid; and long had he wander'd and watch'd by the tide, to claim the fair spirit O'Sullivan's bride!

The maiden, she gazed on the creature of earth, whose voice in her breast to a feeling gave birth; then smiled; and, abashed as a maiden might be, looking down, gently sank to her home in the sea.

Though gentle that smile as the moonlight above, O'Sullivan felt 'twas the dawning of love; and hope came on hope, spreading over his mind like the eddy of circles her wake left behind.

The lord of Dunkerron, he plunged in the waves, and sought through the fierce rush of waters their caves; the gloom of whose depth, studded over with spars, had the glitter of midnight when lit up by stars.

Who can tell or can fancy the treasures that sleep, entombed in the wonderful womb of the deep?—the pearls and the gems, as if valueless, thrown, to lie 'mid the sea-wrack concealed and unknown.

Down, down went the maid—still the chieftain pursued; who flies must be followed ere she can be wooed. Untempted by treasures, unawed by alarms, the maiden at length he has clasped in his arms!

They rose from the deep by a smooth-spreading strand, whence beauty and verdure stretch'd over the land. 'Twas an isle of enchantment! and lightly the breeze, with a musical murmur, just crept through the trees.

The haze-woven shroud of that newly-born isle softly faded away, from a magical pile, a palace of crystal, whose bright-beaming sheen had the tints of the rainbow—red, yellow, and green.

[1] The remains of Dunkerron Castle are distant about a mile from the village of Kenmare, in the county of Kerry. It is recorded to have been built in 1596, by Owen O'Sullivan More.—[*More* is merely an epithet signifying *the Great*.]

And grottoes, fantastic in hue and in form, were there, as flung up—the wild sport of the storm; yet all was so cloudless, so lovely and calm, it seemed but a region of sunshine and balm.

"Here, here shall we dwell in a dream of delight, where the glories of earth and of ocean unite! Yet, loved son of earth! I must from thee away; there are laws which e'en spirits are bound to obey!

"Once more must I visit the chief of my race, his sanction to gain ere I meet thy embrace. In a moment I dive to the chambers beneath: one cause can detain me—one only—'tis death!"

They parted in sorrow, with vows true and fond; the language of promise had nothing beyond. His soul, all on fire, with anxiety burns: the moment is gone—but no maiden returns.

What sounds from the deep meet his terrified ear—what accents of rage and of grief does he hear? What sees he? what change has come over the flood—what tinges its green with a jetty of blood?

Can he doubt what the gush of warm blood would explain?— that she sought the consent of her monarch in vain! For see all around him, in white foam and froth, the waves of the ocean boil up in their wroth!

The palace of crystal has melted in air, and the dyes of the rainbow no longer are there; the grottoes with vapour and clouds are o'ercast, the sunshine is darkness—the vision has past!

Loud, loud was the call of his serfs for their chief; they sought him with accents of wailing and grief: he heard, and he struggled—a wave to the shore, exhausted and faint, bears O'Sullivan More!

IV

THE WONDERFUL TUNE

MAURICE CONNOR was the king, and that's no small word, of all the pipers in Munster. He could play jig and planxty without end, and Ollistrum's March, and the Eagle's Whistle, and the Hen's Concert, and odd tunes of every sort and kind. But he knew one, far more surprising than the rest, which had in it the power to set everything dead or alive dancing.

In what way he learned it is beyond my knowledge, for he was mighty cautious about telling how he came by so wonderful a tune. At the very first note of that tune, the brogues began shaking upon the feet of all who heard it—old or young, it mattered not—just as if their brogues had the ague; then the feet began going—going—going from under them, and at last up and away with them, dancing like mad!—whisking here, there, and everywhere, like a straw in a storm—there was no halting while the music lasted!

Not a fair, nor a wedding, nor a patron in the seven parishes round was counted worth the speaking of without "blind Maurice and his pipes." His mother, poor woman, used to lead him about from one place to another, just like a dog.

Down through Iveragh—a place that ought to be proud of itself, for 'tis Daniel O'Connell's country—Maurice Connor and his mother were taking their rounds. Beyond all other places, Iveragh is the place for stormy coast and steep mountains—as proper a spot it is as any in Ireland to get yourself drowned, or your neck broken on the land, should you prefer that. But notwithstanding, in Ballinskellig Bay there is a neat bit of ground, well fitted for diversion; and down from it, towards the water, is a clean, smooth piece of strand—the dead image of a calm summer's sea on a moonlight night, with just the curl of the small waves upon it.

Here it was that Maurice's music had brought from all parts a great gathering of the young men and the young women—*oh, the darlints!*—for 'twas not every day the strand of Trafraska was stirred up by the voice of a bagpipe. The dance began; and as pretty a rinkafadda it was as ever was danced. "Brave music," said everybody, "and well done," when Maurice stopped.

"More power to your elbow, Maurice, and a fair wind in the bellows," cried Paddy Dorman, a hump-backed dancing-master, who was there to keep order. "'Tis a pity," said he, "if we'd let the piper run dry after such music; 'twould be a disgrace to Iveragh, that didn't come on it since the week of the three Sundays." So, as well became him, for he was always a decent man, says he: "Did you drink, piper?"

"I will, sir," says Maurice, answering the question on the safe side, for you never yet knew piper or schoolmaster who refused his drink.

"What will you drink, Maurice?" says Paddy.

"I'm noways particular," says Maurice. "I drink anything, and give God thanks, barring *raw* water; but if 'tis all the same to you, Mister Dorman, maybe you wouldn't lend me the loan of a glass of whisky."

"I've no glass, Maurice," said Paddy; "I've only the bottle."

"Let that be no hindrance," answered Maurice. "My mouth just holds a glass to the drop; often I've tried it, sure."

So Paddy Dorman trusted him with the bottle—more fool was he; and to his cost, he found that, though Maurice's mouth might not hold more than the glass at one time, yet, owing to the hole in his throat, it took many a filling.

"That was no bad whisky, neither," says Maurice, handing back the empty bottle.

"By the holy frost, then!" says Paddy, "'tis but *cowld* comfort there's in that bottle now. And 'tis your word we must take for the strength of the whisky, for you've left us no sample to judge by." And, to be sure, Maurice had not.

Now, I need not tell any gentleman or lady with common understanding, that if he or she was to drink an honest bottle of whisky at one pull, it is not at all the same thing as drinking a bottle of water; and in the whole course of my life, I never knew more than five men who could do so without being overtaken by the liquor. Of these, Maurice Connor was not one, though he had a stiff head enough of his own—he was fairly tipsy. Don't think I blame him for it; 'tis often a good man's case; but true is the word that says, "When liquor's in, sense is out"; and puff, at a breath, before you could say "Lord save us!" out he blasted his wonderful tune.

'Twas really then beyond all belief or telling the dancing. Maurice himself could not keep quiet; staggering now on one leg, now on the other, and rolling about like a ship in a cross sea, trying to humour the tune. There was his mother, too, moving her old bones as light as the youngest girl of them all; but her dancing—no, nor the dancing of all the rest, is not worthy the speaking about to the work that was going on down on the strand—every inch of it covered with all manner of fish, jumping and plunging about to the music; and every moment more and more would tumble in out of the water, charmed by the wonderful tune. Crabs of monstrous size spun round and round on one claw with the nimbleness of a dancing-master, and twirled and tossed their other claws about like limbs that did not belong to them. It was a sight surprising to behold. But perhaps you may have heard of Father Florence Conry, a Franciscan friar, and a great Irish poet—*bolg an dàna*, as they used to call him—a wallet of poems. If you have not, he was as pleasant a man as one would wish to drink with of a hot summer's day; and he has rhymed out all about the dancing fishes so neatly, that it would be a thousand pities not to give you his verses; so here's my hand at an upset of them into English:

> "The big seals in motion,
>   Like waves of the ocean,
>   Or gouty feet prancing,
>   Came heading the gay fish,
>   Crabs, lobsters and crayfish,
>   Determined on dancing.
>
> "The sweet sounds they follow'd,
>   The gasping cod swallow'd;

'Twas wonderful, really !
And turbot and flounder,
'Mid fish that were rounder,
Just caper'd as gaily.

" John-dories came tripping ;
Dull hake, by their skipping,
To frisk it seem'd given ;
Bright mackerel went springing,
Like small rainbows winging
Their flight up to heaven.

" The whiting and haddock
Left salt-water paddock,
This dance to be put in :
Where skate with flat faces
Edged out some odd plaices ;
But soles kept their footing.

" Sprats and herrings in powers
Of silvery showers
All number out-number'd ;
And great ling so lengthy
Were there in such plenty,
The shore was encumber'd.

" The scollop and oyster
Their two shells did roister,
Like castanets fitting ;
While limpets moved clearly,
And rocks very nearly
With laughter were splitting."

Never was such an ullabulloo in this world, before or since.
'Twas as if heaven and earth were coming together. And all
out of Maurice Connor's wonderful tune !

In the height of all these doings, what should there be dancing
among the outlandish set of fishes but a beautiful young woman
—as beautiful as the dawn of day ! She had a cocked hat upon
her head ; from under it her long green hair—just the colour of
the sea — fell down behind, without hindrance to her dancing.
Her teeth were like rows of pearls ; her lips for all the world
looked like red coral ; and she had an elegant gown, as white
as the foam of the wave, with little rows of purple and red sea-
weeds settled out upon it ; for you never yet saw a lady, under
the water or over the water, who had not a good notion of
dressing herself out.

Up she danced at last to Maurice, who was flinging his feet
from under him as fast as hops—for nothing in this world could
keep still while that tune of his was going on—and says she to
him, chanting it out with a voice as sweet as honey :

> " I'm a lady of honour
>   Who lives in the sea,
> Come down, Maurice Connor,
>   And be married to me.
>
> " Silver plates and gold dishes
>   You shall have, and shall be
> The king of the fishes
>   When you're married to me."

Drink was strong in Maurice's head, and out he chanted in return for her great civility, It is not every lady, maybe, that would be after making such an offer to a blind piper ; therefore 'twas only right in him to give her as good as she gave herself, so says Maurice :

> " I'm obliged to you, madam.
>   Off a gold dish or plate,
> If a king, and I had 'em,
>   I could dine in great state.
>
> " With your own father's daughter
>   I'd be sure to agree ;
> But to drink the salt water
>   Wouldn't do so with me."

The lady looked at him quite amazed, and swinging her head from side to side like a great scholar, "Well," says she, "Maurice, if you're not a poet, where is poetry to be found?"

In this way they kept on at it, framing high compliments, one answering the other, and their feet going with the music as fast as their tongues. All the fish kept dancing too. Maurice heard the clatter, and was afraid to stop playing, lest it might be displeasing to the fish, and not knowing what so many of them may take it into their heads to do to him if they got vexed.

Well, the lady with the green hair kept on coaxing of Maurice with soft speeches, till at last she overpersuaded him to promise to marry her, and be king over the fishes, great and small. Maurice was well fitted to be their king, if they wanted one that could make them dance, and he surely would drink, barring the salt water, with any fish of them all.

When Maurice's mother saw him with that unnatural thing in the form of a green-haired lady as his guide, and he and she dancing down together so lovingly to the water's edge through the thick of the fishes, she called out after him to stop and come back. "Oh, then," says she, "as if I was not widow enough before, there he is going away from me to be married to that scaly woman. And who knows but 'tis grandmother I may be to a hake or a cod. Lord help and pity me, but 'tis a mighty unnatural thing ! And maybe 'tis boiling and eating my own grandchild I'll be, with a bit of salt butter, and I not knowing it ! Oh, Maurice, Maurice, if there's any love or nature left in you, come back to your own *ould* mother, who reared you like a decent Christian ! "

Then the poor woman began to cry and ullagoane so finely that it would do anyone good to hear her.

Maurice was not long getting to the rim of the water. There he kept playing and dancing on as if nothing was the matter, and a great thundering wave coming in towards him ready to swallow him up alive ; but as he could not see it, he did not fear it. His mother it was who saw it plainly through the big tears that were rolling down her cheeks, and though she saw it, and her heart was aching as much as ever mother's heart ached for a son, she kept dancing, dancing all the time for the bare life of her. Certain it was she could not help it, for Maurice never stopped playing that wonderful tune of his.

He only turned the bothered ear to the sound of his mother's voice, fearing it might put him out in his steps, and all the answer he made back was :

"Whisht with you, mother ! Sure, I'm going to be king over the fishes down in the sea, and for a token of luck, and a sign that I am alive and well, I'll send you in, every twelvemonth on this day, a piece of burned wood to Trafraska." Maurice had not the power to say a word more, for the strange lady with the green hair, seeing the wave just upon them, covered him up with herself in a thing like a cloak with a big hood to it, and the wave curling over twice as high as their heads, burst upon the strand with a rush and a roar that might be heard as far as Cape Clear.

That day twelvemonth the piece of burned wood came ashore in Trafraska. It was a queer thing for Maurice to think of sending all the way from the bottom of the sea. A gown or a pair of shoes would have been something like a present for his poor mother ; but he had said it, and he kept his word. The bit of burned wood regularly came ashore on the appointed day for as good—aye, and better than a hundred years. The day is now forgotten, and maybe that is the reason why people say how Maurice Connor has stopped sending the luck-token to his mother. Poor woman, she did not live to get as much as one of them ; for what through the loss of Maurice, and the fear of eating her own grandchildren, she died in three weeks after the dance. Some say it was the fatigue that killed her, but whichever it was, Mrs. Connor was decently buried with her own people.

Seafaring men have often heard, off the coast of Kerry, on a still night, the sound of music coming up from the water ; and some, who have had good ears, could plainly distinguish Maurice Connor's voice singing these words to his pipes :

"Beautiful shore, with thy spreading strand,
Thy crystal water, and diamond sand ;
Never would I have parted from thee
But for the sake of my fair ladie."

NOTE.—The Irish *Merrow* answers exactly to the English Mermaid, being compounded of the sea and a maid. It is also used to express a sea-monster, like the Armoric and Cornish *Morhuch*, to which it evidently bears analogy. The romantic historians of Ireland describe the *Suire* as playing round the ships of the Milesians when on their passage to that island.

LEGENDS OF THE DULLAHAN

I

THE GOOD WOMAN

IN a pleasant and not unpicturesque valley of the White Knight's country, at the foot of the Galtee Mountains, lived Larry Dodd and his wife Nancy. They rented a cabin and a few acres of land, which they cultivated with great care, and its crops rewarded their industry. They were independent and respected by their neighbours ; they loved each other in a marriageable sort of way, and few couples had altogether more the appearance of comfort about them.

Larry was a hard-working and, occasionally, a hard-drinking, Dutch-built little man, with a fiddle head and a round stern ; a steady-going, straightforward fellow, barring when he carried too much whisky, which, it must be confessed, might occasionally prevent his walking the chalked line with perfect philomathical accuracy. He had a moist, ruddy countenance, rather inclined to an expression of gravity, and particularly so in the morning ; but, taken all together, he was generally looked upon as a marvellously proper person, notwithstanding he had, every day in the year, a sort of unholy dew upon his face, even in the coldest weather, which gave rise to a supposition (amongst censorious persons, of course) that Larry was apt to indulge in strong and frequent potations. However, all men of talents have their faults—indeed, who is without them ?—and as Larry, setting aside his domestic virtues and skill in farming, was decidedly the most distinguished breaker of horses for forty miles round, he must be in some degree excused, considering the inducements of " the stirrup-cup " and the fox-hunting society in which he mixed, if he had also been the greatest drunkard in the county ; but, in truth, this was not the case.

Larry was a man of mixed habits, as well in his mode of life and his drink as in his costume. His dress accorded well with his character—a sort of half-and-half between farmer and horse-jockey. He wore a blue coat of coarse cloth, with short skirts and a stand-up collar ; his waistcoat was red, and his lower habiliments were made of leather, which in course of time had shrunk so much that they fitted like a second skin ; and long use had absorbed their moisture to such a degree that they made a strange sort of crackling noise as he walked along. A hat covered with oilskin ; a cutting-whip, all worn and jagged at the end ; a pair of second-hand, or, to speak more correctly, second-footed greasy top-boots, that seemed never to have imbibed a refreshing draught of Warren's blacking of matchless lustre !—and one spur without a rowel, completed the everyday dress of Larry Dodd.

Thus equipped was Larry returning from Cashel, mounted on a rough-coated and wall-eyed nag, though, notwithstanding these and a few other trifling blemishes, a well-built animal ; having just purchased the said nag, with a fancy that he could make his own money again of his bargain, and maybe turn an odd penny more by it at the ensuing Kildorrery fair. Well pleased with himself, he trotted fair and easy along the road in the delicious and lingering twilight of a lovely June evening, thinking of nothing at all, only whistling, and wondering would horses always be so low. "If they go at this rate," said he to himself, "for half nothing, and that paid in butter buyer's notes, who would be the fool to walk ?" This very thought, indeed, was passing in his mind, when his attention was roused by a woman pacing quickly by the side of his horse, and hurrying on as if endeavouring to reach her destination before the night closed in. Her figure, considering the long strides she took, appeared to be under the common size—rather of the dumpy order ; but further, as to whether the damsel was young or old, fair or brown, pretty or ugly, Larry could form no precise notion, from her wearing a large cloak (the usual garb of the female Irish peasant), the hood of which was turned up, and completely concealed every feature.

Enveloped in this mass of dark and concealing drapery, the strange woman, without much exertion, contrived to keep up with Larry Dodd's steed for some time, when his master very civilly offered her a lift behind him, as far as he was going her way. "Civility begets civility," they say ; however, he received no answer ; and thinking that the lady's silence proceeded only from bashfulness, like a man of true gallantry, not a word more said Larry until he pulled up by the side of a gap, and then says he, " *Ma colleen beg*, just jump up behind me, without a word more, though never a one have you spoke, and I'll take you safe and sound through the lonesome bit of road that is before us."

She jumped at the offer, sure enough, and up with her on the back of the horse as light as a feather. In an instant there she was seated up behind Larry, with her hand and arm buckled round his waist, holding on.

" I hope you're comfortable there, my dear," said Larry, in his own good-humoured way ; but there was no answer ; and on they went—trot, trot, trot—along the road ; and all was so still and so quiet that you might have heard the sound of the hoofs on the limestone a mile off : for that matter, there was nothing else to hear except the moaning of a distant stream, that kept up a continued *cronane*, like a nurse *hushoing*. Larry, who had a keen ear, did not, however, require so profound a silence to detect the click of one of the shoes. " 'Tis only loose the shoe is," said he to his companion, as they were just entering on the lonesome bit of road of which he had before spoken. Some old trees, with huge trunks, all covered, and irregular branches festooned with ivy, grew over a dark pool of water, which had been formed as a drinking-place for cattle ; and in the distance was seen the majestic head of Galtee-more. Here the horse, as if in grateful recognition, made a dead halt ; and Larry, not knowing what vicious tricks his new purchase might have, and unwilling that through any odd chance the young woman should get *spilt* in the water, dismounted, thinking to lead the horse quietly by the pool.

" By the piper's luck, that always found what he wanted," said Larry, recollecting himself, " I've a nail in my pocket ; 'tis not the first time I've put on a shoe, and maybe it won't be the last ; for here is no want of paving-stones to make hammers in plenty."

No sooner was Larry off, than off with a spring came the young woman just at his side. Her feet touched the ground without making the least noise in life, and away she bounded like an ill-mannered wench as she was, without saying, "By your leave," or no matter what else. She seemed to glide rather than run, not along the road, but across a field, up towards the old ivy-covered walls of Kilnaslattery Church—and a pretty church it was.

" Not so fast, if you please, young woman—not so fast ! " cried Larry, calling after her ; but away she ran, and Larry followed, his leathern garment, already described, crack, crick, crackling at every step he took. " Where's my wages ? " said Larry. " *Thorum pog, ma colleen oge*—sure, I've earned a kiss from your pair of pretty lips—and I'll have it too ! " But she went on faster and faster, regardless of these and other flattering speeches from her pursuer. At last she came to the churchyard wall, and then over with her in an instant.

"Well, she's a mighty smart creature, anyhow. To be sure, how neat she steps upon her pasterns! Did anyone ever see the like of that before; but I'll not be baulked by any woman that ever wore a head, or any ditch either," exclaimed Larry, as with a desperate bound he vaulted, scrambled and tumbled over the wall into the churchyard. Up he got from the elastic sod of a newly-made grave in which Tade Leary that morning was buried —rest his soul!—and on went Larry, stumbling over head-stones and foot-stones, over old graves and new graves, pieces of coffins, and the skulls and bones of dead men—the Lord save us!—that were scattered about there as plenty as paving-stones; floundering amidst great, overgrown dock-leaves and brambles that, with their long prickly arms, tangled round his limbs, and held him back with a fearful grasp. Meantime the merry wench in the cloak moved through all these obstructions as evenly and as gaily as if the churchyard, crowded up as it was with graves and grave-stones (for people came to be buried there from far and near), had been the floor of a dancing-room. Round and round the walls of the old church she went. "I'll just wait," said Larry, seeing this, and thinking it all nothing but a trick to frighten him. "When she comes round again, if I don't take the kiss, I won't, that's all —and here she is!" Larry Dodd sprang forward with open arms, and clasped in them—a woman, it is true—but a woman without any lips to kiss, by reason of her having no head!

"Murder!" cried he. "Well, that accounts for her not speaking." Having uttered these words, Larry himself became dumb with fear and astonishment; his blood seemed turned to ice, and a dizziness came over him; and, staggering like a drunken man, he rolled against the broken window of the ruin, horrified at the conviction that he had actually held a Dullahan in his embrace.

When he recovered to something like a feeling of consciousness, he slowly opened his eyes, and then, indeed, a scene of wonder burst upon him. In the midst of the ruin stood an old wheel of torture, ornamented with heads, like Cork Gaol, when the heads of Murty Sullivan and other gentlemen were stuck upon it. This was plainly visible in the strange light which spread itself around. It was fearful to behold, but Larry could not choose but look, for his limbs were powerless through the wonder and the fear. Useless as it was, he would have called for help, but his tongue cleaved to the roof of his mouth, and not one word could he say. In short, there was Larry, gazing through a shattered window of the old church, with eyes bleared and almost starting from their sockets; his breast resting on the thickness of the wall, over which, on one side, his head and outstretched neck projected, and on the other, although one toe touched the ground, it derived no support from thence; terror, as it were, kept him balanced. Strange noises assailed his ears, until at last they tingled painfully to the sharp clatter of the little bells, which kept up a continued ding—ding— ding—ding; marrowless bones rattled and clanked, and the deep and solemn sound of a great bell came booming on the night wind.

> " 'Twas a spectre rung
>   That bell when it swung—
>   Swing-swang !
> And the chain it squeaked,
> And the pulley creaked,
>   Swing-swang !

> " And with every roll
>   Of the deep death toll,
>   Ding-dong !
> The hollow vault rang
> As the clapper went bang,
>   Ding-dong !"

It was strange music to dance by; nevertheless, moving to it, round and round the wheel set with skulls, were well-dressed ladies and gentlemen, and soldiers and sailors, and priests and publicans, and jockeys and jennys, but all without their heads. Some poor skeletons, whose bleached bones were ill covered by moth-eaten palls, and were not admitted into the ring, amused themselves by bowling their brainless noddles at one another, which seemed to enjoy the sport beyond measure.

Larry did not know what to think; his brains were all in a mist; and losing the balance which he had so long maintained, he fell head foremost into the midst of the company of Dullahans.

"I'm done for and lost for ever !" roared Larry, with his heels turned towards the stars, and souse down he came.

"Welcome, Larry Dodd, welcome !" cried every head, bobbing up and down in the air. "A drink for Larry Dodd !" shouted they, as with one voice, that quavered like a shake on the bag-pipes. No sooner said than done, for a player at heads, catching his own as it was bowled at him, for fear of its going astray, jumped up, put the head, without a word, under his left arm, and, with the right stretched out, presented a brimming cup to Larry, who, to show his manners, drank it off like a man.

"'Tis capital stuff," he would have said, which surely it was, but he got no further than cap—when decapitated was he, and his head began dancing over his shoulders like those of the rest of the party. Larry, however, was not the first man who lost his head through the temptation of looking at the bottom of a brimming cup. Nothing more did he remember clearly—for it seems body and head being parted is not very favourable to thought—but a great hurry-scurry, with the noise of carriages and the cracking of whips.

When his senses returned, his first act was to put up his hand to where his head formerly grew, and to his great joy there he found it still. He then shook it gently, but his head remained firm enough, and somewhat assured at this, he proceeded to open his eyes and look around him. It was broad daylight, and in the old church of Kilnaslattery he found himself lying, with that head, the loss of which he had anticipated, quietly resting, poor youth, "upon the lap of earth." Could it have been an ugly dream? "Oh, no," said Larry; "a dream could never have brought me here, stretched on the flat of my back, with that death's head and cross marrow-bones forenenting me on the fine old tombstone there that was *faced* by Pat Kearney of Kilcrea— but where is the horse?" He got up slowly, every joint aching with pain from the bruises he had received, and went to the pool of water, but no horse was there. "'Tis home I must go," said Larry, with a rueful countenance; "but how will I face Nancy? What will I tell her about the horse and the seven I.O.U.'s that he cost me? 'Tis them Dullahans that have made their own of him from me—the horse-stealing robbers of the world, that have no fear of the gallows!—but what's gone is gone, that's a clear case!"—so saying, he turned his steps homewards, and arrived at his cabin about noon without encountering any further adventures. There he found Nancy, who, as he expected, looked as black as a thundercloud at him for being out all night. She listened to the marvellous relation which he gave with exclamations of astonishment, and, when he had concluded, of grief, at the loss of the horse that he had paid for like an honest man with seven I.O.U.'s, three of which she knew to be as good as gold.

"But what took you up to the old church at all, out of the road, and at that time of the night, Larry?" inquired his wife.

Larry looked like a criminal for whom there was no reprieve; he scratched his head for an excuse, but not one could he muster up, so he knew not what to say.

"Oh, Larry, Larry!" muttered Nancy, after waiting some time for his answer, her jealous fears during the pause rising like barm; "'tis the very same way with you as with any other man —you are all alike for that matter—I've no pity for you—but confess the truth."

Larry shuddered at the tempest which he perceived was about to break upon his devoted head.

"Nancy," said he, "I do confess. It was a young woman without any head that—"

His wife heard no more. "A woman I knew it was," cried she; "but a woman without a head, Larry! Well, it is long before Nancy Gollagher ever thought it would come to that with her! That she would be left dissolute and alone here by her *baste* of a husband, for a woman without a head! Oh, father, father! and oh, mother, mother! it is well you are low to-day!—that you don't see this affliction and disgrace to your daughter that you reared decent and tender. Oh, Larry, you villian, you'll be the death of your lawful wife, going after such—O—O—O—"

"Well," says Larry, putting his hands in his coat-pockets, "least said is soonest mended. Of the young woman I know no more than I do of Moll Flanders; but this I know, that a woman without a head may well be called a Good Woman, because she has no tongue!"

How this remark operated on the matrimonial dispute history does not inform us. It is, however, reported that the lady had the last word.

II

HANLON'S MILL

ONE fine summer's evening Michael Noonan went over to Jack Brien's the shoemaker, at Ballyduff, for the pair of brogues which Jack was mending for him. It was a pretty walk the way he took, but very lonesome; all along by the river-side, down under the oak-wood, till he came to Hanlon's mill, that used to be, but that had gone to ruin many a long year ago.

Melancholy enough the walls of that same mill looked; the great old wheel, black with age, all covered over with moss and ferns, and the bushes all hanging down about it. There it stood, silent and motionless; and a sad contrast it was to its former busy clack, with the stream which once gave it use rippling idly along.

Old Hanlon was a man that had great knowledge of all sorts; there was not an herb that grew in the field but he could tell the name of it and its use, out of a big book he had written, every word of it in the real Irish *karacter*. He kept a school once, and could teach the Latin; that surely is a blessed tongue all over the wide world; and I hear tell as how "the great Burke" went to school to him. Master Edmund lived up at the old house there, which was then in the family, and it was the Nagles that got it afterwards, but they sold it.

But it was Michael Noonan's walk I was about speaking of. It was fairly between lights, the day was clean gone, and the moon was not yet up, when Mick was walking smartly across the Inch. Well, he heard, coming down out of the wood, such blowing of horns and hallooing, and the cry of all the hounds in the world, and he thought they were coming after him; and the galloping of the horses, and the voice of the whipper-in, and he shouting out, just like the fine old song—

"Hallo, Piper, Lilly, agus Finder !"

and the echo over from the grey rock across the river giving back every word as plainly as it was spoken. But nothing could Mick see, and the shouting and hallooing following him every step of the way till he got up to Jack Brien's door ; and he was certain, too, he heard the clack of old Hanlon's mill going, through all the clatter. To be sure, he ran as fast as fear and his legs would carry him, and never once looked behind him, well knowing that the Duhallow hounds were out in quite another quarter that day, and that nothing good could come out of the noise of Hanlon's mill.

Well, Michael Noonan got his brogues, and well heeled they were, and well pleased was he with them, when who should be seated at Jack Brien's before him but a gossip of his—one Darby Haynes, a mighty decent man, that had a horse and car of his own, and that used to be travelling with it, taking loads like the Royal Mail coach between Cork and Limerick ; and when he was at home Darby was a near neighbour of Michael Noonan's.

"Is it home you're going with the brogues this blessed night ?" said Darby to him.

"Where else would it be ?" replied Mick. "But, by my word, 'tis not across the Inch back again I'm going, after all I heard coming here. 'Tis to no good that old Hanlon's mill is busy again."

"True for you," said Darby. "And maybe you'd take the horse and car home for me, Mick, by way of company, as 'tis along the road you go. I'm waiting here to see a sister's son of mine that I expect from Kilcoleman." "That same I'll do," answered Mick, "with a thousand welcomes." So Mick drove the car fair and easy, knowing that the poor beast had come off a long journey ; and Mick—God reward him for it !—was always tender-hearted and good to the dumb creatures.

The night was a beautiful one ; the moon was better than a quarter old ; and Mick, looking up at her, could not help bestowing a blessing on her beautiful face, shining down so sweetly upon the gentle Awbeg. He had now got out of the open road, and had come to where the trees grew on each side of it : he proceeded for some space in the chequered light which the moon gave through them. At one time, when a big old tree got between him and the moon, it was so dark that he could hardly see the horse's head; then, as he passed on, the moonbeams would stream through the open boughs and variegate the road with light and shade. Mick was lying down in the car at his ease, having got clear of the plantation, and was watching the bright piece of a moon in a little pool at the roadside, when he saw it disappear all of a sudden as if a great cloud came over the sky. He turned round on his elbow to see if it was so; but how was Mick astonished at finding, close alongside of the car, a great, high black coach drawn by six black horses, with long black tails reaching almost down to the ground, and a coachman dressed all in black sitting up on the box. But what surprised Mick the most was, that he could see no sign of a head either upon coachman or horses. It swept rapidly by him, and he could perceive the horses raising their feet as if they were in a fine slinging trot, the coachman touching them up with his long whip, and the wheels spinning round like hoddy-doddies; still he could hear no noise—only the regular step of his gossip Darby's horse, and the squeaking of the gudgeons of the car, that were as good as lost entirely for want of a little grease.

Poor Mick's heart almost died within him, but he said nothing, only looked on; and the black coach swept away, and was soon lost among some distant trees. Mick saw nothing more of it, or, indeed, of anything else. He got home just as the moon was going down behind Mount Hillery, took the tackling off the horse, turned the beast out in the field for the night, and got to his bed.

Next morning early, he was standing at the roadside, thinking of all that had happened the night before, when he saw Dan Madden, that was Mr. Wrixon's huntsman, coming on the master's best horse down the hill, as hard as ever he went at the tail of the hounds. Mick's mind instantly misgave him that all was not right, so he stood out in the very middle of the road, and caught hold of Dan's bridle when he came up.

"Mick dear—for the love of God, don't stop me!" cried Dan.

"Why, what's the hurry?" said Mick.

"Oh, the master!—he's off—he's off—he'll never cross a horse again till the Day of Judgment!"

"Why, what would ail his honour?" said Mick. "Sure, it is no later than yesterday morning that I was talking to him, and he stout and hearty; and says he to me, 'Mick,' says he—"

"Stout and hearty was he?" answered Madden. "And was he not out with me in the kennel last night when I was feeding the dogs? and didn't he come out to the stable, and give a ball to Peg Pullaway with his own hand, and tell me he'd ride the old General to-day? And sure," said Dan, wiping his eyes with the sleeve of his coat, "who'd have thought that the first thing I'd see this morning was the mistress standing at my bedside, and bidding me get up and ride off like fire for Doctor Galway! for the master had got a fit, and—" poor Dan's grief choked his voice—"oh, Mick! if you have a heart in you, run over yourself, or send the gossoon for Kate Finnigan, the midwife; she's a cruel skilful woman, and maybe she might save the master, till I get the doctor."

Dan struck his spurs into the hunter, and Michael Noonan flung off his newly-mended brogues, and cut across the fields to Kate Finnigan's; but neither the doctor nor Katty was of any avail, and the next night's moon saw Ballygibblin—and more's the pity!—a house of mourning.

III

THE HEADLESS HORSEMAN

"God speed you, and a safe journey this night to you, Charley," ejaculated the master of the little shebeen house at Ballyhooley after his old friend and good customer, Charley Culnane, who at length had turned his face homewards, with the prospect of as dreary a ride and as dark a night as ever fell upon the Blackwater, along the banks of which he was about to journey.

Charley Culnane knew the country well, and, moreover, was as bold a rider as any Mallow-boy that ever *rattled* a four-year-old upon Drumrue race-course. He had gone to Fermoy in the morning, as well for the purpose of purchasing some ingredients required for the Christmas dinner by his wife as to gratify his own vanity by having new reins fitted to his snaffle, in which he intended showing off the old mare at the approaching St. Stephen's Day hunt.

Charley did not get out of Fermoy until late; for although he was not one of your "nasty particular sort of fellows" in anything that related to the common occurrences of life, yet in all the appointments connected with hunting, riding, leaping—in short, in whatever was connected with the old mare, "Charley," the saddlers said, "was the devil to *plāse*." An illustration of this fastidiousness was afforded by his going such a distance for his snaffle bridle. Mallow was full twelve miles nearer "Charley's farm" (which lay just three-quarters of a mile below Carrick) than Fermoy; but Charley had quarrelled with all the Mallow saddlers, from hard-working and hard-drinking Tim Clancey, up to Mr. Ryan, who wrote himself "Saddler to the Duhallow Hunt"; and no one could content him in all particulars but honest Michael Twomey of Fermoy, who used to assert—and who will doubt it ?—that he could stitch a saddle better than the lord-lieutenant, although they made him all as one as king over Ireland.

This delay in the arrangement of the snaffle bridle did not allow Charley Culnane to pay so long a visit as he had at first intended to his old friend and gossip, Con Buckley, of the " Harp of Erin." Con, however, knew the value of time, and insisted upon Charley making good use of what he had to spare. " I won't bother you waiting for water, Charley, because I think you'll have enough of that same before you get home ; so drink off your liquor, man. It's as good *parliament* as ever a gentleman tasted—aye, and holy Church too, for it will bear ' X *waters*,' and carry the bead after that, maybe."

Charley, it must be confessed, nothing loth, drank success to Con, and success to the jolly Harp of Erin, with its head of beauty and its strings of the hair of gold, and to their better acquaintance, and so on, from the bottom of his soul, until the bottom of the bottle reminded him that Carrick was at the bottom of the hill on the other side of Castletown Roche, and that he had got no farther on his journey than his gossip's at Ballyhooley, close to the big gate of Convamore. Catching hold of his oilskin hat, therefore, whilst Con Buckley went to the cupboard for another bottle of the " real stuff," he regularly, as it is termed, bolted from his friend's hospitality, darted to the stable, tightened his girths, and put the old mare into a canter towards home.

The road from Ballyhooley to Carrick follows pretty nearly the course of the Blackwater, occasionally diverging from the river and passing through rather wild scenery, when contrasted with the beautiful seats that adorn its banks. Charley cantered gaily, regardless of the rain, which, as his friend Con had anticipated, fell in torrents. The good woman's currants and raisins were carefully packed between the folds of his yeomanry cloak, which Charley, who was proud of showing that he belonged to the " Royal Mallow Light Horse Volunteers," always strapped to the saddle before him, and took care never to destroy the military effect by putting it on. Away he went singing like a thrush—

> " Sporting, belleing, dancing, drinking,
>   Breaking windows—(*hiccup !*)—sinking,
>   Ever raking—never thinking,
>   Live the rakes of Mallow.

> " Spending faster than it comes,
>   Beating—(*hiccup, hic*)—and duns,
>   Duhallow's true-begotten sons,
>   Live the rakes of Mallow."

Notwithstanding that the visit to the jolly Harp of Erin had a little increased the natural complacency of his mind, the drenching of the new snaffle reins began to disturb him ; and then followed a train of more anxious thoughts than even were occasioned by the dreaded defeat of the pride of his long-anticipated *turn-out* on St. Stephen's Day. In an hour of good fellowship, when his heart was warm, and his head not over-cool, Charley had backed the old mare against Mr. Jephson's bay filly Desdemona for a neat hundred, and he now felt sore misgivings as to the prudence of the match. In a less gay tone he continued :

> " Living short but merry lives,
> Going where the devil drives,
> Keeping—"

" Keeping," he muttered, as the old mare had reduced her canter to a trot at the bottom of Kilcummer Hill. Charley's eye fell on the old walls that belonged, in former times, to the Templars ; but the silent gloom of the ruin was broken only by the heavy rain which splashed and pattered on the grave-stones. He then looked up at the sky, to see if there was, among the clouds, any hopes for mercy on his new snaffle reins ; and no sooner were his eyes lowered, than his attention was arrested by an object so extraordinary as almost led him to doubt the evidence of his senses. The head, apparently, of a white horse, with short, cropped ears, large, open nostrils, and immense eyes, seemed rapidly to follow him. No connection with body, legs or rider could possibly be traced—the head advanced—Charley's old mare, too, was moved at this unnatural sight, and snorting violently, increased her trot up the hill. The head moved forward, and passed on. Charley, pursuing it with astonished gaze, and wondering by what means, and for what purpose, this detached head thus proceeded through the air, did not perceive the corresponding body until he was suddenly startled by finding it close at his side. Charlie turned to examine what was thus so sociably jogging on with him, when a most unex-ampled apparition presented itself to his view. A figure, whose height (judging as well as the obscurity of the night would permit him) he computed to be at least eight feet, was seated on the body and legs of a white horse full eighteen hands and a half high. In this measurement Charley could not be mistaken, for his own mare was exactly fifteen hands, and the body that thus jogged alongside he could at once determine, from his practice in horse-flesh, was at least three hands and a half higher.

After the first feeling of astonishment, which found vent in the exclamation, "I'm sold now for ever !" was over, the attention of Charley, being a keen sportsman, was naturally directed to this extraordinary body ; and having examined it with the eye of a connoisseur, he proceeded to reconnoitre the figure so unusually mounted, who had hitherto remained perfectly mute. Wishing to see whether his companion's silence proceeded from bad temper, want of conversational powers, or from a distaste to water, and the fear that the opening of his mouth might subject him to have it filled by the rain, which was then drifting in violent gusts against them, Charley endeavoured to catch a sight of his companion's face, in order to form an opinion on that point. But his vision failed in carrying him farther than the top of the collar of the figure's coat, which was a scarlet single-breasted hunting-frock, having a waist of a very old-fashioned cut reaching to the saddle, with two huge shining buttons at about a yard distance behind. "I ought to see farther than this too," thought Charlie, "although he is mounted on his high horse, like my cousin Darby, who was made barony constable last week, unless 'tis Con's whisky that has blinded me entirely." However, see farther he could not, and after straining his eyes for a considerable time to no purpose, he exclaimed, with pure vexation : "By the big bridge of Mallow, it is no head at all he has ! "

"Look again, Charley Culnane," said a hoarse voice, that seemed to proceed from under the right arm of the figure.

Charley did look again, and now in the proper place, for he clearly saw, under the aforesaid right arm, that head from which the voice had proceeded, and such a head no mortal ever saw before. It looked like a large cream cheese hung round with black puddings ; no speck of colour enlivened the ashy paleness of the depressed features ; the skin lay stretched over the unearthly surface, almost like the parchment head of a drum. Two fiery eyes of prodigious circumference, with a strange and irregular motion, flashed like meteors upon Charley; and to complete all, a mouth reached from either extremity of two ears, which peeped forth from under a profusion of matted locks of lustreless blackness. This head, which the figure had evidently hitherto concealed from Charley's eyes, now burst upon his view in all its hideousness. Charley, although a lad of proverbial courage in the county of Cork, yet could not but feel his nerves a little shaken by this unexpected visit from the headless horseman, whom he considered his fellow-traveller must be. The cropped-eared head of the gigantic horse moved steadily forward, always keeping from six to eight yards in advance. The horseman, unaided by whip or spur, and disdaining the use of stirrups, which dangled uselessly from the saddle, followed at a trot by Charlie's side, his hideous head now lost behind the lappet of his coat, now starting forth in all its horror, as the motion of the horse caused his arm to move to and fro. The ground shook under the weight of its supernatural burden, and the water in the pools became agitated into waves as he trotted by them.

On they went—heads without bodies, and bodies without heads. The deadly silence of night was broken only by the fearful clattering of hoofs and the distant sound of thunder, which rumbled above the mystic hill of Cecaune a Mona Finnea. Charley, who was naturally a merry - hearted and rather a talkative fellow, had hitherto felt tongue-tied by apprehension, but finding his companion showed no evil disposition towards him, and having become somewhat more reconciled to the Patagonian dimensions of the horseman and his headless steed, plucked up all his courage, and thus addressed the stranger :

" Why, then, your honour rides mighty well without the stirrups ! "

" Humph ! " growled the head from under the horseman's right arm.

" 'Tis not an over-civil answer," thought Charley ; " but no matter, he was taught in one of them riding-houses, maybe, and thinks nothing at all about bumping his leather breeches at the rate of ten miles an hour. I'll try him on the other tack. Ahem ! " said Charley, clearing his throat, and feeling at the same time rather daunted at this second attempt to establish a conversation. " Ahem ! that's a mighty neat coat of your honour's, although 'tis a little too long in the waist for the present cut."

" Humph ! " growled again the head.

This second " humph " was a terrible thump in the face to poor Charley, who was fairly bothered to know what subject he could start that would prove more agreeable. " 'Tis a sensible head," thought Charley, " although an ugly one, for 'tis plain enough the man does not like flattery." A third attempt, however, Charley was determined to make, and having failed in his observations as to the riding and coat of his fellow-traveller, thought he would just drop a trifling allusion to the wonderful headless horse that was jogging on so sociably beside his old mare ; and as Charley was considered about Carrick to be very knowing in horses, besides being a full private in the Royal Mallow Light Horse Volunteers, which were every one of them mounted like real Hessians, he felt rather sanguine as to the result of his third attempt.

" To be sure, that's a brave horse your honour rides," recommenced the persevering Charley.

" You may say that with your own ugly mouth," growled the head,

Charley, though not much flattered by the compliment, nevertheless chuckled at his success in obtaining an answer, and thus continued :

"Maybe your honour wouldn't be after riding him across the country ? "

"Will you try me, Charley ? " said the head, with an inexpressible look of ghastly delight.

"Faith, and that's what I'd do," responded Charley ; " only I'm afraid, the night being so dark, of laming the old mare, and I've every halfpenny of a hundred pounds on her heels."

This was true enough. Charley's courage was nothing dashed at the headless horseman's proposal, and there never was a steeple-chase nor a fox-chase, riding or leaping in the country, that Charley Culnane was not at it and foremost in it.

"Will you take my word," said the man, who carried his head so snugly under his right arm, " for the safety of your mare ? "

"Done ! " said Charley, and away they started, helter-skelter, over everything, ditch and wall, pop, pop. The old mare never went in such style, even in broad daylight, and Charley had just the start of his companion, when the hoarse voice called out : " Charley Culnane, Charley, man, stop for your life, stop ! "

Charley pulled up hard. "Aye," said he, " you may beat me by the head, because it always goes so much before you, but if the bet was neck-and-neck, and that's the go between the old mare and Desdemona, I'd win it hollow."

It appeared as if the stranger was well aware of what was passing in Charley's mind, for he suddenly broke out quite loquacious.

"Charley Culnane," says he, " you have a stout soul in you, and are every inch of you a good rider. I've tried you, and I ought to know ; and that's the sort of man for my money. A hundred years it is since my horse and I broke our necks at the bottom of Kilcummer Hill, and ever since I have been trying tc get a man that dared to ride with me, and never found one before. Keep, as you have always done, at the tail of the hounds ; never baulk a ditch, nor turn away from a stone wall, and the headless horseman will never desert you nor the old mare."

Charley, in amazement, looked towards the stranger's right arm, for the purpose of seeing in his face whether or not he was in earnest ; but behold ! the head was snugly lodged in the huge pocket of the horseman's scarlet hunting-coat. The horse's head had ascended perpendicularly above them, and his extraordinary companion, rising quickly after his *avant-coureur*, vanished from the astonished gaze of Charley Culnane.

Charley, as may be supposed, was lost in wonder, delight and perplexity. The pelting rain, the wife's pudding, the new snaffle —even the match against Squire Jephson—all were forgotten ; nothing could he think of, nothing could he talk of, but the headless horseman. He told it, directly that he got home, to Judy ; he told it the following morning to all the neighbours ; and he told it to the hunt on St. Stephen's Day ; but what provoked him after all the pains he took in describing the head, the horse and the man, was that one and all attributed the creation of the headless horseman to his friend Con Buckley's " X water parliament." This, however, should be told, that Charley's old mare beat Mr. Jephson's bay filly Desdemona, by Diamond, and Charley pocketed his cool hundred ; and if he didn't win by means of the headless horseman, I am sure I don't know any other reason for his doing so.

NOTE.—DULLAHAN or DULACHAN signifies a dark, sullen person. The word *Durrachan* or *Dullahan*, by which in some places the goblin is known, has the same signification. It comes from *Dorr* or *Durr*, anger, or *Durrach*, malicious, fierce, etc.

The Death Coach, or Headless Coach and Horses, is called in Ireland " *Coach a bower*," and its appearance is generally regarded as a sign of death, or an omen of some misfortune. The belief in the appearance of headless people and horses appears to be like most popular superstitions, widely extended.

LEGENDS OF THE FIR DARRIG

I

DIARMID BAWN, THE PIPER

ONE stormy night Patrick Burke was seated in the chimney-corner, smoking his pipe quite contentedly after his hard day's work ; his two little boys were roasting potatoes in the ashes, while his rosy daughter held a splinter to her mother, who, seated on a siesteen, was mending a rent in Patrick's old coat ; and Judy, the maid, was singing merrily to the sound of her wheel, that kept up a beautiful humming noise, just like the sweet drone of a bagpipe. Indeed, they all seemed quite contented and happy, for the storm howled without, and they were warm and snug within, by the side of a blazing turf fire. " I was just thinking," said Patrick, taking the dudeen from his mouth and giving it a rap on his thumb-nail to shake out the ashes—" I was just thinking how thankful we ought to be to having a snug bit of a cabin this pelting night over our heads, for in all my born days I never heard the like of it."

" And that's no lie for you, Pat," said his wife ; " but whisht !

what noise is that I *hard?*" and she dropped her work upon her knees, and looked fearfully towards the door. "The *Vargin* herself defend us all!" cried Judy, at the same time rapidly making a pious sign on her forehead, "if 'tis not the Banshee!"

"Hold your tongue, you fool," said Patrick, "it's only the old gate swinging in the wind;" and he had scarcely spoken, when the door was assailed by a violent knocking. Molly began to mumble her prayers, and Judy proceeded to mutter over the muster-roll of saints; the youngsters scampered off to hide themselves behind the settle-bed; the storm howled louder and more fiercely than ever, and the rapping was renewed with redoubled violence.

"Whist, whist!" said Patrick; "what a noise ye're all making about nothing at all. Judy a-roon, can't you go and see who's at the door?" for, notwithstanding his assumed bravery, Pat Burke preferred that the maid should open the door.

"Why, then, is it me you're speaking to?" said Judy, in the tone of astonishment; "and is it cracked mad you are, Mister Burke, or is it, maybe, that you want me to be *rund* away with, and made a horse of, like my grandfather was? The sorrow a step will I stir to open the door, if you were as great a man again as you are, Pat Burke."

"Bother you, then! and hold your tongue, and I'll go myself." So saying, up got Patrick, and made the best of his way to the door. "Who's there?" said he, and his voice trembled mightily all the while. "In the name of Saint Patrick, who's there?" "'Tis I, Pat," answered a voice, which he immediately knew to be the young Squire's. In a moment the door was opened, and in walked a young man, with a gun in his hand and a brace of dogs at his heels. "Your honour's honour is quite welcome, entirely," said Patrick, who was a very civil sort of a fellow, especially to his betters. "Your honour's honour is quite welcome, and if ye'll be so condescending as to demean yourself by taking off your wet jacket, Molly can give you a bran-new blanket, and ye can sit forenent the fire while the clothes are drying."

"Thank you, Pat," said the Squire, as he wrapt himself, like Mr. Weld, in the proffered blanket. "But what made you keep me so long at the door?"

"Why, then, your honour, 'twas all along of Judy there, being so much afraid of the good people; and a good right she has, after what happened to her grandfather—the Lord rest his soul!"

"And what was that, Pat?" said the Squire.

"Why, then, your honour must know that Judy had a grandfather; and he was *ould* Diarmid Bawn, the piper, as personable a looking man as any in the five parishes he was, and he could play the pipes so sweetly, and make them *spake* to such perfection, that it did one's heart good to hear him. We never had anyone, for that matter, in this side of the country like him, before or since, except James Gandsey, that is own piper to Lord Headley —his honour's lordship is the real good gentleman—and 'tis Mr. Gandsey's music that is the pride of Killarney Lakes. Well, as I was saying, Diarmid was Judy's grandfather, and he rented a small mountainy farm; and he was walking about the fields one moonlight night, quite melancholy-like in himself for want of the *tobaccy*, because why, the river was flooded, and he could not get across to buy any, and Diarmid would rather go to bed without his supper than a whiff of the dudeen. Well, your honour, just as he came to the old fort in the far field, what should he see ?—the Lord preserve us !—but a large army of the good people, 'coutered for all the world just like the dragoons ! ' Are ye all ready ? ' said a little fellow at their head dressed out like a general. ' No,' said a little curmudgeon of a chap all dressed in red, from the crown of his cocked hat to the sole of his boot. ' No, general,' said he ; ' if you don't get the Fir Darrig a horse he must stay behind, and ye'll lose the battle.'

" ' There's Diarmid Bawn,' said the general, pointing to Judy's grandfather, your honour ; ' make a horse of him.'

"So with that Master Fir Darrig comes up to Diarmid, who, you may be sure, was in a mighty great fright ; but he determined, seeing there was no help for him, to put a bold face on the matter, and so he began to cross himself, and to say some blessed words, that nothing bad could stand before.

" ' Is that what you'd be after, you spalpeen ? ' said the little red imp, at the same time grinning a horrible grin. ' I'm not a man to care a straw for either your words or your crossings.' So, without more to do, he gives poor Diarmid a rap with the flat side of his sword, and in a moment he was changed into a horse, with little Fir Darrig stuck fast on his back.

"Away they all flew over the wide ocean, like so many wild geese, screaming and chattering all the time, till they came to Jamaica ; and there they had a murdering fight with the good people of that country. Well, it was all very well with them, and they stuck to it manfully, and fought it out fairly, till one of the Jamaica men made a cut with his sword under Diarmid's left eye. And then, sir, you see, poor Diarmid lost his temper entirely, and he dashed into the very middle of them, with Fir Darrig mounted upon his back, and he threw out his heels, and he whisked his tail about, and wheeled and turned round and round at such a rate that he soon made a fair clearance of them, horse, foot and dragoons. At last Diarmid's faction got the better, all through his means ; and then they had such feasting and rejoicing, and gave Diarmid, who was the finest horse amongst them all, the best of everything.

" 'Let every man take a hand of *tobaccy* for Diarmid Bawn,' said the general; and so they did; and away they flew, for 'twas getting near morning, to the old fort back again, and there they vanished like the mist from the mountain.

"When Diarmid looked about, the sun was rising, and he thought it was all a dream, till he saw a big rick of *tobaccy* in the old fort, and felt the blood running from his left eye: for sure enough, he was wounded in the battle, and would have been *kilt* entirely, if it wasn't for a gospel composed by Father Murphy that hung about his neck ever since he had the scarlet fever; and for certain, it was enough to have given him another scarlet fever to have had the little red man all night on his back, whip and spur for the bare life. However, there was the *tobaccy* heaped up in a great heap by his side; and he heard a voice, although he could see no one, telling him, 'That 'twas all his own, for his good behaviour in the battle; and that whenever Fir Darrig would want a horse again he'd know where to find a clever beast, as he never rode a better than Diarmid Bawn.' That's what he said, sir."

"Thank you, Pat," said the Squire; "it certainly is a wonderful story, and I am not surprised at Judy's alarm. But now, as the storm is over, and the moon shining brightly, I'll make the best of my way home." So saying, he disrobed himself of the blanket, put on his coat, and whistling his dogs, set off across the mountain; while Patrick stood at the door, bawling after him: "May God and the blessed Virgin preserve your honour, and keep ye from the good people; for 'twas of a moonlight night like this that Diarmid Bawn was made a horse of, for the Fir Darrig to ride."

II

TEIGUE OF THE LEE

"I CAN'T stop in the house—I won't stop in it for all the money that is buried in the old castle of Carrigrohan. If ever there was such a thing in the world!—to be abused to my face night and day, and nobody to the fore doing it! and then, if I'm angry, to be laughed at with a great roaring ho, ho, ho! I won't stay in the house after to-night, if there was not another place in the country to put my head under." This angry soliloquy was pronounced in the hall of the old manor-house of Carrigrohan by John Sheehan. John was a new servant: he had been only three days in the house, which had the character of being haunted, and in that short space of time he had been abused and laughed at by a voice which sounded as if a man spoke with his head in a cask; nor could he discover who was the speaker, or from whence the voice came. "I'll not stop here," said John; "and that ends the matter."

"Ho, ho, ho! be quiet, John Sheehan, or else worse will happen to you."

John instantly ran to the hall window, as the words were evidently spoken by a person immediately outside, but no one was visible. He had scarcely placed his face at the pane of glass when he heard another loud "Ho, ho, ho!" as if behind him in the hall. As quick as lightning he turned his head, but no living thing was to be seen.

"Ho, ho, ho, John!" shouted a voice that appeared to come from the lawn before the house; "do you think you'll see Teigue? Oh, never! as long as you live! so leave alone looking after him, and mind your business; there's plenty of company to dinner from Cork to be here to-day, and 'tis time you had the cloth laid."

"Lord bless us! there's more of it! I'll never stay another day here," repeated John.

"Hold your tongue, and stay where you are quietly, and play no tricks on Mr. Pratt, as you did on Mr. Jervois about the spoons."

John Sheehan was confounded by this address from his invisible persecutor, but nevertheless he mustered courage enough to say: "Who are you? Come here, and let me see you, if you are a man." But he received in reply only a laugh of unearthly derision, which was followed by a "Good-bye—I'll watch you at dinner, John!"

"Lord between us and harm! this beats all!—I'll watch you at dinner!—maybe you will; 'tis the broad daylight, so 'tis no ghost. But this is a terrible place, and this is the last day I'll stay in it. How does he know about the spoons? If he tells it, I'm a ruined man! There was no living soul could tell it to him but Tim Barrett, and he's far enough off in the wilds of Botany Bay now, so how could he know it?—I can't tell for the world! But what's that I see there at the corner of the wall? 'Tis not a man!—oh, what a fool I am!—'tis only the old stump of a tree! But this is a shocking place—I'll never stop in it, for I'll leave the house to-morrow; the very look of it is enough to frighten anyone."

The mansion had certainly an air of desolation. It was situated in a lawn, which had nothing to break its uniform level, save a few tufts of narcissuses and a couple of old trees coeval with the building. The house stood at a short distance from the road; it was upwards of a century old, and Time was doing his work upon it; its walls were weather-stained in all colours, its roof showed various white patches, it had no look of comfort; all was dim and dingy without, and within there was an air of gloom, of departed and departing greatness, which harmonised well with the exterior. It required all the exuberance of youth and of gaiety to remove the impression, almost amounting to awe, with which you trod the huge square hall, paced along the gallery which surrounded the hall, or explored the long rambling passages below stairs. The ball-room, as the large drawing-room was called, and several other apartments, were in a state of decay: the walls were stained with damp; and I remember well the sensation of awe which I felt creeping over me when, boy as I was, and full of boyish life, and wild and ardent spirits, I descended to the vaults; all without and within me became chilled beneath their dampness and gloom—their extent, too, terrified me; nor could the merriment of my two schoolfellows, whose father, a respectable clergyman, rented the dwelling for a time, dispel the feelings of a romantic imagination, until I once again ascended to the upper regions.

John had pretty well recovered himself as the dinner-hour approached, and the several guests arrived. They were all seated at table, and had begun to enjoy the excellent repast, when a voice was heard from the lawn:

"Ho, ho, ho! Mr. Pratt; won't you give poor Teigue some dinner? Ho, ho! fine company you have here, and plenty of everything that's good. Sure, you won't forget poor Teigue?"

John dropped the glass he had in his hand.

"Who is that?" said Mr. Pratt's brother, an officer of the artillery.

"That is Teigue," said Mr. Pratt, laughing, "whom you must often have heard me mention."

"And pray, Mr. Pratt," inquired another gentleman, "who *is* Teigue!"

"That," he replied, "is more than I can tell. No one has ever been able to catch even a glimpse of him. I have been on the watch for a whole evening with three of my sons, yet, although his voice sometimes sounded almost in my ear, I could not see him. I fancied, indeed, that I saw a man in a white frieze jacket pass into the door from the garden to the lawn, but it could be only fancy, for I found the door locked, while the fellow, whoever he is, was laughing at our trouble. He visits us occasionally, and sometimes a long interval passes between his visits, as in the present case; it is now nearly two years since we heard that hollow voice outside the window. He has never done any injury that we know of, and once when he broke a plate, he brought one back exactly like it."

"It is very extraordinary," said several of the company.

"But," remarked a gentleman to young Mr. Pratt, "your father said he broke a plate; how did he get it without seeing him?"

"When he asks for some dinner, we put it outside the window and go away; whilst we watch he will not take it, but no sooner have we withdrawn, than it is gone."

"How does he know that you are watching?"

"That's more than I can tell, but he either knows or suspects. One day my brothers Robert and James, with myself, were in our back parlour, which has a window into the garden, when he came outside and said: 'Ho, ho, ho! Master James and Robert and Henry, give poor Teigue a glass of whisky.' James went out of the room, filled a glass with whisky, vinegar and salt, and brought it to him. 'Here, Teigue,' said he, 'come for it now.' 'Well, put it down, then, on the step outside the window.' This was done, and we stood looking at it. 'There now, go away,' he shouted. We retired, but still watched it. 'Ho, ho! you are watching Teigue; go out of the room, now, or I won't take it.' We went outside the door and returned; the glass was gone, and a moment after we heard him roaring and cursing frightfully. He took away the glass, but the next day the glass was on the stone step under the window, and there were crumbs of bread in the inside, as if he had put it in his pocket; from that time he was not heard till to-day."

"Oh," said the Colonel, "I'll get a sight of him; you are not used to these things; an old soldier has the best chance. And as I shall finish my dinner with this wing, I'll be ready for him when he speaks next. Mr. Bell, will you take a glass of wine with me?"

"Ho, ho! Mr. Bell," shouted Teigue. "Ho, ho! Mr. Bell; you were a Quaker long ago. Ho, ho! Mr. Bell, you're a pretty boy; a pretty Quaker you were; and now you're no Quaker, nor anything else; ho, ho! Mr. Bell. And there's Mr. Parkes; to be sure, Mr. Parkes looks mighty fine to-day, with his powdered head, and his grand silk stockings, and his bran-new rakish-red waistcoat. And there's Mr. Cole—did you ever see such a fellow? A pretty company you've brought together, Mr. Pratt: kiln-dried Quakers, butter-buying buckeens from Mallow Lane, and a drinking exciseman from the Coal Quay, to meet the great thundering artillery-general that is come out of the Indies, and is the biggest dust of them all."

"You scoundrel!" exclaimed the Colonel; "I'll make you show yourself!" and snatching up his sword from a corner of the room, he sprang out of the window upon the lawn. In a moment a shout of laughter, so hollow, so unlike any human sound, made him stop, as well as Mr. Bell, who, with a huge oak stick, was close at the Colonel's heels; others of the party followed on the lawn, and the remainder rose and went to the windows. "Come on, Colonel," said Mr. Bell; "let us catch this impudent rascal."

"Ho, ho! Mr. Bell, here I am—here's Teigue—why don't you catch me? Ho, ho! Colonel Pratt, what a pretty soldier you are to draw your sword upon poor Teigue, that never did anybody harm."

"Let us see your face, you scoundrel!" said the Colonel.

"Ho, ho, ho!—look at me, look at me! Do you see the wind, Colonel Pratt? You'll see Teigue as soon; so go in and finish your dinner."

"If you're upon the earth I'll find you, you villain!" said the Colonel, whilst the same unearthly shout of derision seemed to come from behind an angle of the building. "He's round that corner," said Mr. Bell—"run, run."

They followed the sound, which was continued at intervals along the garden-wall, but could discover no human being. At last both stopped to draw breath, and in an instant, almost at their ears, sounded the shout:

"Ho, ho, ho! Colonel Pratt; do you see Teigue now? Do you hear him? Ho, ho, ho! you're a fine colonel to follow the wind."

"Not that way, Mr. Bell—not that way. Come here," said the Colonel.

"Ho, ho, ho! what a fool you are. Do you think Teigue is going to show himself to you in the field there? But, Colonel, follow me if you can—you a soldier!—ho, ho, ho!" The Colonel was enraged—he followed the voice over hedge and ditch, alternately laughed at and taunted by the unseen object of his pursuit—(Mr. Bell, who was heavy, was soon thrown out), until at length, after being led a weary chase, he found himself at the top of the cliff, over that part of the River Lee which, from its great depth, and the blackness of its water, has received the name of Hell Hole. Here, on the edge of the cliff, stood the Colonel out of breath, and mopping his forehead with his handkerchief, while the voice, which seemed close at his feet, exclaimed: "Now, Colonel Pratt—now, if you're a soldier, here's a leap for you; now look at Teigue—why don't you look at him? Ho, ho, ho! Come along; you're warm, I'm sure, Colonel Pratt, so come in and cool yourself; Teigue is going to have a swim!" The voice seemed as descending amongst the trailing ivy and brushwood which clothes this picturesque cliff nearly from top to bottom, yet it was impossible that any human being could have found footing. "Now, Colonel, have you courage to take the leap? Ho, ho, ho! what a pretty soldier you are.

Good-bye! I'll see you again in ten minutes above, at the house—look at your watch, Colonel; there's a dive for you!" and a heavy plunge into the water was heard. The Colonel stood still, but no sound followed, and he walked slowly back to the house, not quite half a mile from the Crag.

"Well, did you see Teigue?" said his brother, whilst his nephews, scarcely able to smother their laughter, stood by. "Give me some wine," said the Colonel. "I never was led such a dance in my life; the fellow carried me all round and round, till he brought me to the edge of the cliff, and then down he went into Hell Hole, telling me he'd be here in ten minutes. 'Tis more than that now, but he's not come."

"Ho, ho, ho! Colonel; isn't he here? Teigue never told a lie in his life; but, Mr. Pratt, give me a drink and my dinner, and then good-night to you all, for I'm tired; and that's the Colonel's doing." A plate of food was ordered: it was placed by John, with fear and trembling, on the lawn under the window. Everyone kept on the watch, and the plate remained undisturbed for some time.

"Ah, Mr. Pratt! will you starve poor Teigue? Make everyone go away from the windows, and Master Henry out of the tree, and Master Richard off the garden-wall."

The eyes of the company were turned to the tree and the garden-wall; the two boys' attention was occupied in getting down; the visitors were looking at them; and "Ho, ho, ho!—good luck to you, Mr. Pratt! 'tis a good dinner, and there's the plate, ladies and gentlemen—good-bye to you, Colonel—good-bye, Mr. Bell—good-bye to you all!" brought their attention back, when they saw the empty plate lying on the grass; and Teigue's voice was heard no more for that evening. Many visits were afterwards paid by Teigue; but never was he seen, nor was any discovery ever made of his person or character.

III

NED SHEEHY'S EXCUSE

NED SHEEHY was servant-man to Richard Gumbleton, esquire, of Mountbally, Gumbletonmore, in the north of the county of Cork; and a better servant than Ned was not to be found in that honest county, from Cape Clear to the Kilworth Mountains; for nobody—no, not his worst enemy—could say a word against him, only that he was rather given to drinking, idling, lying and loitering, especially the last; for send Ned off a five-minute message at nine o'clock in the morning, and you were a lucky man if you saw him before dinner. If there happened to be a

public-house in the way, or even a little out of it, Ned was sure
to mark it as dead as a pointer; and, knowing everybody, and
everybody liking him, it is not to be wondered at he had so
much to say and to hear, that the time slipped away as if the
sun somehow or other had knocked two hours into one.

But when he came home, he never was short of an excuse; he
had, for that matter, five hundred ready upon the tip of his
tongue; so much so, that I doubt if even the very Reverend
Doctor Swift, for many years Dean of St. Patrick's, in Dublin,
could match him in that particular, though his Reverence had a
pretty way of his own of writing things which brought him into
very decent company. In fact, Ned would fret a saint, but then,
he was so good-humoured a fellow, and really so handy about a
house—for, as he said himself, he was as good as a lady's-maid—
that his master could not find it in his heart to part with him.

In your grand houses—not that I am saying that Richard
Gumbleton, esquire, of Mountbally, Gumbletonmore, did not
keep a good house, but a plain country gentleman, although he
is second cousin to the last high-sheriff of the county, cannot
have all the army of servants that the lord-lieutenant has in the
Castle of Dublin—I say, in your grand houses, you can have a
servant for every kind of thing; but in Mountbally, Gumbletonmore, Ned was expected to please master and mistress; or, as
Councillor Curran said—by the same token, the councillor was
a little dark man—one day that he dined there, on his way to
the Clonmel Assizes, Ned was minister for the home and foreign
departments.

But to make a long story short, Ned Sheehy was a good butler,
and a right good one too; and as for a groom, let him alone with
a horse—he could dress it, or ride it, or shoe it, or physic it, or do
anything with it but make it speak—he was a second whisperer!
—there was not his match in the barony, or the next one neither.
A pack of hounds he could manage well—aye, and ride after them
with the boldest man in the land. It was Ned who leaped the
old Bounds' Ditch at the turn of the boreen of the lands of
Reenascreena after the English captain pulled up on looking at
it, and cried out it was "No go." Ned rode that day Brian
Boru, Mr. Gumbleton's famous chestnut, and people call it Ned
Sheehy's Leap to this hour.

So, you see, it was hard to do without him. However, many a
scolding he got, and although his master often said of an evening,
"I'll turn off Ned," he always forgot to do so in the morning.
These threats mended Ned not a bit; indeed, he was mending the
other way, like bad fish in hot weather.

One cold winter's day, about three o'clock in the afternoon, Mr.
Gumbleton said to him:

"Ned," said he, "go take Modderaroo down to Black Falvey,
the horse-doctor, and bid him look at her knees, for Doctor
Jenkinson, who rode her home last night, has hurt her somehow.
I suppose he thought a parson's horse ought to go upon its knees;
but indeed, it was I was the fool to give her to him at all, for he
sits twenty stone if he sits a pound, and knows no more of riding,
particularly after his third bottle, than I do of preaching. Now,
mind and be back in an hour at furthest, for I want to have the
plate cleaned up properly for dinner, as Sir Augustus O'Toole, you
know, is to dine here to-day. Don't loiter, for your life."

"Is it I, sir?" says Ned. "Well, that beats anything; as
if I'd stop out a minute!" So, mounting Modderaroo, off he
set.

Four, five, six o'clock came, and so did Sir Augustus and Lady
O'Toole, and the four Misses O'Toole, and Mr. O'Toole, and Mr.
Edward O'Toole, and Mr. James O'Toole, which were all the
young O'Tooles that were at home; but no Ned Sheehy appeared
to clean the plate, or to lay the table-cloth, or even to put dinner
on. It is needless to say how Mr. and Mrs. Dick Gumbleton
fretted and fumed, but it was all to no use. They did their best,
however, only it was a disgrace to see Long Jem, the stable-boy,
and Bill, the gossoon, that used to go of errands, waiting, without
anybody to direct them, when there was a real baronet and his
lady at table, for Sir Augustus was none of your knights. But a
good bottle of claret makes up for much, and it was not one only
they had that night. However, it is not to be concealed that
Mr. Dick Gumbleton went to bed very cross, and he awoke still
crosser.

He heard that Ned had not made his appearance for the whole
night, so he dressed himself in a great fret, and, taking his
horsewhip in his hand, he said:

"There is no further use in tolerating this scoundrel. I'll go
look for him, and if I find him, I'll cut the soul out of his vagabond
body! I will, by—"

"Don't swear, Dick dear," said Mrs. Gumbleton (for she was
always a mild woman, being daughter of fighting Tom Crofts, who
shot a couple of gentlemen, friends of his, in the cool of the
evening after the Mallow Races, one after the other)—"don't swear,
Dick dear," said she; "but do, my dear, oblige me by cutting the
flesh off his bones, for he richly deserves it. I was quite ashamed
of Lady O'Toole yesterday, I was, 'pon honour."

Out sallied Mr. Gumbleton, and he had not far to walk, for not
more than two hundred yards from the house, he found Ned
lying fast asleep under a ditch (a hedge), and Modderaroo standing
by him, poor beast, shaking in every limb. The loud snoring of
Ned, who was lying with his head upon a stone as easy and as

comfortable as if it had been a bed of down or a hop-bag, drew him to the spot, and Mr. Gumbleton at once perceived, from the disarray of Ned's face and person, that he had been engaged in some perilous adventure during the night. Ned appeared not to have descended in the most regular manner, for one of his shoes remained sticking in the stirrup, and his hat, having rolled down a little slope, was embedded in green mud. Mr. Gumbleton, however, did not give himself much trouble to make a curious survey, but with a vigorous application of his thong, soon banished sleep from the eyes of Ned Sheehy.

"Ned!" thundered his master, in great indignation—and on this occasion it was not a word and blow, for with that one word came half a dozen. "Get up, you scoundrel," said he.

Ned roared lustily, and no wonder, for his master's hand was not one of the lightest; and he cried out, between sleeping and waking: "Oh, sir!—don't be angry, sir!—don't be angry, and I'll roast you easier—easy as a lamb!"

"Roast me easier, you vagabond!" said Mr. Gumbleton. "What do you mean? I'll roast you, my lad. Where were you all night? Modderaroo will never get over it. Pack out of my service, you worthless villain, this moment; and indeed, you may give God thanks that I don't get you transported."

"Thank God, master dear," said Ned, who was now perfectly awakened—"it's yourself, anyhow. There never was a gentleman in the whole county ever did so good a turn to a poor man as your honour has been after doing to me; the Lord reward you for that same. Oh, but strike me again, and let me feel that it is yourself, master dear—may whisky be my poison—"

"It will be your poison, you good-for-nothing scoundrel," said Mr. Gumbleton.

"Well, then, *may* whisky be my poison," said Ned, "if 'twas not I was—God help me!—in the blackest of misfortunes, and they were before me; whichever way I turned 'twas no matter. Your honour sent me last night, sure enough, with Modderaroo to Mister Falvey's—I don't deny it—why should I? for reason enough I have to remember what happened."

"Ned, my man," said Mr. Gumbleton, "I'll listen to none of your excuses: just take the mare into the stable and yourself off, for I vow to—"

"Begging your honour's pardon," said Ned earnestly, "for interrupting your honour; but, master, master, make no vows— they are bad things. I never made but one in all my life, which was, to drink nothing at all for a year and a day, and 'tis myself repinted of it for the clean twelvemonth after. But if your honour would only listen to reason: I'll just take in the poor baste, and if your honour don't pardon me this one time may I never see another day's luck or grace."

"I know you, Ned," said Mr. Gumbleton. "Whatever your luck has been, you never had any grace to lose; but I don't intend discussing the matter with you. Take in the mare, sir."

Ned obeyed, and his master saw him to the stables. Here he reiterated his commands to quit, and Ned Sheehy's excuse for himself began. That it was heard uninterruptedly is more than I can affirm; but as interruptions, like explanations, spoil a story, we must let Ned tell it his own way.

"No wonder, your honour," said he, "should be a bit angry—grand company coming to the house and all, and no regular serving-man to wait, only Long Jem; so I don't blame your honour the least for being fretted like; but when all's heard, you will see that no poor man is more to be pitied for last night than myself. Fin MacCoul never went through more in his born days than I did, though he was a great *joint* (giant) and I only a man.

"I had not rode half a mile from the house when it came on, as your honour must have perceived clearly, mighty dark all of a sudden, for all the world, as if the sun had tumbled down plump out of the fine, clear blue sky. It was not so late, being only four o'clock at the most, but it was as black as your honour's hat. Well, I didn't care much, seeing I knew the road as well as I knew the way to my mouth, whether I saw it or not, and I put the mare into a smart canter; but just as I turned down by the corner of Terence Leahy's field—sure, your honour ought to know the place well—just at the very spot the fox was killed when your honour came in first out of a whole field of a hundred and fifty gentleman, and maybe more—all of them brave riders."

(Mr. Gumbleton smiled.)

"Just then, there, I heard the low cry of the good people wafting upon the wind. 'How early you are at your work, my little fellows!' says I to myself; and, dark as it was, having no wish for such company, I thought it best to get out of their way, so I turned the horse a little up to the left, thinking to get down by the boreen, that is that way, and so round to Falvey's; but there I heard the voice plainer and plainer close behind, and I could hear these words:

> "'Ned! Ned!
> By my cap so red!
> You're as good, Ned,
> As a man that is dead.'

'A clean pair of spurs is all that's for it now,' said I, so off I set, as hard as I could lick, and in my hurry knew no more where I was going than I do the road to the Hill of Tarah. Away I galloped on for some time, until I came to the noise of a stream, roaring away by itself in the darkness. 'What river is this?' said I to myself—for there was nobody else to ask. 'I thought,' says I, 'I knew every inch of ground, and of water too, within twenty miles, and never the river surely is there in this direction.' So I stopped to look about; but I might have spared myself that trouble, for I could not see as much as my hand. I didn't know what to do; but I thought in myself, it's a queer river, surely, if somebody does not live near it, and I shouted out as loud as I could: 'Murder! murder! Fire! robbery!' anything that would be natural in such a place—but not a sound did I hear except my own voice echoed back to me, like a hundred packs of hounds in full cry above and below, right and left. This didn't do at all, so I dismounted, and guided myself along the stream, directed by the noise of the water, as cautious as if I was treading upon eggs, holding poor Modderaroo by the bridle, who shook, the poor brute, all over in a tremble, like my old grandmother, rest her soul, anyhow! in the ague. Well, sir, the heart was sinking in me, and I was giving myself up, when, as good luck would have it, I saw a light. 'Maybe,' said I, 'my good fellow, you are only a jacky lantern, and want to bog me and Modderaroo.' But I looked at the light hard, and I thought it was too *study* (steady) for a jacky lantern. 'I'll try you,' says I—'so here goes;' and walking as quick as a thief, I came towards it, being very near plumping into the river once or twice, and being stuck up to my middle, as your honour may perceive cleanly the marks of, two or three times in the *slob*. At last I made the light out, and it coming from a bit of a house by the roadside; so I went to the door, and gave three kicks at it as strong as I could.

"'Open the door for Ned Sheehy,' said a voice inside. Now, besides that I could not, for the life of me, make out how anyone inside should know me before I spoke a word at all, I did not like the sound of that voice, 'twas so hoarse and so hollow, just like a dead man's!—so I said nothing immediately. The same voice spoke again and said: 'Why don't you open the door to Ned Sheehy?' How pat my name is to you,' said I, without speaking out, 'on tip of your tongue, like butter;' and I was between two minds about staying or going, when what should the door do but open, and out came a man holding a candle in his hand, and he had upon him a face as white as a sheet.

"Why, then, Ned Sheehy,' says he, 'how grand you're grown that you won't come in and see a friend as you're passing by.'

"'Pray, sir,' says I, looking at him—though that face of his was enough to dumfounder any honest man like myself—'pray, sir,' says I, 'may I make so bold as to ask if you are not Jack Myers that was drowned seven years ago next Martinmas in the ford of Ah-na-fourish?'

" ' Suppose I was,' says he, ' has not a man a right to be drowned in the ford facing his own cabin-door any day of the week that he likes, from Sunday morning to Saturday night ? '

" ' I'm not denying that same, Mr. Myers, sir,' says I, ' if 'tis yourself is to the fore speaking to me.'

" ' Well,' says he, ' no more words about that matter now ; sure, you and I, Ned, were friends of old. Come in and take a glass ; and here's a good fire before you, and nobody shall hurt or harm you, and I to the fore, and myself able to do it.'

" Now, your honour, though 'twas much to drink with a man that was drowned seven years before in the ford of Ah-na-fourish, facing his own door, yet the glass was hard to be withstood—to say nothing of the fire that was blazing within—for the night was mortal cold. So tying Modderaroo to the hasp of the door—if I don't love the creature as I love my own life—I went in with Jack Myers.

" Civil enough he was—I'll never say otherwise to my dying hour—for he handed me a stool by the fire, and bid me sit down and make myself comfortable. But his face, as I said before, was as white as the snow on the hills, and his two eyes fell dead on me, like the eyes of a cod without any life in them. Just as I was going to put the glass to my lips, a voice—'twas the same that I heard bidding the door be opened — spoke out of a cupboard that was convenient to the left-hand side of the chimney, and said : ' Have you any news for me, Ned Sheehy ? '

" ' The never a word, sir,' says I, making answer before I tasted the whisky, all out of civility ; and, to speak the truth, never the least could I remember at that moment of what had happened to me, or how I got there, for I was quite bothered with the fright.

" ' Have you no news,' says the voice, ' Ned, to tell me from Mountbally, Gumbletonmore, or from the Mill, or about Moll Trantum that was married last week to Bryan Oge, and you at the wedding ? '

" No, sir,' says I ; ' never the word.'

" ' What brought you in here, Ned, then ? ' says the voice. I could say nothing ; for whatever other people might do, I never could frame an excuse ; and I was loth to say it was on account of the glass and the fire, for that would be to speak the truth.

" ' Turn the scoundrel out,' says the voice ; and at the sound of it, who would I see but Jack Myers making over to me with a lump of a stick in his hand, and it clenched on the stick so wicked. For certain, I did not stop to feel the weight of the blow ; so, dropping the glass, and it full of the stuff too, I bolted out of the door, and never rested from running away for as good, I believe, as twenty miles, till I found myself in a big wood.

"'The Lord preserve me! what will become of me now?' says I. 'Oh, Ned Sheehy,' says I, speaking to myself, 'my man, you're in a pretty hobble; and to leave poor Modderaroo after you!' But the words were not well out of my mouth when I heard the dismallest ullagoane in the world, enough to break any-one's heart that was not broke before with the grief entirely, and it was not long till I could plainly see four men coming towards me, with a great black coffin on their shoulders. 'I'd better get up in a tree,' says I, 'for they say 'tis not lucky to meet a corpse. I'm in the way of misfortune to-night, if ever man was.'

"I could not help wondering how a *berrin'* (funeral) should come there in the lone wood at that time of night, seeing it could not be far from the dead hour. But it was little good for me thinking, for they soon came under the very tree I was roosting in, and down they put the coffin, and began to make a fine fire under me. I'll be smothered alive now, thinks I, and that will be the end of me; but I was afraid to stir for the life, or to speak out to bid them just make their fire under some other tree, if it would be all the same thing to them. Presently they opened the coffin, and out they dragged as fine-looking a man as you'd meet with in a day's walk.

"'Where's the spit?' says one.

"'Here 'tis,' says another, handing it over; and for certain they spitted him, and began to turn him before the fire.

"If they are not going to eat him, thinks I, like the *Hannibals* Father Quinlan told us about in his *sarmint* last Sunday.

"'Who'll turn the spit while we go for the other ingredients?' says one of them that brought the coffin, and a big, ugly-looking blackguard he was.

"'Who'd turn the spit but Ned Sheehy?' says another.

"Burn you, thinks I, how should you know that I was here so handy to you up in the tree?

"'Come down, Ned Sheehy, and turn the spit,' says he.

"'I'm not here at all, sir,' says I, putting my hand over my face that he may not see me.

"'That won't do for you, my man,' says he; 'you'd better come down, or maybe I'd make you.'

"'I'm coming, sir,' says I, for 'tis always right to make a virtue of necessity. So down I came, and there they left me turning the spit in the middle of the wide wood.

"'Don't scorch me, Ned Sheehy, you vagabond,' says the man on the spit.

" ' And, my lord, sir, and arn't you dead, sir,' says I, ' and your honour taken out of the coffin and all ? '

" ' I arn't,' says he.

" ' But surely you are, sir,' says I, ' for 'tis to no use now for me denying that I saw your honour, and I up in the tree.'

" ' I arn't,' says he again, speaking quite short and snappish.

" So I said no more, until presently he called out to me to turn him easy, or that maybe 'twould be the worse turn for myself.

" ' Will that do, sir ? ' says I, turning him as easy as I could.

" ' That's too easy,' says he ; so I turned him faster.

" ' That's too fast,' says he ; so, finding that, turn him which way I would, I could not please him, I got into a bit of a fret at last, and desired him to turn himself, for a grumbling spalpeen as he was, if he liked it better.

" Away I ran, and away he came hopping, spit and all, after me, and he but half-roasted. ' Murder ! ' says I, shouting out ; ' I'm done for at long last—now or never ! '—when all of a sudden, and 'twas really wonderful, not knowing where I was rightly, I found myself at the door of the very little cabin by the roadside that I had bolted out of from Jack Myers ; and there was Modderaroo standing hard by.

" ' Open the door for Ned Sheehy,' says the voice—for 'twas shut against me—and the door flew open in an instant. In I ran, without stop or stay, thinking it better to be beat by Jack Myers, he being an old friend of mine, than to be spitted like a Michaelmas goose by a man that I knew nothing about, either of him or his family, one or the other.

" ' Have you any news for me ? ' says the voice, putting just the same question to me that it did before.

" ' Yes, sir,' says I ; ' and plenty.' So I mentioned all that had happened to me in the big wood, and how I got up in the tree, and how I was made come down again, and put to turning the spit, roasting the gentleman ; and how I could not please him, turn him fast or easy, although I tried my best ; and how he ran after me at last, spit and all.

" ' If you had told me this before, you would not have been turned out in the cold,' said the voice.

" ' And how could I tell it to you, sir,' says I, ' before it happened ? '

" ' No matter,' says he, ' you may sleep now till morning on that bundle of hay in the corner there ; and only I was your friend, you'd have been *kilt* entirely.' So down I lay ; but I was dreaming, dreaming all the rest of the night ; and when you, master dear, woke me with that blessed blow, I thought 'twas the man on the spit had hold of me, and could hardly believe my eyes when I found myself in your honour's presence,

and poor Modderaroo safe and sound by my side. But how I
came there is more than I can say, if 'twas not Jack Myers,
although he did make the offer to strike me, or someone among
the good people that befriended me."

"It is all a drunken dream, you scoundrel!" said Mr.
Gumbleton. "Have I not had fifty such excuses from you?'

"But never one, your honour, that really happened before,"
said Ned, with unblushing front. "Howsomever, since your
honour fancies 'tis drinking I was, I'd rather never drink again
to the world's end, than lose so good a master as yourself; and
if I'm forgiven this once, and get another trial—"

"Well," said Mr. Gumbleton, "you may, for this once, go into
Mountbally, Gumbletonmore again. Let me see that you keep
your promise as to not drinking, or mind the consequences;
and, above all, let me hear no more of the good people, for I
don't believe a single word about them, whatever I may do of
bad ones."

So saying, Mr. Gumbleton turned on his heel, and Ned's
countenance relaxed into its usual expression.

"Now, I would not be after saying about the good people
what the master said last," exclaimed Peggy, the maid, who was
within hearing, and who, by the way, had an eye after Ned. "I
would not be after saying such a thing. The good people, maybe,
will make him feel the *differ* (difference) to his cost."

Nor was Peggy wrong; for whether Ned Sheehy dreamt of the
Fir Darrig or not, within a fortnight after, two of Mr. Gumbleton's
cows, the best milkers in the parish, ran dry, and before the week
was out, Modderaroo was lying dead in the stone quarry.

IV

THE LUCKY GUEST

THE kitchen of some country houses in Ireland presents in
no ways a bad modern translation of the ancient feudal hall.
Traces of clanship still linger through its hearth in the numerous
dependants on "the master's" bounty. Nurses, foster-brothers
and other hangers-on, are there as matter of right; while the
strolling piper, full of mirth and music, the benighted traveller,
even the passing beggar, are received with a hearty welcome; and
each contributes planxty, song or superstitious tale towards the
evening's amusement.

An assembly, such as has been described, had collected round
the kitchen fire of Ballyrahenhouse, at the foot of the Galtee
Mountains, when, as is ever the case, one tale of wonder called
forth another, and with the advance of the evening each succeed-

ing story was received with deep and deeper attention. The history of Cough-na-Looba's dance with the black friar at Rahill, and the fearful tradition of *Coum an 'ir morriv* (the Dead Man's Hollow), were listened to in breathless silence. A pause followed the last relation, and all eyes rested on the narrator, an old nurse, who occupied the post of honour, that next the fireside. She was seated in that peculiar position which the Irish name "*Currig-guib*," a position generally assumed by a veteran and determined story-teller. Her haunches resting upon the ground, and her feet bundled under the body; her arms folded across and supported by her knees, and the outstretched chin of her hooded head pressing on the upper arm—which compact arrangement nearly reduced the whole figure into a perfect triangle.

Unmoved by the general gaze, Bridget Doyle made no change of attitude, while she gravely asserted the truth of the marvellous tale concerning the Dead Man's Hollow, her strongly-marked countenance at the time receiving what painters term a fine chiaro-obscuro effect from the fire-light.

"I have told you," she said, "what happened to my own people—the Butlers and the Doyles—in the old times; but here is little Ellen Connell from the County Cork, who can speak to what happened under her own father and mother's roof—the Lord be good to them!"

Ellen, a young and blooming girl of about sixteen, was employed in the dairy at Ballyrahen. She was the picture of health and rustic beauty, and at this hint from Nurse Doyle, a deep blush mantled over her countenance; yet, although "unaccustomed to public speaking," she, without further hesitation or excuse, proceeded as follows :—

"It was one May Eve, about thirteen years ago, and that is, as everybody knows, the airiest day in all the twelve months. It is the day above all other days," said Ellen, with her large, dark eyes cast down on the ground, and drawing a deep sigh, "when the young boys and the young girls go looking after the *Drutheen*, to learn from it rightly the name of their sweethearts.

"My father and my mother, and my two brothers, with two or three of the neighbours, were sitting round the turf fire, and were talking of one thing or another. My mother was hushoing my little sister, striving to quieten her, for she was cutting her teeth at the time, and was mighty uneasy through the means of them. The day, which was threatening all along, now that it was coming on to dusk, began to rain, and the rain increased and fell fast and faster, as if it was pouring through a sieve out of the wide heavens; and when the rain stopped for a bit, there was a wind, which kept up such a whistling and racket, that you would have thought the sky and the earth were coming together. It blew and it blew, as if it had a mind to blow the roof off the cabin, and that would not have been very hard for it to do, as the thatch was quite loose in two or three places. Then the rain began again, and you could hear it spitting and hissing in the fire as it came down through the big *chimbley.*

" ' God bless us ! ' says my mother, ' but 'tis a dreadful night to be at sea,' says she, ' and God be praised that we have a roof, bad as it is, to shelter us ! ' "

" I don't, to be sure, recollect all this, Mistress Doyle, but only as my brothers told it to me, and other people, and often have I heard it, for I was so little then that they say I could just go under the table without tipping my head. Anyway, it was in the very height of the pelting and whistling that we heard something speak outside the door. My father and all of us listened, but there was no more noise at that time. We waited a little longer, and then we plainly heard a sound like an old man's voice, asking to be let in, but mighty feeble and weak. Tim bounced up without a word to ask us whether we'd like to let the old man, or whoever he was, in—having always a heart as soft as a mealy potato before the voice of sorrow. When Tim pulled back the bolt that did the door, in marched a little bit of a shrivelled, weather-beaten creature, about two feet and a half high.

" We were all watching to see who'd come in, for there was a wall between us and the door ; but when the sound of the undoing of the bolt stopped, we heard Tim give a sort of a screech, and instantly he bolted in to us. He had hardly time to say a word, or we either, when the little gentleman shuffled in after him, without a God save all here, or by your leave, or any other sort of thing that any decent body might say. We all, of one accord, scrambled over to the furthest end of the room, where we were, old and young, everyone trying who'd get nearest the wall and farthest from him. All the eyes of our body were stuck upon him, but he didn't mind us no more than that frying-pan there does now. He walked over to the fire, and squatting himself down like a frog, took the pipe that my father dropped from his mouth in the hurry, put it into his own, and then began to smoke so hearty that he soon filled the room of it.

" We had plenty of time to observe him, and my brothers say that he wore a sugar-loaf hat that was as red as blood. He had a face as yellow as a kite's claw, and as long as to-day and to-morrow put together, with a mouth all screwed and puckered up like a washerwoman's hand, little blue eyes, and rather a highish nose ; his hair was quite grey and lengthy, appearing under his hat, and flowing over the cape of a long scarlet coat, which almost trailed the ground behind him, and the ends of which he took up and planked on his knees to dry, as he sat facing the fire. He had smart corduroy breeches, and woollen stockings drawn up over the knees, so as to hide the knee-buckles, if he had the pride to have them ; but at anyrate, if he hadn't them in his knees he had buckles in his shoes, out before his spindle legs. When we came to ourselves a little, we thought to escape from the room, but no one would go first, nor no one would stay last, so we huddled ourselves together, and made a dart out of the room. My little gentleman never minded anything of the scrambling, nor hardly stirred himself, sitting quite at his ease before the fire. The neighbours, the very instant minute they got to the door, although it still continued pelting rain, cut gutter, as if Oliver Cromwell himself was at their heels, and no blame to them for that, anyhow. It was my father and my mother, and my brothers and myself, a little hop-of-my-thumb midge as I was then, that were left to see what would come out of this strange visit ; so we all went quietly to the *labbig* (bed), scarcely daring to throw an eye at him as we passed the door. Never the wink of sleep could they sleep that live-long night, though, to be sure, I slept like a top, not knowing better, while they were talking and thinking of the little man.

"When they got up in the morning, everything was as quiet and as tidy about the place as if nothing had happened, for all that the chairs and stools were tumbled here, there and everywhere, when we saw the lad enter. Now, indeed, I forget whether he came next night or not; but anyway, that was the first time we ever laid eye upon him. This I know for certain, that about a month after that he came regularly every night, and used to give us a signal to be on the move, for 'twas plain he did not like to be observed. This sign was always made about eleven o'clock ; and then, if we'd look towards the door, there was a little hairy arm thrust in through the keyhole, which would not have been big enough, only there was a fresh hole made near the first one, and the bit of stick between them had been broken away, and so 'twas just fitting for the little arm.

"The Fir Darrig continued his visits, never missing a night, as long as we attended to the signal; smoking always out of the pipe he made his own of, and warming himself till day dawned before the fire, and then going no one living knows where ; but there was not the least mark of him to be found in the morning ; and 'tis as true, Nurse Doyle, and honest people, as you are all here sitting before me and by the side of me, that the family continued thriving, and my father and brothers rising in the world while ever he came to us. When we observed this, we used always look for the very moment to see when the arm would come, and then we'd instantly fly off with ourselves to our rest. But before we found the luck, we used sometimes sit still and not mind the arm, especially when a neighbour would be with my father ; or that two or three or four of them would have a drop among them, and then they did not care for all the arms, hairy or not, that ever were seen.   No one, however, dared to speak to it or of it insolently, except, indeed, one night that Davy Kennane —but he was drunk—walked over and hit it a rap on the back of the wrist.   The hand was snatched off like lightning ; but everyone knows that Davy did not live a month after this happened, though he was only about ten days sick.   The like of such tricks are ticklish things to do.

"As sure as the red man would put in his arm for a sign through the hole in the door, and that we did not go and open it to him, so sure some mishap befel the cattle : the cows were elf-stoned or overlooked, or something or another went wrong with them.   One night my brother Dan refused to go at the signal, and the next day, as he was cutting turf in Crogh-na-drimina Bog, within a mile and a half of the house, a stone was thrown at him, which broke fairly with the force, into two halves. Now, if that had happened to hit, him, he'd be at this hour as dead as my great-great-grandfather.   It came whack slap against the spade he had in his hand, and split at once in two pieces. He took them up and fitted them together, and they made a perfect heart.   Some way or the other, he lost it since ; but he still has the one which was shot at the spotted milch cow, before the little man came near us.   Many and many a time I saw that same ; 'tis just the shape of the ace of hearts on the cards, only it is of a dark red colour, and polished up like the grate that is in the grand parlour within.   When this did not kill the cow on the spot, she swelled up ; but if you took and put the elf-stone under her udder, and milked her upon it to the last stroking, and then made her drink the milk, it would cure her, and she would thrive with you ever after.

"But as I said, we were getting on well enough as long as we minded the door, and watched for the hairy arm, which we did sharp enough when we found it was bringing luck to us ; and we were now as glad to see the little red gentleman, and as ready to open the door to him, as we used to dread his coming at first and be frightened of him.   But at long last, we throve so well that the landlord—God forgive him !—took notice of us, and envied us, and asked my father how he came by the penny he had, and wanted him to take more ground at a rack-rent that was more than any Christian ought to pay to another, seeing there was no making it.   When my father—and small blame to him for that —refused to lease the ground, he turned us off the bit of land we had, and out of the house and all, and left us in a wide and wicked world, where my father—for he was a soft, innocent man

—was not up to the roguery and the trickery that was practised upon him. He was taken this way by one, and that way by another, and he treating them that were working his downfall. And he used to take bite and sup with them, and they with him, free enough as long as the money lasted; but when that was gone, and he had not as much ground that he could call his own as would sod a lark, they soon shabbed him off. The landlord died not long after, and he now knows whether he acted right or wrong in taking the house from over our heads.

"It is a bad thing for the heart to be cast down; so we took another cabin, and looked out with great desire for the Fir Darrig to come to us. But ten o'clock came and no arm, although we cut a hole in the door just the *moral* (model) of the other. Eleven o'clock!—twelve o'clock!—no, not a sign of him; and every night we watched, but all would not do. We then travelled to the other house, and we rooted up the hearth—for the landlord asked so great a rent for it from the poor people that no one could take it—and we carried away the very door off the hinges, and we brought everything with us that we thought the little man was in any respect partial to; but he did not come, and we never saw him again.

"My father and my mother, and my young sister, are since dead; and my two brothers, who could tell all about this better than myself, are both of them gone out with Ingram in his last voyage to the Cape of Good Hope, leaving me behind them without kith or kin."

Here young Ellen's voice became choked with sorrow, and bursting into tears, she hid her face in her apron.

NOTE.—FIR DARRIG means the red man, and is a member of the fairy community of Ireland, who bears a strong resemblance to the Shakespearian Puck, or Robin Goodfellow. Like that merry goblin, his delight is in mischief and mockery; and this Irish spirit is doubtless the same as the Scottish *Red Cap*, which a writer in the *Quarterly Review* (No. XLIV., p. 358), tracing national analogies, asserts, is the Robin Hood of England, and the Saxon spirit Hudkin or Hodeken, so called from the hoodakin or little hood wherein he appeared—a spirit similar to the Spanish Duende. The Fir Darrig has also some traits of resemblance in common with the Scotch Brownie, the German Kobold, and the English Hobgoblin. The red dress and strange flexibility of voice possessed by the Fir Darrig form his peculiar characteristics; the latter, according to Irish tale-tellers, is like the sound of the waves; and again, it is compared to the music of angels, the warbling of birds, etc.; and the usual address to this fairy is, *Do not mock us.* His entire dress, when he is seen, is invariably described as crimson; whereas Irish fairies generally appear in a black hat, a green suit, white stockings and red shoes.

TREASURE LEGENDS

——◆——

I

DREAMING TIM JARVIS

TIMOTHY JARVIS was a decent, honest, quiet, hard-working man, as everybody knows that knows Balledehob.

Now Balledehob is a small place, about forty miles west of Cork. It is situated on the summit of a hill, and yet it is in a deep valley; for on all sides there are lofty mountains that rise one above another in barren grandeur, and seem to look down with scorn upon the little busy village which they surround with their idle and unproductive magnificence. Man and beast have alike deserted them to the dominion of the eagle, who soars majestically over them. On the highest of those mountains there is a small, and as is commonly believed, unfathomable lake, the only inhabitant of which is a huge serpent, who has been sometimes seen to stretch its enormous head above the waters, and frequently is heard to utter a noise which shakes the very rocks to their foundation.

But as I was saying, everybody knew Tim Jarvis to be a decent, honest, quiet, hard-working man, who was thriving enough to be able to give his daughter Nelly a fortune of ten pounds; and Tim himself would have been snug enough besides, but that he loved the drop sometimes. However, he was seldom backward on rent-day. His ground was never distrained but twice, and both times through a small bit of a mistake; and his landlord had never but once to say to him: "Tim Jarvis, you're all behind, Tim, like the cow's tail." Now it so happened that, being heavy in himself, through the drink, Tim took to sleeping, and the sleep set Tim dreaming, and he dreamed all night, and night after night, about crocks full of gold and other precious stones; so much so, that Norah Jarvis, his wife, could get no good of him by day, and have little comfort with him by night. The grey dawn of the morning would see Tim digging away in a bog-hole, maybe, or rooting under some old stone walls like a pig. At last he dreamed that he found a mighty great crock of gold and silver—and where do you think? Every step of the way upon London Bridge itself! Twice Tim dreamt it, and three times Tim dreamt the same thing; and at last he made up his mind to transport himself, and go over to London, in Pat Mahoney's coaster—and so he did!

Well, he got there, and found the bridge without much

difficulty. Every day he walked up and down looking for the crock of gold, but never the find did he find it. One day, however, as he was looking over the bridge into the water, a man, or something like a man, with great black whiskers like a Hessian, and a black cloak that reached down to the ground, taps him on the shoulder, and says he: "Tim Jarvis, do you see me?"

"Surely I do, sir," said Tim; wondering that anybody should know him in the strange place.

"Tim," says he, "what is it brings you here in foreign parts, so far away from your own cabin by the mine of grey copper at Balledehob?"

"Please your honour," says Tim, "I'm come to seek my fortune."

"You're a fool for your pains, Tim, if that's all," remarked the stranger in the black cloak. "This is a big place to seek one's fortune in, to be sure, but it's not so easy to find it."

Now Tim, after debating a long time with himself, and considering, in the first place, that it might be the stranger who was to find the crock of gold for him and in the next, that the stranger might direct him where to find it, came to the resolution of telling him all.

"There's many a one like me comes here seeking their fortunes," said Tim.

"True!" said the stranger.

"But," continued Tim, looking up, "the body and bones of the cause for myself leaving the woman and Nelly and the boys, and travelling so far, is to look for a crock of gold that I'm told is lying somewhere hereabouts."

"And who told you that, Tim?"

"Why, then, sir, that's what I can't tell myself rightly—only I dreamt it."

"Ho, ho! is that all, Tim!" said the stranger, laughing. "I had a dream myself; and I dreamed that I found a crock of gold, in the Fort-field, on Jerry Driscoll's ground at Balledehob; and by the same token, the pit where it lay was close to a large furze bush, all full of yellow blossom."

Tim knew Jerry Driscoll's ground well; and moreover, he knew the Fort-field as well as he knew his own potato garden; he was certain, too, of the very furze bush at the north end of it —so swearing a bitter big oath, says he:

"By all the crosses in a yard of check, I always thought there was money in that same field!"

The moment he rapped out the oath, the stranger disappeared, and Tim Jarvis, wondering at all that had happened to him, made the best of his way back to Ireland. Norah, as may well be supposed, had no very warm welcome for her runaway husband—the dreaming blackguard, as she called him—and so soon as she set eyes upon him all the blood of her body in one minute was into her knuckles to be at him ; but Tim, after his long journey, looked so cheerful and so happy like, that she could not find it in her heart to give him the first blow ! He managed to pacify his wife by two or three broad hints about a new cloak and a pair of shoes, that to speak honestly, were much wanting for her to go to chapel in ; and decent clothes for Nelly to go to the patron with her sweetheart, and brogues for the boys, and some corduroy for himself. "It wasn't for nothing," says Tim, "I went to foreign parts all the ways ; and you'll see what'll come out of it—mind my words."

A few days afterwards Tim sold his cabin and his garden, and bought the Fort-field of Jerry Driscoll, that had nothing in it, but was full of thistles and old stones and blackberry-bushes ; and all the neighbours—as well they might—thought he was cracked.

The first night that Tim could summon courage to begin his work, he walked off to the field with his spade upon his shoulder, and away he dug all night by the side of the furze bush till he came to a big stone. He struck his spade against it, and he heard a hollow sound ; but as the morning had begun to dawn, and the neighbours would be going out to their work, Tim, not wishing to have the thing talked about, went home to the little hovel, where Norah and the children were huddled together under a heap of straw, for he had sold everything he had in the world to purchase Driscoll's field, though it was said to be "the backbone of the world, picked by the devil."

It is impossible to describe the epithets and reproaches bestowed by the poor woman on her unlucky husband for bringing her into such a way—epithets and reproaches which Tim had but one mode of answering, as thus : "Norah, did you see e'er a cow you'd like ?" or, "Norah dear, hasn't Poll Deasy a feather-bed to sell ?" or, "Norah honey, wouldn't you like your silver buckles as big as Mrs. Doyle's ?"

As soon as night came, Tim stood beside the furze bush, spade in hand. The moment he jumped down into the pit, he heard a strange rumbling noise under him, and so, putting his ear against the great stone, he listened, and overheard a discourse that made the hair on his head stand up like bulrushes, and every limb tremble.

"How shall we bother Tim ?" said one voice.

"Take him to the mountain, to be sure, and make him a toothful for the *ould sarpint;* 'tis long since he has had a good meal," said another voice.

Tim shook like a potato-blossom in a storm.

" No," said a third voice ; " plunge him in the bog, neck and heels."

Tim was a dead man, barring the breath.

"Stop!" said a fourth ; but Tim heard no more, for Tim was dead entirely. In about an hour, however, the life came back to him, and he crept home to Norah.

When the next night arrived, the hopes of the crock of gold got the better of his fears, and taking care to arm himself with a bottle of potheen, away he went to the field. Jumping into the pit, he took a little sup from the bottle to keep his heart up—he then took a big one — and then, with desperate wrench, he wrenched up the stone. All at once, up rushed a blast of wind, wild and fierce, and down fell Tim—down, down and down he went—until he thumped upon what seemed to be, for all the world, like a floor of sharp pins, which made him bellow out in earnest. Then he heard a whisk and a hurra, and instantly voices beyond number cried out:

> " Welcome, Tim Jarvis dear !
> Welcome, down here ! "

Though Tim's teeth chattered like magpies with the fright, he continued to make answer : " I'm he-he-har-ti-ly ob-ob-liged to-to you all, gen-gen-tlemen, fo-for your civility to-to a poor stranger like myself."   But though he had heard all the voices about him, he could see nothing, the place was so dark and so lonesome in itself for want of the light.   Then something pulled Tim by the hair of his head and dragged him, he did not know how far, but he knew he was going faster than the wind, for he heard it behind him, trying to keep up with him, and it could not.   On, on, on, he went, till all at once, and suddenly, he was stopped, and somebody came up to him, and said : " Well, Tim Jarvis, and how do you like your ride ? "

" Mighty well, I thank your honour ! " said Tim ; " and 'twas a good beast I rode, surely ! "

There was a great laugh at Tim's answer, and then there was a whispering and a great cugger-mugger and coshering, and at last a pretty little bit of a voice said : " Shut your eyes and you'll see, Tim."

" By my word, then," said Tim, " that is the queer way of seeing ; but I'm not the man to gainsay you, so I'll do as you bid me, anyhow."   Presently he felt a small warm hand rubbed over his eyes with an ointment, and in the next minute he saw himself in the middle of thousands of little men and women, not half so high as his brogue, that were pelting one another with golden guineas and lily-white thirteens,[1] as if they were so much dirt. The finest dressed and the biggest of them all went up to Tim, and says he: "Tim Jarvis, because you are a decent, honest, quiet, civil, well-spoken man," says he, "and know how to behave yourself in strange company, we've altered our minds about you, and will find a neighbour of yours that will do just as well to give to the old serpent."

"Oh, then, long life to you, sir!" said Tim, "and there's no doubt of that."

"But what will you say, Tim," inquired the little fellow, "if we fill your pockets with these yellow boys? What will you say, Tim, and what will you do with them?"

"Your honour's honour, and your honour's glory," answered Tim, "I'll not be able to say my prayers for one month with thanking you—and indeed, I've enough to do with them. I'd make a grand lady, you see, at once of Norah—she has been a good wife to me. We'll have a nice bit of pork for dinner, and maybe I'd have a glass, or maybe two glasses; or sometimes, if 'twas with a friend or acquaintance or gossip, you know, three glasses every day; and I'd build a new cabin, and I'd have a fresh egg every morning myself for my breakfast; and I'd snap my fingers at the Squire, and beat his hounds if they'd come coursing through my fields, and I'd have a new plough; and Norah, your honour, would have a new cloak, and the boys would have shoes and stockings as well as Biddy Leary's brats—that's my sister that was—and Nelly would marry Bill Long of Affadown; and, your honour, I'd have some corduroy for myself to make breeches, and a cow, and a beautiful coat with shining buttons, and a horse to ride, or maybe two. I'd have everything," said Tim, "in life, good or bad, that is to be got for love or money —hurra-whoop!—and that's what I'd do."

"Take care, Tim," said the little fellow, "your money would not go faster than it came, with your hurra-whoop."

But Tim heeded not this speech; heaps of gold were around him, and he filled and filled away as hard as he could his coat and his waistcoat and his breeches' pockets; and he thought himself very clever, moreover, because he stuffed some of the guineas into his brogues. When the little people perceived this, they cried out: "Go home, Tim Jarvis, go home, and think yourself a lucky man."

"I hope, gentlemen," said he, "we won't part for good and all; but maybe ye'll ask me to see you again, and to give you a fair and square account of what I've done with your money."

To this there was no answer, only another shout: "Go home,

---

[1] An English shilling was thirteenpence, Irish currency.

Tim Jarvis, go home ; fair play is a jewel ; but shut your eyes, or ye'll never see the light of day again."

Tim shut his eyes, knowing now that was the way to see clearly ; and away he was whisked as before—away, away he went till he again stopped all of a sudden.

He rubbed his eyes with his two thumbs—and where was he ? Where, but in the very pit in the field that was Jer Driscoll's, and his wife Norah above with a big stick ready to beat "her dreaming blackguard." Tim roared out to the woman to leave the life in him, and put his hands in his pockets to show her the gold ; but he pulled out nothing, only a handful of small stones mixed with yellow furze-blossoms. The bush was under him, and the great flagstone that he had wrenched up, as he thought, was lying, as if it was never stirred, by his side ; the whisky-bottle was drained to the last drop ; and the pit was just as his spade had made it.

Tim Jarvis, vexed, disappointed, and almost heart-broken, followed his wife home ; and, strange to say, from that night he left off drinking and dreaming, and delving in bog-holes and rooting in old caves. He took again to his hard-working habits, and was soon able to buy back his little cabin and former potato garden, and to get all the enjoyment he anticipated from the fairy gold.

Give Tim one, or at most, two glasses of whisky-punch (and neither friend, acquaintance, nor gossip can make him take more), and he will relate the story to you much better than you have it here. Indeed, it is worth going to Balledehob to hear him tell it. He always pledges himself to the truth of every word with his forefingers crossed ; and when he comes to speak of the loss of his guineas, he never fails to console himself by adding : " If they stayed with me I wouldn't have luck with them, sir ; and Father O'Shea told me 'twas as well for me they were changed, for if they hadn't, they'd have burned holes in my pocket, and got out that way."

I shall never forget his solemn countenance, and the deep tones of his warning voice, when he concluded his tale by telling me that the next day after his ride with the fairies Mick Dowling was missing, and he believed him to be given to the *sarpint* in his place, as he had never been heard of since. " The blessing of the saints be between all good men and harm," was the concluding sentence of Tim Jarvis's narrative, as he flung the remaining drops from his glass upon the green sward.

II

RENT DAY

" Oh, ullagone, ullagone ! this is a wide world, but what will we do in it, or where will we go ? " muttered Bill Doody, as he sat on a rock by the Lake of Killarney.   " What will we do ?   To-morrow's rent day, and Tim the Driver swears if we don't pay up our rent, he'll cant every *ha'perth* we have ; and then, sure enough, there's Judy and myself and the poor *grawls* (children) will be turned out to starve on the high road, for the never a halfpenny of rent have I !   Oh hone, that ever I should live to see this day ! "

Thus did Bill Doody bemoan his hard fate, pouring his sorrows to the reckless waves of the most beautiful of lakes, which seemed to mock his misery as they rejoiced beneath the cloudless sky of a May morning.   The lake, glittering in sunshine, sprinkled with fairy isles of rock and verdure, and bounded by giant hills of ever - varying hues, might, with its magic beauty, charm all sadness but despair ; for alas !

> " How ill the scene that offers rest,
> And heart that cannot rest, agree ! "

Yet Bill Doody was not so desolate as he supposed ; there was one listening to him he little thought of, and help was at hand from a quarter he could not have expected.

"What's the matter with you, my poor man ?" said a tall, portly-looking gentleman, at the same time stepping out of a furze-brake.   Now Bill was seated on a rock that commanded the view of a large field.   Nothing in the field could be concealed from him except this furze-brake, which grew in a hollow near the margin of the lake.   He was, therefore, not a little surprised at the gentleman's sudden appearance, and began to question whether the personage before him belonged to this world or not. He, however, soon mustered courage sufficient to tell him how his crops had failed, how some bad member had charmed away his butter, and how Tim the Driver threatened to turn him out of the farm if he didn't pay up every penny of the rent by twelve o'clock next day.

" A sad story, indeed," said the stranger ; " but surely, if you represented the case to your landlord's agent, he won't have the heart to turn you out."

" Heart, your honour !   Where would an agent get a heart ! " exclaimed Bill.   " I see your honour does not know him ; besides, he has an eye on the farm this long time for a fosterer of his own ; so I expect no mercy, at all, at all, only to be turned out."

" Take this, my poor fellow—take this," said the stranger,

pouring a purse full of gold into Bill's old hat, which in his grief he had flung on the ground. "Pay the fellow your rent, but I'll take care it shall do him no good. I remember the time when things went otherwise in this country, when I would have hung up such a fellow in the twinkling of an eye!"

These words were lost upon Bill, who was insensible to everything but the sight of the gold, and before he could unfix his gaze and lift up his head to pour out his hundred thousand blessings, the stranger was gone. The bewildered peasant looked around in search of his benefactor, and at last he thought he saw him riding on a white horse a long way off on the lake.

"O'Donoghue, O'Donoghue!" shouted Bill; "the good, the blessed O'Donoghue!" and he ran capering like a madman to show Judy the gold, and to rejoice her heart with the prospect of wealth and happiness.

The next day Bill proceeded to the agent's—not sneakingly, with his hat in his hand, his eyes fixed on the ground, and his knees bending under him—but bold and upright, like a man conscious of his independence.

"Why don't you take off your hat, fellow. Don't you know you are speaking to a magistrate?" said the agent.

"I know I'm not speaking to the King, sir," said Bill; "and I never takes off my hat but to them I can respect and love. The Eye that sees all, knows I've no right either to respect or love an agent!"

"You scoundrel!" retorted the man in office, biting his lips with rage at such an unusual and unexpected opposition, "I'll teach you how to be insolent again — I have the power, remember."

"To the cost of the country, I know you have," said Bill, who still remained with his head as firmly covered as if he was the Lord Kingsale himself.

"But come," said the magistrate; "have you got the money for me?—this is rent day. If there's one penny of it wanting, or the running gale that's due, prepare to turn out before night, for you shall not remain another hour in possession."

"There is your rent," said Bill, with an unmoved expression of tone and countenance; "you'd better count it, and give me a receipt in full for the running gale and all."

The agent gave a look of amazement at the gold; for it was gold—real guineas! and not bits of dirty, ragged, small notes, that are only fit to light one's pipe with. However willing the agent may have been to ruin, as he thought, the unfortunate tenant, he took up the gold, and handed the receipt to Bill, who strutted off with it as proud as a cat of her whiskers.

The agent, going to his desk shortly after, was confounded at beholding a heap of gingerbread-cakes instead of the money he had deposited there.   He raved and swore, but all to no purpose ; the gold had become gingerbread-cakes, just marked like the guineas, with the King's head, and Bill had the receipt in his pocket ; so he saw there was no use in saying anything about the affair, as he would only get laughed at for his pains.

From that hour Bill Doody grew rich ; all his undertakings prospered ; and he often blesses the day that he met with O'Donoghue, the great prince that lives down under the lake of Killarney.

Like the butterfly, the spirit of Donoghue closely hovers over the perfume of the hills and flowers it loves ; while, as the reflection of a star in the waters of a pure lake, to those who look not above, that glorious spirit is believed to dwell beneath.

<hr />

III

LINN-NA-PAYSHTHA

Travellers go to Leinster to see Dublin and the Dargle ; to Ulster, to see the Giant's Causeway, and, perhaps, to do penance at Lough Dearg ; to Munster, to see Killarney, the beautiful city of Cork, and half-a-dozen other fine things ; but who ever thinks of the fourth province ?—who ever thinks of going—

> " —westward, where Dick Martin *ruled*
> The houseless wilds of Cunnemara ? "

The Ulsterman's ancient denunciation " to Hell or to Connaught," has possibly led to the supposition that this is a sort of infernal place above ground—a kind of terrestrial Pandemonium —in short, that Connaught is little better than hell, or hell little worse than Connaught ; but let anyone only go there for a month, and, as the natives say, " I'll warrant he'll soon see the differ, and learn to understand that it is mighty like the rest o' green Erin, only something poorer ; " and yet it might be thought that in this particular " worse would be needless ; " but so it is.

" My gracious me," said the landlady of the inn at Sligo, " I wonder a gentleman of your *teeste* and *curosity* would think of leaving Ireland without making a *tower* (tour) of Connaught, if it was nothing more than spending a day at Hazlewood, and up the lake, and on to the *ould* abbey at Friarstown, and the castle at Dromahair."

Polly M'Bride, my kind hostess, might not in this remonstrance have been altogether disinterested ; but her advice prevailed, and the dawn of the following morning found me in a boat on the unruffled surface of Lough Gill.   Arrived at the head of that splendid sheet of water, covered with rich and wooded islands with their ruined buildings, and bounded by towering mountains, noble plantations, grassy slopes and precipitous rocks, which give beauty, and, in some places, sublimity to its shores, I proceeded at once up the wide river which forms its principal tributary. The "old abbey" is chiefly remarkable for having been built at a period nearer to the Reformation than any other ecclesiastical edifice of the same class. Full within view of it, and at the distance of half a mile, stands the shattered remnant of Breffni's princely hall. I strode forward with the enthusiasm of an antiquary, and the high-beating heart of a patriotic Irishman. I felt myself on classic ground, immortalised by the lays of Swift and of Moore. I pushed my way into the hallowed precincts of the grand and venerable edifice. I entered its chambers, and oh, my countrymen, I found them converted into the domicile of pigs, cows and poultry! But the exterior of "O'Rourke's old hall," grey, frowning and ivy-covered, is well enough; it stands on a beetling precipice, round which a noble river wheels its course. The opposite bank is a very steep ascent, thickly wooded, and rising to a height of at least seventy feet; and, for a quarter of a mile, this beautiful copse follows the course of the river.

The first individual I encountered was an old cowherd; nor was I unfortunate in my cicerone, for he assured me there were plenty of old stories about strange things that used to be in the place; "but," continued he, "for my own share, I never met anything worse nor myself. If it bees ould stories that your honour's after, the story about Linn-na-Payshtha and Poul-maw-Gullyawn is the only thing about this place that's worth one jack-straw. Does your honour see that great big black hole in the river yonder below?" He pointed my attention to a part of the river about fifty yards from the old hall, where a long island occupied the centre of the wide current, the water at one side running shallow, and at the other assuming every appearance of unfathomable depth. The spacious pool, dark and still, wore a deathlike quietude of surface. It looked as if the speckled trout would shun its murky precincts—as if even the daring pike would shrink from so gloomy a dwelling-place.

"That's Linn-na-Payshtha, sir," resumed my guide, "and Poul-maw-Gullyawn is just the very *moral* of it, only that 'it's round, and not in a river, but standing out in the middle of a green field, about a short quarter of a mile from this. Well, 'tis as good as fourscore years—I often *hard* my father, God ¦be merciful to him! tell the story—since Manus O'Rourke, a great buckeen, a cock-fighting, drinking blackguard that was long ago, went to sleep one night and had a dream about Linn-na-Payshtha. This Manus, the dirty spalpeen, there was no ho with him; he thought to ride rough-shod over his betters through the whole country, though he was not one of the real stock of the O'Rourkes. Well, this fellow had a dream that if he dived in Linn-na-Payshtha at twelve o'clock of a Hollow Eve night, he'd find more gold than would make a man of him and his wife, while grass grew or water ran. The next night he had the same dream, and sure enough, if he had it the second night, it came to him the third in the same form. Manus, well becomes him, never told mankind or woman-kind, but swore to himself, by all the books that were ever shut or open, that, anyhow, he would go to the bottom of the big hole. What did he care for the Payshtha-more that was lying there to keep guard on the gold and silver of the old ancient family that was buried there in the wars, packed up in the brewing-pan? Sure, he was as good an O'Rourke as the best of them, taking care to forget that his grandmother's father was a cow-boy to the Earl O'Donnel. At long last, Hollow Eve comes, and sly and silent Master Manus creeps to bed early, and just at midnight steals down to the river-side. When he came to the bank his mind misgave him, and he wheeled up to Frank M'Clure's—the old Frank that was then at that time—and got a bottle of whisky, and took it with him, and 'tis unknown how much of it he drank. He walked across to the island, and down he went gallantly to the bottom like a stone. Sure enough, the Payshtha was there afore him, lying like a great big conger eel, seven yards long, and as thick as a bull in the body, with a mane upon his neck like a horse. The Payshtha-more reared himself up; and, looking at the poor man as if he'd eat him, says he, in good English:

"'Arrah, then, Manus,' says he, 'what brought you here? It would have been better for you to have blown your brains out at once with a pistol, and have made a quiet end of yourself, than to have come down here for me to deal with you.'

"'Oh, plaze your honour,' says Manus, 'I beg my life;' and there he stood shaking like a dog in a wet sack.

"'Well, as you have some blood of the O'Rourkes in you, I forgive you this once; but by this and by that, if I ever see you, or anyone belonging to you, coming about this place again, I'll hang a quarter of you on every tree in the wood.'

"'Go home,' says the Payshtha—'go home, Manus,' says he; 'and if you can't make better use of your time, get drunk; but don't come here, bothering me. Yet, stop! Since you are here, and have ventured to come, I'll show you something that you'll remember till you go to your grave, and ever after, while you live.'

"With that, my dear, he opens an iron door in the bed of the river, and never the drop of water ran into it; and there Manus sees a long dry cave, or underground cellar like, and the Payshtha drags him in and shuts the door. It wasn't long before the baste began to get smaller and smaller and smaller; and at last he grew as little as a taughn of twelve years old; and there he was a brownish little man, about four feet high.

"'Plaze your honour,' says Manus, 'if I might make so bold, maybe you are one of the good people?'

"'Maybe I am, and maybe I am not; but anyhow, all you have to understand is this, that I'm bound to look after the Thiernas[1] of Breffni, and take care of them through every generation; and that my present business is to watch this cave, and what's in it, till the old stock is reigning over this country once more.'

"'Maybe you are a sort of a banshee?'

"'I am not, you fool!' said the little man. 'The Banshee is a woman. My business is to live in the form you first saw me in, guarding this spot. And now hold your tongue, and look about you.'

"Manus rubbed his eyes, and looked right and left, before and behind; and there was the vessels of gold and the vessels of silver, the dishes and the plates and the cups, and the punch-bowls and the tankards; there was the golden mether, too, that every Thierna at his wedding used to drink out of to the kerne in real usquebaugh. There was all the money that ever was saved in the family since they got a grant of this manor, in the days of the Firbolgs, down to the time of their *outer* ruination. He then brought Manus on with him to where there was arms for three hundred men, and the sword set with diamonds, and the golden helmet of the O'Rourke; and he showed him the staff made out of an elephant's tooth, and set with rubies and gold, that the Thierna used to hold while he sat in his great hall, giving justice and the laws of the Brehons to all his clan. The first room in the cave, ye see, had the money and the plate, the second room had the arms, and the third had the books, papers, parchments, title-deeds, wills, and everything else of the sort belonging to the family.

"'And now, Manus,' says the little man, 'ye seen the whole o' this, and go your ways; but never come to this place any more, or allow anyone else. I must keep watch and ward till the Sassanach is druv out of Ireland, and the Thiernas o' Breffni in their glory agan.' The little man then stopped for a while and looked up in Nanus's face, and says to him, in a great passion: 'Arrah! bad luck to ye, Manus, why don't ye go about your business?'

"'How can I? Sure, you must show me the way out,' says

[1] *Tighearna*—a lord. *Vide* O'BRIEN.

Manus, making answer. The little man then pointed forward with his finger.

"'Can't we go out the way we came in?' says Manus.

"'No; you must go out at the other end—that's the rule o' this place. Ye came in at Linn-na-Payshtha, and you must go out at Poul-maw-Gullyawn; ye came down like a stone to the bottom of one hole, and ye must spring up like a cork to the top of the other.' With that the little man gave him one *loise*, and all that Manus remembers was the roar of the water in his ears; and sure enough, he was found the next morning, high and dry, fast asleep, with the empty bottle beside him, but far enough from the place he thought he landed, for it was just below yonder on the island that his wife found him. My father—God be merciful to him!—heard Manus swear to every word of the story."

Note.—As there are few things which excite human desire throughout all nations more than wealth, the legends concerning the concealment, discovery and circulation of money, are, as may be expected, widely extended; yet in all the circumstances, which admit of so much fanciful embellishment, there everywhere exists a striking similarity.

In poor Ireland, the wretched peasant contents himself by soliloquising : "Money is the devil, they say; and God is good that He keeps it from us."

ROCK AND STONE LEGENDS

I

THE LEGEND OF CAIRN THIERNA

FROM the town of Fermoy, famous for the excellence of its bottled ale, you may plainly see the mountain of Cairn Thierna. It is crowned with a great heap of stones, which, as the country people remark, never came there without "a crooked thought and a cross job." Strange it is, that any work of the good old times should be considered one of labour; for round towers then sprung up like mushrooms in one night, and people played marbles with pieces of rock that can now no more be moved than the hills themselves.

This great pile on the top of Cairn Thierna was caused by the words of an old woman, whose bed still remains—*Labacally*, the hag's bed—not far from the village of Glanworth. She was certainly far wiser than any woman, either old or young, of my immediate acquaintance. Jove defend me, however, from making an envious comparison between ladies; but facts are stubborn things, and the legend will prove my assertion.

O'Keefe was Lord of Fermoy before the Roches came into that part of the country; and he had an only son—never was there seen a finer child; his young face filled with innocent joy was enough to make any heart glad, yet his father looked on his smiles with sorrow, for an old hag had foretold that this boy should be drowned before he grew up to manhood.

Now, although the prophecies of Pastorini were a failure, it is no reason why prophecies should altogether be despised. The art in modern times may be lost, as well as that of making beer out of the mountain heath, which the Danes did to great perfection. But I take it, the malt of Tom Walker is no bad substitute for the one; and if evil prophecies were to come to pass, like the old woman's, in my opinion we are far more comfortable without such knowledge.

> " Infant heir of proud Fermoy,
>   Fear not fields of slaughter ;
> Storm and fire fear not, my boy,
>   But shun the fatal water."

These were the warning words which caused the chief of Fermoy so much unhappiness. His infant son was carefully prevented all approach to the river, and anxious watch was kept over every playful movement. The child grew up in strength and in beauty, and every day became more dear to his father, who, hoping to avert his doom, which, however, was inevitable, prepared to build a castle far removed from the dreaded element.

The top of Cairn Thierna was the place chosen; and the lord's vassals were assembled and employed in collecting materials for the purpose. Hither came the fated boy; with delight he viewed the laborious work of raising mighty stones from the base to the summit of the mountain, until the vast heap which now forms its rugged crest was accumulated. The workmen were about to commence the building, and the boy, who was considered in safety when on the mountain, was allowed to rove about at will. In his case, how true are the words of the great dramatist :

> " ——Put but a little water in a spoon,
> And it shall be, as all the ocean,
> Enough to stifle such a *being* up."

A vessel which contained a small supply of water, brought there for the use of the workmen, attracted the attention of the child. He saw, with wonder, the glitter of the sunbeams within it; he approached more near to gaze, when a form resembling his own arose before him. He gave a cry of joy and astonishment, and drew back; the image drew back also, and vanished. Again he approached; again the form appeared, expressing in every feature delight corresponding with his own. Eager to welcome the young stranger, he bent over the vessel to press his lips; and losing his balance, the fatal prophecy was accomplished.

The father in despair abandoned the commenced building, and the materials remain a proof of the folly of attempting to avert the course of Fate.

II

THE ROCK OF THE CANDLE

A FEW miles west of Limerick stands the once formidable castle of Carrigogunnel. Its riven tower and broken archway remain in mournful evidence of the sieges sustained by that city. Time, however, the great soother of all things, has destroyed the painful effect which the view of recent violence produces on the mind. The ivy creeps around the riven tower, concealing its injuries, and upholding it by a tough swathing of stalks. The archway is again united by the long-armed briar which grows across the rent, and the shattered buttresses are decorated with wild flowers, which gaily spring from their crevices and broken places.

Boldly situated on a rock, the ruined walls of Carrigogunnel now form only a romantic feature in the peaceful landscape. Beneath them, on one side, lies the flat, marshy ground called Corcass Land, which borders the noble River Shannon; on the other side is seen the neat parish church of Kilkeedy, with its glebehouse and surrounding improvements; and at a short distance, appear the irregular mud cabins of the little village of Ballybrown, with the venerable trees of Tervoo.

On the rock of Carrigogunnel, before the castle was built, or Brien Boro born to build it, dwelt a hag named Grana, who made desolate the surrounding country. She was gigantic in size and frightful in appearance. Her eyebrows grew into each other with a grim curve, and beneath their matted bristles, deeply sunk in her head, two small grey eyes darted forth baneful looks of evil. From her deeply-wrinkled forehead issued forth a hooked beak, dividing two shrivelled cheeks. Her skinny lips curled with a cruel and malignant expression, and her prominent chin was studded with bunches of grisly hair.

Death was her sport. Like the angler with his rod, the hag Grana would toil and watch, nor think it labour, so that the death of a victim rewarded her vigils. Every evening did she light an enchanted candle upon the rock, and whoever looked upon it died before the next morning's sun arose. Numberless were the victims over whom Grana rejoiced; one after the other had seen the light, and their death was the consequence. Hence came the country round to be desolate, and Carrigogunnel, the Rock of the Candle, by its dreaded name.

These were fearful times to live in. But the Finnii of Erin were the avengers of the oppressed. Their fame had gone forth to distant shores, and their deeds were sung by a hundred bards. To them the name of danger was as an invitation to a rich banquet. The web of enchantment stopped their course as little as the swords of an enemy. Many a mother of a son, many a wife of a husband, many a sister of a brother had the valour of the Finnian heroes bereft. Dismembered limbs quivered, and heads bounded on the ground before their progress in battle. They rushed forward with the strength of the furious wind, tearing up the trees of the forest by their roots. Loud was their war-cry as the thunder, raging was their impetuosity above that of common men, and fierce was their anger as the stormy waves of the ocean!

It was the mighty Finn himself who lifted up his voice, and commanded the fatal candle of the hag Grana to be extinguished. "Thine, Regan, be the task," he said, and to him he gave a cap thrice charmed by the magician Kuno of Lochlin.

With the star of the same evening the candle of death burned on the rock, and Regan stood beneath it. Had he beheld the slightest glimmer of its blaze, he, too, would have perished, and the hag Grana, with the morning's dawn, rejoiced over his corse. When Regan looked towards the light, the charmed cap fell over his eyes and prevented his seeing. The rock was steep, but he climbed up its craggy side with such caution and dexterity, that before the hag was aware, the warrior, with averted head, had seized the candle, and flung it with prodigious force into the River Shannon, the hissing waters of which quenched its light for ever!

Then flew the charmed cap from the eyes of Regan, and he beheld the enraged hag, with outstretched arms, prepared to seize and whirl him after her candle. Regan instantly bounded westward from the rock just two miles, with a wild and wondrous spring. Grana looked for a moment at the leap, and then tearing up a huge fragment of the rock, flung it after Regan with such tremendous force, that her crooked hands trembled and her broad chest heaved with heavy puffs, like a smith's labouring bellows, from the exertion.

The ponderous stone fell harmless to the ground, for the leap of Regan far exceeded the strength of the furious hag. In triumph he returned to Finn:

> " The hero valiant, renowned and learned;
> White-tooth'd, graceful, magnanimous, and active."

The hag Grana was never heard of more; but the stone remains, and, deeply imprinted in it, is still to be seen the mark of the hag's fingers. That stone is far taller than the tallest man, and the power of forty men would fail to move it from the spot where it fell.

The grass may wither around it, the spade and plough destroy dull heaps of earth, the walls of castles fall and perish, but the fame of the Finnii of Erin endures with the rocks themselves, and *Clough-a-Regaun* is a monument fitting to preserve the memory of the deed!

III
CLOUGH-NA-CUDDY

ABOVE all the islands in the lakes of Killarney give me Innisfallen —"sweet Innisfallen," as the melodious Moore calls it. It is, in truth, a fairy isle, although I have no fairy story to tell you about it; and if I had, these are such unbelieving times, and people of late have grown so sceptical, that they only smile at my stories and doubt them.

However, none will doubt that a monastery once stood upon Innisfallen Island, for its ruins may still be seen; neither, that within its walls dwelt certain pious and learned persons called monks. A very pleasant set of fellows they were, I make not the smallest doubt; and I am sure of this, that they had a very pleasant spot to enjoy themselves in after dinner—the proper time, believe me, and I am no bad judge of such matters, for the enjoyment of a fine prospect.

Out of all the monks you could not pick a better fellow nor a merrier soul than Father Cuddy; he sung a good song, he told a good story, and had a jolly, comfortable-looking paunch of his own, that was a credit to any refectory-table. He was distinguished above all the rest by the name of "the fat father." Now, there are many that will take huff at a name; but Father Cuddy had no nonsense of that kind about him; he laughed at it—and well able he was to laugh, for his mouth nearly reached from one ear to the other; his might, in truth, be called an open countenance. As his paunch was no disgrace to his food, neither was his nose to his drink. 'Tis a doubt to me if there were not more carbuncles upon it than ever were seen at the bottom of the lake, which is said to be full of them. His eyes had a right merry twinkle in them, like moonshine dancing on the water; and his cheeks had the roundness and crimson glow of ripe arbutus berries.

"He ate, and drank, and prayed, and slept. What then?
He ate, and drank, and prayed, and slept again!"

Such was the tenor of his simple life; but when he prayed, a certain drowsiness would come upon him, which, it must be confessed, never occurred when a well-filled "black-jack" stood before him. Hence his prayers were short and his draughts were long. The world loved him, and he saw no good reason why he should not in return love its venison and its usquebaugh. But as times went, he must have been a pious man, or else what befel him never would have happened.

Spiritual affairs—for it was respecting the importation of a tun of wine into the island monastery—demanded the presence of one of the brotherhood of Innisfallen at the abbey of Irelagh, now called Mucruss. The superintendence of this important matter was committed to Father Cuddy, who felt too deeply interested in the future welfare of any community of which he was a member, to neglect or delay such mission. With the morning's light he was seen guiding his shallop across the crimson waters of the lake towards the peninsula of Mucruss; and having moored his little bark in safety beneath the shelter of a wave-worn rock, he advanced with becoming dignity towards the abbey.

The stillness of the bright and balmy hour was broken by the heavy footsteps of the zealous father. At the sound the startled deer, shaking the dew from their sides, sprung up from their lair, and as they bounded off—"Hah!" exclaimed Cuddy, "what a noble haunch goes there! How delicious it would look smoking upon a goodly platter!"

As he proceeded, the mountain-bee hummed his tune of gladness around the holy man, save when buried in the foxglove-bell, or revelling upon a fragrant bunch of thyme; and even then, the little voice murmured out happiness in low and broken tones of voluptuous delight. Father Cuddy derived no small comfort from the sound, for it presaged a good metheglin season, and metheglin he regarded, if well manufactured, to be no bad liquor, particularly when there was no stint of usquebaugh in the brewing.

Arrived within the abbey garth, he was received with due respect by the brethren of Irelagh, and arrangements for the embarkation of the wine were completed to his entire satisfaction. "Welcome, Father Cuddy!" said the prior; "grace be on you."

"Grace before meat, then," said Cuddy, "for a long walk always makes me hungry, and I am certain I have not walked less than half a mile this morning, to say nothing of crossing the water."

A pasty of choice flavour felt the truth of this assertion, as regarded Father Cuddy's appetite. After such consoling repast, it would have been a reflection on monastic hospitality to depart without partaking of the grace-cup; moreover, Father Cuddy had a particular respect for the antiquity of that custom.   He liked the taste of the grace-cup well : he tried another—it was no less excellent; and when he had swallowed the third, he found his heart expand and put forth its fibres, willing to embrace all mankind.   Surely, then, there is Christian love and charity in wine !

I said he sung a good song.   Now, though psalms are good songs, and in accordance with his vocation, I did not mean to imply that he was a mere psalm-singer.   It was well known to the brethren, that wherever Father Cuddy was, mirth and melody were with him—mirth in his eye and melody on his tongue, and these, from experience, are equally well known to be thirsty commodities; but he took good care never to let them run dry. To please the brotherhood, whose excellent wine pleased him, he sung, and as *in vino veritas*, his song will well become this veritable history.

THE FRIAR'S SONG

My vows I can never fulfil, until I have breakfasted, one way or other ; and I freely protest that I can never rest till I borrow or beg an egg, unless I can come at the ould hen, its mother. But Maggy, my dear, while you're here, I don't fear to want eggs that have just been laid newly ; for och ! you're a pearl of a girl, and you're called so *in Latin* most truly.

There is most to my mind something that is still upper than supper, tho' it must be admitted I feel no way thinner after dinner; but soon as I hear the cock crow in the morning, that eggs you are bringing full surely I know, by that warning, while your buttermilk helps me to float down my throat those sweet cakes made of oat.   I don't envy an earl, sweet girl, och ! 'tis you are a beautiful pearl.

Such was his song.   Father Cuddy smacked his lips at the recollection of Margery's delicious fried eggs, which always imparted a peculiar relish to his liquor.   The very idea provoked Cuddy to raise the cup to his mouth, and with one hearty pull thereat he finished its contents.

This is, and ever was, a censorious world, often construing what is only a fair allowance into an excess ; but I scorn to reckon up any man's drink, like an unrelenting host ; therefore, I cannot tell how many brimming draughts of wine, bedecked with *the venerable Bead,* Father Cuddy emptied into his "soul-case," so he figuratively termed the body.

His respect for the goodly company of the monks of Irelagh detained him until their adjournment to vespers, when he set forward on his return to Innisfallen.   Whether his mind was occupied in philosophic contemplation, or wrapped in pious musings, I cannot declare, but the honest father wandered on in a different direction from that in which his shallop lay. Far be it from me to insinuate that the good liquor which he had so commended caused him to forget his road, or that his track was irregular and unsteady. Oh, no! He carried his drink bravely, as became a decent man and a good Christian; yet, somehow, he thought he could distinguish two moons. "Bless my eyes," said Father Cuddy, "everything is changing nowadays!— the very stars are not in the same places they used to be; I think *Camcéachta* (the Plough) is driving on at a rate I never saw it before to-night; but I suppose the driver is drunk, for there are blackguards everywhere."

Cuddy had scarcely uttered these words when he saw, or fancied he saw, the form of a young woman, who, holding up a bottle, beckoned him towards her. The night was extremely beautiful, and the white dress of the girl floated gracefully in the moonlight as with gay step she tripped on before the worthy father, archly looking back upon him over her shoulder.

"Ah, Margery—merry Margery!" cried Cuddy; "you tempting little rogue!

> " ' Flos vallium harum,
> Decus puellarum,
> Candida Margarita.'

I see you; I see you and the bottle! Let me but catch you, candida Margarita!" and on he followed, panting and smiling, after this alluring apparition.

At length his feet grew weary and his breath failed, which obliged him to give up the chase; yet such was his piety, that unwilling to rest in any attitude but that of prayer, down dropped Father Cuddy on his knees. Sleep, as usual, stole upon his devotions; and the morning was far advanced when he awoke from dreams, in which tables groaned beneath their load of viands, and wine poured itself free and sparkling as the mountain spring.

Rubbing his eyes, he looked about him, and the more he looked the more he wondered at the alteration which appeared in the face of the country. "Bless my soul and body!" said the good father, "I saw the stars changing last night, but here is a change!" Doubting his senses, he looked again. The hills bore the same majestic outline as on the preceding day, and the lake spread itself beneath his view in the same tranquil beauty, and studded with the same number of islands; but every smaller feature in the landscape was strangely altered. What had been naked rocks, were now clothed with holly and arbutus. Whole woods had disappeared, and waste places had become cultivated fields; and to complete the work of enchantment, the very season

itself seemed changed.   In the rosy dawn of a summer's morning
he had left the monastery of Innisfallen, and he now felt in every
sight and sound the dreariness of winter.   The hard ground was
covered with withered leaves; icicles depended from leafless
branches; he heard the sweet, low note of the robin, who
familiarly approached him; and he felt his fingers numbed from
the nipping frost.   Father Cuddy found it rather difficult to
account for such sudden transformations, and to convince himself
it was not the illusion of a dream, he was about to arise, when lo!
he discovered that both his knees were buried at least six inches
in the solid stone; for notwithstanding all these changes, he had
never altered his devout position.

Cuddy was now wide awake, and felt, when he got up, his
joints sadly cramped, which it was only natural they should be,
considering the hard texture of the stone and the depth his
knees had sunk into it.   But the great difficulty was to explain
how, in one night, summer had become winter, whole woods had
been cut down, and well-grown trees had sprouted up.   The
miracle—nothing else could he conclude it to be—urged him to
hasten his return to Innisfallen, where he might learn some
explanation of these marvellous events.

Seeing a boat moored within reach of the shore, he delayed not,
in the midst of such wonders, to seek his own bark, but seizing
the oars, pulled stoutly towards the island; and here new
wonders awaited him.

Father Cuddy waddled, as fast as cramped limbs could carry
his rotund corporation, to the gate of the monastery, where he
loudly demanded admittance.

"Holloa! whence come you, Master Monk, and what's your
business?" demanded a stranger who occupied the porter's place.

"Business!—my business!" repeated the confounded Cuddy.
"Why, do you not know me?   Has the wine arrived safely?"

"Hence, fellow!" said the porter's representative, in a surly
tone; "nor think to impose on me with your monkish tales."

"Fellow!" exclaimed the father.   "Mercy upon us, that I
should be so spoken to at the gate of my own house!   Scoundrel!"
cried Cuddy, raising his voice, "do you not see my garb—my
holy garb?"

"Aye, fellow," replied he of the keys—"the garb of laziness
and filthy debauchery, which has been expelled from out these
walls.   Know you not, idle knave, of the suppression of this nest
of superstition, and that the abbey lands and possessions were
granted in August last to Master Robert Collam, by our Lady
Elizabeth, sovereign queen of England, and paragon of all beauty
—whom God preserve!"

"Queen of England!" said Cuddy.   "There never was a

sovereign queen of England—this is but a piece with the rest. I saw how it was going with the stars last night—the world's turned upside down. But surely this is Innisfallen Island, and I am the Father Cuddy who yesterday morning went over to the abbey of Irelagh respecting the tun of wine. Do you not know me now?"

"Know you! How should I know you?" said the keeper of the abbey. "Yet, true it is, that I have heard my grandmother, whose mother remembered the man, often speak of the fat Father Cuddy of Innisfallen, who made a profane and godless ballad in praise of fresh eggs, of which he and his vile crew knew more than they did of the Word of God; and who, being drunk, it is said, tumbled into the lake one night and was drowned; but that must have been a hundred—aye, more than a hundred years since."

"'Twas I who composed that song in praise of Margery's fresh eggs, which is no profane and godless ballad—no other Father Cuddy than myself ever belonged to Innisfallen," earnestly exclaimed the holy man. "A hundred years! What was your great-grandmother's name?"

"She was a Mahony of Dunlow—Margaret ni Mahony; and my grandmother—"

"What! merry Margery of Dunlow your great-grandmother!" shouted Cuddy. "St. Brandon help me! the wicked wench with that tempting bottle! Why, 'twas only last night—a hundred years!—your great-grandmother, said you? God bless us! there has been a strange torpor over me; I must have slept all this time!"

That Father Cuddy had done so, I think is sufficiently proved by the changes which occurred during his nap. A reformation, and a serious one it was for him, had taken place. Pretty Margery's fresh eggs were no longer to be had in Innisfallen; and with a heart as heavy as his footsteps, the worthy man directed his course towards Dingle, where he embarked in a vessel on the point of sailing for Malaga. The rich wine of that place had of old impressed him with a high respect for its monastic establishments, in one of which he quietly wore out the remainder of his days.

The stone impressed with the mark of Father Cuddy's knees may be seen to this day. Should any incredulous persons doubt my story, I request them to go to Killarney, where Clough-na-Cuddy—so is the stone called—remains in Lord Kenmare's park, an indisputable evidence of the fact. Spillane, the bugle-man, will be able to point it out to them, as he did so to me.

IV

THE GIANT'S STAIRS

On the road between Passage and Cork there is an old mansion called Ronayne's Court. It may be easily known from the stack of chimneys and the gable-ends, which are to be seen, look at it which way you will. Here it was that Maurice Ronayne and his wife, Margaret Gould, kept house, as may be learned to this day from the great old chimney-piece, on which is carved their arms. They were a mighty worthy couple, and had but one son, who was called Philip, after no less a person than the King of Spain.

Immediately on his smelling the cold air of this world the child sneezed, and it was naturally taken to be a good sign of having a clear head; but the subsequent rapidity of his learning was truly amazing; for on the very first day a primer was put into his hand, he tore out the A, B, C page, and destroyed it, as a thing quite beneath his notice. No wonder, then, that both father and mother were proud of their heir, who gave such indisputable proofs of genius, or, as they call it in that part of the world, *genus*.

One morning, however, Master Phil, who was then just seven years old, was missing, and no one could tell what had become of him. Servants were sent in all directions to seek for him, on horseback and on foot, but they returned without any tidings of the boy, whose disappearance altogether was most unaccountable. A large reward was offered, but it produced them no intelligence, and years rolled away without Mr. and Mrs. Ronayne having obtained any satisfactory account of the fate of their lost child.

There lived, at this time, near Carigaline, one Robert Kelly, a blacksmith by trade. He was what is termed a handy man, and his abilities were held in much estimation by the lads and the lasses of the neighbourhood; for, independent of shoeing horses, which he did to great perfection, and making plough-irons, he interpreted dreams for the young women, sung Arthur O'Bradley at their weddings, and was so good-natured a fellow at a christening that he was gossip to half the country round.

Now it happened that Robin had a dream himself, and young Philip Ronayne appeared to him in it at the dead hour of the night. Robin thought he saw the boy mounted upon a beautiful white horse, and that he told him how he was made a page to the giant Mahon MacMahon, who had carried him off, and who held his court in the hard heart of the rock. "The seven years—my time of service—are clean out, Robin," said he, "and if you release me this night, I will be the making of you for ever after."

"And how will I know," said Robin—cunning enough, even in his sleep—"but this is all a dream?"

"Take that," said the boy, "for a token"—and at the word the white horse struck out with one of his hind-legs, and gave poor Robin such a kick in the forehead that, thinking he was a dead man, he roared as loud as he could after his brains, and woke up calling a thousand murders. He found himself in bed, but he had the mark of the blow, the regular print of a horse-shoe upon his forehead as red as blood; and Robin Kelly, who never before found himself puzzled at the dream of any other person, did not know what to think of his own.

Robin was well acquainted with the Giant's Stairs, as, indeed, who is not that knows the harbour? They consist of great masses of rock, which, piled one above another, rise like a flight of steps, from very deep water, against the bold cliff of Carrig-mahon. Nor are they badly suited for stairs to those who have legs of sufficient length to stride over a moderate-sized house, or to enable them to clear the space of a mile in a hop, step, and jump. Both these feats the giant MacMahon was said to have performed in the days of Finnian glory; and the common tradition of the country placed his dwelling within the cliff, up whose side the stairs led.

Such was the impression which the dream made on Robin that he determined to put its truth to the test. It occurred to him, however, before setting out on this adventure that a plough-iron may be no bad companion, as, from experience, he knew it was an excellent knock-down argument, having, on more occasions than one, settled a little disagreement very quietly; so, putting one on his shoulder, off he marched in the cool of the evening through Glaun a Thowk (the Hawk's Glen) to Monkstown. Here an old gossip of his (Tom Clancey by name) lived, who, on hearing Robin's dream, promised him the use of his skiff, and moreover, offered to assist in rowing it to the Giant's Stairs.

After a supper, which was of the best, they embarked. It was a beautiful, still night, and the little boat glided swiftly along. The regular dip of the oars, the distant song of the sailor, and sometimes the voice of a belated traveller at the ferry of Carrigaloe, alone broke the quietness of the land and sea and sky. The tide was in their favour, and in a few minutes Robin and his gossip rested on their oars under the dark shadow of the Giant's Stairs. Robin looked anxiously for the entrance to the Giant's Palace, which, it was said, may be found by anyone seeking it at mid-night; but no such entrance could he see. His impatience had hurried him there before that time, and after waiting a considerable space in a state of suspense not to be described, Robin, with pure vexation, could not help exclaiming to his companion : " 'Tis a pair of fools we are, Tom Clancey, for coming here at all on the strength of a dream."

"And whose doing is it," said Tom, "but your own ?"

At the moment he spoke they perceived a faint glimmering light to proceed from the cliff, which gradually increased until a porch big enough for a king's palace unfolded itself almost on a level with the water. They pulled the skiff directly towards the opening, and Robin Kelly, seizing his plough-iron, boldly entered with a strong hand and a stout heart. Wild and strange was that entrance, the whole of which appeared formed of grim and grotesque faces, blending so strangely each with the other that it was impossible to define any—the chin of one formed the nose of another—what appeared to be a fixed and stern eye, if dwelt upon, changed to a gaping mouth ; and the lines of the lofty forehead grew into a majestic and flowing beard. The more Robin allowed himself to contemplate the forms around him, the more terrific they became ; and the stony expression of this crowd of faces assumed a savage ferocity as his imagination converted feature after feature into a different shape and character. Losing the twilight, in which these indefinite forms were visible, he advanced through a dark and devious passage, whilst a deep and rumbling noise sounded as if the rock was about to close upon him and swallow him up alive for ever. Now, indeed, poor Robin felt afraid.

"Robin, Robin," said he, "if you were a fool for coming here, what in the name of fortune are you now ?" But as before, he had scarcely spoken when he saw a small light twinkling through the darkness of the distance, like a star in the midnight sky. To retreat was out of the question, for so many turnings and windings were in the passage, that he considered he had but little chance of making his way back. He therefore proceeded towards the bit of light, and came at last into a spacious chamber, from the roof of which hung the solitary lamp that had guided him. Emerging from such profound gloom, the single lamp afforded Robin abundant light to discover several gigantic figures seated round a massive stone table as if in serious deliberation, but no word disturbed the breathless silence which prevailed. At the head of this table sat Mahon MacMahon himself, whose majestic beard had taken root, and in the course of ages grown into the stone slab. He was the first who perceived Robin ; and instantly starting up, drew his long beard from out the huge lump of rock in such haste and with so sudden a jerk, that it was shattered into a thousand pieces.

"What seek you ?" he demanded, in a voice of thunder.

"I come," answered Robin, with as much boldness as he could

put on—for his heart was almost fainting within him—" I come," said he, " to claim Philip Ronayne, whose time of service is out this night."

" And who sent you here? " said the giant.

" 'Twas of my own accord I came," said Robin.

" Then you must single him out from among my pages," said the giant; "and if you fix on the wrong one, your life is the forfeit. Follow me." He led Robin into a hall of vast extent and filled with lights, along either side of which were rows of beautiful children all apparently seven years old, and none beyond that age, dressed in green, and everyone exactly dressed alike.

" Here," said Mahon, " you are free to take Philip Ronayne, if you will; but remember, I give but one choice."

Robin was sadly perplexed, for there were hundreds upon hundreds of children, and he had no very clear recollection of the boy he sought. But he walked along the hall by the side of Mahon as if nothing was the matter, although his great iron dress clanked fearfully at every step, sounding louder than Robin's own sledge battering on his anvil.

They had nearly reached the end of the hall without speaking when Robin, seeing that the only means he had was to make friends with the giant, determined to try what effect a few soft words might have upon him.

" 'Tis a fine, wholesome appearance the poor children carry," remarked Robin, "although they have been here so long shut out from the fresh air and the blessed light of heaven. 'Tis tenderly your honour must have reared them ! "

" Aye," said the giant, "that is true for you; so give me your hand, for you are, I believe, a very honest fellow for a blacksmith."

Robin, at the first look, did not much like the huge size of the hand, and therefore presented his plough-iron, which the giant seizing, twisted in his grasp round and round again as if it had been a potato-stalk. On seeing this, all the children set up a shout of laughter. In the midst of their mirth, Robin thought he heard his name called ; and, all ear and eye, he put his hand on the boy who he fancied had spoken, crying out at the same time : " Let me live or die for it, but this is young Phil Ronayne ! "

" It is Philip Ronayne—happy Philip Ronayne," said his young companions ; and in an instant the hall became dark. Crashing noises were heard, and all was in strange confusion ; but Robin held fast his prize, and found himself lying in the grey dawn of the morning at the head of the Giant's Stairs with the boy clasped in his arms.

Robin had plenty of gossips to spread the story of his wonderful adventure — Passage, Monkstown, Ringaskiddy, Seamount, Carrigaline—the whole barony of Kerricurrihy rung with it.

"Are you quite sure, Robin, it is young Phil Ronayne you have brought back with you?" was the regular question; for although the boy had been seven years away, his appearance now was just the same as on the day he was missed He had neither grown taller nor older in look, and he spoke of things which had happened before he was carried off as one awakened from sleep, or as if they had occurred yesterday.

"Am I sure? Well, that's a queer question," was Robin's reply, "seeing the boy has the blue eyes of the mother, with the foxy hair of the father, to say nothing of the *purty* wart on the right side of his little nose."

However Robin Kelly may have been questioned, the worthy couple of Ronayne's court doubted not that he was the deliverer of their child from the power of the Giant MacMahon, and the reward they bestowed upon him equalled their gratitude.

Philip Ronayne lived to be an old man; and he was remarkable to the day of his death for his skill in working brass and iron, which it was believed he had learned during his seven years' apprenticeship to the Giant Mahon MacMahon.

> "And now, farewell! the fairy dream is o'er;
>   The tales my infancy had loved to hear,
>   Like blissful visions, fade and disappear.
> Such tales Momonia's peasants tell no more!
> Vanish'd are MERMAIDS from the sea-beat shore;
>   Check'd is the HEADLESS HORSEMAN's strange career;
>   FIR DARRIG's voice no longer mocks the ear,
> Nor ROCKS bear wondrous imprints as of yore!
> Such is 'the march of mind.' But did the fays
>   (Creatures of whim—the gossamers of will)
>   In Ireland work such sorrow and such ill
> As stormier spirits of our modern days?
> Oh, land beloved! no angry voice I raise;
> My constant prayer—'May peace be with thee still!'"

APPENDIX

LETTER FROM SIR WALTER SCOTT TO THE AUTHOR OF THE IRISH FAIRY LEGENDS

SIR,—I have been obliged by the courtesy which sent me your very interesting work on "Irish Superstitions," and no less by the amusement which it has afforded me, both from the interest of the stories and the lively manner in which they are told. You are to consider this, sir, as a high compliment from one who holds him on the subject of elves, ghosts, visions, etc., nearly as strong as William Churne of Staffordshire:

> "Who every year can mend your cheer
> With tales both old and new."

The extreme similarity of your fictions to ours in Scotland is very striking. The Cluricaune (which is an admirable subject for a pantomime) is not known here. I suppose the Scottish cheer was not sufficient to tempt to the hearth either him, or that singular demon called by Heywood the Buttery Spirit, which diminished the profits of an unjust landlord by eating up all that he cribbed for his guests.

The beautiful superstition of the Banshee seems in a great measure peculiar to Ireland, though in some Highland families there is such a spectre, particularly in that of MacLean of Lochbŭy ; but I think I could match all your other tales with something similar.

I can assure you, however, that the progress of philosophy has not even yet entirely " pulled the old woman out of our hearts," as Addison expresses it. Witches are still held in reasonable detestation, although we no longer burn or even *score above the breath*. As for the water bull, they live who will take their oaths to having seen him emerge from a small lake on the boundary of my property here, scarce large enough to have held him, I should think. Some traits in his description seem to answer the hippo-potamus, and these are always mentioned in Highland and Lowland story. Strange if we could conceive there existed, under a tradition so universal, some shadowy reference to those fossil bones of animals which are so often found in the lakes and bogs.

But to leave antediluvian stories for the freshest news from Fairyland, I cannot resist the temptation to send you an account of King Oberon's court, which was verified before me as a magistrate, with all the solemnities of a court of justice, within this fortnight past. A young shepherd, a lad of about eighteen years of age, well brought up and of good capacity, and, that I may be perfectly accurate, in the service of a friend, a most respectable farmer at Oakwood, on the estate of Hugh Scott, Esq. of Harden, made oath and said, that going to look after some sheep which his master had directed to be put upon turnips, and passing in the grey of the morning a small copse-wood adjacent to the River Etterick, he was surprised at the sight of four or five little personages, about two feet or thirty inches in height, who were seated under the trees and apparently in deep conversation. At this singular appearance he paused till he had refreshed his noble courage with a prayer and a few recollections of last Sunday's sermon, and then advanced to the little party. But observing that, instead of disappearing, they seemed to become yet more magnificently distinct than before, and now doubting nothing, from their foreign dresses and splendid decorations, that they were the choice ornaments of the fairy court, he fairly turned tail and went "to raise the water," as if the South'ron had made a raid. Others came to the rescue, and yet the fairy *cortége* awaited their arrival in still and silent dignity. I wish I could stop here, for the devil take all explanations, they stop duels and destroy the credit of apparitions, neither allow ghosts to be made in an honourable way, or to be believed in (poor souls!) when they revisit the glimpses of the moon.

I must however explain, like other honourable gentlemen, else-where. You must know, that like our neighbours, we have a school of arts for our mechanics at G——, a small manufacturing town in this country, and that the tree of knowledge there, as elsewhere, produces its usual crop of good and evil. The day before this avatar of Oberon was a fair-day at Selkirk, and amongst other popular divertisements was one which, in former days, I would have called a puppet show, and its master a puppet showman. He has put me right, however, by informing me, that he writes himself *artist from Vauxhall*, and that he exhibits *fantoccini;* call them what you will, it seems they gave great delight to the unwashed artificers of G——. Formerly they would have been contented to wonder and applaud, but not so were they satisfied in our modern days of investigation, for they broke into Punch's sanctuary forcibly, after he had been laid aside for the evening, made violent seizure of his person, and carried off him, his spouse, and heaven knows what captives besides, in their plaid nooks, to be examined at leisure. All this they literally did (forcing a door to accomplish their purpose) in the spirit of science alone, or but slightly stimulated by that of malt whisky, with which last we have been of late deluged. Cool reflection came as they retreated by the banks of the Etterick; they made the discovery that they could no more make Punch move than Lord —— could make him speak; and recollecting, I believe, that there was such a person as the Sheriff in the world, they abandoned their prisoners, in hopes, as they pretended, that they would be found and restored in safety to their proper owner.

It is only necessary to add that the artist had his losses made good by a subscription, and the scientific inquirers escaped with a small fine, as a warning not to indulge such an irregular spirit of research in future.

As this somewhat tedious story contains the very last news from Fairyland, I hope you will give it acceptance, and beg you to believe me very much, your obliged and thankful servant,

WALTER SCOTT.

ABBOTSFORD, MELROSE, *27th April, 1825.*

THE END